CONFERENCING PARENTS OF EXCEPTIONAL CHILDREN

Richard L. Simpson

University of Kansas
Kansas City

AN ASPEN PUBLICATION®
Aspen Systems Corporation
Rockville, Maryland
Royal Tunbridge Wells
1982

Library of Congress Cataloging in Publication Data

Simpson, Richard L.
Conferencing parents of exceptional children.

Includes bibliographies and index.
1. Parent-teacher conferences. 2. Exceptional
children—Education. I. Title.
LC225.5.S55   371.9   82-1770
ISBN: 0-89443-694-5   AACR2

Publisher: John Marozsan
Editorial Director: R. Curtis Whitesel
Managing Editor: Margot Raphael
Editorial Services: Scott Ballotin
Printing and Manufacturing: Debbie Swarr

Library of Congress Catalog Card Number: 82-1770
ISBN: 0-89443-694-5

Printed in the United States of America

2 3 4 5

In Memoriam

To R. Curtis Whitesei, Editorial Director of the Rehabilitation and Special Education Divisions of Aspen Systems, whose untimely death preceded the completion of this text. His encouragement, foresight, support, and stamina were inspirational to the author.

Table of Contents

Preface

The central theme of this text is that educators, including classroom teachers, can and must be involved in aiding parents and families to contend with the various issues that they routinely confront when living with an exceptional child. Suitably trained educators are the most appropriate resource for serving the needs of parents and families with exceptional children, and it was in an effort to provide this training that the writing of this book was undertaken.

Parent conferencing is a subject area that requires both cognitive understanding and related experiences. Thus, while readers should recognize that there is an extensive theoretical and empirical foundation on which parent conferencing is based, they must also accept that the development of skills necessary for meaningful relationships with parents requires appropriate experiences and practice. Accordingly, readers are encouraged to view the included role-playing activities and exercises as an integral and basic component of this book. Though names and other identifying information have been changed to protect the identity of parents and children, the examples and simulation activities are based on the author's clinical experiences.

While the training of educators in parent conferencing skills has historically received limited attention, it is becoming increasingly apparent that competency in this area is necessary for professional success. Only with skill and competence in working with parents and families will educators be able to serve most effectively the needs of their exceptional students.

Richard L. Simpson
May 1982

Part I

The Family of the Exceptional Child

Chapter 1

Families with Exceptional Children

The meaningful relationship between parents and educators is a topic that has received widespread coverage during the past decade. Numerous books, articles, and conferences have been designed to reflect and illustrate the importance of an effective parent-professional relationship and to suggest procedures and models for facilitating such cooperative involvement (Barnard, Christophersen, & Wolf, 1977; O'Dell, 1974). However, in spite of such unprecedented attention, educators and other professionals involved with exceptional children generally are ill at ease and somewhat ineffective about advocating, counseling, and otherwise serving parents. Even educators with expertise in direct service to children and in relating to other professionals seem to experience great difficulty in extending their skills and services to parent-related functions.

The factors associated with this situation are multiple and complicated and, in part, revolve around a lack of perspective regarding the American family and its changing role. In fact, the most salient variable accounting for educators' lack of confidence and dexterity in working with parents is the result of unfamiliarity with and limited insight into the changing structure of the family unit. In order effectively and efficiently to offer appropriate services to parents and families, the professionals involved must possess an understanding of the nature of today's family, its attitudes and values, and the background against which these were developed.

HISTORICAL PERSPECTIVE

The nature and function of the American family has changed dramatically over the past decades, and with it has changed the parents' relationship to their childrens' educational institutions. Prior to the nineteenth century most activities centered almost exclusively around the family. Parents and other members of extended families worked at or near their homes, and the family functioned as the

3

primary educational and social institution for children and youth. In fact, parents frequently were assigned the responsibility of educating their own children. In the mid-seventeenth century, for example, a provision in the Massachusetts Bay Colony stipulated that parents could be fined for failing to educate their children. Early American society was based on an agrarian economy, a way of life that required the participation of entire families, including relatively young children, in producing the basics to sustain life. This society, in which grandparents and other relatives aided parents in serving as adult models, adhered to strict role assignments and well-established family and community values. Thus, rules, policies, and values were reflections of the position of the family and were compatible with the philosophy of rural American society. In keeping with this tradition, schools were designed both to reflect and to perpetuate family and community values and, consequently, involved close cooperation between educators and parents (Bayles & Hood, 1966). Few of the problems experienced by present-day educators were common to that era. It is highly unlikely, for example, that there were debates over the reading series to be used with students, whether a particular teacher-applied punishment procedure might result in a law suit, or whether a pupil's individualized education program had sufficient parental input.

With the Industrial Revolution came the transformation of agrarian life into what was eventually to become modern urban society. This large-scale social and economic development brought about two profound changes: (1) the movement of families from farms to cities and (2) the inclusion of women (and, in some instances, children) in the work force (Goode, 1971). As families moved from farms to cities, contact with extended family members often decreased, thus lessening the opportunity for children to be exposed to a variety of adult family role models. In addition, frequent contacts with other families representing different attitudes and value systems gradually came to exert more influence on the development of attitudes and values than exposure to extended family members and the narrower and more restricted beliefs of small agricultural communities. Furthermore, the induction of women into the work force during the Industrial Revolution resulted in less contact among children, parents, and other adult family members. Almost as a prelude to present-day society, children began to spend relatively long periods of time without parental supervision. Accordingly, their peer groups came to assume a much stronger role in their attitude and value formation.

During the period between the Industrial Revolution and the Civil War, American education began to exhibit many of the characteristics that are prevalent today. Children were given an opportunity to attend publicly supported schools; graded schools and self-contained classrooms proliferated; formal teacher training programs in colleges and universities were developed; curricular options were increased; and consolidated schools staffed and operated by professional educators became the rule.

Since World War II, major technological, political, and economic events have resulted in monumental changes in the American family. Children are presently a part of family units that rarely include grandparents and other extended family members; frequent moves have become commonplace and predictable; single-parent and reconstituted families are increasing in frequency; families in which both parents are employed full time outside the home are becoming the norm; and parents more commonly expect the schools to fulfill roles traditionally assumed by the family.

While disagreement abounds on the nature and ultimate result of these trends (Bronfenbrenner, 1979), it is obvious that schools are the major social institution to feel the impact. The statistics below illustrate the problems facing school personnel and hence the necessity of educators becoming familiar with changes in familial patterns.

- There has been a 700 percent increase in the number of children affected by divorce since the turn of the century.

- It is estimated that over 40 percent of all children born today will spend a portion of their childhood in a single-parent home.

- Fifteen percent of all children are born out of wedlock.

- Thirteen percent of the nation's families are composed of a working father, a nonworking mother, and one or more children.

- Over 50 percent of all mothers with school-age children are employed full time.

- The average 16-year-old will spend more time watching television than spent in school or with parents.

- National Center for Health data suggest that 10 percent of all children between the ages of 12 and 17 will run away from home.

- The incidence of juvenile delinquency is dramatically on the increase; it is estimated that over 10 percent of all teenagers will appear in juvenile court.

- Suicide is the second leading cause of death among teenagers.

Without argument, the family has changed along with the other social institutions in this country. No longer is the family a self-sufficient entity in which parents, children, and other extended family members work together to provide for the economic security of the members and in which most educational, social, and ethical development takes place. Presently, both children and parents spend increased amounts of time outside the home. In spite of indubitable data and other signs of familial change, however, there is little evidence to indicate that the world's oldest social institution will fail to endure. The family continues to serve a major social function and most likely will persist as the major life-style model in the future.

The issue at hand for educators and other professionals involved with children and their families is to recognize the changing family pattern and to develop appropriate programs to serve children and parents. Educators must recognize and accept that many children and families will be impermanent community members; that high divorce rates probably will continue; that heterogeneous values will characterize communities and hence the school population; that schools may function less as recreational and social centers of the community; and that many parents may advocate that the education and socialization of children become an exclusive function of professional educators. At the same time, educators must recognize that parents must be part of any instructional program, especially those designed for exceptional children, and that functional and efficacious models and solutions can be developed to aid in the solution of family problems and in facilitating the growth and development of children.

The individualized and changing nature of most families as well as the ecological issues affecting parents, professionals, and children mandate that the conferencer dispense with cookbook approaches in favor of pragmatic philosophies and strategies. Only with such an approach will today's educators be able to function effectively with parents. Although the challenge is significant, the procedures and technology needed for successful parental involvement can be acquired by those willing to develop appropriate conferencing skills.

While taking into consideration the values and life styles of others, educational conferencers must also be cognizant of their own values and attitudes and, to the maximum extent possible, attempt to accept patterns that otherwise may be contrary to their own personal preferences. While educators are not expected to reinforce or promote individuals raising families outside of marriage, communal living arrangements, or other modes of behavior with which they may not be in agreement, they must recognize that they will likely encounter parents and families who have adopted such life styles. Thus, for educators to be successful they must possess not only personal strategies but also self-understanding and tolerance for modes of behavior that may be contrary to their own.

MAJOR FACTORS INFLUENCING PARENTS AND FAMILIES

Maternal Employment

As noted previously, an increasing number of families are no longer represented by a working father and a housewife mother. Because of either financial need or a desire for a career, women with children are increasingly choosing to become part of the work force (Isakson, 1979). As a function of this trend, educators can neither expect children to receive as much direct parental supervision as may be considered optimal nor expect parents to be available for conferences during working hours. Accordingly, schools and agencies must be willing to schedule conferences at times that are mutually convenient to all participants. Without such flexible scheduling, parents will probably not be active or willing participants in school-related activities.

It is important to remember that while families in which both parents work full time may represent a break with tradition, it cannot be demonstrated that this change is in and of itself either good or bad (Hoffman & Nye, 1974). This particular issue remains clouded by tremendous divergence of opinion and limited data. However, there are indications that the effect of maternal employment on children is directly associated with the mother's attitude toward working. Hoffman and Nye (1974) reported that children benefit most from situations in which attitudes and behavior are congruent. That is, children fare best when mothers desiring to work are able to pursue employment and when those wishing to remain in the home are given that opportunity. Accordingly, professionals must refrain from making the automatic judgment that mothers who are employed may be creating problems for their children.

Single-Parent and Reconstituted Families

Future predictions of the divorce rate show continued increases. As revealed in previously cited statistics, educators can expect to have a significant number of children in their programs who are part of one-parent or reconstituted families. It must be recognized that separation, divorce, and restructuring a family can be traumatizing to children and youth (Wallerstein & Keely, 1976; Martin, 1975) and that it can have severe impact on a child's capacity to function in school (Hetherington & Martin, 1972). As noted by Kauffman (1977), "Not surprisingly, the presence of a good father or other positive male figure in the home and parental harmony in an intact family seem to bode well for children's behavior" (p. 74). Based on these facts, the educational conferencer must accept that breakdowns in family structure will occur and must plan strategies for aiding the children, families, and parents involved. That does not mean that the professional should view every child and single-parent or reconstituted family as being in need of therapy, but rather that special consideration must be given in these situations. In particular, the professional must recognize that single parents may have economic and time constraints beyond those of other families (Karpowitz, 1980); that both parents and children probably will experience increased strain during periods of separation, divorce, and reconstitution (Martin, 1975); and that there may be a period when parents become so involved in their own personal matters that they appear somewhat unconcerned and aloof about their child's school-related problems. Educational conferencers must be reminded that they cannot allow their personal attitudes toward divorce and remarriage to interfere with the interaction process. The success of conferences with single parents or reconstituted parents and families depends to a great extent on the professional's skills in finding ways to make parents a part of their child's school experience. It is also noteworthy that the parent and family involved in a transition probably will be most in need of close contact with school personnel.

Family Mobility

In the past it was not unusual for teachers to be familiar with the parents and families of all the pupils in their classes. Teachers tended to be a part of communities and families who remain for generations in one locale. However, in pursuit of jobs, the "good life," or simply for the sake of change, families are moving more than ever before. In addition, today's educators are much less apt to be a part of the community in which they work.

Notwithstanding arguments from certain businesses and business groups, the effects of frequent moves have not been beneficial to schools, parents, or pupils. Some parents report feeling alienated from their communities and unwilling to invest time and effort in forming new relationships because their efforts would go unrewarded if they were transferred to another area. Some children report difficulty in developing new relationships, adjusting to new schools and schedules, and becoming truly a part of the school or community to which they have moved. One teacher reported that a newly transferred student suggested that the teacher allow him to write his name in pencil in his books owing to his concern that his father might be transferred again before the end of the term. School personnel have also reported that frequently they are unable to establish good relationships with parents and pupils because of their transient life styles. At the same time, school administrators and parents have voiced concern over the high turnover rate among teachers—a trend that is particularly acute for special educators (Needle, Griffin, Svendsen, & Berney, 1980).

While educators may be unable to change the mobile nature of our society, they can work to offset the problems of isolation, detachment, and fragmentation that are often a part of the process. Initial attempts to establish rapport and to familiarize parents and families with their child's educational program may be of significant value. Such efforts may also result in bringing parents and children more closely together at a time when they are most vulnerable to stress.

Changing Role of Schools

Accompanying the technological advances of the past decades has been an increased belief in the value of education and specialization. Notwithstanding frequent criticism of public schools, western society has increasingly become dependent on the supposition that individuals undertaking any task should have specialized training. In keeping with this position, public school educators have managed to convince parents that professional educators, not parents and families, are best qualified to train and educate children and youth. McAfee and Vergason (1979) observed that educators have been able "to convince parents that the values and expertise of the educational system is more desirable and more effective than anything the parents have to offer" (p. 2). As a result, parents have gradually allowed educators increased levels of responsibility for educating their children. Topics that were once considered to be clearly within the domain of parents and the family (e.g., sex education, values, and family planning) are now part of the curriculum of the public schools.

As a logical result of the increased responsibility of the schools for most educational concerns, parents have become systematically eliminated as legitimate educators of their own children. Some parents are overly willing to turn over all responsibility for their child's education to the school and are hence reluctant to participate cooperatively in joint programs with school personnel. Thus, educational personnel may have undermined the very need and basis for parental involvement by convincing the public that schools can be all things to all people.

While educators must continue to play a prominent role in the lives of parents, families, and children, they must also admit that they cannot be all things to all people and that parents and families must take responsibility for certain training areas. As suggested by Isakson (1979), educators must "recognize the strengths in families and capitalize on those so that they can get on with the business they were trained for—teaching" (p. 78). This division of labor will come about only through meaningful and sincere dialogue between parents and professionals. As summarized in one Gallup Poll (1979), "education in the local public schools can be achieved best when parents, the community, and the schools all work together" (p. 41).

Legislation

Parents, especially those with exceptional children, are increasingly being asked to become part of the educational programs provided their offspring and are presently assuming major roles in making educational decisions that will affect their children's future. At least in part, while this heightened involvement has been a result of the acknowledgment by educators and other professionals of the importance of parental participation and cooperation, parents have been able to establish their position and role primarily because of legal, legislative, and political maneuvers. In spite of the obvious role of parents in the development of their offspring, limited support and precedent exist for making them an integral part of the present-day educational system. Thus, only until recently, parents were generally denied opportunities for participating as decision makers in the educational system. Moreover, most parents were not exposed to professionally monitored training procedures with their own offspring in the natural environment. Thus, rather than being considered participants in the educational planning process, parents were more commonly considered unqualified to employ procedures in the natural environment that would facilitate their children's educational or social development or even more inequitably they were routinely looked on as the cause of a child's problems and, thus, in need of treatment themselves.

As a result of this history of conflict, parents were forced to assert their influence by other means. In particular, through parent groups and other legal and legislative avenues, they have been able to establish significant authority relative to the educational provisions for their children. These circumstances have applied most specifically to parents with handicapped children.

As a function of parental action, professionals have been required to accommodate parents as a part of the educational team. Interestingly, this mandated involvement has resulted in increased home-school cooperation and pupil progress (Simpson & Swenson, 1980).

Two landmark cases in the parental struggle for educational service and involvement are *Pennsylvania Association for Retarded Children* v. *Commonwealth of Pennsylvania* (1971) and *Mills* v. *Board of Education, District of Columbia* (1972). In the Pennsylvania case, suit was filed against the State of Pennsylvania for failure to provide a public education for all retarded children. The suit resulted in the issuance of an order for the implementation of educational services for retarded children in the state. Furthermore, the decree stated that it was most desirable for these children to be educated in a program as similar to that of nonhandicapped children as possible. In *Mills* v. *Board of Education* (1976), a class action was filed by parents against the school system for failure to provide a publicly supported education for all children. As in the Pennsylvania case, the court issued a decree for educational opportunity for all children, including the handicapped.

In 1975 the Education for All Handicapped Children   Act (P.L. 94-142) was signed into law, providing for a free and appropriate public education for all handicapped children. This monumental act also provided for significantly increased involvement by parents in school programs. This law, an amendment to the Education of the Handicapped Amendments of 1974 (P.L. 93-380), which in turn augmented and amended the Elementary and Secondary Education Act of 1965 (P.L. 89-10), has significantly increased the rights of handicapped children and youth and the influence of their parents and guardians. In particular, the four basic components of the enactment, (1) assessment safeguards, (2) due process, (3) guarantee of placement in the "least restrictive environment," and (4) an individualized education plan, each allow for parental or guardian involvement and the opportunity for parents and legal custodians to function as advocates for their own children.

As a result of these efforts and programs, parental involvement has undergone significant change. It is obvious that parental participation and influence will continue to characterize program offerings. Meyen (1978), in commenting on developments in the past decade, suggested that "they represent changes so markedly different from the pattern established during the last 20 years that they will not be ignored. The consequences of these changes are so far-reaching that they affect not only the education of exceptional children but the future education of all children" (p. 3).

The legislation and legal transactions of the past few years suggest the appropriateness of at least two basic responses by educators. First, it is mandatory that professionals become familiar with educational legislation; only with knowledge of local, state, and national policies and enactments will they effectively be able to serve the needs of parents. Second, and most importantly, professionals must recognize that parents must voluntarily be provided an opportunity for partnership in their children's education. History attests to the fact that when parents are denied opportunities for participation and involvement, they will seek other avenues of recourse. When parents are forced to exercise their right to input via legal and legislative strategies, everyone suffers. McAfee and Vergason (1979) reported on the shortcomings of legal procedures in effecting the desired parent-educator relationship:

> The real parent-school relationship is not dictated by law. Law may provide an impulse that initiates a change in momentum, but real and meaningful parent involvement grows out of community values, power balances, parent and teacher expectations, economics, and the general social climate existing within the school, the district, the state, and the nation. (p. 3)

Changing Value Systems

Accompanying the technological changes of the past decades have been major value changes. As reported by Kroth and Simpson (1977), "We are not living in a valueless society; nonetheless, it is becoming increasingly difficult to generalize about group, societal, or individual values" (p. 8). That is, there is such variance in the values of people in this country that generalizations tend to be either incorrect or fallacious; furthermore, values are constantly changing.

Educational conferencers must expect children, parents, and families with whom they come into contact to represent a variety of value systems, some of which may be dramatically different from their own. Recognition of this possibility is crucial if the educational conferencer is to work effectively with children, parents, and families with variant socioeconomic, religious, ethnic, and political persuasions. As previously mentioned, educators must be able to understand their own value systems because all individuals, including educators, tend to base their decisions and overall behavior on their own values (Raths, Harmin, & Simon, 1966). Thus, individuals unfamiliar with their personal values may find it exceedingly difficult to understand their interactions or the basis of their behavior. Rutherford and Edgar (1979) observed that, "Behaving in a manner that is congruent with one's beliefs depends on clearly understanding one's values" (p. 41). While clarifying one's own values is not a simple process, conferencers have available several sources to aid them in this effort (Curwin & Fuhrmann, 1975; Kroth & Simpson, 1977; Raths, Harmin, & Simon, 1966; Simon, Howe, & Kirschenbaum, 1972).

In addition, conferencers must be able to understand and accept the values of the different individuals and families with whom they become associated in their professional dealings. Without such understanding the effectiveness of every interaction will be undermined. Perhaps because virtually everyone has had personal school experience most individuals seem to be self-proclaimed experts on the subject of education. Consequently, the conferencer can anticipate that the varying values of parents and families accompanied by their self-proclaimed expertise on the subject of education will result in potential clashes. A simple acknowledgment of the presence of different values and an attempt to understand these systems frequently will serve to turn potential encounters into meaningful and fruitful exchanges.

The educational conferencer must not only recognize that values have changed and will continue to do so but also that such beliefs will be the basis on which meaningful interactions will take place. Value changes are not only major influences on today's family but also salient variables in the determination of the success of the parent-educator conference.

CHANGES IN FAMILIES WITH EXCEPTIONAL CHILDREN

Just as families with nonexceptional children have been changing so, too, have those with children demonstrating special needs. It is logical that families with exceptional children would experience the same ecological changes as others and exist as heterogeneously as other parents and families. Yet, traditionally, parents of exceptional children have been considered as somehow immune to changes experienced by the rest of the world and, in spite of their obvious differences, as having so many commonalities that they exist as a truly homogeneous population. Perhaps in an effort to simplify, parents of exceptional children have often been classified as having unique features not shared by others. However, indications are that parents of exceptional children are as individualized and diversified as those without "special" children; their only common denominator is that they have at least one child who deviates from the norm to such an extent that some type of curriculum modification or specialized educational program is required to help the child function at a level commensurate with ability.

In spite of their heterogeneity, parents and families with exceptional children do appear to experience the common concern of increased levels of frustration and problems not encountered by other parents and families. Equally important, parents of exceptional children may lack feelings of accomplishment and satisfaction so necessary to effective parenthood. That is, the hurt experienced by parents because their child may not one day be an independent adult, the frustration felt when a blind or deaf child lacks the physical capacity to respond to a parent's efforts to interact, or the anger experienced by parents because their child is rejected by other children are experiences common to parents and families with handicapped children. The presence of these children may make some parents perceive themselves as failures or as representative of shattered dreams. Whatever the particular response, it is safe to conclude that it will have significant impact and, in most instances, will intensify stress on the family (Farber, 1968). While this in no way suggests that the presence of a handicapped child precludes family harmony and parental happiness—there are obviously numerous examples to the contrary—it does suggest that parental and family pleasures derived through having a handicapped child may take nontraditional forms. For example, parents and families may find themselves learning to "sign" so they can communicate more effectively with a hearing-impaired child or being satisfactorily involved in a community action program designed to benefit all developmentally disabled individuals. At the very least, the presence of an exceptional child creates unique challenges for both parents and the family (Barsh, 1968; Ross, 1964).

THE EDUCATOR'S ROLE IN SERVING THE NEEDS OF PARENTS AND FAMILIES

The role of educators in serving the needs of parents and families can at best be described as obscure. While educators, particularly teachers, are considered to be legitimate disseminators of educationally related information, they have historically not been perceived as a primary parental counseling resource. It should be noted, for example, that until only a short time ago, most techniques and procedures for confering or counseling with parents of handicapped children were developed by psychologists, psychiatrists, social workers, and counselors. Equally important, these methods were designed primarily for individuals representing these disciplines. Although some attention was focused on the application of accepted procedures by professionals working in the educational environment, especially school counselors and school psychologists, virtually no consideration was given classroom teachers, the professional group having the greatest amount of parental contact. This situation has changed, at least to some extent. Along with the increase in services provided children and youth has been the development of methodology and programs for parental involvement. Thus, most individuals assigned the task of interacting with parents, particularly those with special needs, have acquired some basic conferencing skills (Simpson & Poplin, 1981). Nevertheless, parent conferencing techniques and procedures for educational personnel have been developed and refined at a much closer pace than other educational components. Consequently, even though some advancements have been made in parent conferencing and counseling, this area remains probably the most neglected and underdeveloped skill in the repertoire of most educators. In spite of the fact that educators have not been perceived as primary parental resources, there is evidence to suggest that they can be trained to serve many parental needs (Clements & Alexander, 1975).

Educators represent the most economical and available resource. The concept of the least restrictive alternative refers not only to the placement of handicapped pupils in environments that most closely parallel the "normal" and that provide no greater limitations than are absolutely necessary but also to other dimensions of intervention. Although conclusive data are not available on the specific needs and levels of needs of parents, including those with exceptional children and youth, their needs appear to be normally distributed, with a small percentage of parents requiring either very little or a great deal of support and attention and the largest percentages falling somewhere between the extremes (Kroth, 1980). Thus, most parents will need an opportunity to exchange information with professionals and to receive information on how effectively to use school resources, participate in conferences, and serve as advocates for their own children. A smaller percentage of parents will require training in procedures for enabling them to serve the needs of their own children, such as tutoring or behavior management programs. Only a small percentage of parents will require in-depth counseling or therapy or will be interested in participating in parent advisory or "parent-to-parent" groups. Consequently, in the majority of cases, the parents' needs can be met most expediently and effectively by the classroom teacher or other education personnel. For those parents requiring greater degrees of support or involvement, the services of psychologists, psychiatrists, counselors, and social workers can be made available. However, especially in view of the significant shortage of highly trained mental health personnel, it is unrealistic to expect the most frequent and straightforward needs of parents to be served by highly trained counselors and mental health personnel. By totally relying on this limited and unnecessarily strong resource and by discounting the potential impact of educators, the vast majority of parents might be provided little, if any, appropriate attention.

Educators are in a better position than other professional groups to gain the trust of parents. Ample evidence exists to support the contention that parents, especially those with exceptional children, have frequently experienced frustration and difficulty when attempting to secure diagnostic, placement, and problem-solving services from professionals. Philip Roos, Executive Director of the National Association for Retarded Citizens and himself the parent of an exceptional child, recounted a number of the difficulties that he and his family encountered in attempting to secure appropriate services for their exceptional child. Roos (1978) noted that even though knowledgeable about the system and the procedures involved, "my wife and I embarked on a long series of catastrophic interactions with professionals which echoed the complaints I had heard so often from other parents" (p. 13).

A chronic complaint made by parents of exceptional children with regard to professionals is that these individuals frequently fail to communicate, listen, and provide necessary information or services and that they often give parents the impression that they lack a true commitment to or interest in the child or family. Although it is not being suggested that parents and families do not have some of the same difficulties with educators, these issues are frequently on a much smaller scale and, if they do exist, they are more amenable to change. Since there are probably no significant and consistent attitudinal and interpersonal differences among the various professionals who come into contact with parents and families and since each professional group conceivably strives toward the best interests of children and families with whom they interact, these differences are most likely a function of other factors. One such factor is the parents' opportunity for interacting and establishing rapport with their child's classroom teacher as compared with the other professional groups with whom they come into contact. Frequently, parents report that they simply do not have the opportunity to familiarize themselves with and develop trust in the myriad of professionals involved in the various educational and educationally related processes that determine the future of their child. Consequently, parents often indicate that their lack of familiarity with these individuals and their assigned roles and the infrequent nature of the contacts made with these professionals negate the opportunity to establish the trust and rapport necessary for an adequate conferencing relationship. In addition, since many ancillary professionals who are involved with exceptional children are charged with conveying diagnostic information, parents may understandably associate certain professionals with shock, pain, and despair. McDonald (1962) noted that "when parents of handicapped children meet in small groups for counseling, it may be predicted that an early topic of discussion will be their feelings toward professional workers, particularly those with whom they first discussed their child's problem" (p. 160). Since the educator's role is to serve as an advocate for children and their parents and to influence positively children's development rather than to label, diagnose, or determine the extent of parental responsibility for a problem, it is not surprising that teachers and other educational personnel should be perceived in a relatively positive light. Accordingly, parents may be in a far more favorable position to benefit from conferencing services rendered by educational personnel than by other professionals.

Finally, in spite of changes in societal attitudes, the majority of individuals in our culture are threatened, to some extent, by the prospect of needing the services of certain professional groups, particularly mental health professionals. This fear is well documented in parents of exceptional children and youth. Some parents either perceive counselors as providing few relevant and functional services or consider the role of these professionals exclusively to be the determination of the parents' responsibility for their child's problem. In addition, it is not at all unusual to find that parents of exceptional children are such victims of psychological stress that they deny their need for counseling or conferencing services. Many parents will attempt to avoid contact with certain professional groups because of their perceived threat. Hence, since educators will probably be a far less threatening and more available resource, many conferencing needs can most successfully be served by this group. In instances in which additional services are required, appropriately trained educators who have established a relationship with parents will be able to make the necessary referrals and recommendations.

Educators are in the most satisfactory position to participate in conferences with parents of exceptional children and youth. There is extensive evidence to suggest that education and training programs can function most effectively when parents are used in supportive roles (Berkowitz & Graziano, 1972; Lindsley, 1966; O'Dell, 1974) and when parents and professionals are able to build and maintain satisfactory lines of communication (Duncan & Fitzgerald, 1969). Both subjective and objective documentation indicates that programs demonstrating parental support and cooperation are able to achieve more satisfactory results than those that do not (Kroth, Whelan, & Stables, 1970). One salient feature of good communication with relevance to satisfying certain basic parental needs is the dissemination of accurate and current information. Although parents may have other than information needs, the vast majority of parents are interested in their child's classroom functioning. In addition, it stands to reason that the individual who has the closest and the most consistent contact with the pupil will be most capable of providing information and making necessary procedural changes. Consequently, educators must play an instrumental role in disseminating information to parents. In addition, parents frequently report that they feel most comfortable in discussing their child with the classroom teacher. Not only do educators almost universally have more relevant and current information about the child, but also parents often demonstrate a level of trust and openness toward them not found with many other individuals in the service professions. Therefore, it seems logical to take advantage of this fortuitous position and train educators to serve as many parental and family needs as appropriate.

Developing the Skills Necessary for Conferencing Success

While educators may be in an advantageous position to provide conferencing and counseling services to parents and families, success in this endeavor is ultimately a function of a person's attitude, skills, and conferencing philosophy.

Educators not only must be familiar with and proficient in the use of a variety of general and specific conferencing activities and procedures but also must recognize that for these skills to be implemented successfully they must be based on efficacious human interaction competencies and an individually constructed parent conferencing philosophy. Thus, while conferencing and counseling skills can be taught (Ivey, Miller, Normington, Morrill, & Haase, 1968), it is inaccurate to assume that cookbook approaches and universally applicable solutions will adequately meet the varied needs of parents and families. Basic to success in parent conferencing is the aptitude to interact successfully with others. Such a talent takes precedence over all specific counseling expertise. One generic aptitude associated with successful interaction with others is an interest in and sensitivity to people. Individuals who expect to serve the needs of parents and families must possess a genuine interest in people and a willingness to invest time and energy in arriving at solutions to their problems. Although there need not be an emphasis on "rescuing" another person, there must be an underlying core of humanism on which to draw and build. Rogers (1942) noted that:

> The person who is quite obtuse to the reactions of others, who does not sense the hostility or friendliness which exists between himself and others or between two of his acquaintances, is not likely to become a satisfactory counselor. There is no doubt that this quality can be developed, but unless an individual has a considerable degree of this social sensitivity, it is doubtful that counseling is his most promising field of effort. On the other hand, the individual who is naturally observant of the reactions of others, who can pick out of a classroom group the unhappy child, who can sense the personal antagonism which underlies casual argument, who is alert to the subtle differences in actions which show that one parent has a comfortable relationship with his child, another a relationship full of tensions—such a person has a good natural foundation upon which to build counseling skills. (p. 254)

In the final analysis, an interest in and sensitivity to people may be the most generic and significant determinant of success in the area of parent conferencing and family involvement.

As noted previously, educational conferencers must have a clear understanding of their own values in order to develop their personal conferencing philosophy and to serve a wide range of parents and families. According to Kroth and Simpson (1977), "The importance of assessing your own values or attempting to understand another's values is that ultimately you tend to act on those values you cherish the most" (p. 8). If educators are to serve children, parents, and families, many of whom come from cultures and backgrounds that are different from their own, they must be in a position to understand their own values and those of the individuals with whom they relate.

The process of conflict resolution, information sharing, cooperative planning, and most of the other activities engaged in during conferences with parents will be effective only to the extent that parents, families, and professionals understand and respect the values of one another. Often conflicts between families and professionals arise because the two groups fail to understand each other's values and the significance of individual goals and expectations. Rutherford and Edgar (1979) suggested that, "When a specific school problem already exists, a misunderstanding between parents and teachers of each other's motives or actions causes the additional problem of interpersonal conflict" (p. 40). The lack of value sensitivity can serve not only to increase the probability of conflicts but also to reduce the potential efficacy of intervention and conferencing efforts.

A third generic skill necessary for effective human interaction is the capacity to attend to others effectively. The ability to listen and in turn communicate this attention to parents and families is one of the most basic attributes required for successful conferencing. According to a number of authorities (Benjamin, 1969; Kroth, 1975), the ability to create an effective listening environment and to understand parents and families, including their nonverbal and emotional responses, is such a basic requisite that many other conferencing components and strategies are contingent on this single skill.

Listening is not a passive process. Rather, it involves the professional's full attention to another person. In addition, active listening requires that attention be given to more than manifest verbal messages, including awareness of the affect, body language, pauses, and tone as well as those messages that are hinted at but not actually spoken. While active listening may be discounted because of its elementary nature, it will most likely be one ingredient of any successful conferencing program.

Finally, the conferencer must be able to establish initial trust and rapport with parents and families. This capacity will typically be the basis for future cooperative efforts. Research has clearly documented the utility of initial rapport-building efforts (Duncan & Fitzgerald, 1969). Without a positive interpersonal relationship on which to build, it is highly unlikely that the educator will be in a position to apply specific conferencing and problem-solving procedures. Hence, in addition to the professional's knowledge and skill, there also will be a basic relationship on which to build. Successful conferencing programs seem to occur most frequently when parents and families feel assured that they are a necessary and valued resource and that they are working in concert with professionals in their child's behalf.

Generic skills and an aptitude for parental and family involvement are not sufficient elements of successful conferencing. Included in the competent educator's conferencing repertoire should be the following:

- skill in establishing appropriate information exchange systems

- skill in training parents to be better consumers of and participants in the educational process and thus better advocates for their own children

- skill in training parents and families to employ appropriate behavior management, socialization, and educational procedures for their own children in the natural environment

- skill in arranging for parental and/or family counseling and therapeutic services

- skill in arranging for parents and families to participate in parent-coordinated service programs.

Information Exchange Systems

The educational conferencer must be capable of obtaining relevant facts about the child and family and of providing appropriate information to parents and families. This informational exchange process serves not only to share significant facts and attitudes but also to create a forum for more informal discussions. Such opportunities for parents and family members to share their feelings and attitudes are often more beneficial than exchange of factual data.

Information to parents and family members should include assessment data and a chance for participants to discuss the findings. Even though parents and families may have received an interpretation following an assessment of their child, they will most likely benefit from a review of the information and from an opportunity to discuss the issues involved. Parents and families should also be given a description of the educational program to be provided their child, including the teacher's educational philosophy and strategy, the academic and behavioral remediation programs scheduled for use, the auxiliary services to be provided, and the available parent and family programs. Other information to be disseminated should include an identification of the procedures to be used in evaluation of pupil progress and the manner in which these data will be communicated. Parents and families should also be apprised of problem-solving alternatives, agencies, and resources available to them through the school or community. Finally, parents and families must be given an opportunity to ask specific questions about a child and the child's program and to present any problems they may have.

Information solicited typically includes a parent and/or family impression of a child and a discussion of possible discrepancies between their perception and the manner in which the child is viewed by professionals. Additionally, information should be sought regarding a child's developmental history, personality, strengths and weaknesses, likes and dislikes, school history, and parental and family expectations for the child and the teacher. Finally, information is needed about the home, family, and other social factors.

Consumer and Advocacy Training Programs

Even though parents have been granted significant authority in determining the educational procedures to be used with their children, particularly those with special needs, few provisions have been made for training them in how to serve in this role. Even though parents are eligible to participate in individualized education program conferences and other parent-teacher meetings, they have not been trained in how to do so. If parents are to be expected to function at a level consistent with their assigned rights, they must be provided appropriate training. "In order for professionals to be willing to train parents in procedures for participation in educational conferences and other related activities, they must believe that a majority of parents, with training and encouragement, are willing to become involved with schools in generating and sharing concerns and goals for their child's education and that this participation adds to the school's ability to help the child" (Simpson & Poplin, 1981, p. 21). Unless the parents' need for sufficient information in this area is met, they cannot be expected to participate in parent-teacher conferences in a manner that will maximize the efforts of the school.

Training Programs in Implementing Individualized Programs at Home

Research has confirmed that parents and families can be effectively trained to implement educationally related services with their own children (Berkowitz & Graziano, 1972; O'Dell, 1974). Both as academic tutors and agents of behavior management, parents and other family members have shown themselves to be valuable resources and a means of extending professional intervention and academic programs beyond the classroom setting. Although some parents and families may be unmotivated or unsuited for this role, others will be highly appropriate. Training of parents and families to serve in this role provides a vehicle for extending problem-solving efforts into noneducational environments and for coordinating their motivations for involvement and participation.

Under professional direction, parents and family members can be trained to implement individualized tutoring programs with their own child. Such tutoring serves both to involve these individuals in a child's academic program and to communicate family concern to the child. This activity also provides a means for structuring interactions between the family and child and a way of bridging the gap between the home and school environments.

Parents and families have also been trained to employ behavior management procedures with children. This approach has allowed parents and families to effect planned behavioral changes in the natural environment and thus to extend the therapeutic influence of professionals beyond the classroom.

Counseling, Therapy, and Consultation Services

While the need for in-depth therapeutic and counseling opportunities for parents and families is minimal, resources must be made available for the small percentage of parents and families who require such attention. In most instances, the educator's role in meeting this need will be to put parents in touch with those professionals who are best equipped to serve them. Family counseling, psychotherapy, and other clinical assistance is so significant to parents and families requiring such services that they promptly must be made available.

Parent-Coordinated Service Programs

Some parents and families wish to go beyond the needs of themselves and their offspring to serve the larger community of exceptional children and their families. This might include serving on advisory boards, participating in community service programs or "parent-to-parent" groups, or working as volunteers in programs for exceptional children and youth.

The importance of these activities can be highlighted by noting that basically all major amendments in policies and services for handicapped children have been effected through the work of parent groups. These results, along with the need for continued efforts in this area, may serve as the motivation for certain parents and families to work at local, state, and national levels to secure more and better services for all handicapped individuals. For those parents and families with the time, ability, and energy, opportunities for such service to the larger community of exceptional citizens should be made available.

Developing a Personalized Conferencing Philosophy and Style

The heterogeneous nature and needs of parents and families as well as the variant characteristics of educators necessitates the development of individually formulated conferencing philosophies and styles. Thus, while certain general aptitudes and specific skills are necessary for successful parental and family interaction, these must be applied in accordance with the conferencer's strengths and weaknesses. For reasons discussed previously, ready-made approaches and universally applicable strategies are neither appropriate nor successful with all parents and families.

Consequently, conferencers must work to develop styles that are pragmatic and selective and in harmony with their individual qualities, temperament, and predilections. Furthermore, conferencers must accept each theoretical position as potentially valuable and contributory to the goal of serving parents and families. However, they must recognize the inherent dangers associated with the acceptance of any single position or model as sufficient for meeting the needs of all parents and families. While adherence to a single theoretical model may satisfy a conferencer's need for security, it is rarely adequate for serving a wide variety of parents and families. As previously noted, the American family has undergone significant changes in the past decades. These changed and variant needs can be served most adequately by conferencers who have developed their own personal styles and who are flexible enough to be able to employ different approaches in an effort to meet the varied needs of the parents and families with whom they associate. If educational conferencers are truly to meet the challenge presented by present-day parents and families, they must possess a repertoire and procedures that are in accord with their own character and that can be individualized for use with a variety of parents and families.

CONCLUSION

More than ever before the "average" American family must be considered a nonexistent entity. The needs and characteristics of families are not only varied but also in a state of constant change. Therefore, the educational conferencer must be familiar with the trends impacting on parents and families in addition to having available strategies appropriate for serving their individualized needs.

REFERENCES

Barnard, J.B., Christophersen, E.R., & Wolf, M.M. Teaching children appropriate shopping behavior through parent training in the supermarket setting. *Journal of Applied Behavior Analysis*, 1977, *10*, 49-60.

Barsh, R. *The parents of the handicapped child: The study of child rearing practices*. Springfield, Ill.: Thomas, 1968.

Bayles, E.E., & Hood, B.L. *Growth of American educational thought and practice*. New York: Harper & Row, 1966.

Benjamin, A. *The helping interview*. Boston: Houghton Mifflin, 1969.

Berkowitz, B.P., & Graziano, A.M. Training parents as behavior therapists: A review. *Behavior Research and Therapy*, 1972, *10*, 297-317.

Bronfenbrenner, U. *The ecology of human development: Experiments by nature and design*. Cambridge, Mass.: Harvard University Press, 1979.

Clements, J.E., & Alexander, R.N. Parent training: Bringing it all back home. *Focus on Exceptional Children*, 1975, *7*(5), 1-12.

Curwin, R.L., & Fuhrmann, B.S. *Discovering your teaching self: Humanistic approaches to effective teaching*. Englewood Cliffs, N.J.: Prentice-Hall, 1975.

Duncan, L.W., & Fitzgerald, P.W. Increasing the parent-child communication through counselor-parent conferences. *Personnel and Guidance Journal*, 1969, *47*(6), 514-517.

Farber, B. *Mental retardation: Its social context and social consequences*. Boston: Houghton Mifflin, 1968.

Gallop, G. The eleventh annual Gallop Poll of the public's attitudes toward the public schools. *Phi Delta Kappan,* September 1979, p. 41.

Goode, W.J. World revolution and family patterns. *Journal of Marriage and Family,* 1971, *33,* 624-635.

Hetherington, E.M., & Martin, B. Family interaction and psychopathology in children. In H.C. Quay & J.S. Werry (Eds.), *Psychopathological disorders of childhood.* New York: Wiley, 1972.

Hoffman, L.W., & Nye, F.I. *Working mothers.* San Francisco: Jossey-Bass, 1974.

Isakson, R.L. Whatever happened to the Waltons? *Instructor,* September 1979, pp. 77-79.

Ivey, A.E., Miller, C.D., Normington, C.J., Morrill, W.H., & Haase, R. Micro-counseling and attending behavior: An approach to prepracticum counseling training. *Journal of Counseling Psychology,* 1968, *15*(5), part 2. (Monograph Supplement)

Karpowitz, D.H. A conceptualization of the American family. In M.J. Fine (Ed.), *Handbook on parent education.* New York: Academic Press, 1980.

Kauffman, J.M. *Characteristics of children's behavior disorders.* Columbus, Ohio: Merrill, 1977.

Kroth, R.L. *Communicating with parents of exceptional children.* Denver: Love Publishing, 1975.

Kroth, R. *Strategies for effective parent-teacher interaction.* Institute for Parent Involvement, University of New Mexico, Albuquerque, 1980.

Kroth, R., & Simpson, R. *Parent conferences as a teaching strategy.* Denver: Love Publishing, 1977.

Kroth, R.L., Whelan, R.J., & Stables, J.M. Teacher application of behavior principles in home and classroom environments. *Focus on Exceptional Children,* 1970, *3,* 1-10.

Lindsley, O.R. An experiment with parents handling behavior at home. *Johnstone Bulletin,* 1966, *9,* 27-36.

McAfee, J.K., & Vergason, G.A. Parent involvement in the process of special education: Establishing the new partnership. *Focus on Exceptional Children,* 1979, *11*(2), 1-15.

McDonald, E. *Understanding those feelings.* Pittsburgh: Stanwix House, 1962.

Martin, B. Parent-child relations. In F.D. Horowitz (Ed.), *Review of child development research,* (Vol. 4). Chicago: University of Chicago Press, 1975.

Meyen, E.L. *Exceptional children and youth: An introduction.* Denver: Love Publishing, 1978.

Needle, R.H., Griffin, T., Svendsen, R., & Berney, C. Teacher stress: Sources and consequences. *Journal of School Health,* 1980, *50*(2), 96-99.

O'Dell, S. Training parents in behavior modification: A review. *Psychological Bulletin,* 1974, *81,* 418-433.

Raths, L., Harmin, M., & Simon, S. *Values and teaching.* Columbus, Ohio: Merrill, 1966.

Rogers, C. *Counseling and psychotherapy.* Boston: Houghton Mifflin, 1942.

Roos, P. Parents of mentally retarded children—misunderstood and mistreated. In A.P. Turnbull & N.R. Turnbull (Eds.), *Parents speak out: Views from the other side of the two-way mirror.* Columbus: Merrill, 1978.

Ross, A.O. *The exceptional child in the family.* New York: Grune & Stratton, 1964.

Rutherford, R.B., & Edgar, E. *Teachers and parents: A guide to interaction and cooperation.* Boston: Allyn & Bacon, 1979.

Simon, S.D., Howe, L.W., & Kirschenbaum, H. *Values clarification: A handbook of practical strategies for teachers and students.* New York: Hart, 1972.

Simpson, R., & Poplin, M. Parents as agents of change: A behavioral approach. *School Psychology Review,* 1981, *10*(1), 15-25.

Simpson, R., & Swenson, C. The effects and side-effects of an overcorrection procedure applied by parents of severely emotionally disturbed children in a home environment. *Behavior Disorders,* 1980, *5*(2), 79-85.

Wallerstein, J.S., & Keely, J.B. The effects of parental divorce: Experiences of the child in later latency. *American Journal of Orthopsychiatry,* 1976, *46*(2), 257-269.

Chapter 2

Impact of the Exceptional Child on the Family

Parents and families exert a significant influence on the social and intellectual development of the children with whom they are associated. As noted by Kauffman (1977), "The earliest socialization experiences of children involve a dyadic relationship with the mother, and these initial social interactions are first extended to include other family members" (p. 73). It is also equally obvious that children influence the families of which they are a part. This effect is particularly significant when a child is exceptional (Greer, 1975). While the degree of such an influence is related to a variety of factors, including the severity and nature of a child's exceptionality, any handicapping condition in a family member has a significant effect on the entire family. Buscaglia (1975) observed that "a disability is not a desirable thing and there is no reason to believe otherwise. It will, in most cases, cause pain, discomfort, embarrassment, tears, confusion and the expenditure of a great deal of time and money" (p. 11). Parents and families bear this pain most directly.

Almost without exception parents of exceptional children have reported difficulties directly associated with their child's condition (Turnbull & Turnbull, 1978). Gorham (1975) identified a variety of problems and obstacles that she and her family experienced when securing appropriate services for her handicapped child. While she acknowledged that they were able to survive the ordeal, it was only after "accumulating some scars which clearly mark us parents as members of the 'lost generation' " (p. 522). Gorham further observed the following:

> We are angry. We have gone to the helping profession and have received too little help.
>
> We are still in awe of specialists and intimidated by their expertise.
>
> We are unduly grateful to principals or school directors for merely accepting our children in their programs. The spectre of 24 hour a day, 7 day a week care at home, with the state institution as an alternative, has made us too humbly thankful.

We demonstrate a certain indifference to the latest bandwagon on which the mental retardation experts are riding. Mixed messages have been so much a part of our history that, rather than join the parades we tend to listen politely, then do what we think best for our child. We are often, therefore, accused of apathy.

Many of us have concluded that it is best not to worry about next year (or tomorrow) because things might be better then (or worse). Certainly it seems impossible to 'plan for the future' as most of us are so frequently admonished to do. Generally I have found that those who wanted me to plan for Beckie's future were suggesting that I place her on the roster for permanent residence in the state institution. That is, in fact, the only option available at present. In Maryland, I cannot even provide for her future by putting money aside and setting up an inheritance. If I die, and she must enter an institution, the state's general fund becomes heir to her belongings, and the money saved could go for something as remote to her well being as highway construction. So we worry about the future, but planning for it is not yet really a fruitful activity.

We are tired. We have kept our children at home and raised them ourselves, with all the extra demands on time and energy which that implies—often without much help from the community, neighborhood, professionals, friends, or relatives, and in fact commonly against their well intentioned advice. We have founded parent groups and schools, run them ourselves, held fund raising events to pay teachers and keep our little special schools afloat, organized baby sitting groups, and summer play groups. We have built and repaired special playground equipment for our children's use at home and at school. We have painted classrooms and buildings; we have written legislators and educated them about our children's needs and rights. We have collated and stapled hundreds of newsletters, attended school board meetings, lobbied at the state legislature for better legislation for handicapped children, informed newspaper reporters about inhumane conditions in institutions, and written letters to editors. All this we have done for a decade or more.[1]

It has also been observed (Gorham, Jardins, Page, Pettis, & Scheiber, 1975) that parents of handicapped children are frequently placed in the position of needing to secure services for their children in a society that places little value on the handicapped. Gorham et al. concluded that:

Society does not view their children as worthy of investment; in fact, it disdains those with certain handicaps. The parent, in turn, feels devalued and often is as he proceeds about the business of looking for help for this child. Inevitably he will feel the conflict between his quite natural desire to have 'the best' for his children and the various obstacles to getting it for this child. (p. 155)

The problems and difficulties routinely experienced by parents of exceptional children when attempting to secure appropriate services for their children require educators and other professionals to be able to understand an atypical child's impact on a family system, to have available procedures and strategies for aiding parents and their nonhandicapped children in meeting their own needs, and to provide avenues for allowing parents to serve as effective advocates and agents for their children. Only such a multifaceted thrust will help serve the best interests of both the exceptional child and the family.

Family systems are characterized not only by emotional and biological ties but also by established roles and norms. These traditions and standards structure family members' activities and the manner in which their duties are fulfilled. Reiss (1971) suggested that the introduction of a new child into a family system, either through birth or adoption, results in role changes for the entire family. This change process tends to be most dramatic with the birth of a handicapped child or the discovery of a handicapping condition in one of the family members. Not only can the presence of a "less-than-perfect" child serve to threaten individual family members, but it may also disrupt the normal progression and functioning of the entire family system. Farber (1968) reported that a retarded child disrupts the normal cycle of families. In particular, he noted that while other children in a family become more independent and accept greater amounts of responsibility, the handicapped person remains at various levels of dependency. Farber also found that marital integration and happiness may be reduced by the presence of a handicapped child, particularly when marital difficulties existed prior to the birth of the child.

In her book *The Child Who Never Grew* (1950), Pearl S. Buck wrote "The first cry from my heart, when I knew she would never be anything but a child, was the age old cry that we all make before inevitable sorrow: 'Why must this happen to me?' To this there could be no answer and there was none." Interestingly, Buck's analysis remains relatively current. That is, in spite of the volume of information available on the impact of an exceptional child on the family, there continues to exist a paucity of empirically valid data on the exact nature of this impact. In fact, the majority of the information available on the topic is based on case studies and subjective reports (Turnbull & Turnbull, 1978).

PARENTAL REACTIONS

As a function of its subjective and anecdotal nature, much of the literature dealing with parental reactions to having a handicapped child is characterized by diversity and contrariety. However, in spite of this variance there are some indications that parents of handicapped children experience some commonality of feeling. Love (1970), for example, contended that parents go through a series of emotional reactions, including shock, refusal, guilt, bitterness, envy, rejection, and, finally, adjustment. Others (Cansler & Martin, 1974; Robinson, 1970; Robinson & Robinson, 1965; Weber, 1974) identified similar stages. While different stages and descriptors of stages have been identified, most have included shock, disbelief, and anger at one extreme and emotional and intellectual acceptance at the other. In addition, parents are thought to move from feelings of isolation and total self-concern to a willingness to aid and participate in cooperative ventures with other parents (MacDonald, 1962).

Other researchers have described the reactions of parents of handicapped children in terms of recurrent feelings, including chronic sorrow and inadequacy (Love, 1973). Perske (1973) termed the feelings experienced by parents of exceptional children as "the glooms," "the speeds," "the blocks," "the hurts," "the guilts," "the greats," "the hates," and the "give ups." These reactions are reported not to be experienced by all parents and may vary in duration and strength of response when they do occur. Some researchers perceive the reactions of parents of exceptional children as ego-supportive measures and defense mechanisms that enable them to deal with difficult circumstances.

Finally, it has been suggested that parents' reactions to having an exceptional child parallel reactions to death and dying. Obviously, this pattern is highly correlated with the age of the child at the time of diagnosis, the severity of the handicapping condition, and a host of other factors. Thus, it is unlikely that the parents of a child diagnosed as having a mild learning problem would respond in the same manner as the parents of a child with Down's syndrome or one who is severely handicapped. Nonetheless, it is quite common for parents of handicapped children to respond with emotions similar to those described in terminally ill patients and their families (Kubler-Ross, 1969). In particular, parents have been noted to deny their child's condition (Safford & Arbitman, 1975), to go through a bereavement process (Baum, 1962), or to manifest any one of a number of other emotional reactions before ultimately accepting their child's condition. During particularly difficult periods, parents may manifest both psychologic and somatic symptoms, including somatic distress, preoccupation, guilt, hostility, and anxiety. These patterns appear to be designed to reduce feelings of loss, disappointment, anger, or guilt.

A major topic related to parental reaction has been the manner in which parents were initially apprised of their child's exceptionality. MacDonald (1962) reported that contact with professionals is a topic that parents of exceptional children wish to address. Akerley (1978) clearly articulated her concerns in this area, noting

> We don't begin in anger. We start out the way all parents of all children
> do: with respect, reverence really, for the professional and his skill. The

pediatrician, the teacher, the writer of books and articles on child development, they are the source of wisdom from which we must draw in order to be good parents. We believe, we consult, we do as we are told, and all goes well unless . . . one of our kids has a handicap. (p. 40)

Without attempting to recount the numerous both positive and negative experiences encountered by parents of exceptional children in working and interacting with professionals, suffice it to say that such experiences are frequently identified as the most significant initial encounter parents have. In addition, professionals have been frequently admonished by parents of exceptional children for not being more skillful in this area (Roos, 1978). Parents have recounted instances of gross insensitivity and brusqueness at a time when they are most vulnerable. While parents on occasion may exaggerate their negative experiences with professionals, professionals must become more skillful in their initial contacts with parents, particularly when such contacts involve dissemination of diagnostic and classification information. In particular, professionals must accurately yet compassionately communicate diagnostic findings and recommendations, aid parents in securing appropriate services, utilize suitable and effective language and communication skills, and support parents through what will undoubtedly be an extremely difficult time for them and the rest of their family. As has been suggested previously, such initial positive and supportive interactions with parents will establish a basis for future effective communication and a positive parent-professional partnership.

SIBLING REACTIONS

The position that a handicapped child can have a potentially deleterious influence on other children in the family has existed for a long time (Farber, 1968). Klein (1972), Love (1973), and Telford and Sawrey (1977) all reported that nonexceptional siblings in a family may suffer as a function of their handicapped brother's or sister's condition, particularly when they are required to assume major responsibility for the child's care. These researchers also noted that nonexceptional children frequently feel resentful and neglected because of the immoderate attention given their handicapped sibling.

This negative influence, however, has been refuted by other researchers. Graliker, Fishler, and Koch (1962), for instance, interviewed the teenage siblings of mentally retarded children to determine the effects of having a retarded brother or sister in their school, social, and family life. These researchers reported that the teenage siblings led generally "normal" lives and had adequate social opportunities and peer relationships. In addition, it was revealed that the teenagers had adequate home relationships and understood and accepted their handicapped siblings' condition. Based on this study it was concluded that the presence of a young retarded child in a family did not have an adverse influence on the teenagers sampled.

NEEDS OF PARENTS OF EXCEPTIONAL CHILDREN

Aiding parents in meeting their own needs represents a major component of facilitating the acceptance and accommodation of an exceptional child in a family. While they demonstrate a variety of needs and dimensions of needs, parents of exceptional children frequently have several common desires.

Parents need appropriate educational resources and an opportunity to partici-pate in program planning. While the importance of other needs cannot be denied, it must be acknowledged that these will be secondary to the desire for adequate educational and treatment programs (Justice, O'Connor, & Warren, 1971). Roos (1977) observed that most parent organizations have been formed to promote educational programs for their children. He also noted that these groups have focused on facilitating the involvement of parents in such programs. While the proliferation of educational programs has reduced the conspicuousness of this need, such progress in no way has diminished the importance of appropriate educational resources and programs in the eyes of parents.

Having secured an appropriate educational alternative for their child, many parents want to become actively involved in the program. Blodgett (1971) at-tributed this involvement to a desire on the part of parents to consider their child "normal" and to a frequent parental view of their offspring as having more ability and potential than acknowledged by the child's teachers. In addition, some parents have reported that involvement in their child's educational program and familiarity with educational procedures and protocol enable them to channel their concerns, anger, frustrations, guilt, and energies into more productive areas (Simpson & Poplin, 1981).

While such a desire for participation can frequently result in improved programs and services for children, many parents report that they suffer from a lack of information on how best to become involved in their child's educational program. At present, a major discrepancy exists between the authority and involvement potential of parents of exceptional children and their actual capacity to function. That is, parents not only must be provided the legal authority to aid in formulating and implementing their child's educational program, but they also must be pro-vided the necessary training to permit them to serve in such a capacity. While a number of practitioners have observed that an effective parent-educator relation-ship is contingent on equal role status (Dean, 1975), it is obvious that this relationship can develop only in situations in which parents have sufficient training to function effectively. The competence of parents will be forthcoming only when educators are willing to train parents to serve as advocates for their own children.

Parents should also be provided an opportunity to serve their own children in the natural environment. Such direct service ean take the form of professionally monitored tutoring programs and parent-applied behavior management projects.

Both approaches provide a documented means for allowing parents to become a part of their child's educational program and an efficacious strategy for extending the therapeutic influence of professionals beyond the classroom environment.

Finally, for those parents who have had their own basic needs and those of their offspring satisfied, an opportunity should exist to serve the larger community of exceptional persons and their families. This includes serving on advisory boards, in community service projects, in "parent-to-parent" groups, and as volunteers in programs and organizations. While some parents may lack the interest or ability to be involved in these areas, the opportunity should exist for those parents with the time, ability, and energy.

While not traditionally considered a major need, the involvement of parents in educational, treatment, and related programs can frequently serve to channel their frustrations and other energies into productive efforts. Thus, while not "therapeutic" in the strictest sense of the word, the process can serve both to augment direct pupil services and to allow parents an opportunity to sublimate their faculties into more productive efforts.

Parents need opportunities for communication. Among the most basic and significant needs of parents of exceptional children is the opportunity to communicate with professionals and other persons involved with their children and families. Frequently, parents report that they lack the opportunity to be heard, recognized, and understood (Allen & Cortazzo, 1970). Barsh (1968) observed that most parents have a limited understanding of what goes on in their child's school. Barnes, Eyman, and Engolz (1974) supported this notion, noting that most contact between parents and educators is indirect, either through telephone calls or notes. These researchers further reported that most parent-educator contacts are made in reference to problems, that most parents perceive the concerns of their child's teacher as different from their own, and that most parents are intimidated by school personnel. Without doubt, the majority of parents of exceptional children desire more effective interaction and communication opportunities with the educators who serve their children.

Therefore, professionals must be able to listen with understanding and skill to the parents with whom they interact. Success in communication may in fact be far more a function of an individual's ability to establish conditions favorable to two-way communication than to skill in sending a message (Rogers, 1951). Included in this process must be assurances to parents that they are being heard and understood. Active listening, whereby the conferencer is able to identify and understand what a parent is communicating and feeling, including the message behind the words, often serves as a primary vehicle for aiding parents to understand their own feelings and frustrations relative to having an exceptional child. Professionals who are skillful at attending to parents and whose comments are relevant to the topics under discussion are most effective in meeting the communication needs of parents. Conversely, conferencers who insist on changing the subject and who avoid sensitive issues will communicate an absence of true interest and involvement.

As another component of the effective communication process, parents must be allowed the flexibility of structuring a portion of the format and content of at least some parent-educator conferences. In particular, they must be able to present specific problems and expect the conferencer to provide an appropriate response. Just as importantly, the conferencer must facilitate the discussion of issues and concerns that may lack a simple response. That is, parents must be provided an atmosphere in which they are free to explore certain feelings and attitudes while being exposed to nothing more than an empathic listener. It is not at all unusual for parents of exceptional children to express attitudes, opinions, or feelings about their child that may appear inappropriate, extravagant, or rash. While the conferencer's natural reaction may be to correct the parent's perception or provide a solution or answer, the parent may be seeking nothing more than an opportunity to be heard. Even though it is tempting to "set the record straight" the conferencer must give parents an opportunity to share their perceptions and feelings regarding particular aspects of their child's exceptionality (Schlesinger & Meadow, 1976).

One mother of a severely emotionally disturbed child revealed that she believed her daughter's condition was "God's punishment for my evil ways." She confided that she became pregnant with her daughter out of wedlock, much to the displeasure of her parents. Although she and the child's father, her current husband, were married shortly after the mother learned she was pregnant, she revealed that she remains guilty over the incident. That her later-to-be-diagnosed-autistic daughter was born on Christmas Eve was perceived by the mother to be an omen. During a conference this parent indicated that logically she acknowledged that her daughter's handicap was "not God's punishment;" however, she indicated that "my feelings have remained the same after all these years." Obviously, this mother was not seeking an answer to a question but rather someone to listen and empathize with her situation.

As part of effective communication, parents must also be given the opportunity to have their messages received without distortion. While conferencers may wish to decline support or reinforcement of a particular message, they must nonetheless give parents a chance to be heard. An opportunity to send a message without distortion or denial is a vital component of the communication process. Responses such as, "I know you really don't feel that way," "You don't know what you are saying," "You couldn't possibly mean that," all serve to deny and fail to confirm a parent's thoughts and emotions. These responses place parents in the position of being required either to deny their own perceptions ("I guess I really didn't mean that") or to create a potential conflict ("I meant exactly what I said"). In either case, responses that fail to confirm a parent's message will detract from further attempts at communicating with professionals.

In addition to the more universal requirements of effective communication, sufficient attention must be directed to the interpretation and reinterpretation of diagnostic information during parent conferencing. As suggested by numerous researchers and practitioners (Love, 1970; MacDonald, 1962; Dembinski & Mauser, 1977), this area represents a primary concern for parents. Given the salience of this topic, it is essential that the conferencer allot sufficient time for discussing issues related to the diagnostic process, even in instances in which the parents have previously been provided an interpretation. Included should be a discussion of those issues, concerns, and problems that led to a referral; a summary and discussion of assessment procedures and findings; and a summary and discussion of recommendations and the manner in which they are to be implemented. While most parents receive an interpretation of their child's functioning on diagnostic measures, few are given an opportunity to discuss the findings and their own feelings about the results.

Parents must also be provided an opportunity to obtain more general information. Information to be disseminated during the initial contact with the parents, but which may need to be reviewed periodically, includes items pertaining to individualized education programs, the teacher's educational philosophy, the academic and social intervention programs being employed, ancillary and related services provided, and program and school evaluation procedures. In addition, parents must be provided an opportunity to address items of specific interest or concern to them.

A discussion of the child's future should also be part of the conference. Included should be prognosis, eventual position in society, and postschool alternatives. Although both parents and educators may be somewhat reluctant to address this topic, its significance warrants appropriate attention. While educators obviously lack precise mechanisms for determining a child's future, they can aid parents in identifying and evaluating future options and alternatives. In addition, educators can apprise parents of the postschool dispositions of exceptional children and youth similar to those of their own offspring. The intent of this process is to require parents to address the future and to begin identifying future alternatives. This process necessitates that options other than institutionalization and maintaining a child at home be identified. While many parents may demonstrate some reluctance in discussing this issue, most will acknowledge that "the future" represents a major concern.

Finally, parents of exceptional children may need assurance and confirmation that it is understandable and acceptable to experience negative attitudes and feelings about having an exceptional child. In addition, some parents may need to be encouraged to pursue interests other than serving and advocating for their handicapped child. That is, parents should be encouraged to attend to their own needs and those of other family members and to recognize that being the parent of a handicapped child need not and should not be their sole interest and pursuit.

Overcommitment on the part of parents of exceptional children can sometimes be as detrimental as inattention.

Parents need mechanisms for effectively accommodating the exceptional child in the family structure. The identification of a handicapped child almost universally has significant impact on parents and other family members. A child who is less than a perfect reflection of his or her forefathers and who will alter the family structure will almost without exception generate strong emotions in parents and siblings. Prior to and concurrently with the adjustment to an exceptional child, parents and families will experience a variety of stages and responses, including shock, mourning, denial, blame, guilt, hostility, and depression. To offer assistance to parents of exceptional children, educators must be able to recognize the effect of an exceptional child on the family structure and be able to communicate this potential impact to family members.

According to Simmons-Martin (1976), parents' psychological as well as information needs must be satisfied if they are to understand and plan for an exceptional child. Psychologically, they must be able to understand their own feelings and responses and those of others toward their handicapped child. Information needed for understanding and accommodation by parents includes data on both normal and atypical child development and a knowledge of specific procedures for aiding an exceptional child in functioning at his or her ability level. Parents must also be able to help the exceptional child's siblings understand the situation and their personal feelings regarding their brother or sister. Finally, parents must be aided in comprehending the potential problems associated with placing undue responsibility on nonexceptional children for the care of their exceptional sibling.

Hayden (1976) supported the notion that parents and siblings of exceptional children should be aware of the influence of a handicapped child's condition on the family. In particular, she stressed that some families need a time to adjust to the handicapped child, an opportunity to recognize that they may need help themselves, and encouragement to seek assistance from appropriate agencies. Hayden also suggested that accurate information can often aid parents in understanding the dynamics of their situation. Included should be a discussion of issues about which parents may be afraid to ask and the recanting of misconceptions about various types of handicapping conditions.

Olshansky (1970) also suggested that nonexceptional members of a family may require services and attention and observed that most families with a handicapped child experience "chronic sorrow." In addition, this researcher suggested that quality clinical services, preschool programs, baby-sitting and respite care, and adult education programs can aid parents and families in meeting their own personal needs.

Justice et al. (1971) reported that most parents do not receive assistance for their own problems or those of their families. This is particularly true with regard to minority group parents, who commonly reported being unaware of available services. These parents did, however, identify a need for workshops, recreational alternatives, counseling, respite care, and medical facilities.

While the presence of an exceptional child will inevitably have a significant impact on a family, the deleterious effects of the event may be minimized. A primary goal for educational conferencers and other professionals must be to help parents understand and plan for an exceptional child as a family member. Regardless of their stated job description, educators must be willing to work for the preservation of a family's unity and to employ necessary procedures to ensure that the presence of an exceptional child in a family does not result in the system's destruction.

FACILITATING THE ACCEPTANCE AND ACCOMMODATION OF AN EXCEPTIONAL CHILD IN A FAMILY SYSTEM

Even though the accommodation of an exceptional child in a family will be a gradual transaction associated with a variety of factors that may be beyond the control of the conferencer, the educator can have significant influence on the process. This facilitative influence can be accomplished, however, only with the use of well-planned procedures and strategies. Included should be consideration of the following:

- Listen to parents. This is very frequently what parents are looking for and, therefore, the most therapeutic offering that can be made.

- Avoid hasty attempts at problem solving, advice giving, and information dissemination. Frequently, parents are simply looking for an opportunity to share their concerns with someone who can empathize with their situation.

- Do not attempt to convince parents that a handicapped child is good or beneficial for them and their family. While they can be aided in accommodating the child, they should not be told that the event is advantageous.

- Apprise parents of the potential impact of an exceptional child on the family. The conferencer should not allow problems and conditions to occur without providing some type of appropriate warning.

- Encourage parents and families to pursue interests other than serving their exceptional child. While positive action programs can be beneficial to the larger community of exceptional children, parents should be dissuaded from totally committing their lives to their own exceptional child or programs for exceptional persons.

- Provide parents with alternatives and opportunities for participating appropriately with their own exceptional child and in programs designed to serve other exceptional individuals.

- Encourage parents to assume responsibility for their own child. Do not do everything for them.
- Encourage parents to share their feelings about having an exceptional child. Parents should be made aware of the advantages of having someone to talk with about their concerns.
- Encourage parents to examine their child's future. Included should be the identification of alternatives available to the child and family.
- Identify procedures that the parents can employ with their own child to train and develop functional skills and accomplish agreed-upon goals.
- Aid parents in identifying areas of growth and accomplishment shown by their child.
- Avoid responding negatively or discouragingly to lofty goals set by parents for their exceptional child. A certain measure of overestimation can be advantageous.
- Attempt to aid parents and families in understanding that an exceptional child is only one member of the family and, therefore, should be responded to in that fashion as much as possible.
- Be aware of value system differences between the home and school.
- Do not attempt to produce or use guilt to motivate parents.
- Do not create a false sense of security or progress for parents. Be truthful.
- Be willing to review materials and issues that have previously been discussed; it is not at all unusual for parents to periodically wish to review previously discussed information and to share their perception and feelings regarding it.
- Encourage parents to present their own agendas at conferences.
- Make parents aware of community resources that may facilitate their accommodation of an exceptional child in the family.
- Make parents aware that other children in their family also require attention.

CONCLUSION

An exceptional child will, almost without exception, have a significant impact on the parents and family. While not being able to change this circumstance, the educator can help parents more adequately understand their situation and identify strategies for meeting their own needs and those of their handicapped child.

Provisions for an exceptional child's overall well-being include the availability of appropriate educational resources, opportunities for parental participation in educational and social intervention programs, communication opportunities, and methods for aiding parents accommodate and integrate an atypical child in the family. As any experienced educator can attest, it is only with such efforts that an exceptional child will be able to benefit maximally from professionally planned services and to progress at a rate commensurate with his or her abilities.

Exercises

1. Develop a list of community and school resources that can offer counseling services to parents.
2. Discuss with the parents of an exceptional child the stages they went through after learning of their child's exceptionality.
3. Discuss with the parents of an exceptional child the impact the youngster has had on the family. Discuss with an exceptional child's siblings their relationship with the child.
4. Discuss with the parents of an exceptional child those procedures, techniques, and services that could be made available by professionals to help parents and families more effectively integrate and accommodate an exceptional child.

NOTE

1. Reprinted from "A lost generation of parents" by K.A. Gorman with permission of *Exceptional Children,* © 1975.

REFERENCES

Akerley, M.S. False gods and angry prophets. In A.P. Turnbull & H.R. Turnbull (Eds.), *Parents speak out: Views from the other side of the two-way mirror.* Columbus, Ohio: Merrill, 1978.

Allen, R.M., & Cortazzo, A.D. *Psycho-social and educational aspects and problems of mental retardation.* Springfield, Ill.: Thomas, 1970.

Barnes, E., Eyman, B., & Engolz, M.B. *Teach and reach: An alternative guide to resources for the classroom.* Syracuse, N.Y.: Human Policy Press, 1974.

Barsh, R.A. *The parent of the handicapped child.* Springfield, Ill.: Thomas, 1968.

Baum, M.H. Some dynamic factors affecting family adjustment to the handicapped child. *Exceptional Children,* 1962, *28,* 387-392.

Blodgett, A.E. *Mentally retarded children: What parents and others should know.* Minneapolis: University of Minnesota Press, 1971.

Buck, P. *The child who never grew.* New York: John Day, 1950.

Buscaglia, L. *The disabled and their parents: A counseling challenge.* Thorofare, N.J.: Slack, 1975.

Cansler, D.P., & Martin, G.H. *Working with families: A manual for developmental centers*. Chapel Hill, N.C.: Council for Exceptional Children, 1974.

Dean, D. Closer look: A parent information service. *Exceptional Children*, 1975, *41*, 527-530.

Dembinski, R.J., & Mauser, A.J. Considering the parents of LD children: What they want from professionals. *Journal of Learning Disabilities*, 1977, *10*, 578-584.

Farber, B. *Mental retardation: Its social content and social consequences*. Boston: Houghton Mifflin, 1968.

Gorham, K.A. A lost generation of parents. *Exceptional Children*, 1975, *41*(8), 521-525.

Gorham, K.A., Jardins, C.D., Page, R., Pettis, E., & Scheiber, B. Effect on parents. In N. Hobbs (Ed.), *Issues in the classification of children* (Vol. II). San Francisco: Jossey-Bass, 1975.

Graliker, E.V., Fishler, K., & Koch, R. Teenage reaction to a mentally retarded sibling. *American Journal of Mental Deficiency*, 1962, *66*, 838-843.

Greer, B.G. On being the parent of a handicapped child. *Exceptional Children*, 1975, *41*(8), 519.

Hayden, A.H. A center-based parent training model. In D. Lillie & P.L. Troharris (Eds.), *Teaching parents to teach*. New York: Walker & Co., 1976.

Justice, R.S., O'Connor, G., & Warren, N. Problems reported by parents of mentally retarded children—Who helps? *American Journal of Mental Deficiency*, 1971, *75*(6), 685-691.

Kauffman, J.M. *Characteristics of children's behavior disorders*. Columbus, Ohio: Merrill, 1977.

Klein, S.D. Brother to sister: Sister to brother. *The Exceptional Parent*, 1972, *2*, 10-15.

Kubler-Ross, E. *On death and dying*. New York: Macmillan, 1969.

Love, H.D. *Parental attitudes toward exceptional children*. Springfield, Ill.: Thomas, 1970.

Love, H.D. *The mentally retarded child and his family*. Springfield, Ill.: Thomas, 1973.

MacDonald, E.T. *Understand those feelings*. Pittsburgh: Stanwix House, 1962.

Olshansky, S. Chronic sorrow: A response to having a mentally defective child. In R. Noland (Ed.), *Counseling parents of the mentally retarded*. Springfield, Ill.: Thomas, 1970.

Perske, R. *New directions for parents of persons who are retarded*. Nashville: Abingdon Press, 1973.

Reiss, I.L. *The family system in America*. New York: Holt, Rinehart & Winston, 1971.

Robinson, R. Don't speak to us of living death. In R. Noland (Ed.), *Counseling parents of the mentally retarded*. Springfield, Ill.: Thomas, 1970.

Robinson, H.B., & Robinson, N.M. *The mentally retarded child*. New York: McGraw-Hill, 1965.

Rogers, C.R. *Client-centered therapy*. Boston: Houghton Mifflin, 1951.

Roos, P. Parents of mentally retarded children—misunderstood and mistreated. In A.P. Turnbull & H.R. Turnbull (Eds.), *Parents speak out: Views from the other side of the two-way mirror*. Columbus, Ohio: Merrill, 1978.

Roos, P.A. Parents' view of what public school education should accomplish. In E. Sontag, J. Smith, & N. Certo (Eds.), *Educational programming for the severely handicapped*. Reston, Va.: Council for Exceptional Children, 1977, 72-83.

Safford, P.L., & Arbitman, D.C. *Developmental intervention with young physically handicapped children*. Springfield, Ill.: Thomas, 1975.

Schlesinger, H.S., & Meadow, K.P. Emotional support for parents. In D. Lillie & P.L. Troharris (Eds.), *Teaching parents to teach*. New York: Walker & Co., 1976, 35-49.

Simmons-Martin, A. Facilitating positive parent child interactions. In D. Lillie & P.L. Troharris (Eds.), *Teaching parents to teach*. New York: Walker & Co., 1976, 75-85.

Simpson, R.L., & Poplin, M.S. Parents as agents of change: A behavioral approach. *School Psychology Review*, 1981, *10*(1), 15-25.

Telford, C.W., & Sawrey, J.M. *The exceptional individual*. Englewood Cliffs, N.J.: Prentice-Hall, 1977.

Turnbull, A.P., & Turnbull, H.R. *Parents speak out: Views from the other side of the two-way mirror.* Columbus, Ohio: Merrill, 1978.

Weber, B. A parent of a retarded child gives her idea of services needed. *Child Welfare,* 1974, *53*(2), 98-101.

Chapter 3

The Minority Family and the Exceptional Child

At one parent interpretation and individualized education program planning conference the mother of a recently identified behaviorally disordered child was encouraged to share her perceptions regarding her son and his problems and to react to the information presented by school personnel. This young black woman readily agreed that the concerns of her son's teachers were accurate and that the same problems existed at home. In addition, she discussed several issues that she and her family were attempting to contend with. Perhaps these were not the cause of her son's difficulties, however, they were at least related. This mother of four revealed that she had only the previous week received notice that a reduction in the funds available to the federal agency for which she worked, and through which she was receiving job training, would result in the elimination of her position. She confided that she was anxious over her ability to feed, clothe, and provide a home for her children and frustrated over her capacity to contend with what she considered to be a severe psychological setback. She reported that her ex-husband provided no financial support for the family and that he was, in fact, legally prohibited from having contact with his children because of alleged physical and sexual abuse.

At one point in the conference the discussion focused on the child's problem in developing and maintaining appropriate peer relationships. As a part of this discussion one educator asked the mother if her son interacted with children his own age at home. The mother revealed that while her son had an opportunity to play daily with other children at his baby sitter's house, she was reluctant to allow any of her children to play outside in their own area. She noted that she lived in a federally subsidized housing project "where you keep your doors locked and your kids inside." She also elaborated on various significant problems associated with confining her children to their small apartment.

It is not the intent of the preceding scenario to suggest that a majority of minority children live in housing projects and have abusive fathers or to lend support to any other pernicious or inaccurate stereotype or prejudice of this nature. Abundant evidence exists to support the contention that no cultural, ethnic, or racial group is immune to social problems. Nonetheless, the educational conferencer must be aware that issues related to minority status may commonly require attention. For example, the educator must be sensitive to the fact that minority groups have experienced more than their share of social and economic problems (Makielski, 1973); that minority children have been overly represented in educational programs for exceptional children (Dunn, 1968); and that discriminatory and otherwise biased assessment procedures have long represented significant concerns for minority children experiencing school-related problems (Wallace & Larsen, 1978). Just as significantly, educational conferencers must be sensitive to the communication-related issues that must be dealt with when interacting with minority parents and families of exceptional children.

EXCEPTIONAL CHILDREN AND YOUTH OF MINORITY STATUS

One provision of the Federal Civil Rights Act of 1964 was that the U.S. Office of Education would conduct a study of "the lack of availability of equal educational opportunities for individuals by reason of race, color, religion or national origin in public educational institutions" (Coleman, Campbell, Hobson, McPartland, Mood, Weinfeld, & York, 1966, p. iii). The resulting study, commonly known as the Coleman report, was designed to assess the nature and extent of racial and ethnic public school segregation and the extent of educational inequality among minority children and to correlate academic achievement with minority status and background. This massive research effort yielded several significant findings, including: minority children more commonly attended schools that had larger average class sizes than did nonminority children; minority pupils had less access to educational facilities and experiences related to academic achievement than did nonminority children; minority students were generally taught by less capable instructors; minority students tended to perform more poorly on standardized achievement tests, particularly in the upper grades, than nonminority pupils; and, most significantly, when the students' socioeconomic background was controlled, the availability of school resources (e.g., laboratories, libraries) had only a minor influence on academic achievement. The last finding was not only of surprise to Coleman and his research team but also became the basis for significant interpretation and debate. Jencks (1966) interpreted this finding of the Coleman report to be directly associated with familial and socioeconomic status and opportunity, noting that if children are exposed to homes and environments where verbal and other academically related skills and behaviors are accentuated, they will have a much greater chance of prospering in school. Coleman's (1968) interpretation of the data generated through his study (Coleman et al., 1966) was similar to that of

Jencks, while Bronfenbrenner (1967) also accentuated the finding that a child's home and family experiences are closely associated with academic achievement. Even though the Coleman report (1966) continues to be a controversial document, professionals tend to agree that social influences do correlate closely with children's school-related performance. In particular, the Coleman report further corroborates the notion that schools are limited in their capacity to influence children's performance independent of their social and family experiences and that certain groups, such as minorities, are particularly vulnerable to school-related problems. In addition, the inferences and conclusions based on the Coleman study lend support to the position that unless wide-ranging social intervention programs are made available, including parent training and participation, minority children can be expected to continue to experience severe school-related problems. As suggested by Kosa (1975), majority status tends to be associated with a variety of privileges, including access to facilities and mechanisms for promoting health and healthy and productive life styles.

Compensatory and "special" educational provisions for minority pupils with alleged handicapping conditions also represent a controversial issue. In fact, a number of special education practices have been considered highly discriminatory toward minority groups (Mercer, 1973; Silberberg & Silberberg, 1974). Jones and Wilderson (1976), for example, observed that minority children "were over-represented in special classes, particularly for the mentally retarded" (p. 3); that discriminatory assessment methods and procedures were commonplace; and that educators tended to have negatively biased perceptions of the ability and potential of minority pupils. Jones and Wilderson further suggested that these practices "have served to highlight for many minority parents and professionals the view that institutionalized racism is part and parcel of educational practice" (p. 3).

Johnson (1969), in a further elaboration on this point, accused special education of serving as an alternative placement when the schools failed to motivate and teach children. He specifically postulated that "special education is helping the regular school maintain its spoiled identity when it creates special programs (whether psychodynamic or behavioral modification) for the 'disruptive child' and the 'slow learner' many of whom, for some strange reason, happen to be black and poor and live in the inner city" (p. 245).

While a majority of these indictments were made in the 1960s and 1970s when they had their greatest historical relevance, indications persist that minority children continue to be particularly vulnerable to classification as exceptional (Laosa, 1977) and that many of the same social, political, and economic ills that have been identified in the past as contributing to the educational problems of minority pupils remain (Rudov & Santangelo, 1979). Accordingly, the educational conferencer must be willing to and capable of becoming more responsive to the needs, values, and practices of minority children and their families. Specifically, such responsiveness should be manifested in sensitivity to the political and economic issues affecting minorities; awareness of value differences between nonminority and minority cultures; knowledge of educational procedures that specifically relate to minority pupils; development of an awareness of legislation pertaining to minority students; and development of conferencing strategies appropriate for particular minority groups.

DEVELOPING AN AWARENESS OF THE ISSUES AND PROBLEMS AFFECTING MINORITIES

In his book *36 Children* (1967), Herbert Kohl presented a series of bleak neighborhood descriptions written by fifth-grade students in one Harlem school. The descriptions graphically depicted violence, drugs, poverty, filth, brutality, and urban decay at its worst. Dick Gregory recalled in his autobiography, *Nigger* (1964), that as a child there was rarely enough food for his family and virtually never a regular mealtime. He, too, described the chaos, despair, and rueful conditions that seem to be an all too common part of the lives of urban minority children and their families. Coles and Piers (1969) disputed the notion that many urban minority children are experientially deprived and suggested that these children are actually overstimulated. These researchers specifically noted that many minority children "do not, as a rule, suffer from a lack of experiences. On the contrary, they tend to be helpless victims of a veritable onslaught on the sensorium (p. 167)," being required to suffer through overcrowded living conditions and violence.

Again, the reader must be reminded that while these descriptions may be representative of some of the conditions affecting minority children and their families, they are not intended to be descriptive of the norm. Yet, the educational conferencer must consider that the norm, while perhaps different from the most graphic descriptions given by Gregory (1964) and Kohl (1967), may still be significantly different from typical middle-class experiences. Consider for example the following:

- While blacks comprise only about 12% of the total population, they represent over 30% of the nation's poor; Hispanics and Native Americans also make up a disproportionate number of individuals existing at a poverty level.

- Census Bureau reports reveal that the average yearly income for whites is approximately double that of blacks. In addition, the incomes of other minority groups average far less than that of nonminority.

- The life expectancy for minorities is significantly shorter than for the nonminority population. Malnutrition, infections, and respiratory diseases have in some regions existed at near epidemic levels, and infant mortality rates for racial minorities are about twice those of nonminority infants.

- U.S. health officials report that homicide is the leading cause of death among black men 22 to 44 years old, far surpassing disease and accidents.

- Educational deficiencies, school failure, and dropout rates are common in minority cultures.

- Alcoholism, poverty, unemployment, and economic depression are common among Native Americans, particularly those living on reservations.

- Single-parent families are quite common among minorities. According to Rudov and Santangelo (1979), the highest proportion of divorced people are racial minority women.

As a result of these and similar statistics, the educational conferencer must be particularly cognizant and sensitive to the factors associated with minority status and be willing to accommodate these circumstances. In particular, the conferencer must be aware that the school-related experiences of minority and nonminority students may be quite different. Coles and Piers (1969), for example, commented on the differences in the school-related environments and activities of the two groups. They noted that, on the way to school, the minority child frequently "finds himself in a world of alleyways and broken glass; of addicts; alcoholics, pimps; of idle, bitter men who sit about with little hope for themselves. But when the middle-class child goes to school he is welcomed by the grownups along his path" (p. 34).

Furthermore, minority and nonminority pupils are often differentially perceived relative to their need for compensatory or alternative educational placement. Forer (1970), for instance, observed that minority status is frequently in and of itself cause for "special" educational action or intervention while Cohen, Granger, Provence, and Solnit (1975) observed that "when the troubling or troubled adolescent is poor or a minority group member, he or she is more likely to be referred to the courts for help. Referrals for white, middle-class adolescents are more likely to be made to the mental health system" (p. 113).

While educational conferencers may be able to do little to correct the underlying conditions and inimical circumstances facing many minority families, they must, at a minimum, demonstrate appropriate sensitivity to the circumstances impacting on these groups. Specifically, professionals must be aware that the least of the worries of some parents and families will be their child's poor school performance; that attending school conferences may create significant logistic, economic, and child-care burdens; that trust and rapport with school personnel may be slow in developing; and that the perceived value of education as a facilitator of survival in certain environments may be minimal. Without question, failure to demonstrate such sensitivity will lead to significant communication problems.

DEVELOPING AN AWARENESS OF VALUE DIFFERENCES

Just as Mead (1928) observed differences in the practices and traditions of different cultures, so, too, can subcultural groups be expected to display a unique set of values. These values frequently differ significantly from those held by the predominant culture, particularly with reference to educational issues (Kroth & Simpson, 1977; Rutherford & Edgar, 1979).

One area within the value domain that should receive close individual scrutiny is one's attitudes toward specific minorities. In particular, educators should attempt to become familiar with their personal beliefs, prejudices, fears, and concerns regarding minority groups. In addition, efforts should be made to understand the nature and origin of these perceptions. The middle-class educator should be aware, for instance, that public school curricula and procedures have historically accentuated the "rightness" of the English-speaking tradition. While some schools have attempted to focus on the "melting pot" composition of this country and its ability to accommodate "other peoples," this has traditionally been pursued under the guise that the values, ideals, and practices of the English-speaking culture would eventually be adopted by minority groups. As a result, it is to be expected that an educator reared in the tradition of the dominant culture, particularly if from a middle-class background, has developed certain beliefs and perceptions regarding minority groups as wishing to retain their own traditions and values or having been prevented from becoming a legitimate part of the predominant culture. This should in no way be interpreted as an endorsement of biased or inappropriate attitudes and prejudices; rather, it is a position based on the premise that individuals must first understand their own values and sentiments before being able to communicate effectively with persons of different beliefs (Raths, Harmin, & Simon, 1966). While individuals with particularly strong biases may need to explore strategies for modifying their attitudes, the basic benefit of self-scrutiny is better self-understanding.

As a means of gaining a clearer understanding of one's minority-related beliefs, readers are encouraged to complete the self-assessment survey shown in Exhibit 3-1. It is recognized that some readers of this book will belong to minorities themselves. In such instances, they should complete the form on the basis of their perceptions of other minority groups. For each item, readers are to check the column (e.g., strongly agree, mildly disagree, etc.) that most closely corresponds to their attitude. Participants are encouraged to base their responses on their initial impressions rather than attempting to "talk themselves" into or out of certain choices. After completing and reflecting on their responses, readers are encouraged to ask a colleague to evaluate them using the scale. Areas of discrepancy should be discussed, along with a consideration of attitudes that may require modification. The instrument can also be used to assess patterns of growth and

Exhibit 3-1 Minority Attitude Self-Assessment Survey

	Strongly Agree	Agree	Mildly Agree	Neutral	Mildly Disagree	Disagree	Strongly Disagree
1. I am uncomfortable in conferences with individuals with skin colors different from my own.							
2. I consider minority student educational problems basically to be a function of a lack of parental emphasis on doing well in school.							
3. I am intimidated by individuals from cultures that I do not fully understand.							
4. I believe that the dominant language of the home, even if not English, should be accommodated in public schools.							
5. I believe that the dominant language of the home, even if not English, should be taught in public schools.							
6. I believe that certain minority groups are innately inferior in educational potential to the majority culture.							

Exhibit 3-1 continued

	Strongly Agree	Agree	Mildly Agree	Neutral	Mildly Disagree	Disagree	Strongly Disagree
7. I am uncomfortable in conferences with parents who are unable to speak standard English.							
8. I frequently become angry in conferences with parents who are unable to speak standard English.							
9. I experience many similarities with the minority pupils and families with whom I am associated.							
10. I am usually as satisfied with my conferences with minority parents as with those including nonminorities.							
11. I would prefer to work in a school serving children and families from cultures and backgrounds similar to my own.							
12. I believe that most minority social problems could be solved if groups made up their mind to improve their conditions.							

13. I do not believe that schools can solve many of the problems experienced by minorities.							
14. I am surprised when minority parents show an interest in their child's school-related performance.							
15. I resent certain groups of parents calling me at home more than others.							
16. I am equally at ease in accepting a dinner invitation to the homes of my minority and nonminority students.							
17. I find it easier to empathize with parents whose background is similar to my own.							
18. I am more inclined to give advice to minority parents than to other groups.							
19. I find it easier to admit to a minority parent than a nonminority parent that I was wrong.							
20. I am more inclined to ask minority parents to participate in home-based programs.							

change over time and as a device for soliciting feedback from minority parents and families. While no norms are associated with this scale, it can serve to make educators more familiar with their minority-related values and attitudes. Such self-understanding is the basis for more effective communication and programming efforts.

In addition to self-understanding, educational conferencers also must be willing to invest the efforts necessary to become familiar with the values of the minority families with whom they must interact. Since this understanding will be a basic ingredient of effective communication, it must receive appropriate consideration.

Pepper (1976) identified several value-related differences between Native Americans and the nonminority culture. She observed, for instance, that Native Americans tend to respect and honor their elders more than whites; Native American family life more often includes extended family members; Native Americans more commonly accept and conform to nature while whites concentrate more on attempting to dominate it; Native Americans put less emphasis on competition and prestige than whites; Native Americans more frequently express themselves through their actions than with words; and Native Americans expect that adulthood will commence at an earlier stage than do members of the white race.

It is obvious that the educational conferencer must be knowledgeable of the particular traditions and values of the minority families with whom they are associated. Just as Pepper (1976) observed distinct value characteristics in Native Americans, it can be expected that other minority groups will have their own unique features (Christensen, 1975). Familiarity with and acceptance of these patterns are basic components of conferencing success.

ISSUES ASSOCIATED WITH THE IDENTIFICATION, ASSESSMENT, PLACEMENT, AND EVALUATION OF EXCEPTIONAL MINORITY PUPILS

Conferences with parents of exceptional minority pupils will, at least periodically, focus on issues related to nondiscriminatory assessment, the effects of labeling, and strategies for serving the educational needs of minority students. The significance of these topics to parents of exceptional minority students necessitates that they be effectively dealt with by educational conferencers.

Probably no topic in exceptional education has received as much attention as procedures for conducting nondiscriminatory evaluations of minority pupils. Not only have legal rulings, legislation, and mass media attention sensitized educators and parents to the issues in this area, but ethically professionals are acknowledging the potentially harmful consequences of biased evaluations and the resulting problems of unwarranted labels and incorrect educational dispositions (Goldstein, Arkell, Ashcroft, Hurley, & Lilly, 1975).

It is not without basis that questions regarding nondiscriminatory assessment procedures may arise in conferences with parents of minority pupils. The vast majority of evaluation procedures used by schools have been devised for and standardized on white populations. Until only the past few years there has been little recognition of the potentially discriminatory influence of applying these measures to minority pupils (Oakland, 1973). As a result, historically little attention has been given to the need to consider a child's culture during assessment proceedings (Bryen, 1974) or to the necessity of making a child's ethnic ties a consideration during the evaluation process (Jaramillo, 1974). Currently, however, both professionals and parents are focusing on factors associated with obtaining an accurate and unbiased assessment.

Accordingly, the educational conferencer can anticipate that some parents of minority pupils will want to discuss the assessment and classification systems that have been employed to diagnose a disproportionate number of minority pupils as intellectually subnormal, behaviorally deviant, and educationally deficient (Hurley, 1971; Johnson, 1969; Mercer, 1973), and hence whether or not their own child's diagnosis and placement are associated with such factors. The educator's ability to respond to such questions and to demonstrate to parents that the assessment procedures used with their children were nondiscriminatory, multi-disciplinary, and comprehensive are closely aligned with developing and maintaining rapport, trust, and effective parental involvement.

Also of concern to parents of minority exceptional children are issues related to labeling. Mercer (1970, 1971, 1973, 1975), in her historic "Riverside Study," reported several alarming findings associated with labeling minority groups as handicapped. In particular, she revealed that public schools more commonly diagnosed and labeled individuals exceptional than did other agencies; that those individuals identified by schools as handicapped tended to be more mildly impaired than those identified by other social agencies; that minority pupils were more likely to perform poorly on standardized intelligence tests than their non-minority peers, thus increasing their chance of being identified as retarded; and that children from minority and low socioeconomic groups were more commonly considered to be retarded only during school hours ("six-hour retardates") than nonminority children and pupils from more prosperous homes. While legislation (e.g., P.L. 94-142), court decisions (*Larry P.* v. *Wilson Riles,* 1972; *Diana* v. *California State Board of Education,* 1970), and general attention to this topic (Wallace & Larsen, 1978) have helped to bring about significant improvements in this area, educators who confer with parents and families of minority exceptional children and youth must anticipate that questions regarding this topic will continue to arise in conferences. Educators' ability to deal with these issues effectively will in all likelihood form the basis for future meaningful interactions.

Parents of minority pupils assigned to specialized or modified programs are also interested in the nature of the educational services that will be rendered their children and the manner in which a child's minority status will be accommodated. Parental concerns in this area may focus on the curricula to be used and whether or not it will be compatible with a particular child's background and experiences; the cultural, ethnic, and religious mix of children with whom a child will associate; and the level of acceptance of cultural differences demonstrated by the nonexceptional students in a child's school. While it has been suggested (Johnson, 1976) that the primary goal of minority education should be the achievement of academic gains as opposed to accommodating various cultures, educators must be sensitive and willing to address questions and issues pertaining to minority status. As noted by Meyen (1978), ''If teachers understand a child's uniqueness, respect the child's individuality, and are familiar with the child's cultural background, they are in a better position to make instructional decisions and to establish an environment conducive to learning'' (p. 76). All parents are entitled to such guarantees.

DEVELOPING AN AWARENESS OF LEGISLATION PERTAINING TO EXCEPTIONAL MINORITY PUPILS

Even though the Education for All Handicapped Children   Act of 1975 and Section 504 of the Rehabilitation Act of 1973 are designed to provide procedural safeguards for all exceptional persons, they have particular significance and reference to minorities. For example, P.L. 94-142 provides assurances that assessment procedures employed with minorities ''will be selected and administered so as not to be racially or culturally discriminatory.'' Furthermore, the mandate states that evaluative procedures ''shall be provided and administered in the child's native language.'' The same type of safeguards exist for the other major components of The Education for All Handicapped Children   Act, including provisions for educational placement in the ''least restrictive environment,'' rights to ''due process,'' and guarantees of an ''individualized education program.'' Since legislative attention has been focused on issues relating to minority exceptional children, it is imperative that educators be familiar with the provisions provided through these acts. Only with such familiarity can conferencers be competent to interact with parents of minority pupils within this topical area.

In addition to having a working knowledge of legislation affecting minority exceptional children, educators must also attempt to familiarize parents with this information. Since familiarity can eliminate conceptual biases and misunderstandings and can increase the probability of legitimate parent participation, efforts should be made to acquaint parents with this type of information rather than concealing it from them.

CONFERENCING STRATEGIES APPLICABLE TO PARTICULAR MINORITIES

Meaningful parent-professional interactions are based on a free and accurate exchange of information and an atmosphere of trust, mutual respect, and cooperation. However, interactions between parents and professionals are not always characterized by these factors. In particular, conferences between professionals and minority parents have often been considered replete with misinterpretations and suspicions. Often such communication problems are associated with misread or misunderstood body language, verbalizations, gestures, facial expressions, habits, posture, eye contact, proximity, or other manifestations associated with an individual's culture. Since these and similar manifestations can significantly influence the communication potential in a conference situation, educators must become aware of their own personal interaction style and its effect on specific groups of people. In addition, professionals must be aware of the interaction styles of particular minorities and the impact of this on the conferencing process. One school psychologist, for example, misinterpreted the absence of eye contact in a Native American mother to be a sign of "emotional shock" rather than the cultural manifestation that it indeed was.

It is obviously beyond the scope of this work to identify all the characteristics of minority groups that warrant attention as well as the various idiosyncratic habits of professionals that may impact on certain groups in particular ways. However, conferencers must be willing to analyze their own styles and the cultural norms of the groups with whom they must relate. Awareness and sensitivity to these factors enable professionals to increase their communication effectiveness and to involve parents of minority pupils who might otherwise choose to withhold their cooperation and involvement.

The development of initial rapport may be particularly vulnerable to factors associated with cultural differences. That is, during initial meetings parents and professionals may be adversely influenced by the subtle (and not so subtle) characteristics associated with minority and majority interactions. In particular, professionals may find it difficult to empathize with persons different from themselves; parents from minority cultures, in turn, may doubt the educator's capacity to understand their situation or heritage. Nonetheless, since the development of initial rapport is an essential ingredient of communication success, educators must identify mechanisms for developing at least a measure of fundamental trust. In accordance with this goal, conferencers should become familiar with the effects of different rapport-building procedures with different groups. While it is acknowledged that there will be significant variance within groups, certain commonalities can frequently be identified. For example, some minority groups may be suspicious of "small talk" at the beginning of a conference, believing that such behavior is a delay tactic or a strategy for avoiding an unpleasant topic rather than a device for establishing rapport.

White middle-class conferencers should also become sensitive to and aware that some minority parents may be anxious and suspicious during initial encounters. Since many minority parents will have had prior limited face-to-face contact with educational personnel, they may require support and clarification regarding the nature of the session and their own role in the conference. For example, one Hispanic father who had been asked to attend a progress report conference about his son confided that he had punished his child prior to coming to the meeting because he assumed that the session was designed to focus on his son's "bad classroom behavior."

Educators must also be extremely sensitive to language-related issues when confering with minority parents. In some instances interpreters will be required. However, most frequently language differences will take a more subtle form. For example, the conferencer should be aware that some groups, such as Native Americans, may be quite parsimonious and concrete in their use of language; that many minority parents may fail to use standard English; that even bilingual educators may be unable to converse with some parents because of dialectal differences; and that idioms and phraseology specific to a group or region may be commonly encountered. In situations in which language differences, albeit subtle, are encountered, both educators and parents must feel comfortable in asking for clarification. Failure to do so will severely impede the communication process.

As a general rule, conferencers must be cautious not to be overly sympathetic, indulgent, or patronizing of minority parents. In a like manner, educators should be dissuaded from attempting to convince minority parents that they "truly know" the plight of a particular group (unless, of course, they happen to be a member of that minority or were raised in that culture, for example) or that they are "different" from other professionals with whom the parents may have had contact. While it is hoped that such understanding and trust will develop during the course of the conferencing process, such sentiments should not be expressed in an initial overt message to parents.

Educational conferencers should also recognize the impact of their gender on interactions with some minority parents. Female educators, for example, should be aware that Hispanics, for example, may be reluctant to take advice from women. Conferencers must also be aware that certain groups may avoid making eye contact with an individual solely on the basis of gender.

Above all else, educational conferencers must attempt to understand minority parents in accordance with the culture of which they are a part. They must also recognize that their own demeanor and heritage will impact on any interaction with minority parents. Recognition of these significant factors should result in a more productive conference and increased parental involvement.

CONCLUSION

While the racial and ethnic diversity of Americans has always been recognized, it has, at the same time, been assumed by many that the "melting pot" capabilities of this country would eliminate the qualities differentiating minorities from the nonminority culture. This naive position has been abandoned by most farsighted individuals, including educators, who now recognize that the distinct qualities of these groups must be acknowledged and accommodated.

The role of educational conferencer requires that an educator be able to relate to a variety of parents, including those with different languages, cultural practices, and values. While conferencers must employ the same basic tools and procedures with all parents, these must be applied in a fashion compatible with each parent's background. A willingness and ability to do so on the part of conferencers will increase the probability of conferencing success.

Exercises

1. Complete the Minority Attitude Self-Assessment Survey (Exhibit 3-1) as per the directions and suggestions provided in the chapter.
2. Identify the various minorities in your district or region with whom you might conceivably be required to interact. For each group list particular characteristics that you should consider when providing parent and family conferencing services. Finally, attempt to identify personal patterns of behavior that may facilitate or detract from your ability to interact effectively with particular minority groups.

REFERENCES

Bronfenbrenner, U. The split-level American family. *Saturday Review*, 1967, *50*(40), 60-66.

Bryen, D.M. Special education and the linguistically different child. *Exceptional Children*, 1974, *40*, 589-599.

Christensen, E.W. Counseling Puerto Ricans: Some cultural considerations. *The Personnel and Guidance Journal*, 1975, *53*(5), 349-356.

Cohen, D.J., Granger, R.H., Provence, S.A., & Solnit, A.J. Mental health services. In N. Hobbs (Ed.), *Issues in the classification of children*. San Francisco: Jossey-Bass, 1975.

Coleman, J.S. The concept of equal educational opportunity. *Harvard Educational Review*, 1968, *38*, 7-22.

Coleman, J.S., Campbell, E.Q., Hobson, C.J., McPartland, J., Mood, A.M., Weinfeld, F.D., & York, R.L. *Equality of educational opportunity*. Washington, D.C.: U.S. Office of Education (OE38001), 1966.

Coles, R., & Piers, M. *Wages of neglect*. Chicago: Quadrangle Books, 1969.

Diana v. *State Board of Education*. NOC-70-73-37, U.S. District Court, Northern District of California, 1970.

Dunn, L.M. Special education for the mildly retarded—Is much of it justifiable? *Exceptional Children*, 1968, *34*, 5-22.

Forer, L.G. *No one will listen: How our legal system brutalizes the youthful poor*. New York: John Day, 1970.

Goldstein, H., Arkell, C., Ashcroft, S., Hurley, O., & Lilly, S. Schools. In N. Hobbs (Ed.), *Issues in the classification of children*, (Volume 2). San Francisco: Jossey-Bass, 1975.

Gregory, D. *Nigger*. New York: Pocket Books, 1964.

Hurley, O.L. Special education in the inner city: The social implications of placement. In the President's Committee on Mental Retardation, *Placement of children in special classes for the retarded: Background position papers*. Washington, D.C.: U.S. Government Printing Office, 1971.

Jaramillo, M. Cultural conflict curriculum and the exceptional child. *Exceptional Children*, 1974, *40*, 585-587.

Jencks, C. Education, the racial gap. *New Republic*, 1966, *155*, 21-26.

Johnson, J.L. Mainstreaming black children. In R.L. Jones (Ed.), *Mainstreaming and the minority child*. Minneapolis: Special Education Leadership Training Institute, 1976.

Johnson, J.L. Special education and the inner city: A challenge for the future or another means for cooling the mark out? *Journal of Special Education*, 1969, *3*, 241-251.

Jones, R.L., & Wilderson, F.B. Mainstreaming and the minority child: An overview of issues and a perspective. In R.L. Jones (Ed.), *Mainstreaming and the minority child*. Reston, Va.: Council for Exceptional Children, 1976.

Kohl, H. *36 children*. New York: New American Library, 1967.

Kosa, J. The nature of poverty. In J. Kosa & I.K. Zola (Eds.), *Poverty and health, a sociological analysis*. Cambridge, Mass.: Harvard University Press, 1975.

Kroth, R.L., & Simpson, R.L. *Parent conferences as a teaching strategy*. Denver: Love Publishing, 1977.

Laosa, L.M. Nonbiased assessment of children's abilities: Historical antecedents and current issues. In T. Oakland (Ed.), *Psychological and educational assessment of minority children*. New York: Brunner-Mazel, 1977.

Larry P. v. *Wilson Riles*. NOC-71-2270 RFP, U.S. District Court, Northern District of California, 1972.

Makielski, S.J. *Beleagured minorities: Cultural politics in America*. San Francisco: Freeman, 1973.

Mead, M. *Coming of age in Samoa*. New York: Morrow, 1928.

Mercer, J.R. *Labeling the mentally retarded*. Berkeley, Calif.: University of California Press, 1973.

Mercer, J.R. The meaning of mental retardation. In R. Koch & J.C. Dobson (Eds.), *The mentally retarded child and his family*. New York: Brunner-Mazel, 1971.

Mercer, J.R. Psychological assessment and the rights of children. In Hobbs (Ed.), *Issues in the classification of children*, (Volume 1). San Francisco: Jossey-Bass, 1975.

Mercer, J.R. Sociological perspectives on mild mental retardation. In H.C. Haywood (Ed.), *Social-cultural aspects of mental retardation*. New York: Appleton-Century-Crofts, 1970.

Meyen, E.L. An introductory perspective. In E.L. Meyen (Ed.), *Exceptional children and youth: An introduction*. Denver: Love Publishing, 1978.

Oakland, T.D. Assessing minority group children: Challenges for school psychologists. In T.D. Oakland & B.N. Phillips (Eds.), *Assessing minority group children*. New York: Behavioral Publications, 1973.

Pepper, F. Teaching the American Indian child in mainstreaming settings. In R.L. Jones (Ed.), *Mainstreaming and the minority child*. Minneapolis: Special Education Leadership Training Institute, 1976.

Raths, L., Harmin, M., & Simon, S. *Values and teaching*. Columbus, Ohio: Merrill, 1966.

Rudov, M.H., & Santangelo, N. *Health status of minorities and low-income groups*. Washington, D.C.: U.S. Department of Health, Education and Welfare, Public Health Service, 1979.

Rutherford, R.B., & Edgar, E. *Teachers and parents: A guide to interaction and cooperation*. Boston: Allyn & Bacon, 1979.

Silberberg, N.E., & Silberberg, M.C. *Who speaks for the child*. Springfield, Ill.: Thomas, 1974.

Wallace, G., & Larsen, S.C. *Educational assessment of learning problems: Testing for teaching*. Boston: Allyn & Bacon, 1978.

Chapter 4

Age Considerations in Parent and Family Conferencing

Even though parental involvement has become a fundamental feature of many educational programs, as a result of the well-documented need for cooperative parent-professional relationships and efforts (Appell, Williams, & Fishell, 1964; Boyd, 1979) most of these opportunities and programs have been aimed primarily at parents of elementary-age children. Within the past few years, however, there have been increased attempts to involve parents of preschool children, adolescents, and young adults. With this increased attention on parents of non-elementary-age children has come the realization that the child's age is a salient factor in parent conferencing and that the needs of parents and families will vary with the stages of a child's development.

The increased attention given parents and families of children of all ages is a function of at least three major factors. First, growing evidence indicates that parents and families play a prominent role in a child's development and, consequently, must be made a significant component of any educational program, regardless of the child's age. As observed by Bronfenbrenner (1974), "evidence indicates that the family is the most effective and economical system for fostering and sustaining development of the child. The evidence indicates further that the involvement of the child's family as an active participant is critical to the success of any intervention program" (p. 55). The significance of the concept "any program," including those designed for very young children, youth, and young adults, appears at last to have been recognized (Hobbs, 1978; Shearer & Shearer, 1972).

A second factor associated with the increased attention given involvement of parents of non-elementary-age children relates to the legislative advances that have taken place in behalf of the handicapped. Specifically, the passage of the Education for All Handicapped Children Act of 1975 (P.L. 94-142) and Section 504 of the Rehabilitation Act of 1973 have redefined and expanded the educational and treatment provisions available to handicapped individuals, including those not of traditional school age. Owing to concurrent attempts to involve parents and families, the availability of parent programs and involvement opportunities have increased significantly.

Finally, the expectations of both parents and professionals regarding the need for parental and family involvement programs have been expanded. Perhaps because the need for parental involvement has been so widely discussed and documented (Gordon, 1970; McAfee & Vergason, 1979; O'Dell, 1974) and because parents and professionals are becoming more accustomed to working with one another, parents are demanding and professionals are acknowledging that parents of *all* children and youth, particularly those classified as exceptional, must be made a part of their offspring's program.

Expansion of the population of parents and families to whom involvement, conferencing, and counseling services are being made available has resulted in the realization that the age of a child or youth determines various parental and family needs and, subsequently, the services to be rendered. The most frequent need of parents of preschool children, for example, relates to information on normal child growth and development, appropriate expectations for their offspring, as well as home- and community-based resources and programs. Parents and families of young handicapped children may also require emotional support and information on how to interact with their child.

Parents of elementary-age children most often request information relating to their child's academic and social progress, strategies for developing a cooperative partnership with educational personnel, mechanisms for influencing the policies of schools and agencies, and methods for augmenting school programs through home-based efforts.

Parents and legal custodians of adolescents, particularly those with exceptionalities, most frequently request information on how to become involved in their child's school program, how to aid their child in making plans for the future, and how to contend with issues such as sex, drugs, alcohol, and rebellious behavior.

Parents of young adults, in turn, frequently require information and options for facilitating independence and adjustment to the postschool world. Often these parents are more interested in focusing on community- and work-related concerns than school-related issues.

The conferencer must be aware that a child's age is a significant factor in providing useful parent conferencing services and be able to individualize accordingly. While certain basic and generic skills are associated with any successful conference with a parent, such skills must be applied in an individualized fashion, with a child's developmental stage being one critical consideration.

PARENTS AND FAMILIES OF YOUNG EXCEPTIONAL CHILDREN

A variety of reports published within the past decade have supported the efficacy of early intervention with handicapped and disadvantaged children (Hayden & McGinness, 1977; McDaniels, 1977). Such reports, in conjunction with earlier research on cognitive development (Bloom, 1964; Piaget, 1952) and the effects of early environmental experiences on school achievement (Caldwell & Yahraes, 1975), have served as the basis for the development of early childhood programs designed to stimulate intellectual development. Furthermore, subsequent reports have identified parental support and participation as a basic ingredient in the success of these programs (Holmes, Simpson, & Brittain, 1979).

Head Start, a federally supported project initially funded in 1965, is one of the first and most comprehensive early childhood models. This experimental program, designed to provide comprehensive educational, health, and social services to low-income families, has from its inception focused on making parental involvement an integral and basic component. While the overall impact of Head Start has been questioned by some (Westinghouse Study, 1969), the parental participation component of the program is generally considered to be exemplary. Parental involvement in Head Start continues to be pervasive, with parents routinely having a part in developing and operating all components of the program. In particular, parents work in cooperation with Head Start staff to select curricula, carry out daily activities, and recruit and hire staff.

Other early childhood programs including home-based intervention projects (Gordon, 1971; Levenstein, 1970) and preschool programs with home training and parental involvement components (Gray & Klaus, 1965; Karnes, Teska, Hodgins, & Badger, 1970; Weikart, 1970) have also revealed the necessity of active parental participation. In fact, because parents are the major source of information, stimulation, and social influence for children, their involvement is indispensible. As concluded by Honig (1975), parental involvement in early childhood programs is essential "to sustain the often considerable cognitive gains demonstrated during the child's participation in a program" (p. 10).

Efforts to involve and serve parents and families with preschool children must be based on the premise that a variety of individuals and needs must be served (Coletta, 1976). Nonetheless, in spite of the heterogeneous nature of parents and families, their needs will tend to cluster in three general areas: (1) emotional support needs, (2) information exchange opportunities, and (3) strategies for securing and utilizing services for child and family. While these needs exist in every family with preschool-age children, they are most dramatic in families of exceptional children.

Need for Emotional Support

The birth of a handicapped child or later identification of an exceptionality will almost universally have a significant impact on both the parents and the ecology of the family. A less than perfect reflection of the family is typically associated with anxiety and strong emotion and may also serve to make members of the family more vulnerable to otherwise normal pressures and frustrations of life. Farber (1968) reported that a severely handicapped child will frequently cause the family to focus their attention on problems within the family to the exclusion of community concerns. Such a reaction may be seen as a necessary behavior since "failure to do so may lead to conflict and disturbance of family relationships" (p. 174).

Often the need for emotional support in parents and families with young handicapped children can most effectively be served by providing them an opportunity to express their perceptions, ideas, feelings, and concerns to an interested and nonjudgmental listener. In addition, support can be provided by aiding them in comprehending the stages they are apt to go through while adjusting and accepting an exceptional child. Karnes and Lee (1980) suggested that conferencers should be "sensitive to stages of parental reaction and to attempt to counsel parents through each stage of adjustment" (p. 208), including denial, anger, guilt, shame, blame, overprotection, and adaptation. While these stages are routinely experienced by all parents and families with exceptional children, it appears that the intensity of this response is most dramatic when the child of concern is of preschool age (McDonald, 1971).

As part of the emotional and psychological support services to parents and families of young handicapped children, Hayden (1976) stressed the importance of accepting their child's condition. She noted that parents and families should be allowed to reach a determination on their own that they require such services and then to seek appropriate options independently rather than having these thrust upon them. Sullivan (1976) supported this position, adding that parents and families must be allowed to determine their own emotional needs as opposed to those thought to exist by professionals. One father of a child diagnosed as an infant having cerebral palsy revealed that he and his wife became extremely irritated at one professional who persisted in attempting to identify their "stages" of acceptance and in having them "share their true feelings." While this parent confided that he and his wife would have enjoyed the opportunity to discuss their feelings about their handicapped daughter with a supportive professional, they were unwilling to confide in the individual who was so ostensibly attempting to aid them.

While it is obvious that a variety of factors will determine the need for emotional support in parents and families of young handicapped children, it is equally certain that virtually all will experience this need to some degree. Accordingly, professionals must be willing and able to develop appropriate strategies and alternatives for serving parents and families in this significant area.

Need for Information Exchange Opportunities

Probably the most common and generic need experienced by parents and families of young exceptional children is for effective communication opportunities. Of particular significance to parents of young exceptional children are opportunities to discuss the nature and etiology of their child's exceptionality. Barsch (1968) reported that a high percentage of parents of young handicapped children first become concerned about their child's condition within the first six months following birth. Of particular concern to parents are delays in motor and speech development. All too frequently parents report that they are provided insufficient opportunities to discuss their concerns with professionals and, in instances when a diagnosis has been made, to share and receive information about the demonstrated exceptionality (McDonald, 1971).

Most parents of young children who have suspicions about their child's normality make their first professional contact with a physician. Such contacts clearly differentiate parents of young children from their counterparts with older offspring, whose most frequent contacts on the child's behalf tend to be interactions with school and other nonmedical professionals. Whether rightly or wrongly, physicians, more than any other professional group, have been criticized for their demeanor and communication style toward parents with young exceptional children (Akerley, 1978; Farber, 1968; McDonald, 1971). Barsch (1968) reported that the majority of parents of handicapped children considered the time allotted them by their physician for discussion of their child's diagnosis to be inadequate; over one-third of the parents in his study "felt that the physician was abrupt, blunt and completely objective showing little concern for the individuality of their problem" (p. 85). While parents must be provided straightforward and accurate information in as timely a manner as possible, the information must be disseminated in a manner that suits individual family needs. Failure to do so will most likely result in a failure to satisfy the information needs of parents.

Children who are diagnosed as exceptional prior to the time they enter school tend to have conditions that are more severe or overt than those diagnosed in the elementary grades. Many parents of preschool exceptional children will have received a definitive diagnosis and associated information within the first year of life. Barsch (1968), for example, reported that 80% of Down's syndrome, 66% of cerebral-palsied, 61% of blind, and 40% of deaf children are diagnosed within 12 months of birth. It can thus be assumed that the nature of a child's condition, development, and subsequent problem will at least partly determine the type and specificity of the information to be disseminated to parents and families. Likewise, it can be assumed that parents whose children have not received a definitive diagnosis will also require appropriate attention, including an opportunity to exchange information. Therefore, parents of children with unspecified developmental lags may suffer through a relatively lengthy period of anxiety and uncertainty unless given adequate chances to communicate. While information exchange opportunities may not eliminate much concern, they will typically aid parents and families in more effectively dealing with the situation.

Although the informational needs of parents and families of young exceptional children vary, most frequently these individuals tend to be interested in discussing future expectations for independent functioning, available treatment and educational opportunities, and their children's performance in an intervention program. Siladi (1980), in a study conducted with parents of preschool-age severely handicapped children assigned to a transdisciplinary setting, reported that parents were most interested in discussing their child's progress in the program, teaching and intervention strategies being employed, and educational objectives associated with future public-school placement. Results also revealed that parents most preferred to meet with their child's teacher, program coordinator, physical therapist, and speech therapist, respectively. Parents least preferred to confer with the programs' parent consultant, other parents, and social workers, respectively.

Without doubt, parents of young exceptional children require adequate opportunities for communicating with professionals. Such opportunities will most likely be the basis for other successful parent-related program efforts.

Service and Advocacy Needs

Hayden (1979) observed that exceptional children from birth to three years of age require not only medical intervention but also educational attention. She specifically stressed that "while nonhandicapped young children may make acceptable progress without early educational intervention, handicapped or at risk children do not. To deny them the attention that might increase their chances for improved functioning is not only wasteful, it is ethically indefensible" (p. 510). Others (McDaniels, 1977; Simmons-Martin, 1976) have also advocated appropriate educational intervention opportunities for young exceptional children, noting that such services are an indispensable component of any efficacious program.

A variety of noneducational services have also been identified as necessary to satisfy the needs of exceptional children and their families. Olshansky (1966) recommended that the following four types of services be made available: (1) medical, (2) baby-sitting, (3) respite care, and (4) parent education. Others (Kentowitz, Gallagher, & Edgar, 1977) have stressed the need for community-based programs, while some (Justice, O'Connor, & Warren, 1971) have noted the severe paucity of services available, particularly for minority families.

Although only a small percentage of parents and families of young handicapped children can be expected to require counseling and therapy, such services must be available when needed. An increasing percentage of parents and families can be anticipated to need training in the use of behavioral and educational methodology applicable in the natural environment. In both areas parents have demonstrated themselves to be valuable resources and a means of extending professionally monitored intervention programs into a variety of settings. Employment of parents in this fashion also has the advantages of establishing appropriate child advocacy expectations and training parents in the use of strategies that can be used with their children at other times in their lives.

PARENTS AND FAMILIES OF ELEMENTARY-AGE EXCEPTIONAL CHILDREN

While the needs of parents with elementary-age exceptional children are as varied and individualized as those with preschool-age exceptional children, they tend to fall within the same basic areas; that is, emotional support and understanding; information exchange opportunities; and mechanisms for identifying, implementing, and evaluating services required by the child and family.

Need for Emotional Support

Identification of an elementary-aged child as exceptional has a significant impact on both the parents and the family structure. In some instances the identification and diagnostic process serves to confirm the previously undefined concerns of a family; in other cases the process comes as an unexpected shock. While the identification occurs at a time subsequent to that of infancy and preschool, and even though the exceptionality is frequently less severe and obvious than those found in preschoolers, the impact can be expected to be no less significant. While attempting to accept a handicapping condition, benefit from involvement with professionals, and facilitate their child's development, parents and families of exceptional children must be allowed to satisfy their own emotional needs. Coletta (1977) applied Maslow's hierarchy of needs to parents of exceptional children, noting that these individuals must have their physical, psychologic, emotional, self-esteem, and fulfillment needs met prior to accommodating and serving an exceptional child.

When parents and families become aware of a handicap in a family member, they will not only experience a variety of strong emotional reactions but may also lack experience or confidence in their ability to accommodate and serve the child. Thus, while few family members are trained for their respective roles, whether it be parent or sibling, they typically have the benefit of role models and direction from adult figures in the family. However, it is not at all unusual for families to feel somewhat overwhelmed and bewildered because they lack a frame of reference for interacting with an exceptional child and because the adults in the family may consider the needs of the handicapped child to be beyond their parenting skills.

Aiding parents and families to understand their emotional experiences and concerns is not a simple matter. However, the process can be facilitated by providing opportunities for discussing affective issues and understanding reactions such as shock, denial, fear, guilt, bereavement, anger, and depression. The mother of a recently diagnosed learning-disabled child indicated that even though she had read and heard of the strong reactions parents sometimes had when hearing of their child's exceptionality she was surprised at her own intense feelings of anger and frustration. She did note, however, that having an opportunity to discuss these feelings with her child's resource room teacher was extremely beneficial.

Need for Information Exchange Opportunities

Parents of elementary-age children frequently report that one of their most prominent needs is to meet and exchange information with the individuals assigned the task of educating their sons and daughters. This need seems particularly acute at the time when a child is initially identified as exceptional and assigned to a "special" program (Simpson & Whorton, 1982). Even though parents may have been provided an interpretation following their child's assessment, they will frequently benefit from an opportunity to discuss this information with their child's teacher after having had an opportunity to ruminate over its content and implications.

Parents should also be given information about their child's educational program and provided an opportunity to discuss it. Specifically, they should be made aware of the procedures and curriculum to be used in implementing each individual program, ancillary services to be employed, and the manner in which their child will be evaluated. In addition, they should be advised of the availability of school and community resources that may be required by the family. Finally, subsequent to a child's placement in a special program, parents should receive progress report information from school personnel at regularly scheduled intervals. Such sessions should not only consist of a review of a child's academic, social, behavioral, and physical progress but also include an opportunity to ask specific questions, discuss problems, and present agenda items of their own.

The importance of providing adequate opportunities for exchange of information between parents and educators has been highlighted by a number of professionals (Yoshida & Gottlieb, 1977). However, concerns and problems within this domain still abound. Dembinski and Mauser (1977), for example, asked parents of gifted children to react to questions about their interactions with school personnel. The results of this survey indicated that approximately 60% of the parents sampled felt uncomfortable about asking questions of professionals. These researchers suggested that professionals must create an atmosphere that encourages free discussions. Only under such conditions will parents' information needs be met.

While the information needs of parents and families of elementary-age children are just as significant as those of parents with younger children, the focus of the parent-professional discussions at this level shifts from community to public school and from readiness and development to more traditional academic concerns. As noted previously, the need for information remains among the most generic parental needs and, consequently, the services associated with it become the basis for effective program progress (Davis & Davis, 1981).

Service and Advocacy Needs

Initially, parents of school-age exceptional children can be expected to be most concerned about locating appropriate educational and treatment alternatives for their children. Fortunately, increased availability of educationally related alternatives for exceptional children has aided in satisfying this need. However, even though federal legislation and school policy changes have resulted in an increased number of program options for exceptional children, thus relieving many parental concerns for direct service, the legitimate and meaningful involvement of parents in their child's school experience remains less than optimal. This issue is nowhere more apparent than at the elementary level, where parents are frequently highly interested in augmenting professional services and meeting the school-related needs of their children and where school personnel, in turn, may be less than totally willing to establish a partnership. According to Yoshida and Gottlieb (1977), parental dissatisfaction over this situation prompted many parents to search for a more equal power distribution within the school structure.

The motivation of many parents and families to be involved in their exceptional child's educational program is matched by their ability to augment and support school-related programs and to carry out independent home projects. Parents have, for example, demonstrated the ability to use educational and behavioral principles systematically in cooperative school-home programs (Baker, Brightman, Heifetz, & Murphy, 1973; Walker, 1979) and to be generally capable of facilitating their child's development under structured conditions (Barnard, Christophersen, & Wolf, 1977; O'Dell, 1974). Berkowitz and Graziano (1972) suggested that parents must play a key role in the programs provided their children, noting that "parents have assumed the major moral, ethical, and legal responsibility for their children, they generally have the greatest degree of contact with the children, and greatest control over the natural environment, and they are typically both willing and fully capable of assuming and carrying out detailed therapeutic measures" (p. 299).

However, in spite of the proved effectiveness of parents in supporting school-related intervention programs, they have traditionally been provided little support and structure for doing so. Consequently, even though parents have been granted significant authority in determining the nature of their child's program and in being involved in subsequent implementation of intervention strategies, they have received limited attention and training on how to exercise these privileges. Goldstein, Strickland, Turnbull, and Curry (1980) proposed that parents be trained to participate in their children's individualized education program conference. Without such training, only limited parental participation and involvement can be expected. Simpson and Whorton (1982) supported this position, stating that while "parents will want to be involved in facilitating and augmenting the educational and intervention processes employed with their handicapped children, they can be expected to do so only with appropriate training. Thus, opportunity and encouragement must be accompanied by training if parents' needs are to be met" (p. 13).

Finally, in addition to advocacy and involvement training, parents and families must be directed to appropriate counseling, therapy, and social agencies whenever appropriate. As suggested previously, the infrequency of this need in no way discounts its overall importance.

PARENTS AND FAMILIES OF EXCEPTIONAL YOUTH AND YOUNG ADULTS

During the past few years we have witnessed a significant increase in the availability of programs and services for exceptional youth and young adults. Primarily as a function of legislative mandates and litigation, secondary-age pupils and young adults with special needs are beginning to receive at least some of the services they have so long been denied. While the increased availability of services for exceptional youth has been paralleled, to some extent, by increased parent-related programs and involvement efforts, the true proliferation of parent-related services has been relatively slow. Siegel (1975) reported that many parents lose faith and interest in being involved in their offspring's program after watching their child fail for an extended period of time and after often determining that professionals lack a "cure" for their child's condition. Kronick (1975) supported this notion, observing that as an exceptional child grows older, the parents demonstrate less motivation and stamina to serve the child's needs. As a result, some professionals have concluded that parents of older children lack the interest in being involved in their child's program and, consequently, thus failed to put forth the efforts necessary to encourage such participation. Nonetheless, in spite of this notion, there are ever-increasing signs that parents and families of exceptional youth and young adults are motivated to work with schools, agencies, and professionals in behalf of their offspring. In addition, these parents and families appear to require services and, therefore, must be afforded the same opportunities for involvement as their counterparts with younger children (Alley & Deshler, 1979). In fact, while the specific needs of parents and families of exceptional youth and young adults are different from those of parents with younger children, their needs generally fall within the same domain. Specifically, they can be expected to experience a need for emotional support, information exchange opportunities, and appropriate service options.

Need for Emotional Support

While not as widely recognized in parents and families of exceptional adolescents and young adults, these individuals and units nonetheless require emotional support and attention to help them cope with their exceptional child or family member. Such a need exists regardless of time lapsed since the initial diagnosis and interpretation and the services that have been rendered. The mother of an autistic adolescent reported that she periodically breaks into tears when seeing her handicapped son, who was diagnosed as an infant, attempting to interact with his normal siblings. Accordingly, the conferencer must be aware and sensitive to the needs of parents and families for support independent of a child's age. Such sensitivity and awareness must be manifested by recognizing the feelings and attitudes of individual family members relative to living with an exceptional individual, being willing to listen to their concerns and perceptions, and being attentive to issues that families must deal with. The mother of an 18-year-old son with Down's syndrome reported that, whereas her neighbors at one time considered her son to be "cute," he was currently considered by many to be a threat even though he had never shown any aggressive or antisocial inclinations. Another set of parents of a moderately retarded and physically impaired adolescent girl revealed that they experienced their family recontending with emotional issues and reexperiencing emotional stages that they thought had been resolved years before. These parents noted, for example, that with their daughter's passage into puberty came the realization that her condition was truly permanent. Specifically, they experienced renewed feelings of anger and frustration over knowing that she would never be able to live independently or function as a normal adult. Other parents of older exceptional children have reported problems in dealing with such issues as institutionalization, sex, employment, and marriage.

When youth and young adults who were classified as exceptional on the basis of school-related criteria and who will be able to function independently in normalized settings upon leaving school grow older, their parents generally experience a sense of relief. Conversely, parents whose children have more severe handicaps will encounter even more frustration as they see their offspring growing up. Accordingly, the educational conferencer must be reminded that parents' emotional support needs can in no way be expected to vanish once a child leaves an elementary-level program (Hobbs, 1975).

Need for Information Exchange Opportunities

The nature of the psychological and developmental changes associated with adolescence and young adulthood is such that even in the most normal situations this period can be highly unpredictable. The interaction of adolescence and a handicapping condition can result in a period of even greater instability for a youth and the family (Nelson & Polsgrove, 1981). While adolescence is typically a period when parents are replaced by a youth's peer group as the primary social influence (Muuss, 1976), an exceptionality may require parents of a handicapped adolescent to continue to serve in a more prominent and supportive role. Accordingly, parents frequently desire information relating to the changes associated with their offspring's puberty and the many issues associated with this period. In addition, many parents want an opportunity to share information about their child with the child's teacher and other professionals. Warfield (1975), in a report of the results of interviews conducted with mothers of retarded children in their judgment of various components of a parent program, noted that parents judged as most favorable that information that focused on "problems of adolescence," interpretation of test results, and planning for a child's future. McDowell (1981) listed some of the particular youth-related problems on which parents desire information as drug and alcohol abuse, juvenile delinquency, suicide, sex, and marriage. The obvious significance of these and related issues makes it apparent that parents of exceptional youth, contrary to popular opinion, will be highly motivated to interact with professionals for the purpose of exchanging relevant information.

It is also significant to note that, based on research findings, parents of exceptional adolescents and young adults can be expected to be interested in discussing the results of various types of assessment measures descriptive of their offspring's abilities. Thus, rather than parents being satiated or totally familiar with their adolescent son's or daughter's strengths and weaknesses, they will most likely have a strong interest in this variety of information. Perhaps because these parents and families are moving toward the consideration of nonacademic alternatives for their children, or because they are more realistic about a handicap, diagnostic data appear to be a topic of great interest during this period of a child's life. While parents of elementary-age children may be most interested in discussing the educational implications of a handicapping condition or school-related progress, they will probably be far more concerned with the implications of assessment data on a child's future when the child is older.

One of the most prominent information exchange needs is a discussion of a child's future between parents and families and teachers and other professionals. In some instances this exchange may take the form of determining whether or not an individual's needs can be best served in an institutional setting (Farber, 1968), whether or not a youth is eligible or appropriate for particular types of services, and the impact of an exceptionality on a youth's postschool adjustment. The importance of encouraging discussions of this nature is emphasized in Clements and Alexander's report (1975), for example, that "many parents believe that their children's disabilities will disappear, contingent upon a number of years in special education" (p. 3).

Finally, many parents of exceptional children, particularly those with severe disabilities, will be interested in discussing the options available to their son or daughter upon their death. While some parents of exceptional youth may be reluctant to initiate discussions that focus on their child's future, this reticence in no way can be interpreted as a lack of interest in the topic.

Service and Advocacy Needs

The historical paucity of services for exceptional adolescents and young adults (Alley & Deshler, 1979) and the notable absence of parental involvement programs at the secondary level (Kroth, 1981) have currently resulted in significant efforts on the part of parents of these individuals at acquiring appropriate programs for their children. Thus, in the future many parents of handicapped youth and young adults can be expected to focus most notably on identifying acceptable direct-service options for their sons and daughters.

In addition to direct services, educators and other professionals must be able to identify or coordinate other types of services. Alexander, Kroth, Simpson, and Poppelreiter (1982) suggested that professionals must be willing to aid parents in securing appropriate psychological, social, and academic services for exceptional youth and families. In particular, the conferencers must be willing and able to serve as a crisis intervention resource, community liaison, and educational referral agency. Alexander et al. emphasized that professionals must be familiar with resources outside public school settings if they are to serve the needs of exceptional youth and their families. Educators must "be capable of coordinating existing community, federal and state services to meet the needs of a student or family. These services may include welfare, medical, dental, child protection, psychological, social, psychiatric, vocational and alternatives to traditional family living" (Alexander et al., p. 304).

Parents of exceptional adolescents and young adults may require the assistance of the educational conferencer in structuring their home environment and developing behavior management strategies. Obviously, some of the parent-applied procedures and consequences appropriate for managing the behavior of adolescents and young adults are different from those applicable with younger children. The mother of a 200-pound mentally retarded teenage boy remarked, for example, that a "time out" procedure would no longer be effective the day her son told her that he would no longer go to the time out area voluntarily.

One of the basic issues related to the provision for services and involvement opportunities to parents and families of exceptional youth and young adults has been the assumption of familial indifference. Unfortunately, a number of educators and other professionals have judged parents and families of exceptional youth to be generally phlegmatic with regard to their children and to lack the motivation to be involved in their children's education or treatment. Alexander et al. (1982), however, identified several factors related to this legacy of parental uninvolvement that were independent of motivation or interest in a child. In particular, those authors noted the following to be possible explanations for this pattern: the history of conflict that has characterized parent-educator relationships; the complexity of secondary and postschool programs and the large number of educators, support personnel, and other professionals parents must relate to in these programs; the complex and changing nature of families, including the high incidence of single-parent and reconstituted families; the lack of continuity in parent education programs and the paucity of resources commensurate with parent and family needs; and finally, "parent burnout."

While each of the above factors must be considered to be valid and significant explanations for parental noninvolvement, it should be noted that most of these issues can be abated, at least to some extent, by educational conferencers. Educators must consider their role to consist, in part, of finding ways of facilitating the cooperative involvement of parents and families within an educational program. Above all, conferencers must search for ways to facilitate cooperative involvement with parents and families as opposed to assuming that they are not interested in their child's program and unwilling to be involved.

CONCLUSION

More than ever before educators and other professionals are acknowledging that parents and families are the most significant individuals to impact on the lives of children and youth. Accordingly, increased efforts have been made to serve the needs of all parents and families of exceptional children, including those of preschool age, secondary level, and young adulthood. With the increased emphasis on serving the needs of this broader spectrum of parents and families has come the realization that a child's age is closely correlated with the needs of families and the types of services to be rendered. Therefore, while all parents and families will have general needs for emotional support, information, and service options, the particular needs and requirements for the delivery of related services will vary with the age of a child. Hence, the educational conferencer must be able to offer services based on age considerations.

Exercises

1. Compare the parental and family needs of the children with whom you are most involved with those of different ages. Note areas of similarity and difference.
2. Conduct a survey of the parents in your class or program to identify their emotional support, informational, and service and advocacy needs. Next, identify resources within your school agency or community for most effectively serving these needs. Finally, compare your information with that of other individuals who are involved with a different age-group.

REFERENCES

Akerley, M.S. False gods and angry prophets. In A.P. Turnbull & H.R. Turnbull (Eds.), Parents speak out: *Views from the other side of the two-way mirror.* Columbus, Ohio: Merrill, 1978.

Alexander, R., Kroth, R., Simpson, R., & Poppelreiter, T. The parent role in special education. In R. McDowell, G. Adamson, & F. Wood (Eds.), *Teaching emotionally disturbed children.* Boston: Little, Brown, in press.

Alley, G., & Deshler, D. *Teaching the learning disabled adolescent: Strategies and methods.* Denver: Love Publishing, 1979.

Appell, M.J., Williams, C.M., & Fishell, L. Changes in attitudes of parents of retarded children. *American Journal of Mental Deficiency,* 1964, *68,* 807-812.

Baker, B.L., Brightman, A.S., Heifetz, L.J., & Murphy, D.M. *The READ project series.* Cambridge, Mass.: Behavioral Education Projects, 1973.

Barnard, J.B., Christophersen, E.R., & Wolf, M.M. Teaching children appropriate shopping behavior through training in the supermarket setting. *Journal of Applied Behavior Analysis,* 1977, *10,* 49-60.

Barsch, R.H. *The parent of the handicapped child.* Springfield, Ill.: Thomas, 1968.

Berkowitz, B.P., & Graziano, A.M. Training parents as behavior therapists: A review. *Behavior Research and Therapy,* 1972, *10,* 297-317.

Bloom, B.S. *Stability and change in human characteristics.* New York: Wiley, 1964.

Boyd, R. Systematic parent training through a home-based model. *Exceptional Children,* 1979, *45*(3), 647-648.

Bronfenbrenner, U. *A report on longitudinal evaluations of preschool programs: Is early intervention effective?* (Vol. 2). Washington, D.C.: Department of Health, Education and Welfare, Office of Human Development, 1974.

Caldwell, B.M., & Yahraes, H. The effects of early experience on a child's development. In J. Segal (Ed.), *The mental health of the child.* Washington, D.C.: Department of Health, Education and Welfare, 1975.

Clements, J.E., & Alexander, R.N. Parent training: Bringing it all back home. *Focus on Exceptional Children,* 1975, *7*(5), 1-12.

Coletta, A.J. *Parent involvement: A resource guide for teachers.* Wayne, N.J.: William Patterson College Services, 1976.

Coletta, A.J. *Working together: A guide to parent involvement.* Atlanta: Humanities Limited, 1977.

Davis, D.H., & Davis, D.M. Managing parent teacher conferences. *Today's Education,* 1981, *70*(2), 40-44.

Dembinski, R.J., & Mauser, A.J. Considering the parents of LD children: What they want from professionals. *Journal of Learning Disabilities,* 1977, *10,* 578-584.

Farber, B. *Mental retardation: Its social context and social consequences.* Boston: Houghton Mifflin, 1968.

Goldstein, S., Strickland, B., Turnbull, A., & Curry, L. An observational analysis of the IEP conference. *Exceptional Children,* 1980, *46*(4), 278-286.

Gordon, I.J. *A home learning center approach to early stimulation.* Gainesville, Fla.: Institute for Development of Human Resources, 1971.

Gordon, T. *Parent effectiveness training.* New York: New American Library, 1970.

Gray, S., & Klaus, R. Experimental preschool program for culturally deprived children. *Child Development,* 1965, *36,* 887-898.

Hayden, A. A center-based training model. In D. Lillie & P.L. Trohanis (Eds.), *Teaching parents to teach*. New York: Walker & Co., 1976.

Hayden, A.H. Handicapped children, birth to age 3. *Exceptional Children*, 1979, *45*, 510-516.

Hayden, A.H., & McGinness, G.D. Bases for early intervention with handicapped infants. In E. Sontag, J. Smith, & N. Certo (Eds.), *Educational programming for the severely and profoundly handicapped*. Reston, Va.: Council for Exceptional Children, 1977.

Hobbs, N. Classification options: A conversation with Nicholas Hobbs on exceptional child education. *Exceptional Children*, 1978, *44*(7), 494-497.

Hobbs, N. *The futures of children*. San Francisco: Jossey-Bass, 1975.

Holmes, G., Simpson, R., & Brittain, L. Effect of an infant stimulation program on children with developmental disabilities. *Educational Considerations*, Fall 1979, pp. 22-26.

Honig, S. *Parent involvement in early childhood education*. Washington, D.C.: National Association for the Education of Young Children, 1975.

Justice, R.S., O'Connor, G., & Warren, N. Problems reported by parents of mentally retarded children—who helps? *American Journal of Mental Deficiency*, 1971, *75*(6), 685-691.

Karnes, M., & Lee, R. Involving parents in the education of handicapped children. In M. Fine (Ed.), *Handbook on parent education*. New York: Academic Press, 1980.

Karnes, M., Teska, J., Hodgins, A., & Badger, E. Educational intervention at home by mothers of disadvantaged infants. *Child Development*, 1970, *41*, 925-935.

Kentowitz, L.A., Gallagher, J., & Edgar, E. Generic services for the severely handicapped and their families: What's available? In E. Sontag, J. Smith, & N. Certo (Eds.), *Educational programming for the severely profoundly handicapped*. Reston, Va.: Council for Exceptional Children, 1977.

Kronick, D. *What about me?* San Rafael, Calif.: Academic Therapy Publications, 1975.

Kroth, R.L. Involvement with parents of behaviorally disordered adolescents. In G. Brown, R.L. McDowell, & J. Smith (Eds.), *Educating adolescents with behavior disorders*. Columbus, Ohio: Merrill, 1981.

Levenstein, P. Cognitive growth in preschoolers through verbal interaction with mothers. *American Journal on Orthopsychiatry*, 1970, *40*, 426-432.

McAfee, J.K., & Vergason, G.A. Parent involvement in the process of special education: Establishing the new partnership. *Focus on Exceptional Children*, 1979, *11*(2), 1-15.

McDaniels, G. Successful programs for young handicapped children. *Educational Horizons*, 1977, *56*(1), 26-33.

McDonald, E. *Understand those feelings*. Pittsburgh: Stanwix House, 1971.

McDowell, R.L. Adolescence. In G. Brown, R.L. McDowell, & J. Smith (Eds.), *Educating adolescents with behavior disorders*. Columbus, Ohio: Merrill, 1981.

Muuss, R.E. The implications of social learning theory for an understanding of adolescent development. *Adolescence*, 1976, *11*, 61-85.

Nelson, C.M., & Polsgrove, L. The etiology of adolescent behavior disorders. In G. Brown, R.L. McDowell, & J. Smith (Eds.), *Educating adolescents with behavior disorders*. Columbus, Ohio: Merrill, 1981.

O'Dell, S. Training parents in behavior modification: A review. *Psychological Bulletin*, 1974, *81* (7), 418-433.

Olshansky, S. Parent responses to a mentally defective child. *Mental Retardation*, 1966, *4*, 21-23.

Piaget, J. *The origins of intelligence in children*. New York: International Universities Press, 1952.

Shearer, M., & Shearer, D. The Portage Project: A model for early childhood education. *Exceptional Children*, 1972, *39*, 210-217.

Siegel, E. *The exceptional child grows up.* New York: Dutton, 1975.

Siladi, M.S. *A survey of parental preferences in types of involvement, interactions and information in the education of severely handicapped children.* Unpublished master's thesis, University of Kansas, 1980.

Simmons-Martin, A. Facilitating positive parent-child interactions. In D. Lillie, & P.L. Trohanis (Eds.), *Teaching parents to teach.* New York: Walker & Co., 1976.

Simpson, R.L., & Whorton, D. Education exceptional children: Parental involvement. In E.L. Meyen & D. Lehr (Eds.), *Exceptional children and youth in today's schools.* Denver: Love Publishing, 1982.

Sullivan, R. The role of the parent. In M.A. Thomas (Ed.), *Hey, don't forget about me.* Reston, Va.: Council for Exceptional Children, 1976.

Walker, H.M. *The acting out child: Coping with classroom disruption.* Boston: Allyn & Bacon, 1979.

Warfield, G.J. Mothers of retarded children review a parent education program. *Exceptional Children*, 1975, *42*, 559-562.

Weikart, D. *Longitudinal results of the Ypsilanti Perry preschool project.* Ypsilanti, Mich.: High-Scope Educational Research Foundation, 1970.

Westinghouse Learning Corporation and Ohio State University. *The impact of Head Start: An evaluation of the effects of Head Start on children's cognitive and affective development.* Springfield, Va.: Clearing House for Federal Scientific and Technical Information, 1969.

Yoshida, R., & Gottlieb, J. Model of parental participation in the pupil planning process. *Mental Retardation*, 1977, *15*, 17-20.

Chapter 5

Involvement with Single-Parent and Reconstituted Families

The formation of a new family system occurs with each marriage. Each family functions as a microcosm of society and as such is governed by differing rules, values, and norms, all of which are designed to perpetuate the structural integrity of the familial unit. The rules and norms for each family are products of the personalities, family histories, experiences, values, and expectations of each husband-wife team. The incorporation of children into a family system, either through birth or adoption, impacts on both the child and other family members. Accordingly, infants must contend with an environment wholly different from that experienced in utero while new parents must make time, priority, and financial adjustments. However, in spite of the significant impact a child will have on a family system, even if he or she is exceptional, it is the child who is expected to adapt to the rules and expectations of the family and to eventually carry on its traditions.

Normally, families with children follow a series of set developmental stages after marriage, beginning with the birth of a first child and ending with the departure from home of the youngest offspring. This normal progression, however, is increasingly being disrupted by divorce and/or family reconstruction (Skolnick & Skolnick, 1977). The trauma associated with parental separation and divorce or the reconstitution of a family will have a significant effect on both the adults and children associated with the process (Landis, 1960; McDermott, 1970; Tooley, 1976). The educator, although not typically a marital or family counselor, must nonetheless contend with the effects of family disruption. The conferencer must be able to comprehend the circumstances involved in this family change process and possess procedures and strategies for facilitating the growth of involved family members. Moreover, the professional must recognize that the separation, divorce, or reconstitution process will most likely be further complicated when a child (or children) in an involved family is exceptional (Turnbull & Turnbull, 1978).

EFFECTS OF SEPARATION AND DIVORCE ON FAMILIES

According to the U.S. Department of Commerce, there were approximately 1,770,000 divorces granted in 1980, up more than 65 percent from 1970. The steady rise in the divorce rate leads some demographers to estimate that nearly half of the infants born today will live in one-parent families for at least part of their childhood. While there is some variation in the estimates presented, there is agreement that divorce is a national trend that shows no sign of diminishing.

Impact on Children

While the overall impact of separation and divorce on children remains a poorly researched area that is clouded by speculation and personal belief, there is good accord that the event can have a profound influence (Johnson & Lobitz, 1974). Kelly and Wallerstein (1976), in a study of early latency age children, reported that patterns of "pervasive sadness," denial, and fear were common. These researchers also discovered that the relationship of the children to their parents changed after the separation or divorce. Those assigned to live with their mothers reported feelings of paternal abandonment and rejection, and most children considered the visitation schedule of two weekends per month to be insufficient for maintaining contact with their fathers. Kelly and Wallerstein also reported that some children had feelings of anger toward their mothers, allegedly for causing the separation or driving their fathers from the home. Other children reportedly had fears of antagonizing their mothers, believing that unless they appeased her they, too, would be driven from the home. Many children reported conflicts in maintaining loyalty to both parents following separation and divorce. Although there were inconsistent school progress patterns for the children following the separation and divorce, few children evinced better academic progress after the exit of one of the parents.

In a similar study of children in older latency, Wallerstein and Kelly (1976) disclosed that more mature boys and girls also suffered from the divorce experience. In particular, it was reported that the older children felt anger, just as did those of a younger age, but that the emotion was better organized and more object directed, usually toward one or both of the parents. In addition, a number of children were found to have diminished perceptions of identity, somatic complaints, weakened school performance, and impaired peer relationships. Finally, it was revealed that it was not uncommon for older children to change significantly their relationship with their custodial parent; in several instances there were reports of parent-child interdependence and support.

The impact of separation and divorce, while significant for all children and youth, appears to have different degrees of influence for different groups. Wallerstein and Kelly (1975) suggested that preschool children are least equipped to accept and contend with divorce. Others (Rutter, 1971; Tuckman & Regan, 1966) have noted that divorce may have a more deleterious influence on boys than girls. In particular, boys are more apt to demonstrate aggressive, impulsive, and anti-social behavior following a divorce than are girls.

The influence of separation and divorce on the academic progress of children is also a topic clouded by equivocal results and positions. While it has been demonstrated that children from homes where fathers are absent do not function as well in school as those where fathers are present (Chapman, 1965), the contributing factors responsible for this finding are not clearly understood. Coleman (1966), for example, suggested that these differences are more a function of racial and economic factors than the absence of a paternal figure. In support of this position, Herzog and Sudia (1973) noted that "the critical element [in poorer school performance] is not father's absence itself, but rather a complex of interacting family, economic and community factors" (p. 156). In the final analysis it does not appear that parents' separation and divorce will typically serve as an academic facilitator for children; however, the complexity of the factors involved and the precise relationship of parental divorce to school achievement serve to make this issue an unresolved empirical question.

All in all, there are strong indications that separation and divorce can have a deleterious influence on children (Biller, 1970; Shinn, 1977). Yet, the complexity of the variables involved requires that a thorough analysis be made of factors such as the age of the child at the time of separation, the relationship of the child and parents prior to the family disruption, the relationship of the parents at the time of the separation and divorce, and the interpersonal atmosphere of the family before such definitive conclusions can be drawn. As noted by Hetherington and Martin (1979), "specific characteristics of the child such as sex, age at testing, race, socioeconomic status, and birth order influence the impact of separation and growing up in a single parent home. No studies have adequately controlled or assessed the influence of all these variables" (p. 270).

Finally, it must be noted that studies have clearly demonstrated that warm and effective single-parent homes are more advantageous to children than conflict-torn nuclear families (McCord, McCord, & Thurber, 1962). Although a cliché, it seems apparent that the quality of parent contact in a home is far more significant to children than the number of parents in the home.

Impact on Parents

The impact of separation and divorce is no less severe for parents than children. In particular, mothers, the most prominent custodial parent, seem to experience a number of problems and issues directly associated with divorce and the resulting responsibility of raising a family without the support of a mate. As well as being cognizant of the potential impact of the family change on a child, the educator also must be aware of the changes that will result for parents. This knowledge is indispensable in the parent and family conferencing process.

It is estimated that more than 11,500,000 children are living in one-parent homes, up over 40 percent since 1970. The vast majority of these homes are headed by women, even though there has been an increase in custodial male parents (Brandwein, Brown, & Fox, 1974). Mothers who head families seem to encounter problems in three primary areas: (1) financial, (2) family management, and (3) personal. For many women, gaining resolution to these issues is complicated because they not only have not had to deal with problems related to divorce but also may, for the first time in their lives, be accepting sole responsibility for any significant matter. The degree to which they are successful in contending with these problems will not only determine whether they grow personally but also the degree to which they will be able to develop and maintain a supportive family environment for their children

Financial Problems

A major issue facing many single parents, particularly mothers, is economic survival. According to Bane (1976), the 1974 mean family income of families headed by mothers was less than half that of families headed by fathers; this same researcher reported that over half of the children in homes headed by mothers were members of families existing below the poverty level. Furthermore, a significant percentage of fathers failed to make their agreed-upon child support payments after the first year (Brandwein et al., 1974).In some instances women find themselves in a position following their divorce of needing to find permanent employment without the benefits of marketable skills, training, or experience. Even women who have worked while married frequently discover that rather than working to supplement the family income they become the sole means of support for their families. While both men and women will typically have a lower standard of living after their divorce, it is the mother-headed family that seems to be most vulnerable to financial problems (Ruma, 1976). Accordingly, women who head homes must concern themselves not only with the impact of personal economic change at a time when they are most vulnerable but also with the influence of this change on their children. That children may hold their mothers personally responsible for their lower standard of living can further heighten the problem.

One recently divorced woman revealed that one problem she had not considered when seeking a divorce from her husband of 14 years was financial. Although she had volunteered at a hospital and worked part time as a clerk in a fabric store, she found that she was unprepared for what she considered to be "good jobs." Furthermore, she found that even when she was able to gain full-time employment, her income was far below what she and her children had formerly had when she was married. This mother was particularly distressed because, in spite of her efforts, her children held her personally responsible for their change in life style.

Without question, the educator must be aware of the economic issues facing divorced parents and be sensitive to the fact that it will not be at all uncommon for these individuals to have concerns that they consider to be far more significant than their child's performance in school. Such awareness and sensitivity will be the initial step in establishing effective communication.

Family Management Problems

Custodial parents routinely experience family management problems not shared by two-parent families. These concerns are attributable, at least in part, to the increased responsibility assigned the custodial parent and to the change in life style that can accompany a divorce. Women, for example, may find that in addition to child care, domestic responsibilities and a full-time job that they have inherited tasks previously held by their husbands. Single-parent fathers may also find themselves in the position of being responsible for the first time for meal preparation and child care. All in all, separation and divorce is usually associated with at least short-term family disruption and disorganization (Hetherington, Cox, & Cox, 1977).

One obvious and common concern of single parents is related to assuming total responsibility for child rearing. Mothers, in particular, report feeling ''trapped'' and unable to free themselves from the responsibilites of 24 hour-a-day child management. That there is not another parent to spell the mother must be considered to be the basic part of the issue. In a similar fashion, single parents frequently voice concern because they must serve as the sole role model for their children.

Single parents may also experience problems in discipline and child management beyond those encountered in two-parent homes. Particularly vulnerable are boys in families headed by mothers; these children tend to be more aggressive, impulsive, and prone to delinquency than boys in two-parent families (Santrock, 1975). The factors associated with this situation are not clearly understood and may in fact not even be primarily a function of a father's absence from a home. Herzog and Sudia (1973), for example, noted that the issues may be more related to ''stress and conflict within the home [and the] inability of the mother to exercise adequate supervision'' (p. 154). Hetherington et al. (1977) suggested that this pattern is related to changes in parent-child interactions following a divorce. In particular, it was noted that custodial mothers tended to become more restrictive, less affectionate, and more inconsistent in their discipline while noncustodial fathers tended to be overly permissive and indulgent. These patterns, which could obviously explain many of the problems identified in the literature, tend to reverse themselves with time. In particular, mothers who head families typically become significantly more effective as single parents after one to two years and noncustodial fathers tend to become less indulgent and permissive.

One mother who headed her family reported that while prior to her divorce she had been the primary disciplinarian in the family, she could rely on the support of her husband in carrying out punishment. She noted that she could tell her three preadolescent sons, if need be, that their father would aid in carrying out prescribed contingencies. She revealed, however, that after her divorce her sons tended to be extremely belligerent and frequently ignored her commands. She also reported that her sons complained that she was always "picking on them." She did confess that her anger towards her ex-husband and her frustration with her "plight" may have contributed to the deteriorated relationship she had with her sons.

Single parents, particularly women, must also convince their children (and sometimes themselves!) that they are in control of family-related matters. In many instances they must be successful at somewhat routine tasks, albeit those that they may have never contended with before. Thus, they must be able to deal with repairmen, utility companies, other agencies, and their overly aggressive children. As one seemingly bright spot in this area, Tooley (1976) observed that "while divorce is gruelingly stressful for these mothers and children, it also represents a developmental opportunity for the women involved: They could never, would never, be that helpless and overwhelmed again" (p. 40).

Personal Problems

The personal problems of divorced parents, particularly women, have been widely discussed (Newland, 1979). Mothers who head their homes have been described as vulnerable to economic hardships, isolation, discrimination, and anxiety over establishing new relationships. In short, these circumstances can serve to heighten the problems associated with divorce and family change.

Discrimination is one commonly voiced concern of divorced women (Lewis, 1977). While enactments such as the Equal Credit Opportunity Act, designed to ease credit discrimination, Title VII of the 1964 Civil Rights Act, which prohibits discrimination on the basis of race, color, religion, sex, or national origin, and the Equal Pay Act of 1963, which requires equal pay for equal work regardless of sex, have reduced the overtness of discriminatory procedures, discrimination allegedly continues to exist (Weitz, 1977). As noted by Frieze, Parsons, Johnson, Ruble, and Zellman (1978), "When equal pay for equal work became the law, many employers renamed jobs and gave men slightly more to do in order to justify paying them more" (p. 286).

Single parents have also revealed that in addition to their increased responsibilities, divorce may be associated with feelings of isolation, loss of status in their neighborhood and community, and rejection by friends, neighbors, and relatives. While the prevalence of divorce and single-parent families has aided in instilling new attitudes, many divorced parents have commented that it remains a problem. Finally, divorced parents have reported that forming new relationships, with both men and women, can be a difficult and anxiety-provoking experience (Frieze et al., 1978).

One recently divorced mother of two children indicated that she not only had far more responsibility and was working longer hours than when she was married but that she had experienced an erosion of support in her friends and neighbors. Particularly from her married friends and neighbors she felt a "coolness" following her separation and divorce. This young mother noted that along with her other new responsibilities she did not have time to go out and make friends. However, she did reveal that she did need someone with whom to talk.

RECONSTITUTED FAMILIES

The reconstituted family is a symbol of the decade. In fact, the reconstituted family is nearly as common as the traditional family and is gaining in acceptance daily. The high divorce rate data cited previously correlate closely with the figures on reconstituted families. That is, the majority of divorced men and women remarry, most within a few years. In addition, a number of these remarriages will involve stepchildren.

Along with the rewards of reorganizing a family will be a series of problems, all of which will impact on a child's performance in school and thus affect the role of the educational conferencer. The conferencer must be cognizant and sensitive to such matters as previous emotional ties and loyalties of children to their noncustodial parents and other relatives, the distribution of authority within the family structure, and role development and enforcement. Each of these areas will be associated with the effective reconstitution of a family.

Frequently, individuals assuming the role of stepparent will enter a family system with lofty, albeit somewhat unrealistic expectations. Some may envision themselves as perfect parents who will be able instantly to love and gain the love of their stepchildren and immediately to unite a new family into a closely bonded unit. Many will expect that their stepchildren will automatically love and respect them, and few will probably consider the resentment and anger that their children may feel over their marriages and the family reconstitution process. These negative feelings are frequently heightened when both parents contribute children to a new family.

Probably the most significant adjustment that must be made in reconstitution will be by a new parent who has never had children. This adjustment will probably be even more prominent when the person inheriting a family is a woman who is expected to assume a child care and domestic role.

The educational conferencer must be able to serve as a knowledgeable and available resource to reconstituted families. In particular, the conferencer should be familiar with the major issues that must be faced by these families, including clarification of lines of authority, financial concerns, loyalty to natural parents and siblings, and need for effective communication.

Clarifying Lines of Authority

It is not at all unusual for the natural parent of children in a reconstituted family to be perceived as "the parent" and the stepparent as somehow different. Children in reconstituted families may resist complying with the wishes of stepparents, natural parents may not want their spouse disciplining their children, and stepparents may feel uncomfortable in assuming a parent role. Each of these and other factors will obviously skew the communication process and subsequently the effective reconstitution process. Frequently the educator will be asked to become involved in formulating disciplinary techniques and developing strategies for clarifying authority and communication lines. The conferencer must recognize this issue as not only common in reconstituted families but also an area in which resolution must occur if the family is to function effectively (Melville, 1977).

Financial Issues

Just as with single-parent families, reconstituted families must contend with a change in the amount and distribution of money. The reconstitution of a family may in some instances be associated with conflicts over whether or not to support a particular project and resentment because of expenditures for items for individuals who were not members of an original family. Thus, for example, more than the typical amount of animosity might be anticipated because the orthodontic work needed by a new child in a family takes precedence over a family vacation. While educational conferencers are not expected to do financial counseling, any more than they are expected to be marital therapists, they should be aware and sensitive to this issue.

The Issue of Loyalty

By its very nature the reconstitution process involves the incorporation of individuals from different parentages and connections into a single family unit. It can be anticipated that many children will experience conflict in remaining loyal to a natural parent while living and relating to a stepparent or interacting with a stepbrother or stepsister in the same manner as a natural sibling.

The conferencer must be able to aid stepparents in recognizing that they must not expect nor demand that their stepchildren will respond to them as a natural parent nor that their children will not have feelings of allegiance for their natural parents. Furthermore, they must not expect that children brought together into a family through marriage will have the same feelings of loyalty and allegiance as those connected by blood. Finally, members of reconstituted families should be shown that there are advantages to their familial relationships. For example, stepparents should recognize that unlike a natural parent, they are not required to love their child unconditionally but rather that they have the advantage of allowing a more natural relationship, based on individual characteristics, to develop.

The Need for Effective Communication

The reconstitution process can be expected to create at least short-term disorder and turmoil (Duberman, 1975). Family members must adjust to the incorporation of new personalities into the unit, and with them a new set of values and expectations. Furthermore, the reconstitution process will most likely be associated with role changes for all family members.

While the processes associated with establishing a new family order can be anxiety provoking and formidable, they can also be exciting and rewarding if honesty and open communication prevail. Although a bit of a cliché, open communication (James & Jongeward, 1971) is a sine qua non to effective reconstitution and an area in which most families can benefit from objective input. Therefore, conferencers must not only recognize the importance of this issue but also acknowledge their role in aiding reconstituted families to establish effective avenues of communication.

THE ROLE OF THE EDUCATIONAL CONFERENCER IN SERVING SINGLE-PARENT AND RECONSTITUTED FAMILIES

Regardless of the attitude and personal position assumed by an educational conferencer relative to the increased prevalence of single-parent and reconstituted families, it must be considered that these trends do represent reality. Educational conferencers have no choice but to contend, either effectively or ineffectively, with these situations. While educators may not be trained to provide family or marital counseling, they must nonetheless be sensitive to the issues facing single-parent and reconstituted families and be cognizant of the special needs of these groups. Furthermore, they must recognize that the changes associated with divorce and family reconstruction will impact significantly on both children and adults. The conferencer must recognize that only with sensitivity and the application of appropriate strategies can the special needs of these families and children be met. The forthcoming are considerations for the conferencer relative to serving the special needs of single-parent and reconstituted families.

Be able to suggest resources and services for single-parent and reconstituted families. While the educational conferencer must not automatically assume that single-parent and reconstituted families will universally require community and professional services, he or she must recognize that these families will in many cases be in their most vulnerable state. Therefore, the conferencer should have available a list of appropriate resources to serve the various needs of these families. Included should be family counseling, mental health, and social agency contact persons; support groups for adults and children encountering divorce; agencies that can aid divorcées in such areas as establishing credit, securing child support and alimony, and understanding their various rights under the law; community recreation facilities and programs; day-care programs; and other problem-solving agencies. Even though not able to provide all the services needed to satisfy the varied needs of these families, the educator can effectively assume the essential role of referral agent.

Be aware that the priority concerns of single-parent and reconstituted families may be different from those of the educator. Even though most parents will be concerned about the progress of their children in school, it must be recognized that recently divorced parents and those involved in reconstituting a family will have concerns that they may consider to take priority. This is not to suggest that these parents should not be apprised or allowed to be involved in their child's educational program but rather that the educator should be aware of the other issues that may be impinging on these families. A recently divorced mother who is having difficulty earning sufficient money to feed and shelter her children may be understandably callous to learn that her daughter is having difficulty in math. Therefore, the educator must be able to apprise and involve parents in their child's educational program while allowing them to put school-related concerns in proper perspective.

Be aware that single parents may have severe time, energy, and financial restrictions. As noted previously, single-parent families are routinely beset by monetary problems and time restrictions. One recently divorced mother reported that her day started at 5:15 A.M. and ended at about 9:30 P.M. She confessed that even though she was deeply concerned about her child's school progress that she had neither the time nor energy to be closely involved. This common issue for single-parent homes should sensitize educators to the need for flexible conference schedules, alternatives to face-to-face contacts (e.g., notes and telephone calls) and properly spaced contacts.

Attempt to include noncustodial parents in conferences and programs. Even though a child may be legally assigned to live with one parent or may be part of a reconstituted family, it must be recognized, both by parents and conferencers, that they still may have another parent with whom they have regular contact. Efforts must be extended to apprise parents of their child's school-related progress and to include them in intervention programs. Such measures not only allow disrupted families to receive significant information but also extend therapeutic programs to a greater number of settings within the natural environment.

Recognize the importance of listening to parents. Notwithstanding the importance of entering each conferencing session with a structured agenda, the educational conferencer must also recognize the value of allowing single parents and those involved in reconstituting families an opportunity to be heard. The value of effective listening has been well documented (Rogers, 1961) and must be considered a highly effective strategy for meeting a basic human need. While all parents must be afforded an appropriate listening environment, this need appears particularly acute with parents of families undergoing change. Hence, the educator must allow the parent an opportunity to deviate periodically from a set agenda and to present concerns related to other matters. Individuals who chronically insist on discussing matters only peripherally related to the purpose of the conference should be apprised of the necessity of staying on task and schedule or referred to a professional who can provide appropriate counseling.

While the educational conferencer may consider this investment of time a waste, it must be recognized that listening is not only a basis for any human interaction but also a vehicle for establishing the rapport and trust necessary for any program to operate. Furthermore, the conferencer should recognize that divorced parents may not have anyone with whom they can discuss their problems. Consequently, the educator must initially establish an appropriate listening atmosphere for parents and then offer alternatives for allowing further interactions to occur (e.g., groups, friends, or others who can serve in a listening role).

Become familiar with your family-related values. The importance of value familiarity in parent conferencing is that individuals tend to act on their values (Kroth & Simpson, 1977). Hence, the attitudes and perceptions that educators have toward marriage, divorce, and family reconstitution will undoubtedly effect the manner in which they relate to individuals involved in family change. Simply becoming aware of one's values in this area can significantly improve the conferencing process.

Be able to apprise parents and family members of the potential impact of divorce and reconstitution on the family structure. It is not at all unusual for the educational conferencer to be a major referral and support resource for single-parent and reconstituted families. In fulfilling this role the educator must be able to inform parents of the potential impact of the change process. In some instances this will take the form of providing reassurance that turmoil and confusion are expected by-products of divorce and family reconstitution and that these problems will eventually be replaced by more satisfying experiences. In other situations the role of the conferencer may be to direct families in procedures for facilitating the growth and stabilization of the family unit. Finally, the conferencer may find it appropriate to relate to parents that cooperation between home and school can serve to stabilize and hold constant at least one significant environment for children in the face of an otherwise changing world. Regardless of the role played, the conferencer must have at least a basic understanding of the potential impact of divorce and family reconstitution on families and be able to relate this information appropriately to parents.

Aid divorced parents and stepparents to be effective in their respective roles. Above all, the conferencer must not be a source of additional problems for families undergoing change. Care must be taken not to accuse parents of contributing to their child's problems through undergoing divorce or family reconstitution, to set rigid schedules for conferences that may be difficult for single parents to meet, or to insist on the use of a traditional family model in the face of familial change.

Aiding parents to fulfill their respective roles will involve the use of effective listening techniques, including attention to feelings, exercising care in voicing opinions about an individual's life style and behavior (e.g., "I just don't think divorced ladies with children should date"); avoiding the taking of sides in marital and family conflicts; and making available appropriate intervention strategies and resources for solving particular problems.

With support and appropriate resources most parents who are single or involved in family reconstitution can learn to serve the needs of their children effectively. It is mandatory that the educator be available to serve as a facilitator in this process.

Anticipate atypical behavior in parents and children experiencing turmoil and change. As suggested previously, parents and children involved in a divorce or family reconstitution will experience a significant amount of pressure and family turmoil. Frequently these influences can produce significant changes in behavior. The conferencer should be sensitive to deviations in academic and social behavior in children involved in a change process and willing to take necessary actions to reduce their long-term injurious effects. In the same manner the conferencer must recognize that many changes in parental behavior, including even irrational behavior, may be a function of the difficult situation a person is in. Hence, the conferencer must be cautious in drawing hasty conclusions under these circumstances.

CONCLUSION

Single-parent and reconstituted families are a common component of today's changing world and as such will impact significantly on those educators assigned the role of interacting with parents. While the issues involved in divorce and reconstitution are significant, the conferencer can serve as a valuable stabilizing force for families undergoing change. With the cooperation of parents, the educational conferencer, and other significant individuals, the long-term deleterious influence of these change processes frequently can be reduced.

Exercises

1. Identify services available through your school, agency, or community that can be used to aid parents and families contending with divorce or family reconstitution.
2. Interview parents and family members who have undergone a divorce or reconstitution regarding their needs during this period. Request that they indicate those measures that could be employed by educators to facilitate the process.

REFERENCES

Bane, M.J. Marital disruption and the lives of children. *Journal of Social Issues,* 1976, *32*, 103-117.

Biller, H.B. Father absence and the personality development of the male child. *Developmental Psychology,* 1970, *2*, 181-201.

Brandwein, R.A., Brown, C.A., & Fox, E. Mothers and their families. *Journal of Marriage and the Family,* 1974, *36*(30), 498-515.

Chapman, A.H. *Management of emotional problems of children and adolescents.* Philadelphia: Lippincott, 1965.

Coleman, J.S. *Equality of educational opportunity.* Washington, D.C.: Department of Health, Education and Welfare, U.S. Office of Education, OE38001, National Center for Educational Statistics, 1966.

Duberman, L. *The reconstituted family.* Chicago: Nelson-Hall, 1975.

Frieze, I.H., Parsons, J.E., Johnson, P.B., Ruble, D.N., & Zellman, G.L. *Women and sex role: A social psychological perspective.* New York: Norton, 1978.

Herzog, E., & Sudia, C.E. Children in fatherless families. In B.M. Caldwell & H.N. Ricciuti (Eds.), *Review of child development research* (Volume 3). Chicago: University of Chicago Press, 1973.

Hetherington, E.M., Cox, M., & Cox, R. The aftermath of divorce. In J.H. Stevens & M. Matthews (Eds.), *Mother-child, father-child behaviors.* Washington, D.C.: National Association for the Education of Young Children, 1977.

Hetherington, E.M., & Martin, B. Family interaction. In H.C. Quay & J.S. Werry (Eds.), *Psychopathological disorders of childhood.* New York: Wiley, 1979.

James, M., & Jongeward, D. *Born to win.* Reading, Mass.: Addison-Wesley, 1971.

Johnson, S.M., & Lobitz, G.R. The personal and marital status of parents as related to observed child deviance and parenting behaviors. *Journal of Abnormal Child Psychology,* 1974, *3*, 193-208.

Kelly, J.B., & Wallerstein, J.S. The effects of parental divorce: Experiences of the child in early latency. *American Journal of Orthopsychiatry,* 1976, *46*(1), 20-32.

Kroth, R.L., & Simpson, R.L. *Parent conferences as a teaching strategy.* Denver: Love Publishing, 1977.

Landis, J. The trauma of children when parents divorce. *Marriage and Family Living,* 1960, *22*, 7-13.

Lewis, D.K. A response to inequality: Black women, racism, and sexism: Signs. *Journal of Women in Culture and Society,* 1977, *3*(2), 339-361.

McCord, W., McCord, J., & Thurber, E. Some effects of paternal absence on male children. *Journal of Abnormal and Social Psychology,* 1962, *64*, 361-369.

McDermott, J. Divorce and its psychiatric sequelae in children. *Archives of General Psychiatry,* 1970, *23*, 421-428.

Melville, K. *Marriage and family today.* New York: Random House, 1977.

Newland, K. *The sisterhood of man.* New York: Norton, 1979.

Rogers, C.R. *On becoming a person.* Boston: Houghton Mifflin, 1961.

Ruma, E.H. Counseling the single parent. In G.S. Belkin (Ed.), *Counseling: Directions in theory and practice.* Dubuque, Iowa: Kendall-Hunt, 1976.

Rutter, M. Parent-child separation: Psychological effects on the children. *Journal of Child Psychology and Psychiatry,* 1971, *12*, 233-260.

Santrock, J.W. Father absence, perceived maternal behavior, and moral development in boys. *Child Development,* 1975, *46*, 753-757.

Shinn, M. Father absence and children's cognitive development. *Psychological Bulletin,* 1978, *85*, 295-324.

Skolnick, A.S., & Skolnick, J.H. *Family in transition.* Boston: Little, Brown, 1977.

Tooley, K. Antisocial behavior and social alienation post divorce: The "man of the house" and his mother. *American Journal of Orthopsychiatry,* 1976, *46*(1), 33-42.

Tuckman, J., & Regan, R.A. Intactness of the home and behavioral problems in children. *Journal of Child Psychology and Psychiatry,* 1966, *7*, 225-233.

Turnbull, A.P., & Turnbull, H.R. (Eds.). *Parents speak out: Views from the other side of the two-way mirror.* Columbus, Ohio: Merrill, 1978.

Wallerstein, J.S., & Kelly, J.B. The effects of parental divorce: Experiences of the preschool child. *Journal of the American Academy of Child Psychiatry,* 1975, *14*, 600-616.

Wallerstein, J.S., & Kelly, J.B. The effects of parental divorce: Experiences of the child in later latency. *American Journal of Orthopsychiatry,* 1976, *46*(2), 256-269.

Weitz, S. *Sex roles.* New York: Oxford University Press, 1977.

Part II

Technical Skills and Strategies for Successful Conferencing

Chapter 6

Listening to Parents

Without doubt, listening is the key to effective communication. As noted by Langton and Scott (1959), "the teacher should be willing to listen as well as to talk" (p. 86). It is obvious, however, that most professional people, including educators, are far more adept at talking than listening. Kroth (1980), for example, observed that "one of the problems that teachers often have is that they are quite verbal people; they abhor silence. As a result, if there is quiet during the conference the teacher is apt to step in and talk" (p. 64).

While listening may be a skill that is frequently taken for granted, its salience to the successful conference is such that it cannot be underestimated. In addition, contrary to popular belief, it is not a behavior that is a natural aptitude of most people. Benjamin (1974) noted that true listening requires diligence and practice and that the listening process rarely occurs spontaneously. Others (Larsen & Poplin, 1980) have also reported that listening is a difficult skill that requires discipline and concentration to master.

SIGNIFICANCE OF GOOD LISTENING SKILLS

John Dewey (1938) observed that one of man's strongest urges is to be important. Listening, and the attention that accompanies the process, is a primary means of facilitating a feeling of acceptance and value in another person. Others have also made note of the impact of the attention that is a part of good listening. For example, Publilius Syrus, the famous poet of ancient Rome, remarked that "we are interested in others when they are interested in us" and Dale Carnegie (1936) observed that a demonstration of interest in another person is the most effective means of establishing rapport.

While these phrases may be ancestral in some respects, they are by no means out-of-step with current parent conferencing goals and practices. Without question, the ability to communicate interest and attention will largely be dependent on the educator's ability to follow the topics of the parent and to communicate an accurate understanding of what is being said and felt. As suggested by Rogers (1962), "I believe the quality of my encounter is more important in the long run than is my scholarly knowledge, my professional training, my counseling orientation, the techniques I use in the interview" (p. 416). Accordingly, educators should be reminded that one of their most important assets will be the ability to attend and listen to parents.

DEVELOPING LISTENING SKILLS

Although not an easy task, the capacity to listen can be learned. Ultimately this skill will take the form of simply allowing another person the opportunity to talk, with assurance that what is being communicated is important enough to require the full attention of another concerned individual.

Ivey, Normington, Miller, Morrill, and Haase (1968) successfully employed a video training procedure to instruct students in the use of basic counseling skills, including listening. This training program focused on developing "attending behaviors" and reflecting and summarizing the feelings of others. Ivey and his colleagues reported that they were able to develop basic counseling skills in a relatively short period of time using the video strategy.

According to Kroth (1975) there are two varieties of listeners: passive and active. The passive listener allows another individual the opportunity to talk without playing an overly intense role and without making numerous responses. Passive listeners are frequently sought out by others primarily because they offer another person the opportunity to hear themselves out. This type of listener, although perhaps not appropriate in all situations, may offer parents of exceptional children what they most need, the chance to talk about their attitudes and feelings relative to having an exceptional child to an interested, yet quietly accepting professional person. An example of passive listening is provided by Carnegie (1936), who relates the story of how Abraham Lincoln sought out a friend during the Civil War to discuss the issue of slavery. As the story was related, President Lincoln spent a great deal of time verbalizing the pro's and con's of abolishing slavery. After having spent hours talking about the situation, without asking for his friend's opinion, Lincoln thanked his friend for "talking" with him. Carnegie noted that "Lincoln hadn't wanted advice. He had wanted merely a friendly, sympathetic listener to whom he could unburden himself. That's what we all want when we are in trouble" (p. 113). Moreover, others, including parents of exceptional children, frequently desire and require nothing more than the opportunity to be listened to. While educators must be able to disseminate information and to respond to questions when information is truly being requested, they must also allow parents the opportunity to derive the benefits of a good listening atmosphere.

As observed by Johnson (1956), an attentive listener is the most effective physician.

Active listeners, on the other hand, will assume a far more vigorous and enthusiastic role in the parent-educator conference (Kroth, 1975). This intensity will take the form of increased levels of eye contact, responding, body animation, and asking questions. Active listening also implies a well-established degree of rapport between respondent and listener. Fine (1979) noted that effective communication is associated with acceptance and interpersonal security. In particular he noted that in instances of effective communication "you seem to understand what your friend is attempting to communicate, and your friend seems to understand you" (p. 103).

Gordon (1970) identified active listening as a basic means of communicating with another person. He noted that the process takes the form of attempting to relate to "What it is the sender is feeling or what his message means. Then he puts his understanding into his own words (code) and feeds it back for the sender's verification. The receiver does not send a message of his own—such as an evaluation, opinion, advice, logic, analysis, or question" (p. 53).

Davis (1977) offers several suggestions for facilitating the listening process. These suggestions include giving another individual an opportunity to talk; establishing an environment in which the person feels comfortable in speaking; demonstrating interest in the person and the subject; removing distracting stimuli; being empathic; allowing sufficient time in each session for the respondents to complete their agenda; avoiding becoming angry, argumentative, or critical; and demonstrating interest by asking appropriate questions.

As noted previously, effective communication between parents and professionals will not occur independently of an adequate listening environment. While listening is a behavior that can be trained, it must be developed and practiced. Consequently, the listening process must include a willingness to listen to parents and their points of view. The professional who attempts to respond to parents prior to listening to them or the educator who too hastily assumes the position of "telling" parents what to do or who "answers" their questions when they simply desire the opportunity to talk will rarely offer the most satisfactory conferencing relationship. Parents have repeatedly observed that educators routinely fail to meet their listening needs (Turnbull & Turnbull, 1978). In particular, parents have observed the following listening traits of some educators:

- Some educators listen with one ear, waiting for the parent to finish speaking so that they can make their point or explain the way it "really is."

- Some educators merely tolerate the parents' talking without really listening.

- Some educators use the analytical process of reducing and analyzing the content of the parents' messages.

- Some educators seem preoccupied while parents are talking; they obviously have something else on their minds.

- Some educators seem to go through the mechanics of listening, but their responses make it apparent that they do not understand.

- Some educators respond critically to things related by parents or attempt to provide suggestions when all the parent really wants (and needs) is an opportunity to talk.

DEVELOPING THE LISTENING ENVIRONMENT

In order for effective communication to occur, an appropriate listening atmosphere must be created. This atmosphere will include both external factors and components internal to the parent and educator. Kroth and Simpson (1977) identified several external factors that should be evaluated, including assurances of privacy and suggestions for arranging the physical environment. These authors suggested that "It is possible that negative environmental variables may neutralize other efforts that may be employed by the interviewer to communicate interest and sensitivity" (p. 77).

In addition to providing an acceptable external setting, educational conferencers must also strive to create an acceptable interpersonal setting. This should include the establishment of a psychological atmosphere that will serve to impart a sense of well-being and security for parents of exceptional children. In particular, educators should attempt to achieve a professional, yet relaxed atmosphere.

While a warm and relaxed atmosphere is most likely a climate of universally agreed-upon importance, the mechanism for achieving this condition may not be readily apparent. However, there are a variety of factors that counselors may wish to employ to produce the most desirable conferencing conditions. These include the following:

Be prepared. No single preparatory measure will facilitate the desired psychological climate of the conference as much as being prepared. Both parents and professionals alike tend to report feelings of being qualified, confident, and relaxed when they are well prepared for a conference. Accordingly, a thorough review of a child's folder and an assessment of progress and problems experienced together with an outline of agenda items to be pursued will typically aid in creating the conditions necessary for a meaningful interaction to occur.

Arrange for a private, professional setting for the conference. Attention to the physical setting may not always enhance the overall success of the parent-professional conference; however, failure to attend to this important feature may significantly interfere. Consequently, it is important to arrange for a professional setting where privacy and confidentiality can be assured. The classroom setting may or may not serve this purpose.

Arrange for appropriate furniture. In order to create an atmosphere conducive to discussing parent-educator matters, all parties should be provided comfortable, adult-sized seating. Not only will such physical considerations facilitate an adult-to-adult conversation, but failure to attend to this factor may significantly impair the parent and/or educator's capacity to attend.

Schedule relaxation time prior to the conference. Conferences scheduled back-to-back, which prohibit an educator from taking a short break, frequently serve to increase the anxiety of a conference. While breaks between parent sessions may be considered a luxury by some administrators, their overall importance should serve to make them a mandate. Some educators have taken the few minutes prior to a conference to jog in place, breathe deeply, engage in passive mental imagery (visualizing a relaxing scene), and attempt deep-muscle relaxation exercises. While the means for best achieving a relaxed state will tend to vary from person to person, educational conferencers must remember that these efforts will aid in creating an appropriate climate for the conference.

Reduce anxiety for the parents. Educational counselors should keep in mind that the functional interaction between parent and teacher will at least in part be dependent on the capacity of the professional to put the parents at ease. Consequently, it is essential that in preparation for the conference the educator attempt to reduce anxiety for the parents. This process will at least in part consist of reducing uncertainty for the parents. Included should be a specification of the time of the conference, the amount of time allotted, the location of the school and meeting room, the purpose of the session, and the information that the parent should be prepared to receive or share.

Maintain a natural demeanor in the conference. During the conference, the educational counselor should attempt to be as natural as possible. Rather than adopting a style that may be somewhat contrived simply to simulate what may be considered to be a desired counselor style, the professional would be far wiser to assume as natural a posture as possible. Such a strategy will serve to both put the counselor and parent at ease.

Recognize that eye contact is a basic component of good listening. Adequate eye contact has been identified as a necessary and basic means of creating and maintaining an appropriate listening atmosphere (Ivey et al., 1968). The significance of good eye contact dictates that educational counselors be aware of the necessity of this behavior. Hence, rather than attempting to augment the gaze intensity, educational counselors should simply concentrate on communicating that they are listening to the parent with whom they are interacting via the attention of their eyes.

Be sensitive to the emotions of parents. In addition to attending to the manifest content of the verbalizations of parents, educational conferencers should also be aware of the tone, gestures, expressions, and other affective responses made. As observed by Ekman (1964), individuals should listen not only with their ears but also their eyes, minds, and hearts. Accordingly, professionals must be sensitive to feelings as well as to manifest content.

EMPATHY: A BASIS FOR LISTENING

Effective communication appears to be most feasible in situations in which the educator is able to listen empathetically to parents. *Empathy*, a Greek term which literally means "suffering in," connotes an attitude of understanding that goes beyond the surface. The ability to empathize is an attempt to experience and understand another person's world and situation in a fashion similar to what that person is experiencing. Although obviously the process of empathy can never totally be achieved, the climate created through attempting to understand another person's view can establish an attitude of acceptance that will facilitate the conferencing process.

The ultimate goal of empathy is to facilitate the listening process by means of increasing the acceptance of the parents' position. Empathic listeners are able, within obvious limits, to relate to another individual's frame of reference as if it were their own. By relating and understanding the internal world of the parent, the educator is better able to create an accepting and supportive listening environment. While the empathic relationship is desirable, it is important for the educational conferencer to be aware that this type of understanding is rare in interpersonal relationships. Rather than attempting to understand the position and perception of parents, educators far more commonly attempt to analyze the situation or arrive at a solution to the parent's problem. While these strategies are not necessarily incorrect, they are frequently incompatible with true understanding and effective listening. According to Benjamin (1974) "The empathic interviewer so cares for the self of the interviewee and so wants him to learn to care that he is willing to abandon temporarily his own life space and try to think and act and feel as if the life space of the other were his very own" (p. 48). Once this atmosphere has been achieved, educators should have the trust of the parent, the appropriate relationship, and the necessary information to be able to meet the needs of the person with whom they are working.

The empathic process also involves an attempt to understand and relate to the emotions that are being experienced by the parent. Carkhuff and Berenson (1967) suggested that the empathic counselor must be able "to allow himself to experience or merge in the experience of the client, reflect upon this experience while suspending his own judgments, tolerating his own anxiety, and communicating this understanding to the client" (p. 27). Accordingly, the empathic process must go beyond the mere cognitive level and include an understanding of the emotions and feelings being experienced by the parent.

SPECIFIC LISTENING TECHNIQUES

The effective listener, in addition to demonstrating the skills of attending, acceptance, and empathy, must also possess specific listening strategies for facilitating the communication process. Included is knowledge in the use of door-opening statements, clarifying responses, restatements, reflecting, and summarization.

Door-Opening Statements

Door-opening statements are designed to demonstrate an interest by the conferencer in the parent and to indicate a willingness to listen. These efforts at initiating the interaction process are not pointed attempts to interrogate or analyze a situation but rather simply an indication of an interest in the parent and a willingness to attend. Door-opening statements and questions are not necessarily attempts at soliciting particular units of information or a means of establishing a routine of questions and answers. Rather these responses are designed simply to set the tone for a meaningful interaction. Implicit in the use of door-opening statements is the message that the professional does not intend to do all the questioning and the parent all the answering. In addition, these responses are not designed to establish an interaction set whereby the professional is the expert who will be able to solve all the parent's problems. Rather, door-opening statements are designed to maintain the proper problem ownership while allowing the parents an opportunity to talk about the situation.

Questions by the conferencer such as "Can you tell me about how you see the matter?" "How do you feel about having a handicapped child?" and "Can we talk about that?" illustrate this variety of statement. In addition, there are door-opening responses that can be made to specific parent-initiated comments. The examples provided below are designed to illustrate this use.

> *Parent:* "Nothing seems to go right at home anymore."
> *Educational Conferencer:* "Oh."
>
> *P:* "Parent-teacher conferences always seem to upset me."
> *EC:* "Sounds frustrating."

Clarifying Statements

Clarifying statements are designed to bring into focus information that requires additional elaboration or which the conferencer was unable to understand. In situations in which the conferencer, for whatever reason, is unable to follow or understand the parent, it is best to ask for clarification. Statements such as "I'm not sure exactly what you mean'' or ''Could you state that again?'' are examples of requests for clarification. This same strategy can also apply in situations in which the educational conferencer desires feedback regarding whether or not he or she has been understood correctly. ''What is your understanding of all of this?'' is illustrative of this type of clarifying statement.

Finally, and perhaps most commonly, clarifying responses can be employed to prompt the parent in making further elaborations on a point or concept. Again, the intent of these responses is to indicate the conferencer is attending and listening and is interested in having additional information. Examples of this type of clarifying statement include ''You mentioned feeling guilty about not giving as much attention to your nonhandicapped kids. What do you mean?'' and ''Can you describe more fully how you felt when you learned your child was mentally retarded?''

Restating Content

Listening can also be conveyed by restating to the parent that which was presented. The intent of restating is threefold. First, this process serves to demonstrate to the parent that the conferencer is in fact listening and is requesting further information and elaboration. Second, the process allows the parents an opportunity to hear themselves through the conferencer. Since parents may be more able to absorb and understand their own thoughts and motivations when echoed through another person, this process can be highly beneficial.

Finally, the restatement process can serve to secure consensus and agreement between what is said and perceived. Consensus and understanding in the conferencing and counseling process is a basic component without which little progress and rapport can be anticipated. The restatement of content act will frequently take the form of ''You seem to be saying that you don't understand the nature of your son's special education program'' or ''If I understand correctly, you would like to see more emphasis put on vocational training for Jennifer.''

Reflecting Affect

Along with attention to the manifest content of a parent's message must also be sensitivity to the feelings and emotions being expressed. To be in a position to reflect accurately, the listener must be able to empathically follow the parents. Empathy, as noted by a number of authorities (Carkhuff & Berenson, 1967; Rogers, 1951) is so integral a component of accurately responding to affect that the process can be legitimately undertaken only after this basic listening condition has been achieved. The reflection process, just as is the case with restating content, is undertaken for three reasons. First, these responses communicate to the parent that the educator is listening to more than the manifest content of the message; that is, the parents' feelings are also being followed and understood by the conferencer. This act serves to legitimize the feelings of the parent and to communicate that it is acceptable and understandable to have and demonstrate emotions. This simple act of acknowledging the acceptability of parents' feelings can greatly enhance the communication and rapport building process. Failure to acknowledge or adequately respond to the feelings of parents is frequently interpreted as an indication that feelings are not an acceptable component of the conference or that the conferencer is either uninterested or unqualified to respond to affect. Either situation can be devastating to the conferencing process. While educators may consider themselves to be most qualified to deal with agenda items unrelated to affect, the nature of the parent population dictates that the professional has no alternative but to be able to respond to emotion.

The reflection process also allows the parents an opportunity to hear their own emotions being expressed through a concerned and involved professional. Since emotions may or may not be evident to the parent, this mirroring process can frequently play an insightful role for parents.

Finally, reflecting feelings serves to confirm the accuracy of the conferencer's perceptions. While parents may not always acknowledge their feelings, even when correctly identified by the conferencer, this process nonetheless does communicate the sensitivity and attentiveness of the professional and allows the parent an opportunity to clarify the perception of the professional. Thus, for example, parents may indicate that they are not angry at the physician who diagnosed their cerebral-palsied child, as suggested by the conferencer, but that they were extremely "hurt."

As suggested, the reflecting process takes the form of accurately understanding and expressing for the parent those feelings that are present. According to Benjamin (1974), "reflection consists of bringing to the surface and expressing in words those feelings and attitudes that lie behind the interviewee's words" (p. 117). Thus, the educational conferencer plays the role of a mirror, reflecting both those feelings expressed by the parent and those observed by the professional but not directly stated by the parent.

Ivey et al. (1968) identified three major components of the reflecting process. First is a sensitivity to the emotions of another person. Second, the conferencer must be able to time the reflecting comments appropriately. It was suggested by Ivey and his colleagues that professionals not attempt to respond to every comment but rather that they wait for those fortuitous occasions when the response will be most meaningful and when it will facilitate rather than interfere with the interaction process. The third component of the reflecting process is to restate for another person the emotion that was originally expressed.

While conceptually valid, the reflection process has been severely admonished in recent years, primarily because of inappropriate and rigid use. In instances in which counselors attempt to rely on this procedure in the absence of other

established listening and conferencing techniques and when the reflecting response takes a hackneyed and routine format, its efficiency will be greatly
diminished. Undoubtedly most educators have encountered at least one aspiring
therapeutic agent whose entire counseling repertoire consists of an overused
phrase like "It appears that you feel . . ." or "I hear you saying you feel. . . ." In
instances in which this strategy is rigidly followed, minimal success can be
expected. This is particularly true in educational settings where parents are
typically not seeking therapy for themselves and where they request that other
items be covered within a relatively short period of time. However, it is also
important for educators to remember that they must have strategies for responding
to affect. When emotional content is the most salient feature, educational conferencers must respond appropriately. To not do so will undoubtedly undermine
other aspects of the parent-teacher interaction and the future goals of the relationship. Thus, conferencers must concentrate on developing an authentic and spontaneous style compatible with their personality but which is also appropriately
responsive to the emotions of the parent.

Illustrative examples of reflecting affect are provided below:

> *P:* "It's just heartbreaking to see Tommy floundering in school and not
> being able to do anything to help."
> *EC:* "It's really frustrating."
>
> *P:* "We could have just shot the psychologist who told us our son was
> retarded. He was so cold."
> *EC:* "You feel like he wasn't very sensitive to your feelings."

Summarizing

A final listening technique is to summarize for the parents, at periodic intervals,
information and affect that has been generated or observed. Summarizing statements can thus occur at points in the conference other than at the end and can be
designed to respond to both manifest content and affect. Again, the intent of these
comments is to communicate to parents that the professional is interested and
sensitive to what they are saying and that the professional is attempting to interpret
their world and experience in the same fashion that they are. Summarizing
statements can also serve to clarify the perceptions of the parent and to synthesize
and integrate affect. Illustrative examples of these types of statements include
"Can we say then, that you felt most uncomfortable about special education
placement because you didn't understand the diagnostic testing and because you
felt powerless to help your son?" and "To summarize, it appears that you have
identified three major concerns."

CONCLUSION

As noted throughout this chapter, the ability to listen accurately and to communicate this interest to parents is one of the most basic attributes of the successful conferencer and a primary basis for obtaining and disseminating information. Successful educational conferencers have clearly established that the ability to create an appropriate listening environment is so basic a part of the parent-educator communication network that other conferencing components will be dependent on the mastery of this single skill.

Exercises

1. Identify an individual (preferably a friend rather than a parent) to relate a topic of interest to you. Practice the following:
   a. putting yourself and the person with whom you are relating at ease
   b. maintaining good eye contact
   c. being an empathic listener
   d. making use of specific listening behaviors, including door-opening statements, clarifying statements, restatements of content, reflecting affect, and summarization statements.
   Discuss with the person the reactions that you both had to the various procedures.
2. Make an attempt to observe other people, including the students in your class, as they manifest different emotions and feelings. Pay particular attention to the way in which their nonverbal cues (e.g., posture and expressions) communicate the way in which they feel.
3. Attend to individuals whom you consider to be good and poor listeners. Try to identify the particular characteristics that lead you to categorize them as you do.

REFERENCES

Benjamin, A. *The helping interview*. Boston: Houghton Mifflin, 1974.

Carkhuff, R.R., & Berenson, B.G. *Beyond counseling and therapy*. New York: Holt, Rinehart & Winston, 1967.

Carnegie, D. *How to win friends and influence people*. New York: Simon & Schuster, 1936.

Davis, K. *Human behavior at work: Organizational behavior*. New York: McGraw-Hill, 1977.

Dewey, J. *Experience and education*. New York: Collier, 1938.

Ekman, P. Body position, facial expression, and verbal behavior during interviews. *Journal of Abnormal and Social Psychology*, 1964, *68*, 295-301.

Fine, M. *Parents vs children: Making the relationship work*. Englewood Cliffs, N.J.: Prentice-Hall, 1979.

Gordon, T. *Parent effectiveness training*. New York: Wyden, 1970.

104   Conferencing Parents of Exceptional Children

Ivey, A.E., Normington, C.J., Miller, D.C., Morrill, W.H., & Haase, R.F. Microcounseling and attending behavior: An approach to prepracticum counselor training. *Journal of Counseling Psychology, Monograph Supplement*, 15(5), Part 2, September, 1968.

Johnson, W. *Your most enchanted listener*. New York: Harper, 1956.

Kroth, R.L. *Communicating with parents of exceptional children*. Denver: Love Publishing, 1975.

Kroth, R.L., & Simpson, R.L. *Parent conferences as a teaching strategy*. Denver: Love Publishing, 1977.

Kroth, R.L. *Strategies for effective parent-teacher interaction*. Institute for Parent Involvement, University of New Mexico, Albuquerque, 1980.

Langton, G., & Scott, I.W. *Teacher-Parent interviews*. Englewood Cliffs, N.J.: Prentice-Hall, 1959.

Larsen, S., & Poplin, M. *Methods for educating the handicapped: An individualized education program approach*. Boston: Allyn & Bacon, 1980.

Rogers, C.R. *Client-centered therapy*. Boston: Houghton Mifflin, 1951.

Rogers, C.R. The interpersonal relationship: The core of guidance. *Harvard Educational Review*, 1962, *32*(4), 416-429.

Turnbull, A.P., & Turnbull, H.R. (Eds.). *Parents speak out: Views from the other side of the two-way mirror*. Columbus, Ohio: Merrill, 1976.

Chapter 7

The Development of Trust in the Parent-Educator Relationship

A basic concept of parent conferencing is that the process is not something that is applied to parents by the professional but rather that the act involves the joint participation of both groups. The cooperative participation of parents and educators, however, will largely depend on the capacity of the professional to establish conditions conducive to a cooperative effort. Paramount among the factors associated with the development of this environment will be the educator's ability to establish a relationship based on trust. Without trust, the ability of parents and professionals to communicate effectively and work together will be significantly impaired. As suggested by Rutherford and Edgar (1979), "When teachers and parents find themselves in adversary roles, distrusting each other, children suffer" (p. 20). Others (Benjamin, 1974; Hammond, Hepworth, & Smith, 1977) have also identified trust as a sine qua non of any therapeutic relationship.

While trust in the counseling relationship is typically thought of as an atmosphere that is created for parents, it is equally important for the professional to have trust in parents. Since the educational conferencer is not an unfeeling technician who is simply programmed to disseminate and interpret information, but rather an individual who is profoundly affected by the attitudes and responses of parents, educators must be able to both create and receive trust. It is simply unrealistic for the educational conferencer to attempt to establish a relationship in which parents are expected to trust the professional without a reciprocating response. Unfortunately, this futile strategy has been actively pursued and may be one of the primary reasons why the parent-professional relationship has not been noted for its high levels of mutual trust.

THE NATURE OF TRUST

Trust, as used in the context of the parent-professional relationship, is the basic ingredient on which the conditions for achieving educational objectives are based.

In fact, both in professional and business affairs, little can be accomplished without an acceptable level of trust. Even though definitions of this rather nebulous term may fail to describe its precise characteristics, professionals are in agreement as to its significance (Rogers, 1969; Truax & Carkhuff, 1967).

Kroth and Simpson (1977) defined trust ''as the belief that another person will act honestly or perform reliably and, therefore, can be depended upon'' (p. 34). Others have noted that trust is a necessary condition that must occur if change and growth are to occur. In particular, Combs, Avila, and Purky (1971) noted that ''an atmosphere which makes exploration possible must be established'' (p. 210) if one individual is to help another.

While the characteristics and distinct features of trusting associations will vary from situation to situation, there are qualities that typify these relationships. One particular feature of individuals in a trusting relationship is a heightened willingness to take interpersonal risks and to reveal elements of themselves to another person. Risk taking, in this context, is a willingness to make oneself vulnerable without fear of deleterious results. That is, parents and educators involved in trusting relationships display confidence that agreed-upon patterns of behavior will prevail. While similar in some respect to gambling, trusting is more strongly suggestive of a reliance on the occurrence of previously agreed-upon standards. Whereas gambling involves a situation in which one ventures a small risk to possibly secure a large gain, interpersonal risk taking is more closely aligned with confidence in a previously identified outcome. In gambling, an individual does not expect to be consistently reinforced. However, interpersonal risk taking, and the trust on which it is based, requires confidence that that which is anticipated will in fact occur. Thus, for example, when parents confide in a teacher, taking the risk that their confidence will be maintained, they expect (and trust) that this expectation will be upheld. Accordingly, it is apparent that a willingness to venture, which is a direct manifestation of a trusting relationship, must not be associated with the properties of uncertainty.

The trusting relationship, on which the conditions of change and growth are based, involves three basic components. First, professionals must create, with the aid of parents, an atmosphere in which a shared feeling of safety exists. Second, the educational professional must provide reassurance and a model for risk taking. Finally, both the professional and parent must reinforce one another for their risk-taking efforts.

Creating the Conditions of Safety

One of the primary ways in which educational conferencers will be able to establish a safe, trusting, and secure atmosphere will be through a display of warmth for the parents with whom they work. Rogers (1962) suggested that counselors who are authentically warm and positive toward the individuals with whom they are working are more likely to produce desired therapeutic gains. He termed this attitude "positive regard." This researcher, along with others (Truax & Carkhuff, 1967), has convincingly articulated the need and value of establishing a supportive atmosphere for individuals involved in a conferencing relationship.

An atmosphere of safety will also be facilitated when educational conferencers are comfortable with themselves and when they are willing to enter the relationship without a facade. Truax and Mitchell (1971) suggested that the ability to display nonpossessive therapeutic warmth is dependent on the "ability to feel a receptivity and warmth for our own self—an openness to both the good and bad that lives within us" (p. 317).

One mother of a severely emotionally disturbed adolescent revealed to the program staff serving her son that she was only able to put her trust in them after having had an opportunity to "do some testing." In particular, this involved an assessment of the extent to which the program staff were willing to follow through with requests made by the mother and with what they said they would do. Although in previous programs the mother had also been promised numerous things, little follow through was provided. After the program staff had convinced the mother that they were willing to make good on their promises, the mother was more willing to enter into a trusting relationship.

Providing Reassurance and a Model for Interpersonal Risk Taking

In addition to developing the atmosphere of trust and safety, educational conferencers must also be willing to provide cues and reassurances for parental risk taking and a model for this behavior. Hence, in spite of the degree of safety and rapport that is developed, parents must be provided reassurance that educational conferencers will maintain their trust even under vulnerable conditions. In addition, professionals must not expect the parent to display a willingness to venture in the interpersonal relationship when the stage has not been set for this response. While it is not being suggested that professionals must always become vulnerable in order to secure a reciprocal response from the parent, conferencers must nonetheless demonstrate a willingness to make themselves human and to suggest that they may not have all the answers. One mother of an elementary-age behaviorally disordered boy confided that it was only after a teacher acknowledged that she did not have all the solutions to her son's problems that she felt willing to share information. She noted in particular that she had been exposed to a series of professionals who gave the impression that her child's behavior could be easily managed if the right techniques were used, implying that she was not using the right approach. Only after being asked to help develop a cooperative plan was she willing candidly to provide information needed to develop the intervention strategy.

A willingness to expose oneself in a parent-educator relationship must also be based on an attitude of security and a belief in joint responsibility and solutions. While agreement on the relationship between an educator's attitudes and the development of security with parents may exist, the methodology for identifying the precise nature of these attitudes may be much more difficult to secure.

The risk-taking questionnaire shown in Exhibit 7-1 serves as one means for allowing educational professionals an opportunity to gain feedback relative to their capacity to create conditions of safety for parents. The format for using the instrument is simple. Place a checkmark in the column that most accurately describes your degree of comfort for each item (e.g., you are very comfortable, somewhat uncomfortable, etc.). This measure can be used at a later time to assess changes that have occurred. Finally, have a co-worker or supervisor who knows you well do a rating of you. Compare the perceptions you have of yourself with those held by your colleagues.

Providing Reinforcement for Risk Taking and Growth

An amendment to the adage "Behold the turtle; it makes progress only when it sticks its neck out" might be that it is willing to stick out its neck only because that behavior was followed by a positive consequence. Accordingly, both parents and professionals must be reinforced for their honesty, sincerity, and willingness to share relative information. While a safe atmosphere in and of itself will provide the means for allowing a parent and/or educator the opportunity to secure positive internal feedback for their risk-taking behavior, this willingness can be greatly augmented by appropriate positive feedback. One parent related that a teacher's feedback on how pleased he was about the parent's openness was of tremendous personal value. While positive reinforcement may be considered applicable only with children in classroom settings, it should be remembered that there are ample demonstrations and suggestions of the efficacy of operant conditioning on adult behavior (Skinner, 1948). With specific regard to the counseling situation, Siegman and Pope (1972) reported that a reduction in interviewer feedback was directly associated with a reduction in verbal productivity. Again, overwhelming evidence exists to support the contention that positive verbal feedback will facilitate the rapport building and general communicative process.

FACTORS ASSOCIATED WITH THE DEVELOPMENT OF A TRUSTING RELATIONSHIP

While it can be argued that the foremost requirement for professional status is technical competence, an equally compelling argument can be presented to support the contention that in the area of parent conferencing the professional must be equally skilled in gaining trust. Regardless of technical competence, the educational conferencer must first be able to secure the confidence of the parent. Only in instances when this trust and rapport have been developed will the conferencer be able to utilize whatever technical skills he or she may have. Thus, the efficacy of essentially every strategy and technique of the educational professional will be intricately tied to the relationship that has been developed with the parents.

Even though there has been a great deal said about the erosion of trust in parent-educator relationships, it is significant to note that good and trusting parent-educator relationships do exist. An analysis of factors associated with the development or dissolution of confidence and trust reveals several elements that must be given close scrutiny.

Parents and teachers must be willing to give if trust is to develop. The trusting relationship must be one in which both parents and educators are willing and comfortable in contributing to a common cause. One father of a severely physically handicapped child reported that he enjoyed contributing time and energy to community programs for handicapped children and adults. When asked about his efforts for all handicapped individuals he commented that he made these contributions because it was personally gratifying. Likewise, educators who have successfully conducted parent-oriented programs have commented that they are willing to invest the necessary time and effort in these endeavors because they enjoy the results or recognize the ultimate benefits as worthwhile. In virtually every instance the trusting relationship is based on a willingness to give that is not motivated by a hope for reciprocation. These individuals do not need to keep score (''If I do this for you, what will you do for me?''), nor are they motivated by a need to think of themselves as martyrs making a sacrifice. They fulfill their own needs by responding to the needs of others.

Both parents and educators must acknowledge that they both have a commitment to children. It is not uncommon for parents to be heard to say that professionals can never truly understand the plight of parents because they are only with the child for a few hours daily and because they are being paid for their services. Educators, on the other hand, have been heard to say that parents fail to take responsibility for their children or that the child's problems are directly related to the parents' problems. Unfortunately, such an attitude will almost universally serve to impede the development of a trusting relationship. Parents and professionals must acknowledge that they are both actively committed to the child and that only through the concerted effort of educators and parents will progress be forthcoming.

Both parents and educators must assertively serve as an advocate for children. While cooperation is an obvious component of the successful parent-educator relationship, so is the need for strong advocacy. The two positions are not in opposition and, in fact, there are many indications that respect and trust are most prevalent when both parties can candidly share their perceptions and positions. Following a conference, one mother revealed to a teacher that she was elated at the

Exhibit 7-1 Risk-Taking Questionnaire

How comfortable are you in	Very Comfortable	Somewhat Comfortable	Neutral	Somewhat Uncomfortable	Very Uncomfortable
1. telling parents you don't know					
2. telling parents that you made a mistake					
3. suggesting to parents that another professional made an error					
4. suggesting to parents that they should consider therapy for themselves					
5. telling parents that there are behaviors displayed by their children that you dislike					
6. displaying your emotions in a parent-educator conference					
7. confronting parents with their failure to follow through on agreed-upon plans					
8. talking about your own problems in a parent-educator conference					
9. praising parents for things they do well					
10. having parents take notes during conferences					

11. allowing parents to observe in your class while you are teaching								
12. allowing parents to tutor their own child at home								
13. allowing parents to use behavior modification procedures with their own child at home								
14. telling parents their "rights" under P.L. 94-142								
15. having parents assume an active role during individualized education program conferences								
16. having parents ask you to defend your teaching strategies								
17. having parents bring a friend to individualized education program conferences								
18. having parents call you at home about a problem their child is having at school								
19. having parents recommend specific curriculum for use with their child.								
20. having parents review school records on their child								

teacher's willingness to argue a point strongly. This mother, who had gained the reputation of being somewhat disagreeable, indicated it was a pleasure not to be patronized. She further revealed that the teacher's willingness to stand up for her beliefs relative to her child was interpreted as an indication of the teacher's commitment to the child.

A positive outlook is essential to the development of trust. Inevitably, there will be periods of difficulty for both parents and educators of handicapped children and youth. However, in instances when both parties firmly believe that the situation will improve and when they are willing to actively work together to accomplish this goal, the relationship will survive the ups and downs of the child. Trust will be forthcoming in situations in which every change in a child's behavior or progress is welcomed as an opportunity to determine what the parents (or the teacher) did to create the situation.

Educators and parents must be willing to both reinforce and confront one another. A goal for both parents and teachers of exceptional children is to acknowledge that they are equals. Accordingly, both parents and teachers must not become so immersed in the "cooperative relationship" that they lose their independent perspective. Only when parents and educators are able to analyze and respond to particular situations independently will true trust be earned. Both groups must be able and willing selectively and appropriately to praise the other for things that are done well and to confront or disagree on matters about which a difference of opinion exists.

Parents and educators must maintain a sensitivity to each other's needs. A fundamental component of the trusting relationship is the ability to demonstrate sensitivity to the needs of another person. This skill requires that parents and educators concentrate on recognizing one another's positions and feelings. For the educators, this will involve attempting to understand the parents rather than to analyze the appropriateness or logic of their needs or positions. Furthermore, this process will involve the ability to listen and respond to the affective elements of the parents' world. Thus, while assertively advocating their own position for a child, parents and educators must also be sensitive to the position of others.

Parents and teachers must want to trust one another. Rather than waiting to be "shown," parents and teachers must actively take the position of wanting to trust. While trust must be earned, it is counterproductive to adopt an attitude of distrust until reasonable evidence to the contrary has been presented. This suggests that both parents and professionals must avoid restricting trust only to situations in which another person has been manipulated into responding in an acceptable manner or when trust-related responses have not been observed. Rather, a willingness to trust must be pervasive and relatively contingency free.

As a further component of this concept, educators and parents must be willing and able to understand and accept themselves. Only through the demonstration of this attitude can they be expected to have others trust them.

Honesty is an essential ingredient of trust. Regardless of whatever other positive characteristics professionals may have, they must be honest if they are to earn the trust of parents. While there is a difference between honesty and outspoken veracious candor, there is no excuse for dishonesty in the parent-educator conference. If, for example, educators are not able to promise complete confidentiality, they must make that matter clear to the parents. McDonald (1962) noted that a "willingness to supply correct information about the nature of a child's handicapping condition will help create a climate of acceptance" (p. 48). Langdon and Stout (1954) also suggested the salient nature of honesty in parent-educator conferences, noting the positive effects that are derived when parents know that they are able to "get an honest answer, to know that they will be told truthfully how their youngster is doing in school, to know that whatever the teacher says can be depended upon to be honestly spoken" (p. 296).

Honesty is also demonstrated through conferencer authenticity. The educational conferencer must strive to be as genuine as possible and to avoid the temptation of setting a tone or creating a facade that may create barriers. Rogers (1969), in commenting on the need for authenticity, noted that "when the facilitator is a real person, being what he is, entering into a relationship with the learner without a front or facade, he is more likely to be effective" (p. 106).

Be aware of some basic do's and don'ts of parent-educator relationship building. While lists seldom provide a comprehensive statement of desired outcomes, they can serve to remind individuals of certain basic elements that need to be considered. This statement also applies to the creation of trust between parents and educators.

Do's:

- Maintain a sense of humor.
- Be accepting of yourself and the parents with whom you work.
- Demonstrate warmth and sensitivity.
- Be positive.
- Demonstrate respect for the parents with whom you work.
- Be sincere.
- Listen.
- Use language that parents can understand.
- Attend to the emotions and body language of parents.
- Reinforce parents when it is appropriate.

Don'ts:

• Don't attempt to be a sage who has all the answers.

• Don't make premature judgments.

• Don't be overly critical.   .

• Don't threaten, ridicule, or blame parents.

• Avoid arguing with parents.

• Avoid strong expressions of surprise and concern.

• Avoid making promises and agreements that you may not be able to keep.

• Don't patronize parents.

• Avoid making moralistic judgments.

• Don't minimize what parents have to say about their child.

VALUES AND THE DEVELOPMENT OF TRUST

There is currently tremendous concern with value issues, particularly those value differences that exist between students and their parents, students and educators, and parents and educators. Since values are the very beliefs, convictions, and other persuasions through which individuals structure their lives, they will exist as a paramount factor in establishing and maintaining a trusting conferencing relationship. Given the salient nature of values, it is obvious that conflicts and dissonance can arise because professionals and educators are unaware of their own values or the values of others. That is, a failure to recognize one's own values or the importance of another's values may be the basis for a severe breakdown in the communication process.

While the significance of values to the communication process may be somewhat disconcerting, it is not difficult to understand. The technological advances of the past decades combined with the ever-changing divergent and contradictory values of our society serve to obscure the validity of even the most basic convictions and principles. In fact, more than ever before, individuals (including parents and educators) are questioning the existence of any universal values. In addition, an individual's values are not rigidly maintained but are dynamic and constantly changing. And yet, given the tenuous and ethereal nature of values, they exist as a basic determinant of the parent-educator relationship and thus an aspect that must be understood and dealt with if trust is to be developed and maintained.

The need for the educational conferencer to understand the nature of values is primarily based on the role of values in decision making. In particular, both parents and professionals tend to utilize their personal value systems in making education-ally related decisions. As noted by Kroth and Simpson (1977), "The importance of assessing your own values or attempting to understand another's values is that ultimately you tend to act on those values you cherish the most" (p. 8). That is, individuals, contrary to what they may believe or have people think, tend to respond on the basis of their values, rather than logic or empirical facts. Values, for example, are frequently the basis for a professional choosing one therapeutic approach over another. In addition, conferencing goals are frequently more an extension of a professional's values than of the needs of the individual being counseled (Wiener & Ehrlich, 1960). Finally, the efficacy of a particular strategy will often be related to the extent to which certain terminal behaviors are in keeping with a particular value system. Thus, for example, an educational conferencer may consider a particular parent to have made significant growth if the family spends additional time together when in fact the parents' relationship with their handi-capped child has not changed. Hence, it is undeniable that values in a parent-educator relationship are a primary factor in the communication process.

The goal of value clarification and assessment is typically not to change an individual's values but rather to make the person aware of his or her own value patterns and the values of other people. An acknowledgment of the differences in individuals' values will conceivably make the educational conferencer more empathic and knowledgeable of the basis for parent-professional conflicts.

The task of clarifying one's own values and becoming sensitized to others' values has been undertaken by several different researchers (Raths, Harmin, & Simon, 1966; Simon, 1974). Simon, Howe, and Kirschenbaum (1972) developed an entire book of activities for aiding in the clarification of values. Kroth and Simpson (1977) also adapted a number of value clarification activities for training teachers to work with parents. In all instances, these procedures are not designed to instill a particular set of values or change a person's value system; rather these activities are designed to sensitize a person to his or her own values and to the values of another. The accomplishment of this goal will, without question, be closely tied to the development of a trusting and secure interpersonal relationship.

CONCLUSION

Without trust as a basis on which to build, the relationship between parents and educators will at best be impaired. Strategies and procedures for establishing trust exist and must be actively pursued by professionals. While trust may be considered to be so elementary as to defy attention, its importance to the communication process makes it a component that must be assigned a prominent position by professionals who aspire to meet the needs of parents.

Exercises

1. Identify the characteristics of a friend or relative whom you trust. Translate these behaviors into procedures that you can use to increase the trust level of the parents with whom you work.
2. Recall and analyze the feelings you have had in instances when you felt trusted or not trusted. Attempt to identify situations in which you felt parents displayed extremely trusting attitudes. Are there particular conditions or behaviors that you can identify that resulted in these attitudes?
3. Obtain a copy of Simon, Howe, and Kirschenbaum's (1972) book or Kroth and Simpson's (1977) text and complete some of the values clarification exercises. Note the manner in which a sensitivity to this factor can improve your relationship with parents.

REFERENCES

Benjamin, A. *The helping interview.* Boston: Houghton Mifflin, 1974.

Combs, A.N., Avila, D.L., & Purky, W.W. *Helping relationships: Basic concepts for the helping professions.* Boston: Allyn & Bacon, 1971.

Hammond, D.C., Hepworth, D.H., & Smith, V.G. *Improving therapeutic communication.* San Francisco: Jossey-Bass, 1977.

Kroth, R.L., & Simpson, R.L. *Parent conferences as a teaching strategy.* Denver: Love Publishing, 1977.

Langdon, G., & Stout, I.W. *Teacher-parent interviews.* Englewood Cliffs, N.J.: Prentice-Hall, 1954.

McDonald, E.T. *Understand those feelings.* Pittsburgh: Stanwix House, 1962.

Raths, L.E., Harmin, M., & Simon, S.B. *Values and teaching: Working with values in the classroom.* Columbus, Ohio: Merrill, 1966.

Rogers, C.R. *Freedom to learn.* Columbus, Ohio: Merrill, 1969.

Rogers, C.R. The interpersonal relationship: The core of guidance. *Harvard Educational Review,* 1962, *32*(4), 416-429.

Rutherford, R.G., & Edgar, E. *Teachers and parents: A guide to interaction and cooperation.* Boston: Allyn & Bacon, 1979.

Siegman, A.W., & Pope, B. The effects of ambiguity and anxiety on interviewee verbal behavior. In A.W. Siegman and B. Pope (Eds.), *Studies in dyadic communication.* Elmsford, N.Y.: Pergamon Press, 1972.

Simon, S.B. *Meeting yourself halfway.* Niles, Ill.: Argus Communications, 1974.

Simon, S.B., Howe, L.W., & Kirschenbaum, H. *Values clarification: A handbook of practical strategies for teachers and students.* New York: Hart, 1972.

Skinner, B.F. *Walden Two.* New York: Macmillian, 1948.

Truax, C.B, & Carkhuff, R.R. *Toward effective counseling and psychotherapy: Training and practice.* Chicago: Aldine, 1967.

Truax, C.B., & Mitchell, K.M. Research on certain therapist interpersonal skills in relation to process and outcome. In A.E. Bergin and S.L. Garfield (Eds.), *Handbook of psychotherapy and behavior change.* New York: Wiley, 1971.

Wiener, D., & Ehrlich, D. Values and goals. *American Journal of Psychotherapy,* 1960, *73*, 615-617.

Chapter 8

Interviewing Methods

Plato's creed that "the beginning is the most important part" seems to be particularly well suited in describing the initial contact that takes place between parents and educators. This preliminary conference will, in most instances, establish the tenor under which future contacts will operate and as such should be considered among the most significant of all parent-school sessions. Since the nature and timing of the initial session will be dictated by a number of factors, this conference will in many instances vary from situation to situation. It should be noted, however, that regardless of other factors, the classroom teacher should always be involved in the initial contact process.

The initial contacts that take place between parents and schools can take one of several forms. For example, diagnosticians may request or be asked by parents to meet and discuss the nature of the problems and issues involved prior to or concurrently with the initial conference session. Thus, one primary form of the initial conference will be an interview conducted as part of the diagnostic evaluation. A second form of this conference may occur during the parent interpretation conference. Although not nearly as fortuitous a time for the session, the conferencer will cover many of the same points as during the ones held concurrently with the student evaluation. Finally, the conference may occur concurrently with the development of the individualized education program (IEP) or the placement of a pupil in a special education program. While it might be argued that the frequent opportunities for contact between professionals and the parents diminishes the necessity of the teacher being involved in the initial interview, the educator's prominent position in the service delivery system demands his or her involvement. Consequently, the teacher cannot idly sit by and assume that the right information will be obtained and disseminated. Rather, given the unique job description of the educator, this individual must be in a position of providing input in his or her speciality area.

PURPOSES OF THE INITIAL CONFERENCE

The initial conference is first and foremost conducted for the purpose of establishing rapport with parents. In addition to this primary purpose, the initial conference is also designed to solicit information and history from parents that may be pertinent to the accurate assessment and educational programming of a pupil. A third purpose of the conference will be to provide parents basic information regarding their son or daughter's handicapping condition and the remediation strategy to be employed. Finally, the initial conference provides an opportunity to evaluate and better understand the parents, under the premise that if the school or agency is to orchestrate cooperative efforts between the home and school success-fully, procedures must be employed to ensure that the educational personnel fully understand and are able to capitalize on the parents' strengths and weaknesses. The initial conference will be discussed with regard to each of these purposes.

Establishing Rapport

A basic reason for conducting the initial interview conference is that such contact can facilitate a future positive working relationship. Positive initial contact with individual parents has been shown to be a vehicle for increasing the proba-bility of success with students and also for providing the basis for other types of parent-school interaction. Duncan and Fitzgerald (1969), for example, investi-gated the effects of establishing a positive parent-school relationship with indi-vidual parents prior to a pupil's entrance into junior high school. These researchers reported that initial positive parent contacts significantly increased not only the amount of parental interest in the school but also the attendance, grade-point average, drop-out rate, and number of disciplinary referrals of the pupils whose parents participated in the initial contact sessions. If for no other reason than the rapport that can be established, educators should attempt to make initial contact with the parents of each student referred because of a school-related problem. Even in instances when other professionals have made prior contact with the parents, the teacher should attempt to facilitate future positive contact by means of conducting an initial conference.

An additional argument in favor of conducting the initial interview session, relative to the establishment of rapport, is that such contact can facilitate the cooperation and participation of the parents in developing and monitoring their son or daughter's IEP. As a function of the Education for All Handicapped   Children Act (P.L. 94-142), each handicapped pupil must have an individualized program that outlines the goals and strategies to be employed in the educational process. This document is jointly developed by a representative of the school or agency (other than the teacher), the teacher(s), the parents or legal custodians, the student (when appropriate), and other individuals, at the discretion of the parents or school/agency. The law specifies that the IEP must be in effect prior to the time that a child is placed into a program. Although the concept of an IEP represents a monumental step toward providing needed services for exceptional children and youth, the participation of parents in the process is not automatically guaranteed. That is, even though parents are theoretically equal partners in the IEP development process, they are frequently placed in the position of having their initial face-to-face contact with professional staff at the IEP conference. It is also frequently at this same conference that they are provided interpretative information and apprised of the IEP process. Given that many parents will be intimidated, emotionally upset over the diagnosis and placement of their child in a program, or simply unfamiliar with the myriad of professionals in attendance at IEP meetings, it is quite unlikely that they can or will be contributing and functioning members of the IEP team. Consequently, if the goal is to secure participation from parents in this highly significant conference, procedures must be employed for obtaining their participation. Clearly, the most simplistic and efficient means of accomplishing this goal is to meet with and establish a working relationship with parents prior to the IEP conference. Once this has been accomplished, the process of educating a pupil can become a truly cooperative endeavor between home and school. ·

The need for an initial relationship cannot be underestimated and must consistently exist as the primary purpose for conducting the initial parent session. As noted by Conant (1971), ''If schools do not acknowledge this responsibility in their [parents] role as the formal educational agents of society, they will find themselves reacting rather than acting—and not always constructively—to the demands of the parents for more information, more involvement, and more control of school policies and practices'' (p. 114).

Obtaining Information

As previously suggested, each of the reasons for conducting the initial parent-educator conference is related to the supposition that parents have a significant impact on a child or adolescent's abilities to function in educational settings and that programs with which parents are familiar and including information they have provided will be most successful. One of the most obvious reasons for obtaining background information from parents early in the educational planning process is that in a number of instances this solicitation may lead to the securing of data not previously available. Programs for the handicapped have historically provided a high percentage of their services to children and adolescents from minority groups and lower socioeconomic strata. These disadvantaged clients have frequently not been followed by other professional groups. Thus in a number of instances educators and related school personnel have been the single professional group to come into contact with all school-age children identified as handicapped. Therefore, it becomes readily apparent that if the assessment or educational planning process is to be based on a pupil's individual history (which it obviously should), then it is essential that the educational community secure that information necessary for maintaining a child advocacy role and for guaranteeing necessary services. This position thus requires that educators function in such a manner as to ensure that no pupil is denied necessary services because of a lack of relevant information. It thus becomes necessary that educators function to obtain relevant information consistent with optimal educational planning.

Most educational interviewers report they find it beneficial to use an interview outline when they conduct the initial session. However, with experience, many interviewers find that they are able to obtain the needed information in an organized fashion without rigidly adhering to a set format. The format to be proposed in this section is designed to allow for the solicitation of information most commonly of value to the educator. However, since each initial session will have its own unique emphasis and purposes, the forthcoming general format must be adapted as per the requirements of each situation. Therefore, even though a basic format can be used, this approach will be functional only when adapted to meet the specific needs of the interviewer. Consequently, it is necessary for the educator to adapt the content, structure, and sequence to each different child and the parents' specific situation. For example, if certain information is available through previous interviews or if particular units of information are considered irrelevant, the interviewer is encouraged to modify the content. The interviewer should be highly sensitive to not duplicating previous efforts. With great regularity, parents have reported that they are extremely irritated by interviewers from the same agency who ask the same questions.

Format for Obtaining Initial Information from Parents

Parents' Statement of the Problem. Even though the interviewer may conceivably have access to detailed diagnostic information regarding a child's school-related problem, it is suggested that the initial interview commence with a request for the parents to discuss their perception of the problem. This area of content is dealt with first in the session for four basic reasons. First, even though educators and other diagnosticians may have conducted a thorough and multidisciplinary evaluation of a child, no one will have more information about the child than the parents. Thus, parents should always be tapped for data because they will know the child's history better than anyone else. A second reason for beginning the session by asking for a statement of the problem is that it is the most effective way of getting the parents to talk. Obviously, if the session is to operate with even basic utility, it is necessary that the parents discuss, in relative detail, the history and other factors sought in the session. The most satisfactory means of obtaining adequate responses from the parents is to begin the session in the area that they feel comfortable in discussing. In addition, once the parents have begun to discuss the problem, it is possible for the interviewer to direct the session, based on information generated by the parents, into those areas that appear to be worthy of further pursuit.

An additional reason for beginning the session with a discussion of the problem is to determine whether or not accurate diagnostic information has been previously provided the parents. Although it is almost universally assumed that parents are provided an interpretation, it is significant to be aware that this may be a faulty assumption, or if an interpretation was conducted, it may have consisted of inaccurate information or data that the parents were unable to comprehend. Since there are a number of instances in which parents were not given information or did not comprehend the feedback, it is necessary to evaluate the extent of the parents' knowledge relative to this issue early in the conference. The most efficient means of obtaining this data is to request that the parents begin the session by discussing the nature of the child's problems.

Finally, the strategy of requesting a statement of the problem is employed to determine if the parents' perception of the child's problem is consistent with that of the professionals who assessed the child. In cases of gross discrepancy, the educator will need to clarify the nature of the incongruence as well as to plan a strategy for bringing about greater insight. In instances in which there is a significant discrepancy, the interviewer should attempt to determine whether the parents are reflecting inaccurate information provided them in an interpretation or whether they have misinterpreted or are denying information provided them in an earlier interpretation. Although the interviewer may choose to avoid dealing in depth with a discrepancy issue during the initial interview, it will nonetheless be an area that needs to be explored.

History of Development. Although a handicapped child's developmental history is of significance when developing an educational program, it may not be necessary for the educational interviewer to obtain that information directly. That is, in situations in which it is apparent that another professional (e.g., school nurse, physician, social worker, psychologist) has previously obtained and recorded a child's developmental history, the educator need not invest time in this area. However, in situations in which it is doubtful that a child's developmental history has been previously obtained, it should be taken. Since school personnel are sometimes the only professionals to have sustained contact with exceptional children, it is mandatory that this group act to ensure that a pupil is not denied appropriate services because of a lack of knowledge regarding the developmental history.

A child's developmental history will consist of those significant events that have occurred since the time of conception. Consequently, the interviewer must be sensitive to unusual events that occurred during the pregnancy, birth, newborn, or childhood periods. Specifically, events such as emotional stress or unusual circumstances that occurred during the pregnancy; complications or difficulties during the delivery; and complications, illnesses, or serious accidents that occurred during the infant or childhood stages should be explored. Since parents may have a tendency to respond that "nothing" of significance occurred, even in describing highly bizarre situations, it is essential that discussions in this area be designed to require more than a simple "yes" or "no" response. Specifically, the interviewer should require elaboration and specific data such as the parents' perception of the child's development and the age at which specific developmental landmarks were reached. Since parents are frequently poor informants, it is suggested that the interviewer request information only in significant developmental and historical areas, such as the age at which the child talked, walked, developed bowel and bladder control, and had specific illnesses, accidents, and behavioral manifestations. A preferable strategy would be to employ a developmental history questionnaire, which should be sent to the parents prior to the session. Then, during the conference attention can be directed at following up on areas needing clarification. One developmental history form is provided as an example (Exhibit 8-1).

Again, it must be emphasized that the information generated from developmental history questioning may not be directly translated by educators into educationally related recommendations. For that reason, educators who find themselves in the position of needing to solicit developmental information must be willing to make referrals to professionals who have more expertise in making use of this variety of data.

Parents' Analysis of Child's Attitudes. This particular section of the interview is designed to allow the parents an opportunity to comment on their son or daughter's attitudes toward such things as school, home, and friends and to provide them a chance to discuss their child's likes and dislikes, hobbies, and leisure activities. It is also an opportunity for behavioral and social traits and tendencies to be discussed. Behavioral traits that the interviewer should be sensitive to include patterns of antisocial or withdrawn behavior, temper tantrums, aberrant sleeping patterns, enuresis or encopresis, hyperactivity, or destructive or overaggressive responses.

Discussions revolving around a child's attitudes and personality are not only designed to provide information that can be used in the educational planning process but also to provide the parents an opportunity to comment on the child's areas of strengths. Since the initial parent interview is basically oriented around a child's problems, it is important to allow parents an opportunity to talk about their youngster's strengths. If in fact the parents are unable to provide information on the child's strengths, the educator has still obtained valuable information.

Exhibit 8-1 Developmental History Form

Name of Child _____

Address _____

Date of Birth _____ Age _____

Father's Name _____ Birth Date _____
   Occupation _____

Mother's Name _____ Birth Date _____
   Occupation _____

Legal Relationship of Parents to Child (please check)

   Natural Parent: Mother _____ Father _____
   Adoptive Parent: Mother _____ Father _____
   Stepparent: Mother _____ Father _____
   Foster Parent: Mother _____ Father _____
   Relative: _____

Family Physician _____

Address _____
               Street   City   State   Zip Code

Phone _____

Listing of Persons Living in the Home:

Name	Age	Relation to Child

Developmental History

1. *Pregnancy*

Was medical care provided? _____ By whom _____

Address of person providing medical care _____
                                              Street

_____
            City   State   Zip Code

Exhibit 8-1 continued

Medical care was begun in _____ month of pregnancy.
Was any attempt made to abort pregnancy? _____
How much weight was gained during the pregnancy? _____ lbs.
Check any of the following that occurred during pregnancy

		When
Excessive nausea and vomiting	__	_____
Rh incompatability	__	_____
High blood pressure	__	_____
Toxemia	__	_____
Severe headaches	__	_____
Bleeding	__	_____
False labor	__	_____
German measles	__	_____
Chickenpox	__	_____
Virus infection	__	_____
Other illnesses	__	_____
Serious accident	__	_____
Drugs or medications	__	_____
What kind and amount	__	_____
X-rays	__	_____
Special diet	__	_____
Unusual physical strain	__	_____
Unusual emotional strain	__	_____

2. *Birth*

Where was the baby born? _____
How long was labor? _____
Birth was: Normal __ Cesarean __ Breech __ Multiple births __
Were forceps used? ____ What was the mother's condition? ____

3. *Early Childhood*

Birth weight _____ Length at Birth _____
What was the baby's condition at birth? _____
Did the baby need medical assistance in breathing? _____
If so, how long before normal breathing was established? _____

Exhibit 8-1 continued

What means were used? _____
Was baby in incubator? _____ If so, how long? _____
Did the baby receive oxygen? _____ If so, how long?_____
Check any of the following that the baby had in first month of life:
   Cyanosis (turned blue) _____ Deformity _____
   Jaundice (yellow) _____ Feeding difficulty _____
   Convulsions _____ Swallowing or sucking
   Hemorrhage _____   difficulty _____
   Skin eruption _____ Excessive crying _____
   Injury _____ Infection _____

Feeding: Breast _____ How long? _____
        Formula _____ Kind(s) _____
        At what age was baby weaned? _____
        Was baby's weight gain unusual in any respect? _____
        How? _____

4. Child's Development

General impression of baby's development:
Slow _____ Normal _____ Advanced _____
Describe the baby's activity level: _____
_____

Give age at which the baby first did the following:
   Smiled _____ Followed objects with eyes ____
   Held head up _____ Noticed noises _____
   Rolled over _____ Cut tooth _____
   Sat without support _____ Crawled _____
   Stood alone _____ Walked alone _____
   Fed self with spoon _____ Said his first word _____
   Completed toilet   Used two- or three-word
     training _____   sentences _____

Check those statements that best describe your child's speech development:
   Understands simple commands _____
   Understands everything said to him _____
   Speech is limited to single words and/or simple phrases _____
   Speech is mainly short sentences _____
   Converses without apparent handicap _____

Exhibit 8-1 continued

5. *Past Illnesses*

	Age	Complications
__ Measles	_____	_____
__ Scarlet fever	_____	_____
__ Chickenpox	_____	_____
__ Diphtheria	_____	_____
__ Mumps	_____	_____
__ Polio	_____	_____
__ Encephalitis	_____	_____
__ Ear infections	_____	_____
__ Visual problems	_____	_____

Serious accident or injuries _____

Does your child take medication on a regular basis? _____

For what purpose? _____

6. *Other Problems*

	Age		Age
__ Falls frequently _____		__ Allergies _____	
__ Eye or visual problems ____		__ Frequent colds _____	
__ Ear or hearing		__ Poor appetite _____	
problems _____		__ Convulsions or	
__ Abdominal pain _____		"spells" _____	
__ Vomits frequently _____		__ Diarrhea frequent ____	
__ Constipation frequent ____		__ Speech problems ____	
__ Pain or weakness			
of muscles _____			

7. *Emotional Development*

Check any of the below listed that apply to your child:

	Yes	No	Sometimes
Difficult to discipline	__	__	_____
Becomes upset easily	__	__	_____
Has temper tantrums	__	__	_____

Exhibit 8-1 continued

Has unreasonable fears   — — _____
Has difficulty sleeping   — — _____
Wets bed   — — _____
Is destructive   — — _____
Prefers to be alone   — — _____
Lives in a world of his or her own — — _____
Unusually active   — — _____
Other _____

Source: Children's Rehabilitation Unit, University of Kansas Medical Center.

History of Past School Performance. Although the educational interviewer will in most instances have access to documents providing information on the pupil's school-related history, it is nonetheless important for the parents to be given an opportunity to comment on this area. Specifically, parental perceptions of successes and failures in school and their causes, academic performance, as compared with the child's peer group, and those areas of academics in which the parents would like to see the greatest investment of effort should be focused on. In addition, the content in this area of the interview should be structured in such a fashion as to allow the parents a chance to discuss previous relationships they and their child have had with school personnel. This area of content has frequently been reported to be among the most beneficial for educators to explore.

Finally, the interviewer should discuss with the parents any measures that they have employed to deal with the problem. It is not at all uncommon for parents of even mildly handicapped children to have had contact with a number of professionals. Not only can a knowledge of the findings of their evaluations and remediation strategies aid in planning for the pupil in the classroom but also a discussion of these procedures can allow the parents to vent their anger and frustration over many of the problems associated with gaining an evaluation of their exceptional child.

Goals and Expectations of the Parents. The goals and expectations that parents have for their handicapped children and the educators of these children will have a significant impact on the relationship that exists between the parents and the school personnel. Consequently, an analysis must be made of this extremely significant variable. First, a determination must be made of the goals that parents have for their children and whether or not a child's abilities are commensurate with these goals. Educators must obtain parents' information on their expectations in order to aid them accomplish these goals or to attempt to develop more realistic aspirations for the child.

Educators should also solicit information from parents regarding the expectations that are held for the educator, school (or agency), and community. For example, it is not unusual for parents to assume that special education placement will result in almost instantaneous improvements and that the placement of a pupil in special education will be for a much shorter period of time than is realistic. Although some of these expectation discrepancies may be amenable to resolution at IEP conferences, it is obviously necessary for the educator to obtain the perceptions of parents relative to their goals prior to planning a strategy for reducing discrepancies.

Sociological Information. An area of significant educational interest, and thus a topical item for the initial conference, will be the ecological and sociological aspects of the child's environment. Since an adequate understanding of the family and the environment will enable the educators to more adequately understand and plan for the pupil, this area should be considered among the most significant of the items covered in the initial session.

Areas of specific concern in this area will include the following:

- socioeconomic status of the family
- individuals living in the home
- physical and mental health of individuals residing in the home
- ethnic, cultural, or religious backgrounds and beliefs of the family that may have an influence on the parents' attitudes toward educational planning
- languages other than English used by individuals in the home
- child rearing practices and attitudes of the parents and family members
- the supervision provided the handicapped child or adolescent after school, including those individuals the educational personnel should contact regarding the implementation of after school programs.

Although interviewers have long agreed that care must be taken to avoid asking "personal" questions, it is nonetheless necessary to address the various issues related to gaining an understanding of the family. Even though no simple strategy for securing this sometimes sensitive material exists, it can be obtained most frequently by developing an adequate interpersonal relationship with the parents, which it is hoped will encourage the parents to discuss candidly information of significance.

Providing Parents Information

Although it might be argued that parents have ample opportunities for receiving information about the educational program that their handicapped child is scheduled to enter as a function of the numerous preliminary contacts that occur (i.e., meetings occurring prior to or concurrently with assessment and placement), indications are that these sessions, including the interpretation and IEP meetings, provide few of the actual facts that parents are interested in receiving. One obvious explanation for this deficit is that the classroom teacher, the individual most knowledgeable about the educational program, may have, at best, only marginal involvement in these early meetings with parents. Likewise, those professionals frequently having the most initial involvement with the parents may simply be unable to provide basic information about the classroom operation. As noted by one father following an interpretation conference, "Those may have been smart people, but they never did tell me what time school started and ended, what supplies he would need and how the class would be different from his other one." Given that this situation may occur on a regular basis, it is mandatory that parents have an opportunity to meet individually with the classroom teacher, the one individual most capable of meeting the information needs of the parents.

Just as educators expect parents to be able to provide basic information, so should parents anticipate that educators will meet their information needs by discussing those educational procedures to be employed with their child. Although a logical and basic concept, this process has historically not been the norm. Rather, teachers and other educational personnel have been far more concerned with obtaining information from parents than with the parents' right to acquire information. Consequently, it is imperative to the success of the initial parent-teacher conference that the same degree of importance allotted the acquiring of information from parents be given the dissemination process.

Although the specific information to be disseminated will be a function of the needs of the parents, of the condition of the pupil, and of the educational program to be utilized, the process will encompass certain generic elements. These factors will include a discussion of the assessment and diagnostic procedures; the educational program to be employed with the pupil; the methodology for evaluating the progress of the pupil and the manner in which this information will be communicated to parents; and problem-solving alternatives and other resources available to the parents through the school and community.

Assessment and Diagnostic Information

The heavy emphasis on the use of formal assessment procedures with exceptional children and adolescents has been criticized by a number of authorities. Nonetheless, testing results continue to be not only a major means of drawing diagnostic inferences but also more importantly the basis for making educational programming decisions. Consequently, the importance of assessment in any diagnostic and remediation program must not be underestimated.

In a similar fashion, parents frequently relate that one of their strongest and most immediate needs is to obtain interpretative information about their son or daughter. The fact that parents may have received prior information following the evaluation may do little to offset this need. Rather, even in instances in which interpretative data have been previously given, many parents indicate the need for further information. Although the reasons for this situation may vary, there appear to be several basic considerations. First, even though parents may be physically involved in the interpretation process, and even in instances in which the interpretation is skillfully conducted, they may be intellectually and emotionally detached from the conference. It is not at all uncommon to find that parents are overwhelmed by the quantity and sophistication of material covered in the conference or are in a state of emotional shock over the diagnostic classification or the finality of the educational disposition. Parents have frequently reported that they were only able to "hear" information presented up to the point that the term *mentally retarded,* *emotionally disturbed,* or *brain damaged,* for example, was used. Consequently, even though some parents may appear attentive and involved in the conference, they may actually comprehend little of the information presented.

Second, parents appear to be much more comfortable in receiving information from teachers, as opposed to other professionals whose role, identity, mission, and commitment may be less clearly understood. Teachers have been the brunt of much recent criticism; yet it remains true that they, as a group, are among the most respected and endeared of all professionals.

Third, it is frequently related by parents that the initial interpretation of testing results was so muddled by esoteric language and terminology, anachronisms, and other confusing information that they were unable to benefit effectively from the information. Although teachers are obviously not immune to the same type of error, it appears that as a group they tend to engage less in this nonfunctional behavior than certain other professional groups. In addition, classroom teachers tend to have more samples of behavior on which to base their inferences and it is hoped that they will be in a position to augment standardized testing results with informal measures and observations that are more closely aligned with remediation programs.

As implied earlier, parents frequently experience a number of concerns at the time of the evaluation and placement of their handicapped child. These concerns can take a number of forms but frequently are expressed as questions. Kanner (1957) listed a series of questions frequently asked by parents of retarded children, many of which surface at the time of the initial parent-teacher conference. These questions included the following:

- What is the cause of our child's condition?
- Have we personally contributed to his condition?
- Why did this have to happen to us?
- What about heredity?
- Is it safe to have another child?
- Is there any danger that our normal children's offspring might be similarly affected?
- How is his (or her) presence in the home likely to affect our normal children?
- How shall we explain him (or her) to our friends and neighbors?
- How shall we explain him (or her) to our normal children?
- Is there anything that we can do to brighten him (or her) up?
- Is there an operation that might help?
- What about glutamic acid?
- Will our child ever talk?
- What will our child be like when he (or she) grows up?
- Can we expect graduation from high school?
- Would you advise a private tutor?
- Should we keep our child at home or place him (or her) in a residential school, and, if so, how long will he (or she) have to remain there?
- What specific school do you recommend?
- Will our child become alienated from us if placed in a residential school?
- Will our child ever be mature enough to marry?
- Do you think that our child should be sterilized and, if so, at what age?

It is important to note that these difficult questions, many of which lack answers, are frequently a vehicle for parents to vent anger, fear, and frustration and may be most typically experienced in follow-up conferences. That is, while they may occur only periodically during the initial interpretation session they may occur on a regular basis in ensuing sessions. Many parents, even when given the opportunity, may not be at a point at which they are capable of making these emotionally laden comments during the initial interpretation; however, they seem to have less difficulty in doing so during conferences that follow.

In brief, the actual reinterpretation process should focus on the following: a clarification of the purpose of the evaluation and the expectations that were held for the assessment; an opportunity for the parents to ask questions about the assessment procedures; a presentation of the evaluation findings in summarized form; an opportunity for the parents to raise questions about or discuss the findings; a restatement of the recommendations; an opportunity for the parents to raise questions about or discuss the recommendations; a discussion of the manner in which the recommendations are to be implemented; and an identification of those individuals responsible for the implementation. It is also important to note that since the needs of parents will vary, the individual conducting the conference must determine the needs of the parents and respond accordingly. Thus, while some individuals may need only a brief review of this information, others will require a more thorough discussion.

Clarify the Purpose and Expectations for the Evaluation. Although more and more professionals are acknowledging the limitations of tests the public still attributes powers to these instruments that often outweigh their capabilities. Consequently, the purpose of the testing, the capabilities of the instruments used, and the expectations of the diagnostic team should be shared. Without such a candid statement, the parents cannot truly be expected to be equal and participating members of the remediation process.

Discuss the Assessment Procedures. Frequently assumed by professional diagnosticians is that parents either understand or do not really need to understand the nature of the assessment procedures used. There has, for example, been a tendency for results of testing to be provided without an explanation of what the tests involve. Consequently, if parents are informed that their son or daughter has a perceptual motor deficit, emotional disturbance, specific learning disability, or similar problem, it is important to apprise parents of the manner in which the condition was identified. Although it is not the intent of this process to enter into discussions regarding the validity of particular tests, it is necessary to inform parents of the nature of a particular handicap. In addition, parents can frequently augment specific findings once informed of the types of behaviors sampled. Again, without this discussion parents can neither be expected to have an understanding of the evaluation process nor to be a functioning member of the team.

Summarize the Analysis of the Findings. The results of the assessment process should be given to the parents in abbreviated form, with attention given to those areas considered to be of greatest significance. Since most assessment techniques are designed to yield data in the intellectual, educational (achievement), emotional/personality, physical/sensory, or ecological area, the summarized interpretation should also follow this outline.

Allow Opportunities for Questions. As noted previously, parents may be far more able to ask questions after having had initial interpretative information. Consequently, the reinterpretative process, perhaps even more so than the initial interpretation, must provide opportunities for parents to address issues of concern or confusion. The counselor should, of course, focus on items of concern to the parents and explain accordingly. The interpreter should also be prepared to entertain difficult questions related to the diagnostic and placement process. Questions such as "Is he mental?" "Will he be able to marry?" "Did we cause this?" "Will his offspring have the same problems?" are not at all uncommon. Although it is unrealistic to look for easy answers with such difficult issues (there are none), there are some rules. These include having the parents define what they mean by their terms (e.g., mental and clumsy), determining whether the parents are looking for an answer or structuring an opportunity to offer their own views (frequently, parents who ask these types of questions are looking for no more than an opportunity to talk), allow the parents an opportunity to discuss their feelings and perceptions, and, finally, attempt to answer their questions candidly. However, it is important to keep in mind that an "I don't know" response may be the most appropriate statement that can be made.

Restate Recommendations. Not only must recommendations be reviewed, especially from the standpoint of the specifics that the teacher can address and clarify, but the parents must be given an opportunity to raise questions about the remediation strategies. Since this is probably the most frequently glossed over component in the initial interpretation, and obviously a major need for parents, it should be planned for accordingly.

Educational Program to be Employed

Although individuals who routinely conduct interpretation and disposition conferences may be relatively proficient at meeting many of the basic needs of parents, they are routinely quite lacking in their capacity to offer specifics on the operation and nature of the educational program and remediation strategies to be provided. Consequently, even though descriptors such as *low pupil-teacher ratio, individualized program,* and *structured classroom* may be adequate for "selling" the program and as an indication of the type of model to be provided, it is an area that requires further clarification for the parents. Topics that should be discussed are classroom and school schedules; classroom and school philosophy and administration; academic remediation programs (goals and objectives for the pupil and the manner in which the personnel and program will be able to satisfy these needs); classroom management and emotional social remediation strategies; ancillary personnel and programs to which the child will be exposed; and parent/family programs that are available.

Classroom and School Schedules. Without question, parents will be extremely interested in the educational and treatment schedule and routine their son or daughter will follow. Included will be the bus schedule; school starting and stopping times; the activity schedule the pupil will follow both in and out of the special program; lunch, recess, and break periods; the school calendar that will be followed, including vacations and special events; and a schedule of those activities that the pupil will be exposed to in the special program. Both day-to-day and long-term activity schedules should be shared with the parents.

Classroom and School Philosophy and Administration. Since the philosophy of the teacher and administration will dictate the general approach to be employed, it is essential that this information be provided to parents, albeit in a manner that they can understand. For example, educational programs serving the emotionally disturbed can follow any one of a number of orientations, including behavioral, psychoeducational, or ecological. Although each of these approaches will have many similarities, there will also be distinct differences. Consequently, in language they can understand, the parents should be oriented to the philosophy of the program.

Academic Remediation Programs. As noted previously, individuals who interpret test information and make program recommendations for parents frequently have limited information regarding the specific academic remediation programs to be employed. Thus, even though a deficit area may have been identified, the precise manner in which this concern will be dealt with may receive little attention. Thus, program components such as the degree of structure, curricula, specific procedures and equipment, and teaching strategies should be outlined. Attention should be focused on the goals and objectives identified in the IEP and to other areas in which the teacher considers to need further clarification or in which the parent raises a question.

Classroom Management and Emotional/Social Remediation Programs. Just as the specifics of the academic intervention programs should be outlined, so should emotional/social intervention strategies. However, this orientation will include both an analysis of the manner in which IEP goals and objectives will be accomplished and overall classroom management techniques. Special attention should be given procedures that may be considered controversial or based on reward systems or punishment contingencies. Token economy systems, time out, and making lunch or school dismissal contingent on classroom productivity or behavior, for example, should of course be discussed.

Ancillary Personnel and Related Services. Related services, or those activities required for a pupil to benefit from a special program, include:

transportation and such development, corrective, and other supportive services as are required to assist the handicapped child to benefit from special education, and includes speech pathology and audiology, psychological services, physical and occupational therapy, recreation, early identification and assessment of disabilities in children, counseling services, and medical services for diagnostic and evaluation purposes. The term also includes school health services, social work services, and parent counseling and training. (Implementation of Part B of the Education of the Handicapped Act, 1977, p. 42479)

These related services are designed to augment the impact of the special education program. Since they frequently involve resources and personnel that the parents may not be familiar with, it will of course require careful explanation. One vehicle for providing this explanation will be to provide parents with information on the role and function of the various personnel who will be involved with the pupil. The example listed below, taken from a booklet entitled *Who Can Help?* (1977), describes the role of the physical therapist in language that parents can understand.

The Physical Therapist:
If your child has a certain type of physical disability, he may benefit from the assistance of a physical therapist. The physical therapist is concerned with developing the strength and endurance of the body parts and in developing normal motor patterns, and in helping your handicapped child move easily so he becomes as independent as possible.
The physical therapist has completed a program of training in the therapeutic use of movement and physical activity. He holds either the Bachelor's degree (B.A., B.S.) or Master's degree (M.A., M.S.) in the specialty of physical therapy. The Licensed Physical Therapist (L.P.T.) has also completed a state examination and is licensed to practice in Pennsylvania. The physical therapist is usually affiliated with an agency, clinic, or school which offers a team approach for the treatment of handicapped children. He will see your child only upon the referral of a licensed physician. The referring physician may be a pediatrician, neurologist, or orthopedist. The physical therapist will often train you, as parents, in daily treatment procedures to help your handicapped child at home. You may be taught to assist your child in a program of exercises or you may be asked to participate in certain play activities at home that will help your child build physical strength and endurance.

Parent/Family Programs. Since many special education programs include parents in their programs it is necessary that the teacher review for the parents the schedules, expectations, and procedures associated with this component of the program. Individual and group conference dates, workshop schedules, and resources available to the parents and family (through both the school and community) should be reviewed. In addition, since many parents are interested in augmenting classroom academic programs through home tutorial procedures, the teacher should be able to structure or provide input and/or material into the teaching activities for the parents. Finally, parents should be provided information regarding procedures associated with visiting the classroom, general expectations for them, materials/equipment that they should supply, and other related items.

As suggested, the process of disseminating information implies that the educator will respond to questions and areas of parental concern. Thus, providing information to parents implies a process entailing much more than a simple and straightforward dissemination process.

Since the material to be provided parents is extremely noteworthy and will in all likelihood be needed by the parents for future reference, a handbook may prove to be an excellent resource, both for the parent and the teacher. According to Kroth (1975), a handbook "should be short, attractive, inclusive, and written on a level the parents can understand" (p. 56). With regard to content this same author suggests that "anything that all parents of children in that classroom need to know should be included" (p. 57).

An example of part of one teacher's handbook, geared to behaviorally disordered children, is provided in Exhibit 8-2 for illustrative purposes.

Procedures for Evaluating the Pupil's Progress and Disseminating This Information to the Parents

Assessing the progress of students and communicating this information to parents is a basic and necessary element of any good educational programs. Although the Education for All Handicapped Children   Act mandates that the progress of students be assessed, the fact that this accounting must be made only annually and that only short-term objectives be evaluated makes it of rather dubious utility for parents. Thus, since the evaluation and communication of progress to parents should be an ongoing activity, alternative evaluation procedures need to be developed. Alternatives (in addition to parent-teacher conferences) appropriate for this purpose include telephone contacts, daily or weekly report cards, and letters/notes. In all instances it is recommended that these parent-educator communication procedures be used on a regular basis and that they be designed to communicate progress more than problem areas.

Telephone Contacts. The telephone can serve as an unmatched instrument for apprising parents of their child's progress in a school or program. Not only is the telephone convenient and inexpensive, but it also can serve to overcome the problem of parents' inability or unwillingness to attend face-to-face conferences.

Exhibit 8-2 Example of a Teacher's Handbook

INTRODUCTION

I view education, be it regular or special, as an active process between a child and his environment. It is a period of discovery, within and around a child. Learning centers around communication. Communication, in turn, creates participation, which is essential for any learning process to take place. I see my role as a facilitator of change and a source of information that the children may or may not use. I feel the responsibility for educational success rests firmly with the teacher. Through constant self-evaluation as well as the evaluation of the student's performance, I hope to provide optimal conditions for educational, social, and personal growth. Education requires mutual cooperation between teacher, parent, and child. I feel it is important for the parents of my students to become familiar with the activities and operation of my class and with me personally and be active in helping work with the child whose individual learning styles dictate my approach. Real individualization of education must begin with the acceptance of the child as the central focus of concern. I intend to respond to the needs of the child rather than relate to his label. The focus of my class is on the individual learner in relation to cognitive material and on his learning and adaptive behaviors in the educational setting. My concern is directed toward the whole child, the integrity of the whole person and his ideals, as well as his academic advancement—this is special education.

A child learns 90 percent of all he will learn in his first five years of life. This fact places a tremendous responsibility on parents as well as teachers. The early years at home and in the classroom must be geared to help the child reach his fullest potential for growth and development.

EMOTIONALLY DISTURBED??

The term *emotionally disturbed* is a label placed on certain children in our society. It is a very arbitrary title and is only definable in a larger social context. It is of use to professionals who relate in similar ways across categories such as teaching, psychology, medicine, and school administration. It is also a national term that the federal government uses and allocates funds to.

Exhibit 8-2 continued

To me, an educator of children with this label, it is somewhat global and vague. I feel these children have behavioral difficulties not unlike other so-called regular children. Our children merely have too much or too little of a certain behavior that is viewed as socially unacceptable. The causation of such problems could be the topic (and is) of thousands of books. I tend to place some responsibility on education in general and some on society for not taking a more active role in viewing uniqueness as an asset rather than labeling it a deviance. A child placed in special education is one who has not gained from regular education. A child like this needs individual help and concentrated academic remediation.

Through a structured learning experience and the expansion of a child's behavioral pattern, positive changes can take place. Concentration on a child's strengths is the starting point to produce real and lasting academic as well as behavioral changes.

DURATION OF PLACEMENT

A child will be in this special class as long as he is benefiting from the placement. Children do not have to be lost in the specializing process and never heard of again. Your child's improvements and movements will be carefully evaluated and his time in a special education classroom will be as brief as possible. It is the intention of special education to prepare the child for return to the regular class environment. As the child progresses through my program he is gradually expected to maintain certain regular classroom behaviors and will, with time, be slowly mainstreamed into regular class activities. In our school we have a resource room where the child is given support during his initial entrance back into regular education. The child gradually participates in regular classes and his time is split between the resource room and the regular class. When the child and his teachers feel he is ready, the process of return can be completed.

CLASSROOM PROCEDURES AND POLICIES

Before a child's entrance into my classroom, I have the child come in for informal testing. This usually takes a half of a day and is not a standardized procedure where the child slaves over a computer-designed form with a large, messy black pencil. I take a survey of his

Exhibit 8-2 continued

academic skills—discover his strengths and weaknesses, find out his interest areas, and introduce him to the room with all its different areas and materials. After this procedure, I know where to start the child's individual academic programming and also have knowledge of what may be possibly appealing to him in relation to interest activities.

The children in the class are gradually phased in so as to make the transition smooth. During this time I discover how the children relate to each other and see if any conflicts may arise or if any children are especially compatible with each other.

My class is behaviorally oriented in that I deal with strengthening some positive behaviors while decreasing or eliminating other inappropriate behaviors. The use of contingencies is prevalent whereby the child comes to realize he can earn positive privileges by finishing assigned work, displaying appropriate behaviors, or generally improving. Reinforcement is also used. In this aspect the child is given praise, rewards, or other incentives for maintaining expectations. These expectations are realistic and geared to each child individually. I believe a teacher receives from his student what he expects. If the expectations are high, the performance of the child will increase accordingly.

Source: Courtesy of Allen Dodge, Kansas City, Mo.

Contacting parents by telephone is most appropriate as a means for providing reinforcement and feedback, scheduling conferences, and obtaining information on changes in behavior or performance. However, in spite of the advantages of telephone contacts, there are several potential problems. First, it is important to determine whether or not parents want to be contacted by telephone. Independent of whether or not the call is scheduled for a convenient time, some parents simply do not wish to be telephoned at home. Second, it is important that telephone conferences not take the place of regularly scheduled sessions. While a convenient means of communicating, telephone contacts must never be thought of as substitutes for ongoing conferences. Finally, the telephone should not be used to confront parents or discuss sensitive material. Agenda items of this type should always be dealt with in a face-to-face fashion.

Daily or Weekly Report Cards. As noted by Rutherford and Edgar (1979), "of all written methods, report cards are used most frequently" (p. 6). However, to be most effective, these reports must be sent on a regular basis. Since the intent of this strategy is to provide ongoing information to parents and to provide them a basis for reinforcing the pupil, the system must be positively oriented. Examples of reporting systems used to communicate with parents are provided in Figures 8-1 and 8-2.

Figure 8-1 Sample Parent Report

	Reading	Math	Language Arts	Science	Social Studies	Health
Leroy had satisfactory social behavior						
Leroy completed his work independently						
Leroy participated in group activities						

Figure 8-2 Sample Parent Report

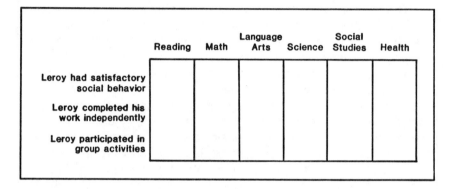

U WERE THE 🍎

OF MY 👁 TODAY!

_____

HAD GOOD BEHAVIOR.

_____
TEACHER

Letters and Notes. As is the case with telephone contacts and report cards, letters and notes sent to parents can be useful communication tools. Specifically, they are most appropriate as a vehicle for reinforcing the parents and/or child and exchanging information. Just as with the telephone, however, letters and notes should not be used as a means of sharing sensitive information or other potentially inflammatory materials or of criticizing parents or children.

Problem-solving Alternatives and Other Parental Resources in the School and Community

It is quite possible that parents and families of exceptional children will have needs that will require the services of community agencies or school district support services. The educator should be able to provide parents information on how and where to secure the services that they require, even though these services may be for the parents or family as opposed to the exceptional child. Included should be an awareness on the part of the educator of welfare services; respite care programs; baby-sitting services for the handicapped children and youth; psychiatric, psychological, and counseling services; and social agencies. Finally, the educational conferencer should be aware of crisis-intervention programs that exist to serve the immediate needs of parents and families. While many parents may not need access to this type of information, there will frequently be a small number who will. In addition, parents requiring supportive, ancillary, or crisis-intervention services should be given immediate attention. Such attention will require that the conferencer be in a position of providing immediate and appropriate alternatives for the parents.

Evaluating the Parents

A fourth major purpose for conducting the initial conference is to assess the strengths and weaknesses of the parents. This process is based on the supposition that in order for an educator to make use of the resources that parents have, these assets must first be understood. It is important to recognize that while this information is critical, it is not recorded. Rather, the educator must simply make determinations of the parents' strengths and weaknesses without attempting to make a written record of the assessment process.

Both popular and professional literature reflect abundant concern for the influence that parents have on the development of their offspring (Martin, 1975). It has not only been suggested but also actually demonstrated that parents and families can have a profound influence on the development and later school-related performance of children. However, whereas attention was at one time almost totally focused on the influence of parents as a causal variable for certain types of problems, consideration is more and more being directed at procedures for enlisting the aid of parents in accomplishing specified goals and in better understanding the impact of the parents on the pupil. Thus, rather than being totally perceived as a factor responsible for certain types of educationally related problems, parents have begun to be entrusted with the title of "colleague," and in keeping with this role are being offered the opportunity, under structured conditions, to augment their son or daughter's program through the use of home-based procedures. Although this process has been demonstrated to be a logical and economical use of available resources, it does necessitate that the strengths and weaknesses of the parents be carefully evaluated. Just as children have different strengths and weaknesses, so do the parents. It is an analysis and understanding of these areas that will determine the effectiveness of any parent-educator program. In the same manner that a teacher would implement an educational program only after determining the abilities of the pupil he or she is working with, so must the educator take careful stock of those things the parents will be able to do before establishing programs.

Although each of us constantly evaluates individuals with whom we have contact using individualized criteria consistent with our own value structure and needs, educational planning strategies must be tempered in more objective criteria. These should include the intellectual abilities of the parent, level of educational training, physical and health-related factors, personality characteristics, and ecology of the home.

Intellectual Abilities

Although educators may not consider themselves psychometrists or psychologists who are capable of estimating the intellectual capabilities of another person—especially in the absence of formal testing—it must be remembered that it is possible to make reasonably accurate estimates of intelligence based totally on verbal interactions. Although it must be considered that little validity can be placed in the preciseness of this procedure, it is possible in many instances to determine whether or not an individual is functioning at or near an average intellectual level. Above and beyond that, this gross procedure is not particularly useful. However, based on the information provided by the parent, especially that which relates to occupation, education, verbal fluency, memory, and demeanor of an individual, it is frequently possible to draw reasonably accurate intellectual inferences. Although this process can be a useful tool in the arsenal of the educational conferencer, the rationale for undertaking the intellectual analysis must be kept firmly in mind. This gross screening index should serve as a reminder that different parents will need different programs. It should not be employed as a basis of etiology for a pupil's handicap nor as a discriminator for services.

Educational Level

In a great many instances parents will volunteer the extent to which they have been formally educated; in other instances this information can be inferred from their occupation, vocation, or behavior. Again, just as in the case of making intellectual judgments, the intent of this process is to determine whether the parents are literate and, if so, the extent to which they will be capable of utilizing self-directed programs or to participate as tutors with their own child. Although this process may appear on the surface to be an invasion of privacy, it should be recalled that the success of any program will be founded on just such information. Consequently, the conferencer would be remiss if he or she were not to give adequate attention to this area.

Physical and Health Factors

Physical and health considerations of the parents include their ages, health, physical limitations, sensory deficits, and other related factors. Although a particular program might be effective under normal circumstances, modifications will most likely be needed for a physically handicapped or health-impaired parent. Even though this may appear to be a rather straightforward and obvious consideration, who can argue that many parent-educator programs have been formulated with little or no attention to these and equally important factors.

Personality Factors

Although personality factors are probably the most significant variables in determining the success or failure of many home-school programs, they are also the most elusive. In addition, teachers frequently report that they simply feel unprepared to "analyze" the personality of another adult. While the intent here is not to suggest that this area can be dealt with effectively by an individual with little or no formal training in psychology or counseling, it is suggested that observations of the parents' style and strategies can be useful in determining the manner in which a program can be most beneficial.

One mother, for example, repeatedly referred to herself in a conference as highly dependent on other individuals in providing care for her mentally retarded son. She revealed that she relied heavily on friends and relatives in making even minor parenting decisions and reported feeling overwhelmed at the prospect of making independent decisions and assuming total responsibility for the care of her child. While the educational conferencer identified independent functioning as a goal for this mother, she wisely adopted the strategy of initially working with the mother with the aid of one of her support personnel. To have done otherwise would have been to deny a major segment of information on the parent's personality.

Ecological Considerations

Ecological concerns, or information related to the social and familial nature of the home, must also be considered when determining how the educators and parents may best work together. However, since the information of concern will typically be the same as that solicited under "sociological information" in the initial information-gathering conference this data need not be gathered separately.

CONCLUSION

The initial interview must be considered to be a basic and essential process for consummating the parent-educator relationship and for most effectively sharing information. The four components of this conference, (1) establishing rapport, (2) obtaining information, (3) providing information, and (4) evaluating the parents, are undertakings that can facilitate the educational process of the pupil and the positive working relationship of the parents and educators.

Exercise

Complete a simulation conference using the role-playing materials in Appendix A. Materials are provided for the exceptionalities of mental retardation, physically handicapped, learning disabled, behaviorally disordered, and gifted. Consequently you should use those materials most closely aligned with the pupils you are associated with or aspire to educate.

In conducting the simulation exercise, one individual should assume the part of the parent, using those materials labeled "for parents." Another person, taking the part of the teacher, should structure responses around the teacher materials. A third individual should assume the role of the evaluator, using the evaluation form provided.

In disseminating information about "your program" to the person playing the part of the parent, talk about an actual program you would employ with this pupil.

Individuals should change roles after completing the exercise.

REFERENCES

Conant, M.M. Teachers and parents: Changing roles and goals. *Childhood Education,* 1971, *48,* 114-118.

Duncan, L.W., & Fitzgerald, P.W. Increasing the parent-child communication through counselor-parent conferences. *Personnel and Guidance Journal,* 1969, *47*(6), 514-517.

Kanner, L. Parents' feelings about retarded children. In C. Stacey (Ed.), *Counseling and psychotherapy with the mentally retarded.* Glencoe, Ill.: Free Press, 1957.

Kroth, R.L. *Communicating with parents of exceptional children.* Denver: Love Publishing, 1975.

Martin, B. Parent-child relations. In F.D. Horowitz (Ed.), *Review of child development research* (Volume 4). Chicago: University of Chicago Press, 1975.

Rutherford, R.B., & Edgar, E. *Teachers and parents: A guide to interaction and cooperation.* Boston: Allyn & Bacon, 1979.

Who can help? Philadelphia: National Learning Resource Center of Pennsylvania, 1977.

Chapter 9

Training Parents to be Treatment Agents with Their Own Children

The process of aiding parents of exceptional children to serve their own children effectively requires that they be instructed in the use of basic behavioral change strategies. This approach allows parents to affect planned behavioral changes in the natural environment and thus to extend the therapeutic influence of professionals beyond the classroom setting. This robust procedure can be used to abate problem behaviors occurring exclusively in the home setting and problem behaviors occurring simultaneously in the home and school environments and as a means of involving parents in the management of school-based behavioral problems.

HISTORICAL PERSPECTIVE

Ample historical and empirical documentation exists to support the contention that the parent-child relationship affects behavior (Harlow, 1958; Kauffman, 1977; Quay & Werry, 1972). Consequently, it is not surprising that professionals have attempted to influence the behavior of children through work with parents. However, until only recently, parents have not been provided the training by professionals necessary to allow them to apply therapeutic and educational strategies with their own children. Rather, the predominant approach used with parents was a counseling model. That is, attempts were made to facilitate the development and progress of children through counseling or therapy with parents. This position resulted in parents not only being denied access to strategies and procedures that would allow them to become members of a ''therapeutic alliance'' (Berkowitz & Graziano, 1972) but further made many parents the object of therapists' crafts. These procedures were, and in some instances continue to be, designed to uncover factors associated with developmental and school-related difficulties through an analysis of the parent-child relationship. It is also apparent that since teachers and most school personnel were not trained to provide therapy for parents, few problem-solving procedures involving parents were employed in school environments. Almost without exception, parents were not perceived as a resource that could serve to augment school-applied procedures.

This position has, however, undergone significant change, and parents are, with ever-increasing regularity, being trained to use problem-solving procedures with their own children in the natural environment.

One of the most prominent and efficacious of the problem-solving alternatives available to parents is behavior modification. This approach is based on the application of an experimental analysis strategy to specific human behaviors and on the assumption that parents should be given an opportunity to assume an active role in the intervention programs that are implemented with their children rather than being required to be passive onlookers.

The procedures associated with behavior modification are designed to focus on observable and measurable behaviors. Behavior, as used in the model discussed later, refers to any observable and external response (Sulzer & Mayer, 1972). In addition, the model is based on the assumption that the operant responses of children can be controlled through the systematic application of learning theory principles. Finally, since the model assumes that behavioral principles can be taught to parents and that ''problem behaviors'' represent inadequate or incorrect learning, rather than evidence of underlying pathology on the part of the parent or child, parents can be taught ways of teaching their offspring to make more appropriate and developmentally mature responses. Thus, the behavioral model, in the present context, assumes that parents will function in a structured and systematically designed training role with their own children.

The procedures associated with behavior management techniques are designed to modify the frequency, rate, duration, or intensity of some specific behavior through the systematic application of learning theory principles (Ross, 1972). The selection of appropriate observable and overt behaviors is a basic concept in behavior modification; only with the consideration of this component can appropriate evaluation techniques be applied. For example, if the parents were allowed to apply behavioral principles to increase their child's actualization of potentiality, great difficulty would undoubtedly be experienced in obtaining agreement among independent observers not only on the frequency, rate, intensity, or duration of the behavior but also on the effectiveness of any intervention procedure that might be applied. However, while ''actualization of potential'' is very difficult to define and measure, the parents could be instructed in determining precisely the number of minutes their child studied at home each evening. Only with such precision can the techniques associated with behavior modification be effectively utilized. It is significant also to note that the strategy of concentrating on overt behaviors enables the person devising a program to eliminate from consideration not only unobservable behaviors and processes but also indirect intervention approaches. Thus, it could be argued from a behavioral position that a child's lack of social interest does not necessarily indicate a "personality problem" or other equally unobservable explanation. In addition, any intervention procedure that might be implemented would be designed to train the subject in more appropriate and useful interpersonal skills rather than to remediate a defective personality. Thus, although a child's personality might improve as a function of an intervention procedure, the intervention would be designed to modify directly some observable and measurable behavior.

Since behavioralists assume that observable environmental events that precede and follow a response are the agents responsible for the existence of the behavior and that the systematic manipulation of these factors will be associated with predictable changes in behavior, a situation conducive to the utilization of parents as agents of change is established. That is, the procedures associated with behavior modification are of such a nature that parents can be instructed in applying them with their own children and consequently in extending the treatment process to the natural home setting for an extended period of time. More traditional therapeutic approaches, on the other hand, focus on more unobservable variables and intervention techniques that, in addition to being difficult to evaluate, are not possible to transmit and apply by parents who have extensive contact with the individual of concern in the natural environment.

One additional benefit to the behavioral approach is the wide applicability of the technique. Even though as many as 10 percent of all children and youth may be considered exceptional, this in no way should be interpreted to mean that the remaining 90 percent do not have problems. Obviously the parents of even the most well-adjusted child would acknowledge that management and structuring techniques will be needed from time to time. Consequently, because of the complexity of child development and child rearing and because parents are not trained for their role, each will be faced with a difficult task for which they have little or no preparation. The techniques associated with applied behavior analysis and behavior modification become applicable and appealing to all parents because of the effectiveness and ease of dissemination of the procedures and because virtually every parent, including those with exceptional children, will find the techniques useful. In addition, behavior modification is one of the few procedures that does not automatically assume abnormality and that therefore carries the virtue of not "labeling" individuals with whom the technique is used. Since behavioral principles assume that all maladaptive behaviors are governed by the same laws that govern adaptive behaviors, no attempt is made to differentiate between "normality" and "abnormality." Rather, behaviors are evaluated relative to their own unique adaptiveness and techniques are differentially developed for behaviors deemed to be maladaptive.

USING PARENTS AS AGENTS OF CHANGE

Obviously a question that must be addressed relative to the use of parents as planned facilitators of change, regardless of the technology employed or the orientation favored, is the rationale for such a procedure. Since parents have historically not been involved as agents of therapeutic change with their own children, the issue of a rationale for such a process must be provided. One justification for the use of parents as agents of change is related to the paramount role they play in child development. As noted previously, parents are the most significant influence in a child's life, especially during the formative years. Since a relationship has been demonstrated for the influence of parents on their child's development, it is obvious that techniques for training parents to be more effective would be important. O'Dell (1974) suggested not only that there are numerous benefits to utilizing parents as a legitimate resource but also that parents should specifically be trained to use a learning theory approach. O'Dell noted a number of advantages to this strategy:

- Behavior modification techniques can be transmitted to individuals with little or no knowledge of traditional therapeutic procedures.

- Behavior modification is an orderly and empirically based model.

- Groups of individuals can be trained in the technology of behavior modification simultaneously.

- Individuals can be trained to use the procedures in a relatively short period of time.

- The procedures allow for the maximum use of professional staff talent.

- The model does not assume "sickness" as the basis for the problem.

- A majority of childhood behavior problems are responsive to the approach.

- A behavioral approach allows for treatment in the natural environment by the individuals who routinely experience the problem.

As a further argument for the development of parent-implemented behavioral programs, O'Dell suggested that "parents must become involved if effective preventive mental health programs hope to meet the demand for professional services. Also, parent training follows the growing trend toward working in the natural environment and behavior modification offers a relatively easily learned and empirically derived set of concepts for such a parent training model" (p. 419).

Williams (1959) was among the first to report the use of a simple extinction procedure by parents to eliminate bedtime tantrums in a 21-month-old child. Williams reported that the parents were able to achieve cessation of bedtime crying in a relatively short period of time and that the problem behavior did not reappear at a later date. Although not extraordinary in its methodology or results, this study demonstrated that parents could be taught to utilize behavior modification procedures effectively in a natural environment. Thus, in essence, this study initiated a new era of parental participation in the training of their own children. Since the time of Williams' study there have been innumerable other research reports that have unequivocally demonstrated the efficacy of employing parents as behavioral change agents (Bernal, Williams, Miller, & Reagor, 1972; Christophersen, Arnold, Hill, & Quilitch, 1972).

Even though the principles of behavior modification have been empirically derived and the technology has been found to be highly efficacious, even when applied by parents in the home environment, the ultimate success of the procedures will be a function of the skill of the individuals using them. Even the most efficient and well-planned parental strategy must be correctly implemented if it is to produce change. As a means of isolating factors that may be correlated with the successful application of behavior modification techniques by parents, several researchers have attempted to evaluate the characteristics of the individuals with whom they have worked. Mira (1970) failed to find a relationship between the intellectual abilities, education, and socioeconomic status of parents and their ability to employ behavior modification procedures. However, Mira used a direct teaching format rather than a lecture or reading approach. Others (Patterson, Cobb, & Ray, 1972) have suggested that lower socioeconomic parents lacking formal educational training are difficult to instruct and that families lacking integration and cooperation and individuals evidencing psychopathology are poor candidates for the role of therapeutic intervener (Bernal et al., 1972; Patterson, 1965).

Although problems and issues do exist relative to the application of behavioral techniques by parents, data suggest that when appropriately trained in the use of behavior modification procedures, parents can be effective in the role of therapeutic change agent. In addition, it seems logical that when parents are trained to manage maladaptive behavior in the environment in which the response is manifested, the greatest degree of success and generalization will be realized. As suggested by Ross (1972), "If behavior is to be modified, the modification must take place when and where the behavior manifests itself. This is rarely the therapist's consulting room, and as a consequence, behavior therapists working with children frequently find themselves working through the adults who are in a position to be present when the target behavior takes place, and who have control over the contingencies of reinforcement" (p. 919).

CONCEPTUALIZING THE PROBLEM

Children are exposed to two primary environments, the home and school. In addition, they may also spend time in other settings, such as a church or the home of relatives or a baby sitter. It is in these settings that behavioral excesses and deficits will be manifested and problems inferred. As revealed in Table 9-1, problem behaviors can occur in the primary setting of the home or school, in environments other than these primary settings, or in any combination of these environments.

In addition a problem-solving strategy can be initiated in any one or a combination of these settings. That is, a problem can occur primarily at home and be dealt with in that setting; a problem can occur at school and be treated by the parents at home; a problem can occur in all environments and be dealt with only at school; or any one of 46 other combinations can exist.

The site at which the problem is manifested and the locale at which the intervention is applied will be directly related to problem ownership and the level of anticipated parent and educator involvement. That is, some parents may have limited motivation to participate in solving a program occurring exclusively in the classroom or educators may be unmotivated to serve as a resource for problems occurring at a baby sitter's or at Sunday School. It is as a result of these factors that the primary responsibility for problems and their solutions must be determined.

As suggested by Gordon (1970) and Kroth (1975), until the ownership for any problem has been identified, the various problem-solving strategies will be rather ineffective. That is, until the parents and educator can agree as to the nature of the problem, the influence it has on adjustment, and the person most responsible for its occurrence, the intervention cannot be expected to be effective.

A MODEL FOR IMPLEMENTING PARENT-APPLIED BEHAVIORAL CHANGE PROGRAMS

The following section presents methods and procedures for implementing parent-applied behavioral change programs. This methodology, presented as objectives and related activities, is applicable to problems occurring and being dealt with in home, school, or other than home-school, or a combination of these settings. However, since the success of any change program will be a function of both the skill with which the various components are implemented and the motivation of the participants, careful consideration must be given the anticipated level of motivation and responsibility of those individuals involved. In particular, the model to be presented is most appropriate for problems occurring in the home environments or other settings where parents are most apt to be responsible or motivated to bring about change in their child's behavior.

Table 9-1 Behavioral Problem and Consequence Paradigm

Site of Problem

	(A) Home	(B) School	(C) Other	(A/B) Home/School	(A/C) Home/Other	(B/C) School/Other	(A/B/C) Home/School/Other
(A') Home	A/A'	B/A'	C/A'	(A/B)/A'	(A/C)/A'	(B/C)/A'	(A/B/C)/A'
(B') School	A/B'	B/B'	C/B'	(A/B)/B'	(A/C)/B'	(B/C)/B'	(A/B/C)/B'
(C') Other	A/C'	B/C'	C/C'	(A/B)C'	(A/C)C'	(B/C)/C'	(A/B/C)/C'
(A'/B') Home/School	A/A'B'	B/A'B'	C/A'B'	(A/B)/A'B'	(A/C)A'B'	(B/C)/A'B'	(A/B/C)/A'B'
(A'/C') Home/Other	A/A'C'	B/A'C'	C/A'C'	(A/B)/A'C'	(A/C)/A'C'	(B/C)/A'C'	(A/B/C)/A'C'
(B'/C') School/Other	A/B'C'	B/B'C'	C/B'C'	(A/B)/B'C'	(A/C)/B'C'	(B/C)/B'C'	(A/B/C)/B'C'
(A'/B'/C') Home/School/Other	A/A'B'C'	B/A'B'C'	C/A'B'C'	(A/B)/A'B'C'	(A/C)/A'B'C'	(B/C)/A'B'C'	(A/B/C)/A'B'C'

Site of Intervention

Problems occurring exclusively in classroom settings are the responsibility of educators. While parents can be involved in better understanding and reaching solutions to these problems, the primary impetus for change must come from the educator. These issues, consequently, are typically not amenable to solution via the model to be presented. The procedures to be discussed must be applied only when parents can be assured of assuming at least partial problem ownership.

The model discussed in this section provides only the basics of the technology used in training parents to be agents of change with their own children. Consequently, it should be remembered that the success of this program will be a function not only of the skill with which the various components are implemented but also of the effectiveness with which the behavioral engineer attends to basic counseling skills (e.g., establishes preliminary rapport, uses active listening skills). Without adequate attention to these factors the behavioral counselor cannot expect to be successful, regardless of how skillfully the technology is applied.

As noted in the procedural outline below, the development and implementation of a successful behavior management program cannot be established in a single conference session. The model listed below is time sequenced for procedural objectives and activities. In addition, this procedural model was developed under the assumption that individuals utilizing these procedures would have a basic working knowledge of operant conditioning and applied behavior analysis procedures. Individuals not meeting this basic criterion are encouraged to supplement this outline with basic behavioral information.

Parent-Applied Behavior Modification Technology and Training Procedures

Procedural Steps in Session I	*Specific Activities*
Identify and operationally define the most significant problem response.	List and operationally define the parents' concerns about specific problem behaviors shown by the child.
	Priorate the concerns of the parents.
	Identify the adaptive, positive and desirable behaviors of the child.
	Select one problem behavior for modification, choosing a behavior for which success is probable.
Identify those environments and situations in which the target behavior most frequently occurs.	Determine the individuals, situations, times, and circumstances surrounding the occurrence of the problem behavior.

Identify contingencies operating to support the target behavior.

Determine the responses of the parents, family members, and others in the environment following the emission of the target response.

Train the parents to identify, observe and record the target behavior.

Identify and demonstrate simple observation and recording procedures to the parents.

Aid the parents in applying these systems in order to evaluate the target behavior in the home environment.

Train parents in procedures for establishing reliability.

Make adjustments in the observation and recording systems based on feedback from the parents.

Procedural Steps in Session II

Specific Activities

Train the parents to chart and inspect the target behavioral data.

Train parents to use simple visual displays to chart the target behavior.

Train parents to record daily observations on the chart.

Train parents to inspect the baseline data for variability and trend.

Establish intervention procedures and performance goals.

Select with the parents appropriate consequences for modifying the target behavior. Intervention procedures should be positive (if possible), practical, economical, simple, and realistic.

Establish appropriate performance expectations.

Train parents to apply the consequences in the home setting, employing the behavioral principles of consistency, constancy, and immediacy.

Train parents to continue observing, recording, charting, and analyzing the target behavior after the intervention procedures have been applied.

Procedural Steps in Session III and Subsequent Meetings	*Specific Activities*
Show parents methods of analyzing and interpreting data relative to the target behavior.	Aid parents in inspecting and analyzing the data with respect to expectation goals.
Make changes in recording, charting, and intervention procedures, as needed.	Implement program modifications as needed.
Encourage parents to maintain contact with the behavioral conferencer and to apply the same model with other behaviors or children.	Suggest a follow-up schedule for parents to use in reporting the success of the home-based program.
	Encourage parents to apply the general model techniques with other problems and children.

Session I Procedures

Identify and Operationally Define a Behavior of Concern

An initial step in establishing a parent-coordinated behavior management program is to solicit a statement of concern from parents, specifically including those behaviors they consider to be most in need of change. It is obvious that this basic step in the process is contingent on parental motivation and at least partial acceptance of ownership for the problem. The educational conferencer cannot expect parents to identify "problem behaviors" that may not be perceived as problems in the home setting or to accept ownership of problems occurring exclusively in the classroom. Consequently, the conferencer must be able to verify that the parents are truly seeking aid and that partial responsibility for the problem has been accepted.

Even though applied behavior analysis principles are characterized by tremendous versatility and adaptiveness, they offer utility only when observable and measurable responses can be pinpointed. Furthermore, the response pinpointed for modification must be defined in such a fashion as to allow the various individuals involved with the child to perceive the behavior in an identical manner. For example, to one parent hyperactivity may consist of crying, screaming, and distractibility while to another it may consist primarily of failing to complete homework assignments. Consequently, it is essential to the success of any applied behavior analysis program that each individual participating in a change program be trained to observe the target behavior in the same way.

The educator implementing an applied behavior analysis program, in addition to determining that the target behavior is observable, measurable, and defined in such a manner as to allow for reliability, must solicit other basic information from the parents. First, a determination must be made as to whether or not the pinpointed behavior is under the child's control. Behaviors such as taking out the trash, fighting, and studying are responses typically under a child's control, while parasympathetic functions, such as sweating, breathing, and salivating are beyond a child's influence. Although not an infallible rule, the process of determining whether a behavior is under an individual's control, and consequently the type of behavior analysis procedure to be employed, usually consists of determining whether the problem behavior follows or precedes a controlling environmental stimulus. Respondent behavior (classical conditioning) is a response elicited by a stimulus. That is, the presentation of a particular stimulus event will provoke a response. Respondent behavior typically includes involuntary responses such as those involving the smooth muscles or glands of the body. Respondent behavior would be exemplified by a child sweating profusely and becoming agitated when his father calls him for dinner. Thus, a respondent behavior is typically a function of a stimulus event that occurs prior to a response. Operant behaviors, in contrast, are a consequence of the stimulus events that follow them (Wagonseller & McDowell, 1979). Operant responses are under the voluntary control of a child and are maintained by the environmental events that follow them. It is obvious that the behavioral counselor must be able to discriminate between a respondent and operant behavior since the change process will involve an understanding of the controlling environmental stimuli. Although behavioral principles can be employed with respondent types of behaviors, the most efficacious use of the principles for the behavioral counselor will be with operant responses. Consequently, primary attention will be focused on the use of the model with operant behaviors.

The behavioral counselor employing a behavioral strategy must also determine, either through interviewing or direct observation, whether or not the proposed target behavior contains movement. Applied behavior analysis techniques are designed for use with responses that contain movement. For example, parents can be trained to see a child wash the dinner dishes or hit a sibling. In the same manner, behaviors that contain minimal movements are difficult to analyze. Sleeping, for example, would typically not be as acceptable a choice of target behavior as a response containing more movement.

An additional consideration relative to the selection of an appropriate target behavior is to determine whether the response selected by the parents for modification is repeatable. In spite of the fact that the parents of a child who engages in severe temper tantrums may wish to modify the response, the fact that the behavior occurs only once per month would make it a poor choice for an applied behavior analysis program.

Another variable that should be evaluated prior to developing a parent-applied behavior modification program is to determine whether or not the response selected for change has a definite starting and stopping point. For most efficient management a target behavior should have a definitive cycle of repeatable movement. In order for parents to measure a behavior accurately, it should consist of a relatively short cycle that contains both a definite starting and stopping point. Completing an assigned task or throwing objects, for example, both have these cyclical characteristics. Sleeping, on the other hand, has relatively obscure starting and stopping points, not to mention that it involves a cycle far too lengthy for most parents to measure accurately.

A major task of the behavioral counselor is to translate the concerns that parents have about their child's behavior, and thus targets for modification, into operational definitions containing the before-mentioned characteristics. Typically the listing of their behaviors will be reasonable easy for the parents to provide if the task has been adequately explained and if the parents are motivated to effect change. Although not a significant problem, the educational counselor may discover that the parents can identify only one behavior in need of change. In instances in which this is the case and in which the response appears appropriate for modification via an applied behavior analysis approach, the single target behavior will suffice. This limiting process will of course make the establishment of priorities for change an easy matter. Even in instances in which a number of "problem responses" can be generated, parents will typically have fixed in their own minds a priority problem most in need of modification.

In situations in which a problem response occurs exclusively in a school environment but parents are involved in the management process (e.g., home reinforcement for acceptable school behavior) the conferencer will be responsible for operationally defining the behavior. The same procedures identified previously for aiding parents identify a behavior will be followed by the conferencer.

Asking parents to focus attention on those positive or adaptive behaviors shown by their child cannot be underrated in importance. This tactic can serve to provide a sense of perspective to the parents regarding their child's overall behavioral pattern. For example, it is not at all unusual for a single behavioral excess or deficit in a child to generalize in the minds of the parents such that the youngster is perceived as having virtually no positive qualities. Statements such as "He always causes problems at home—he just can't seem to do anything right" are quite common. However, the process of pinpointing a behavioral excess or deficit for modification coupled with an analysis of a child's strengths can serve to place the complaint in proper perspective. Identifying a child's strength may consist of the one positively oriented component of an otherwise "problem oriented" model, thus making it an extremely significant program feature and one that cannot be underestimated in importance.

Although the motivation and interests of parents must be carefully considered in selecting a target behavior for modification, care must also be taken in selecting a response with which success is a possibility. Especially in programs designed for handicapped children, behaviors should not be initially selected that have been totally unresponsive to other treatments. Although behavioral counselors should be responsive to the goals of parents in applying the technology, care should be taken to ensure that success will be forthcoming. Thus, for example, even though the parents of a ten-year-old nonverbal autistic child might understandably want their son to talk, this behavior would be a poor initial target choice. After the counselor has established his or her own validity and the validity of the procedures, and after the parents have determined their capabilities for successful modification, more difficult problem responses can be considered.

Identify Environments and Situations in which the Target Behavior Occurs

In addition to identifying an appropriate target behavior for change, the behavioral conferencer must also seek information regarding the environments and circumstances surrounding the occurrence of the response. Although frequently overlooked in importance, gaining an understanding of the relationship of the environment to the response, including whether the response is generalized across settings or is environmentally specific, is extremely significant.

The behavioral conferencer will also want to inquire about the individuals most frequently in contact with the child when the problem response is manifested. In very few instances will the response pattern be independent of the individuals involved, thus necessitating an understanding of this factor. As noted by Bandura (1969), "under naturalistic conditions behavior is generally regulated by the characteristics of persons toward whom responses are directed, the social setting, temporal factors, and a host of verbal and symbolic cues that signify predictable response consequences" (p. 25).

In addition to needing environmental and situational facts to construct a functional behavior management program, this information will aid in determining the appropriateness of a behavior management strategy. That is, in the course of obtaining information regarding the environments and situations surrounding the problem the conferencer may conclude that a behavioral strategy is not appropriate and that other solutions should be considered.

For example, one mother requested an appointment with her son's classroom teacher to discuss "problems" that she was having at home in controlling his behavior. In the course of discussing the circumstances surrounding the situations, it was discovered that the problem ("antisocial behavior") occurred only when the child was at the baby sitter's during a two-hour period in the late afternoon. Further discussion revealed that the baby sitter frequently abandoned the child during the time he should have been under her care, and that the "antisocial" act consisted of "wandering around" an adjacent neighborhood. On the basis of this information the teacher suggested the appointment of another baby sitter instead of developing a behavior modification program.

Although this component of the behavioral model may not be particularly familiar to many, its importance cannot be minimized. As noted by Bersoff and Grieger (1971) "obtaining knowledge about environments and situations in which the behavior appears is a necessity" (p. 487).

Identify Contingencies Operating to Support the Target Behavior

According to the tenets of operant conditioning, both adaptive and maladaptive behaviors are controlled by environmental conditions (Bandura, 1969). Consequently, it must be assumed that a problem behavior occurring in or around the home environment is a function of existing stimulus conditions. Functionally, for the behavioral counselor this requires an understanding of those variables associated with the maintenance of the problem response. Although only the most naive behavioral counselor would expect to discover, among the multitude of causal factors, a straightforward and easily interpreted understanding of the contingencies for any behavior, it is nonetheless necessary that an attempt be made to determine major environmental events correlated with the occurrence of the target response. Specifically, the major factors of concern are the discriminative stimulus, or that environmental circumstance alerting the subject to the fact that conditions are correct for a particular response; the operant response itself; and the reinforcing or consequent stimulus. It must be emphasized in this paradigm and to the successful construction of an applied behavior analysis program, that any operant response is a function of its consequences, thus requiring an understanding and modification of the contingencies controlling the behavior.

Although contingencies are most frequently thought of as intervention techniques, they also involve antecedent conditions. Therefore, the task in this significant area is to solicit information from the parents regarding what happens prior to and immediately after the occurrence of the target behavior. Questions such as "What happens right before he has a tantrum?" "What happens right after the tantrum starts and ends?" and "How do others in the family respond to the tantrums?" serve to generate information in this highly significant area. Bersoff and Grieger (1971) suggest that conferencers focus on the interactions that take place between the parents and child, the parents' perception of these interactions, the punishment tactics employed by the parents, and the manner in which expectations, praise, and punishment are presented to the child by the parents.

Train Parents to Identify, Observe, and Record the Target Behavior

In keeping with standard behavior management procedures, parents must be instructed to employ simple measurement and evaluation procedures. Even though some parents may appear to be threatened and overwhelmed by this seemingly difficult task, the conferencer should be able to quell these feelings. First, the conferencer can inform parents of the importance of accurate behavioral measurements and that this feature of the model is an integral and basic element of successfully employing the system (Phillips, 1978). Parents being counseled in the use of the system can typically be convinced to participate in the measurement process by pointing out to them that only through measurement can a thorough analysis of the behavioral excess or deficit and its antecedent and consequent events be gained and that without measurement activities no overall determination can be made regarding whether or not the contingencies being manipulated are having the desired results.

The second strategy relative to achieving compliance in measurement-related activities is to invest the resources necessary to ensure success in the activity. Unfortunately, educational conferencers who have a behavioral approach have frequently made the erroneous assumption that the measurement process is so simplistic that it needs little or no explanation or that parents are already competent in this activity and thus require little or no formal instruction in the data collection procedures. Because of these historic problems it is mandatory that carefully considered explanations, programming, and modeling methodology accompany each set of procedures. Only when parents have been provided proper instruction can assurances of competence be assumed. Since remaining components of the model will be contingent on the successful completion of this task, it is essential that appropriate attention be given measurement methodology.

Almost without exception parents should be advised to use observational recording techniques. Hall (1970) identified five varieties of observational recordings, all of which can be employed by parents. Included are (1) continuous, (2) event, (3) duration, (4) interval, and (5) time sample recordings.

Continuous measurements (anecdotal records) involve the tedious process of having parents record the various responses manifested by a child over a given period of time. Although this procedure allows the parents an opportunity to record a variety of behaviors, it lacks reliability and requires an investment of resources that may not be available to parents. In very few instances would this alternative be useful for parents being counseled in the use of behavior management methodology.

Event recording techniques, on the other hand, are typically very functional for parental use. These procedures consist of making a cumulative account of specific behavioral events. For example, parents can use an event recording system to note the number of words a child pronounces correctly or the frequency of one child kicking another. In addition to being relatively easy for parents to understand, event recording systems are highly adaptable to the needs of parents and the target behavior under scrutiny.

Duration recording, another observational system highly appropriate for parental use, involves having the parents calculate the amount of time their child engages in a particular target behavior. This alternative is most preferable when the length of time the behavior occurs is considered to be the most significant response descriptor. For example, the amount of time a child is engaged in having a tantrum may be a far more accurate descriptor of the behavior than the frequency with which it occurs.

Interval recording systems involve the division of a predetermined observation period into equal time segments. Parents using this procedure should be advised to record whether the target response occurs during each interval. Although this recording technique requires the undivided attention of the parent conducting the observations, it has the advantages of allowing the person to observe more than a single target behavior.

Time sampling, although similar to interval recording, has the advantage of not requiring continuous observations. Parents are trained to determine whether or not the child being observed is engaging in the target behavior at the end of a specific time interval. For example, a child's study behavior might be observed by his parents for one hour, with recordings made at the end of each five-minute period. Every five minutes the parent would observe whether or not the child was studying. This procedure has the advantage of generating a significant amount of data while at the same time allowing the parents to be involved in other activities.

The above-described procedures are the basic arsenal used in training parents to assess the frequency, rate, duration, or intensity of a target response. Regardless of which measurement alternative the behavioral counselor selects for use by the parents, it is essential that care be taken to determine that they have a thorough working knowledge of the procedure. Thus, rather than advising parents to "record the number of times John refuses to comply with a request you make," it is necessary that more precise steps be taken. Included should be the specific time period during the day when the measurement will occur and the specific procedure (e.g., tally sheet, golf counter, kitchen timer, stopwatch) for measuring and recording. This information should be provided in clear and concise written language for the parents to use as a reference. Regardless of how mundane the behavioral counselor may consider this information to be, it is absolutely mandatory that these procedures be clearly understood by the parent.

As a related agenda item, the behavioral counselor, during this initial conference, should also provide the parents with a format for recording the target behavior. Since graphing and charting procedures should be pursued during the second conference, this format can, and should, be as simple as possible. An example of a format appropriate for this task is shown in Exhibit 9-1.

Exhibit 9-1 Sample Recording Form

Child's name _____		
Observer's name _____		
Target behavior _____		
Operational definition of behavior _____		
Time of observation _____		

Date	Frequency of duration	Comments

The baseline observation should be structured such that it can be completed within five to ten days. Fewer observation days will provide a less than adequate picture of the response, and longer baseline demands may endanger the willingness of parents to participate in the program.

Although reliability procedures are an excellent addition to the behavioral system, this component should not be perceived as a sine qua non in the model. That is, if obtaining reliability data appears to present a problem for the parents, this component should be eliminated. Even though one of the major advantages of the reliability process is that it allows for the active participation of more than a single parent or other participant, it should not exist as a deterrent to the overall program.

Finally, during that period of time in which the baseline data are obtained the parents should be able to consult freely with the behavioral engineer. At a minimum, the conferencer should make at least one telephone contact with parents. In addition, the parents must feel free to contact the educator if problems or questions arise.

Although each of the procedural steps involved in the development of a successful parent-applied behavior management program is critical, the importance of being successful in the first session is paramount. Specifically, the majority of "failures" can be traced to procedural problems occurring in the initial behavioral planning session. If the behavioral counselor can successfully establish his or her own validity and the validity of the program, select an appropriate target behavior for management, accurately analyze the environments, situations, and contingencies surrounding the response, and obtain measurement data from the parents, the probability that overall success with the program will be forthcoming will be significantly increased. Again, one essential ingredient in the process must be to convince the parents to follow through with each of the components of the program. If parents can be successfully directed to complete the activities in session I, their probability of effectively influencing a target behavior will increase significantly.

Session II Procedures

Train Parents to Chart and Analyze the Behavioral Data

One of the initial tasks in the second session of the behavior management training sequence will be to demonstrate graphing and charting procedures. When parents are able to return for the second conference with accurate baseline data, in a form similar to the one shown in Figure 9-1, this training process becomes relatively simple. This simplicity is augmented when the parent conferencer has access to a graph on which the raw data can be plotted. Thus, prior to meeting with the parents the educator should construct a demonstration graph similar to the one shown in Figure 9-1. As illustrated this form should have all components labeled and completed except the actual data points.

By using a form similar to the one shown, the behavioral counselor can demonstrate the manner in which data points are inserted and connected. This same training format can be used to indicate the charting procedures for the remainder of the program. The essential ingredient in successfully developing this charting and graphing competency in parents will be to make available modeling procedures and tangible products. With careful planning the otherwise-complicated features associated with explaining the concept of a baseline become extremely straightforward and easy for most parents to grasp.

During this same training session the behavioral counselor should attempt to acquaint parents with the information being derived from the baseline data and the manner in which these data will be compared with subsequent measures. Finally, the counselor should attempt to apprise the parents of concepts related to baseline trend and variability. The extent to which this task will be pursued will in large measure be a function of the interest and abilities of parents.

Figure 9-1 Demonstration Graph Form

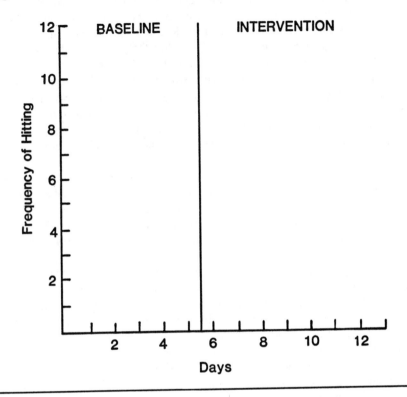

Establish and Implement Intervention Procedures and Performance Goals

Parents involved in applied behavior analysis programs with their own children are confronted with target behaviors that can be classified as either behavioral excesses or deficits. That is, parents may consider their offspring lacking in some particular response, such as completing homework assignments or engaging in desirable social interactions with neighborhood children. In a similar manner they may consider their child to be excessive in some dimension of behavior. For example, parents may consider their child to cry or quarrel too often or manifest an unnecessary level of another behavior. Consequently, because of the nature of the model and the manner in which problem responses are operationally defined, behavioral principles are designed to either increase or decrease the occurrence of some specific behavior under specific conditions. This task is accomplished via the systematic manipulation of reinforcers and punishers. Operationally, an operant reinforcer is an environmental event that strengthens the behavior it follows

(Skinner, 1953). A punisher (or aversive consequence) on the other hand is an environmental event that weakens the behavior it follows (Millenson, 1967). Hence, a concept that must be communicated to parents is that if an environmental event fails to change a behavior, then it does not operationally qualify as a meaningful consequence, regardless of whether the parents or the behavioral counselor perceive it to be impressive. In addition, this concept implies that the only valid strategy for judging whether a stimulus event will be effective is to observe its influence on the behavior it follows. For that reason, parents must again be reminded that measurement procedures must be continued throughout the program as a means of determining the influence of a consequence.

The selection of an effective consequence is not an easy task. However, through observing children, asking them about their preferences, and creatively devising reinforcers that may be potentially motivating, this task can be pursued with increased confidence. Very often parents will be able to identify or educe a number of potentially useful consequences. Others (Edlund, 1969; Homme, 1969) have reported that a reinforcement menu, or a listing of possible reinforcers from which a child may choose, is an excellent strategy for making a variety of positive consequences available.

Even though punishers and negative consequences may have some appeal, it is highly recommended that parents be encouraged to utilize positive contingencies. A number of researchers have clearly demonstrated that parents can be effective in modifying the behavior of their own children through reliance on positive reinforcement programs. Risley and Wolf (1966), for example, used shaping and reinforcement procedures to train an institutionalized severely emotionally disturbed child in more adaptive behaviors. After successful results had been achieved in a laboratory setting, the child was returned to the home environment where the mother was instructed in applying the same behavioral techniques. This transfer of the intervention procedure to the home resulted in a significant increase in adaptive behavior.

Hawkins, Peterson, Schweid, and Bijou (1966) trained mothers in procedures for interacting with their own children in the natural environment. These training efforts resulted in improved interactions between the parents and children and generally improved child behavior.

Others (Reith & Hall, 1974; Haring & Phillips, 1962) have engineered reinforcement programs in the home to increase desirable school behavior. Edlund (1969) reported that parents were able to promote desirable school behaviors through reinforcing their children for completing assignments and engaging in acceptable social behavior. Kroth, Whelan, and Stables (1970) also reported that they were able to accelerate academic and social progress in school by means of training parents to apply behavioral change techniques in the home.

Token reinforcement programs have also been successfully used by parents with their own children. Specifically, parents have been trained to reward desired behaviors with tokens, which can be exchanged at a later time for some reinforcer. O'Leary, O'Leary, and Becker (1967) reported that they were able to train the parents of a six-year-old aggressive child to employ a token economy system effectively. Initially, the parents were trained to provide verbal praise and food reinforcement when the subject and his brother were involved in cooperative play activities. Tokens, which were exchangeable for reinforcers, were phased successfully into the program. Within a relatively short time, the parents were able to employ all of the procedures originally developed by the behavioral counselor. The parents reported that as a result of this program their son became more cooperative in this play behavior and that his other social skills began to improve.

The selection of an appropriate behavioral consequence should be based not only on an evaluation of the child but also on the parents. That is, compatibility should exist between the parents' demeanor, skills, and resources and the contingency selected. In particular, consequences that are realistic, feasible, economically within the reach of the parents, and practical will tend to be most effective. For example, the parents of a nine-year-old son were extremely concerned about his nocturnal enuresis. According to his parents, the boy wet the bed at least five or six nights a week. During an informal conference the parents asked their son's learning disabilities teacher for assistance. The teacher recommended that the parents purchase a "P-P-Vigilante," a monitoring device designed to awaken a youngster when be begins to urinate. Unfortunately, the device, which cost $589.00, was far beyond the financial means of the parents.

As suggested in the above example, a number of parent-related factors must be considered in selecting an appropriate consequence. While the child must serve as the most significant factor determining the intervention stimulus to be used, the parents must also be given consideration.

The communication of the agreed-upon experimental procedures should be provided in both verbal and written form. That is, rather than simply explaining to parents what they should do in the program, they should be provided a simple plan sheet that details the procedures to be followed. Then if parents forget or do not clearly understand particular segments of the verbal explanation they will have access to a written procedural plan. An example of one procedural plan sheet is shown in Table 9-2.

The "Description of Program" column is reserved for a general statement of the objectives of the project, including who will be responsible for carrying out the procedures; what times (hours) of the day the program will be in effect; where the program will be implemented (e.g., home, neighborhood, or store); and the contingencies that will be involved. This component of the plan sheet is designed to provide an overview of the program, particular areas of responsibility, and specifics for successfully carrying out the project.

The "Description of Target Behavior" column provides for an operational definition of the behavior. This description, of course, should be made in such a

Table 9-2 Procedural Plan Sheet for Parent-Applied Behavioral Program

Child's Name   Chuck Jones

Parent's Name   Ms. Jones

Date Started   October 19 —

Description of Program	Description of Target Behavior	Procedures Prior to Observation of Target Behavior	Procedures Following Observation of Target Behavior
The program is designed to reduce Chuck's ruminating. The program will take place at home on a daily basis during times when Chuck is awake. Chuck's mother will carry out all procedures.	Rumination is operationally defined as vomiting food into the oral cavity or from the oral cavity. Most frequently this behavior will consist of vomiting food into the mouth and then reswallowing it. It is not necessary for the vomitus to be visible for the behavior to be recorded. Rumination will be evaluated daily at home by the mother using an interval recording procedure (same as procedure explained and used during baseline data collection).	Chuck will be told following baseline that it is not appropriate to ruminate. In addition, his mother will maintain the meal schedule presently in effect.	When observed to be ruminating, Chuck is to be told "No, swallow it" (or "No") in a bland tone. If he fails to comply with this command, place one hand over his mouth and squeeze his cheeks, forcing him to swallow. Next, lemon juice is to be squirted into Chuck's mouth, and he is required to swallow the substance. Then Chuck is to be taken to a sink where his lips and mouth will be washed with soap and water for 30 seconds. After his mouth and lips are dried, face cream is to be massaged on his lips and mouth for 45 seconds. Following this, the child is is allowed to return to his previous activity.

fashion as to guarantee comprehension by the parents. In addition, a brief description of the strategy to be used in measuring the target behavior should be made.

The third column, "Procedures Prior to Observation of Target Behavior," allows for a description of any responses and structuring procedures pertinent to the program. For example, if a parent-applied behavior management program was designed to decrease tantrums at bedtime, specific instructions would be required in order for the parents to structure conditions such that the target behavior could occur. That is, the parents would need to be instructed that at a certain time each evening they should announce to their child to prepare for bed. These instructions, in order to be consistent with the intervention program, would need to be delivered in a systematic fashion. Likewise, if a program were established to increase compliance behavior, parents would need to be instructed in when and how to deliver commands. Although this significant program component will be closely aligned with success, it is frequently neglected. Without question, the conferencer must give careful attention to this program feature by carefully programming the parents.

The fourth column, "Procedures Following Observation of Target Behavior," serves to describe for the parents in specific and sequential fashion, the consequences to be applied in the event the target behavior occurs. It is essential that this information be provided in a way that can be easily comprehended by the parents.

Above all else, the plan sheet should be written for the benefit of the parents, for whom it was designed. An example of a plan sheet developed for the parent of a ten-year-old boy is provided for illustrative purposes. In this study (Simpson & Sasso, 1978) an effort was made to eliminate the voluntary rumination of a severely emotionally disturbed child:

> The subject for the study was a 10-year-old male who had previously been diagnosed as severely disturbed and functionally retarded, and who had been in programs for the handicapped since he was 2 years of age. He was described as "nonverbal, having little or no interest in establishing or maintaining appropriate social relationships and prone to engage in aggressive and self-destructive behaviors." The subject was born with a cleft lip and palate deformity, which were surgically corrected at the age of 15 months. Even though this child engaged in a number of highly deviant social behaviors, his rumination was of the greatest concern to his parent and teacher. Although the subject's mother was not able to identify the age of onset of his rumination, the behavior was described as a chronic problem, having continued since infancy. The subject's rumination most frequently took the form of vomiting previously consumed food into his mouth, holding and rechewing it for several seconds, and then reswallowing it. The regurgitation process was accomplished by quick thrusts of the stomach and abdominal

muscles. Although the child most frequently held the vomitus in his mouth, resulting in a "full cheeked" appearance, he periodically would allow the regurgitated materials to flow out his mouth.[1]

The procedural plan sheet shown in Table 9-2 depicts the intervention program designed for the above described child's mother. Again, the necessity for preparing a written plan sheet for use by parents cannot be overemphasized. This procedure appears to be one basic way of reducing uncertainty for parents while increasing their faith in the program, thus increasing the overall probability of success.

Modeling, demonstration, and monitoring techniques should also be utilized by conferencers to aid parents in implementing agreed-upon procedures. Therefore, as a means of augmenting the verbal and written intervention program instructions, actual demonstration or modeling should be used. Verbal and written instructions can be easily misunderstood; however, a demonstration of the actual behavior to be employed in the program or feedback on the parent's application of techniques is far less apt to be misinterpreted.

The importance of this process was found in the implementation of a parent-applied behavior management program with a six-year-old mentally retarded boy. A behavior management program was developed in order to reduce the child's negativism. In particular, both parents had experienced marked difficulty in getting the child to obey parental requests or commands; the subject was described as "headstrong" and "set in his ways." Although expressive language was not his primary mode of communication, he did use phrases such as "No-No," "I won't," and "I can't" at a high rate of frequency.

Negative behavior was operationally defined as a refusal, either verbal or nonverbal, to obey a parental request or command. An event recording procedure was employed to measure oppositional behavior daily between the hours of 2:00 and 4:00 P.M. and 6:30 and 8:30 P.M. Both observation and experimental procedures were carried out in the child's home.

Baseline data indicated the subject to display an average of 21.85 specific instances of negative behavior per day (median 23). This measure was found to be fairly stable, although slightly ascending, during the seven days of baseline.

Following baseline procedures, learning theory principles and procedures that had proved effective with other children in decreasing oppositional episodes were discussed with the parents. A two-point program of experimental procedures was agreed upon, with the goal being to diminish oppositional behavior. Contingency procedures were as follows: the parents were instructed to eliminate attention for oppositional behavior, while introducing contingencies for cooperative behavior; and the parents were instructed to isolate the subject for three minutes immediately following each instance of oppositional behavior.

During the initial phases of the experimental procedures, the designer of the program received several anxious phone calls from the subject's mother; during each contact the mother appeared to be more upset and less sure of her ability to carry out the prescribed program. Supportive efforts proved to be only marginally successful. The subject was described as "uncontrollable" when attempts were made to implement the time out procedures; he was said to "kick the wall and me (mother)," "chew on his chair," and "scream" when placed in the time-out room. The child's mother also stated that only by physically holding her son could the time-out procedure be implemented.

The child and his mother returned to the behavioral counselor's office shortly thereafter for further instruction. Since it was apparent that specific instructions were needed, a telecoaching device was devised whereby the mother could follow via a radio and earplug verbal instructions that the child was unable to hear. The behavioral counselor stood on one side of a one-way mirror and specifically told the mother what to say and do (i.e., when to reinforce, ignore, and implement time-out procedures). Comments such as "tell him that was very good," "ignore that," and "take him to the time-out room now" were representative of these comments. Following a single instruction period the mother left, commenting that she felt much more knowledgeable as to what her role "really was."

Following this training session there was a significant decrease in the number of negative episodes. The mean number of oppositional incidents was reduced to three (median = two).

According to subjective parental comments, the subject was described as much easier to live with. He was also noted to use expressive language more, arguing against requests rather than totally refusing. This tactic, although still negative, was felt to be more sophisticated than "no."

Even though these procedures were time consuming, the benefits were obvious. While most parents will not require such graphic training, most can benefit from behavioral demonstrations and modeling procedures. The conferencer must, without exception, be assured that parents are familiar with the procedures to be followed. To do otherwise is dooming any project to failure.

As a related feature, the conferencer must play an active role in aiding parents to establish acceptable program goals. Without doubt, the technology associated with applied behavior analysis can be effectively utilized to change behavior (Berkowitz & Graziano, 1972; O'Dell, 1974; Zielberger, Sampsen, & Sloane 1968); therefore, as a part of training parents to apply these powerful procedures the conferencer must play a prominent role in determining that goals are acceptable. Without this safeguard, the conferencer has no ethical basis for training parents to apply experimental procedures with their children. The conferencer must not allow parents to determine indiscriminately that they will totally eliminate a behavior that should only be reduced. It is highly acceptable to make parents a part of their child's management program, but only when accompanied by professional monitoring considerations.

Session III and Subsequent Meetings

Follow-up meetings are primarily designed to assess the influence of the program procedures, establish and modify performance goals, and make program changes. Although parents must have access to the behavioral engineer at other than established follow-up meeting times, it will be at these sessions when most modifications will be made.

The conferencer must be cautious in suggesting or allowing contingency changes. That is, it is important that consequences be given ample opportunity to be successful. While amendments should obviously be made in instances in which consequences lack efficacy, it is important that the process not involve capricious changes. Such behavior will do nothing more than undermine the parents' faith in the behavioral counselor and the program.

Finally, subsequent sessions must be structured in such a fashion as to provide reinforcement for the parents' efforts. Since parents will obviously be instrumental in determining the success of any program and their behavior will be a function of consequent stimuli (Skinner, 1953), plans must be made for providing positive feedback. This often-neglected element is frequently found to be the basis for successful program results.

CONCLUSION

As noted throughout this chapter, behavioral principles can be effectively applied by parents of exceptional children in natural environments. However, the success of the model will be most prominently associated with the skill of the conferencer in translating behavioral tenets into functional procedures. Consequently, the conferencer must recognize that program success (or failure) will probably not be a function of the technology; the technology works! Rather, success will be determined by the behavioral counselor's skill as an educational conferencer. Accordingly, the conferencer must recognize applied behavior analysis as a tool that can only be effectively applied through effective conferencing skills. Without attending, listening, rapport, and other basic conferencing elements, this approach will fail to accomplish the goals set forth for it.

The primary issue confronting educational conferencers is not whether the behavioral approach is efficacious but rather whether it is the best strategy for a particular situation and, if it is, the specific components that will make it effective. The educational conferencer must first acknowledge that a behavioral approach may not be the most appropriate tool for all problems. In addition, when a behavioral approach is selected it is necessary that the procedures be structured to meet the needs of the child and appropriate resources made available to the parents.

Exercise

Conduct a behavioral simulation conference using the materials in Appendix B. Descriptions are provided for the cases previously presented for the initial interview role-play exercise (i.e., mentally retarded, physically handicapped, gifted, behaviorally disordered, and learning disabled). Consequently, you should use those materials most aligned with your area or those that you have used in the previous role-playing exercise (Appendix A).

In conducting the simulation exercise, one individual should assume the part of the parent, using those materials labeled "Parent Role." The conference should be parent initiated; that is, it is to be assumed that the parent in the exercise contacted the educator regarding aid for a home-based problem.

The individual playing the role of the conferencer will not have materials. However, background information on each case can be obtained from the descriptions provided for the earlier simulation conference. A third individual should play the role of evaluator, using the attached evaluation forms.

The behavioral conference should be separated into two separate sessions. The first session should comprise those elements identified in the chapter as "Procedural Steps in Session I." At the completion of this first session, individuals playing the part of the parent should generate baseline data on the identified target behavior. This information should be written on a form similar to the one shown in Exhibit 9-1, Sample Recording Form.

Following the first segment, individuals assuming educator roles should prepare a graph similar to the one shown in Figure 9-1 to demonstrate how baseline data is to be transferred on a chart. These individuals should also develop a list of possible consequences to discuss with parents and a procedural plan sheet as shown in Table 9-2. The plan sheet, of course, cannot be completed until the second session.

During the second phase of the simulation conference, "Procedural Steps in Session II" should be followed. This session, as noted previously, will make use of the data generated by parents following the first conference; the graph for allowing the educator to translate the parent-generated data; the possible consequences generated by the educator; and the educator-developed plan sheet.

Individuals should change roles after completing both phases of the conference.

NOTE

1. Reprinted from "The modification of rumination in a severely emotionally disturbed child through an overcorrection procedure" by R.L. Simpson and G.M. Sasso with permission of the *AAESPH Review*, © 1978.

REFERENCES

Bandura, A. *Principles of behavior modification*. New York: Holt, Rinehart & Winston, 1969.

Berkowitz, B.P., & Graziano, A.M. Training parents as behavior therapists: A review. *Behavior Research and Therapy*, 1972, *10*, 297-317.

Bernal, M.E., Williams, D.E., Miller, W.H., & Reagor, P.A. The use of videotape feedback and operant learning principles in training parents in management of deviant children. In R.D. Rubin, H. Festerheim, J.D. Henderson, and L.P. Ullman (Eds.), *Advances in behavior therapy*. New York: Academic Press, 1972.

Bersoff, D.N., & Grieger, R.M. An interview model for the psycho-situational assessment of children's behavior. *American Journal of Orthopsychiatry*, 1971, *41*(3), 483-493.

Christophersen, E.R., Arnold, C.M., Hill, D.W., & Quilitch, H.R. The home point system: Token reinforcement procedures for application by parents of children with behavior problems. *Journal of Applied Behavior Analysis*, 1972, *5*, 485-497.

Edlund, C.V. Rewards at home to promote desirable school behavior. *Teaching Exceptional Children*, 1969, *1*, 121-127.

Gordon, T. *Parent effectiveness training*. New York: Wyden, 1970.

Hall, R.V. *Behavior modification: The measurement of behavior*. Merriam, Kans: H & H Enterprises, 1970.

Haring, N.G., & Phillips, E.L. *Educating emotionally disturbed children*. New York: McGraw-Hill, 1962.

Harlow, H.F. The nature of love. *The American Psychologist*, 1958, *13*, 673-685.

Hawkins, R.P., Peterson, R.F., Schweid, E., & Bijou, S.W. Behavior therapy in the home: Amelioration of problem parent-child relations with the parent in a therapeutic role. *Journal of Experimental Child Psychology*, 1966, *4*, 99-107.

Homme, L.H. *How to use contingency contracting in the classroom*. Champaign, Ill.: Research Press, 1969.

Kauffman, J. *Characteristics of children's behavior disorders*. Columbus, Ohio: Merrill, 1977.

Kroth, R.L. *Communication with parents of exceptional children*. Denver: Love Publishing, 1975.

Kroth, R.L., Whelan, R.J., & Stables, J.M. Teacher application of behavior principles in home and classroom environments. *Focus on Exceptional Children*, 1970, *3*, 1-10.

Millenson, J.R. *Principles of behavior analysis*. New York: Macmillan, 1967.

Mira, M. Results of a behavior modification training program for parents and teachers. *Behavior Research and Therapy*, 1970, *8*, 309-311.

O'Dell, S. Training parents in behavior modification: A review. *Psychological Bulletin*, 1974, *81*, 418-433.

O'Leary, K.D., O'Leary, S., & Becker, W.C. Modification of deviant sibling interaction patterns in the home. *Behavior Research and Therapy*, 1967, *5*, 113-120.

Patterson, G.R. A learning theory approach to the treatment of the school phobic child. In L.P. Ullman & L. Krasner (Eds.), *Case studies in behavior modification*. New York: Holt, Rinehart & Winston, 1965.

Patterson, G.R., Cobb, J.A., & Ray, R.S. A social engineering technology for restraining aggressive boys. In H. Adams & L. Unikel (Eds.), *Georgia Symposium in Experimental Clinical Psychology* (Volume II). Springfield, Ill.: Thomas, 1972.

Phillips, L.W. The soft underbelly of behavior therapy: Pop behavior mod. *Journal of Behavior Therapy and Experimental Psychiatry*, 1978, *2*, 139-140.

Quay, H.C., & Werry, J.S. *Psychopathological disorders of childhood.* New York: Wiley, 1972.

Reith, H.J., & Hall, R.V. *Responsive teaching model readings in applied behavior analysis.* Lawrence, Kans.: H & H Enterprises, 1974.

Risley, T.R., & Wolf, M.M. Experimental manipulation of autistic behaviors and generalization into the home. In R. Ulrich, T. Stachnik, & J. Mabry (Eds.), *Control of human behavior.* Glenview, Ill.: Scott, Foresman, 1966.

Ross, A.O. Behavioral therapy. In B.B. Wolman (Ed.), *Manual of child psychopathology.* New York: McGraw-Hill, 1972.

Simpson, R.L., & Sasso, G.M. The modification of rumination in a severely emotionally disturbed child through an overcorrection procedure. *AAESPH Review,* 1978, *3*(3), 145-150.

Skinner, B.F. *Science and human behavior.* New York: Macmillan, 1953.

Sulzer, B., & Mayer, G.R. *Behavior modification procedures for school personnel.* Hinsdale, Ill.: Dryden Press, 1972.

Wagonseller, B.R., & McDowell, R.L. *You and your child: A common sense approach to successful parenting.* Champaign, Ill.: Research Press, 1979.

Williams, C.D. The elimination of tantrum behavior by extinction procedures. *Journal of Abnormal and Social Psychology,* 1959, *59*, 269.

Zeilberger, J., Sampen, S.E., & Sloane, H.M. Modification of a child's problem behavior in the home with the mother as therapist. *Journal of Applied Behavior Analysis,* 1968, *1*, 47-53.

Part III

Regularly Occurring and Ongoing Conferencing Activities

Chapter 10

Legal and Legislative Considerations

A basic prerequisite to effective functioning as an educational conferencer and as an advocate for children and their parents is familiarity with legal and legislative information. With respect to parents of exceptional children, this translates into cognizance and insight into the Education for All Handicapped Children Act of 1975 (P.L. 94-142).

INTRODUCTION TO THE EDUCATION FOR ALL HANDICAPPED CHILDREN ACT

Without argument, the most comprehensive and significant legislation yet proposed and enacted for meeting the educational needs of handicapped children and youth has been the Education for All Handicapped Children Act of 1975. This law, an amendment to the Education of the Handicapped Amendments of 1974 (P.L. 93-380), which in turn clarified, expanded, and amended the Elementary and Secondary Education Act of 1965 (P.L. 89-10), is so significant and far-reaching that it dominates every prior piece of legislation that has been enacted for the handicapped. The impact of P.L. 94-142 is complemented and augmented by Section 504 of the Rehabilitation Act of 1975. Although both laws share a similar purpose, that is, to promote the rights of the handicapped, Section 504 of the Rehabilitation Act of 1975 broadens the range of individuals affected by expanding the age and definitional parameters. In addition, Section 504 widens the contingencies for noncompliance. Together, these two enactments have more significantly affected the education of handicapped individuals than any other prior legislation.

The Education for All Handicapped Children Act of 1975 was designed to ensure a free and appropriate public education for all handicapped children and youth. This law, signed into effect by President Gerald Ford on November 29,

1975, following nearly four years of legislative proceedings, provides guidelines for aiding states and individual agencies in offering suitable educational experiences to the handicapped and in ensuring that the rights of these individuals and their families are protected. Many of the specific procedures involved in P.L. 94-142 are contained in individual "state plans," which are documents explaining the precise manner in which each state will provide educational provisions and alternatives for the handicapped. Although the present section is not intended to be a comprehensive review of this monumental act, the relationship this law has with parental issues is so significant that to fail to deal with at least the most basic concepts would constitute a significant deficiency for any work claiming to address the issues of parent conferencing. However, since the present chapter is not intended to be a thorough analysis of the various components involved, the reader is directed toward documents designed to provide this information.

According to MacMillan (1977), P.L. 94-142 is designed to provide for the following:

1. Protection against discriminatory testing in diagnosis, which ensures against possible bias in tests used with ethnic minority children.
2. The right to due process, which protects the individual from erroneous classification, capricious labeling, and denial of equal education.
3. Placement in an educational setting that is the least restrictive environment, which protects the individual from possible detrimental effects of segregated education for the handicapped.
4. Individualized program plans, which ensures accountability by those responsible for the education of the handicapped (p. 1).

As suggested previously, the participation of parents in the various activities associated with diagnosing, placing, and programming for exceptional children and youth is extremely significant. Thus, parents and legal custodians cannot be considered simply an appendage to the system or process but rather must be made a component that must be effectively integrated if the procedures are to operate smoothly. Although future reference will be made only to parents, the reader should be reminded that the same principles will apply to other legal custodians.

PROTECTION AGAINST DISCRIMINATORY ASSESSMENT

The Education for All Handicapped Children   Act of 1975 requires

> procedures to assure that testing and evaluation materials and procedures utilized for the purposes of evaluation and placement of handicapped children will be selected and administered so as not to be racially or

culturally discriminatory. Such materials or procedures shall be provided and administered in the child's native language or mode of communication, unless it clearly is not feasible to do so, and no single procedure shall be the sole criterion for determining an appropriate educational program for a child.

Identification and diagnostic procedures are the preliminary measures employed in providing appropriate services to exceptional children and youth. These screening and evaluation processes are designed to identify and assess those pupils encountering significant educational difficulties and to generate functional intervention strategies.

The role of parents in the diagnostic process is so significant that the procedures themselves hinge on the ability of the diagnostic team to secure permission to conduct the evaluation. Specifically, parents of children or youth considered by educational personnel to be a potential beneficiary of further investigation must be notified and apprised of the need for evaluation prior to the initiation of any assessment procedures. The notification, which can and should be given orally but which must also be given in written form, should provide a rationale for the proposed evaluation and a description of the tests and procedures to be employed. In addition, the notice should indicate the approximate duration of the evaluation and the anticipated benefits to the pupil. This information must be presented in a fashion that can be understood by the parents.

Upon receipt of the request for permission to evaluate, parents can make one of three possible responses. First, they can grant permission for the child to be evaluated. Once permission has been granted the evaluation can commence immediately. Second, parents can choose to deny permission to have their son or daughter evaluated. In fact, the right of parents to deny permission for their offspring to be assessed must be made known to them. In the event that parents choose to exercise their denial privileges and school district or agency personnel are not successful in convincing the parents of the need for the assessment, the district or agency can either accept the parents' position or, if they believe the pupil's best interests demand the investigation, they can request a court order to conduct the evaluation or seek permission to conduct the evaluation via a due process hearing. Due process procedures will be discussed in a later section.

Finally, parents can choose to not respond to the request to permit an evaluation. If follow-up contacts are not successful in gaining a response from the parents, the district or agency must interpret the parents' failure to reply as an indication that they are opposed to the evaluation. Accordingly, the same procedures applicable to a "no" response apply to a failure to respond.

For example, a mother and father were both angry and frightened when they received a request from the school district to conduct an evaluation on their first-grade daughter. The notice from the school and a follow-up conversation with the child's teacher indicated that their daughter was having "difficulty keeping up with the rest of the class." Although the district's school psychologist attempted to assure the parents that the evaluation would be "routine" and that it would not necessarily lead to special education placement but rather to "a better understanding so that more appropriate educational provisions can be made," they were suspicious. Their 14-year-old nephew had been tested and subsequently placed in a "special education class" when he was 8 and, according to his parents, this event produced "nothing but problems." The mother's sister and brother-in-law have, on numerous occasions, expressed the position that their son only began to have "problems" after being placed in special education. After learning that the parents had received a request for permission to evaluate, their relatives strongly recommended that they "fight."

Fortunately, however, a single session with the school psychologist and classroom teacher convinced these parents that the best interests of their daughter would be served by allowing the evaluation to take place. In addition, the parents were notified that their prior approval would be required before any change in their child's educational placement could be initiated.

It should be noted that requests for evaluation can be made not only by schools but also by parents. Parents can, in fact, request an evaluation or reevaluation of their offspring at any time they deem appropriate. However, the school district has the choice of conducting or not conducting the evaluation. In the event the district concedes to the request for an evaluation, they must still obtain written permission from the parents prior to actually conducting the assessment. If the district takes the position that an evaluation is not needed, they must notify the parents, in writing, of their decision. This notice must also inform the parents that if they desire, they can request a due process hearing to arbitrate differences of opinion between the school and themselves regarding the need for an evaluation.

One mother believed strongly that her 12-year-old son was "learning disabled" and should be provided special class placement. Even though he had been evaluated twice in six years by the school district's diagnostic team and once by an educational psychologist in private practice, all at the mother's request, to determine his need for special intervention procedures, and even in spite of the fact that each of the evaluations failed to indicate learning or behavior problems, she requested an additional assessment session. Since the child's mother had failed to participate in a recommended counseling program offered by the county mental health association and because classroom reports and observations did not justify the need for an additional evaluation, the mother's request was denied. Although the mother initially filed for a due process hearing, she later decided to move to a neighboring district in order to obtain "the right program" rather than attempting to secure the evaluation via rights available to her under P.L. 94-142.

Candidly explicit in the Education For All Handicapped Children Act is the directive that requests for permission to evaluate must be in a language that is understandable to the child's parents. If the parents' primary language is not English, the notice must be provided in the major language of the home. In the event that the parents' primary language or mode of communication is nonwritten, or if the parents are unable to interpret written materials, it is the responsibility of the school district to take whatever steps are necessary to ensure that the parents understand the content of the notice. Districts should also be cautioned that it is necessary that they be sensitive to dialectal and regional variables when selecting appropriate communication modes for seeking permission to evaluate.

The parents of an 11-year-old son had both been profoundly deaf since infancy. They had met while students at a state school for the deaf and had married shortly after completing their programs at the institution. Although both were gainfully employed, and had been for over eight years, neither was able to communicate effectively via an oral means. In addition, neither had more than the most minimal academic survival skills. They were able to sign manually, however, and essentially all of the communication that took place between the parents and the "hearing world" occurred via manual signing. When the school district made contact with the parents to solicit their permission to evaluate their son because of alleged "learning and behavior problems," they not only sent a letter to the parents explaining the procedure but also sent an individual to their home to "sign" the contents of the letter and to further elaborate on the need for the evaluation.

Historically, evaluation efforts have accentuated procedures associated with labeling and justifying the placement of handicapped children and youth in special education programs (Wallace & Larsen, 1978). However, this emphasis has been at the expense of generating information that can be used in formulating an appropriate individualized teaching strategy. This pattern has specifically been characterized by an overreliance on a limited number of procedures that have extremely dubious levels of utility and by evaluations conducted by individuals with somewhat narrow perceptions of the needs of handicapped children and youth. These evaluative shortcomings have, at least to some extent, been positively modified by the implementation of P.L. 94-142, which directly requires a comprehensive evaluation by a multidisciplinary staff. A comprehensive and multidisciplinary evaluation, just as the concepts suggest, involves a complete assessment prior to the initiation of any program modification. In order for an evaluation to meet the spirit of comprehensiveness, it should involve consideration of not only the child's ability to function on standardized and teacher-made instruments but also an analysis of relevant home, school, and community variables that appear to be having an impact on the pupil's ability to function. Consequently, the evaluation must provide data relating to the physical, psychological, sociological, and educational status of each pupil being evaluated. Furthermore these evaluations must be made by a variety of "experts" representing their respective disciplines as opposed to a single diagnostician. That is, in addition to informal assessment procedures, direct observations, and related techniques commonly employed by classroom teachers, the input of individuals representing other disciplines must also be considered. Even though the roles of the individuals involved will vary with the diagnostic questions under consideration, they will commonly represent the disciplines of school psychology, social work, physical and occupational therapy, speech pathology, audiology, medicine, nursing, counseling, and school administration. Input from these professional groups will, of course, be considered along with that provided by the parents or legal custodians.

Each individual involved in the assessment process is charged with utilizing his or her expertise and the technology associated with the respective discipline to provide relevant information. The importance of accuracy in this function was underscored by Turnbull and Turnbull (1978): "Misclassifying children as handicapped when they are not, or classifying them inaccurately with respect to their handicaps, can result not only in denying them their rights to an educational opportunity (not to mention their rights to an appropriate education), but also in unjustifiably stigmatizing them" (p. 85).

Implicit in the above discussion and expressly a component of P.L. 94-142 is the mandate that pupils under evaluation not be discriminated against in the assessment process, either as a function of the handicapping condition itself or racial, language, or cultural factors. With regard to the latter, the Education of All Handicapped Children Act requires that the following assessment procedures be followed prior to any program modification:

    (a) Tests and other evaluation materials
        (1) Are provided and administered in the child's native language or other mode of communication, unless it is clearly not feasible to do so;
        (2) Have been validated for the specific purpose for which they are used;
        (3) Are administered by trained personnel in conformance with instructions from the producer;
    (b) Tests and other evaluation materials include those tailored to assess specific areas of educational need and not merely those which are designed to provide a single general intelligence quotient;
    (c) Tests are selected and administered so as best to insure that when a test is administered to a child with impaired sensory, manual or speaking skills, the test results accurately reflect the child's aptitude or achievement level or whatever other factor the test purports to measure, rather than reflecting the child's sensory, manual, or speaking skills (except where those skills are the factors which the test purports to measure);

(d) No single procedure is used as the sole criterion for determining an appropriate educational program for a child and placement;
(e) The evaluation is made by a multidisciplinary team or group of persons, including at least one teacher or other specialist with knowledge in the suspected disability;
(f) The child is assessed in all areas related to the suspected disability, including, where appropriate, health, vision, hearing, social and emotional status, general intelligence, academic performance, communicative status, and motor abilities.

Not only are the above-mentioned procedures mandatory components of determining the most appropriate educational programs for a pupil and for complying with federal and state guidelines but they have special significance for parental involvement. Although with various degrees of difficulty, program modifications may (or may not) be effected without parental permission, the desired option is of course to obtain parental input and support for the recommendations made. Consequently, the diagnostic team must be able to present data justifying the conclusions drawn and recommendations made. Since staffing and interpretative conferences are frequently the initial contacts that take place between parents and school personnel, and thus set the tone for future interactions, it is crucial that both the evaluation process itself and the interpretation of results be the basis for future positive contacts. Finally, since parental or legal guardian permission must be obtained prior to placing, reassigning, or transferring an exceptional pupil, it is essential that supporting data and attitudes assure the parents that their child is being provided the most appropriate education possible. This does not imply that educational diagnostics and staffings must take on a game atmosphere, in which parents are wiled into complying (to the detriment of their child) with the wishes of educators, but rather that appropriate procedures and data, including legitimate parental input, be the basis for program recommendations. Only with the adoption of such standards can the arduous and unrewarding task of arbitrating differences through due process hearings be avoided. Although the due process alternative is a legitimate right that schools and parents may choose to exercise in select instances, rigid assessment procedures, meaningful parental involvement, and adequate interpretative standards can effectively increase the working relationship between educators and parents and reduce the need for more formal recourse procedures.

RIGHT TO DUE PROCESS

Probably no single term in education produces such a visceral response as "due process." Both parents and educators alike seem to associate the term with legal involvement, conflict, and proceedings more aligned with a courtroom than an educational setting. However, the provisions of due process, as specified in the

Education of All Handicapped Children   Act, which so closely govern the assessment, educational placement, transfer, and the rights of exceptional children and youth, are nothing more than the parent's or pupil's right to challenge a course of action recommended because of an alleged exceptionality. The basic concepts associated with educational due process were initially articulated in *Pennsylvania Association for Retarded Children* v. *Commonwealth of Pennsylvania* (1972). In their decision, the court stipulated that ''no child who is mentally retarded can be assigned initially or reassigned to either a regular or special education status, or excluded from a public education without a prior recorded hearing before a special hearing officer.'' The court decision was also accompanied by a series of steps detailing the operational elements of due process, much of which is currently, at least in concept, a part of the due process proceedings contained in P.L. 94-142. The primary due process procedures afforded parents and children under P.L. 94-142 include parental access to records, independent evaluations, surrogate parents, parental notice, and right to a hearing.

Parental Access to Records

Parents or legal custodians are afforded access to all records and data pertaining to the identification, assessment, and placement of their child. As noted in the assessment section, this component accentuates not only the need for a complete and thorough evaluation but also an accurate and professional report of the findings and recommendations to parents.

Independent Evaluation

Parents and legal custodians are also entitled to obtain an evaluation of their son or daughter from qualified (licensed or certified) examiners not affiliated with the district or agency recommending the action. Again, the importance of initial rapport and an adequate multidisciplinary and comprehensive evaluation cannot be overemphasized since parents are entitled to present data from an alternate source in instances in which they question or are dissatisfied with the findings and recommendations presented them. Since dissatisfaction is frequently associated with a lack of parental input or involvement, diagnostic teams should both be able to support their findings and to provide parents with the opportunity for input into the analysis of the problem and intervention strategies.

Even though parents are entitled to seek their own independent evaluation and even though schools or agencies may be required to recommend appropriate individuals to conduct the evaluation, the parents may be required to assume the costs of the testing. Only in instances in which hearing officers request additional independent data or in which schools or agencies acknowledge, or parents can demonstrate in a hearing, that the evaluation conducted was deficient or biased, can the parents be exempted from assuming financial responsibility. However, regardless of the financial responsibility issue, assessment data solicited from independent diagnosticians must be considered by individuals charged with making disposition recommendations.

In this example, the parents acknowledged that their son had a "learning problem," but they questioned the ability of the school district's diagnostic team to conduct an adequate evaluation. They consequently sought out community professionals to assess their son simultaneously with the evaluation being conducted by school district personnel. Since the majority of the private evaluation findings were identical to those obtained by school district personnel, the parents were required to assume financial responsibility for the private testing. The one exception was the audiological exam conducted by a private practitioner. Since the school district did not assess the child's hearing, and because this was considered to be potentially related to his problem, the district did agree to pay for this service. In all instances the information generated by private professionals was considered by district personnel.

Appointment of Surrogate Parents

In instances in which a child or adolescent is a ward of the state, or the parents are unavailable or unknown, the appointment of a surrogate parent must be made. Surrogate parents are commissioned to represent the child in all matters pertaining to evaluation and placement. The criteria for the selection of a surrogate parent is that the appointee have the necessary competence to represent an exceptional child or adolescent and that no conflict of interest exists. Thus, individuals employed by or affiliated with an institution or setting in which a child or adolescent is a resident may not serve as surrogate parents. Due process hearings exist as the means for resolving conflicts over the appointment of parent surrogates.

Right to Parental Notice

As discussed earlier, parents, legal custodians, or surrogates must be provided written notice whenever a school or agency proposes to conduct an evaluation or make a change in the educational program for a pupil. This requirement also applies in instances in which parents request changes or evaluations. As previously noted, these formal notices must follow a written format and be in the parents' or guardian's native language. In instances in which the parents are unable to read, or if the native language is not a written language, it becomes the responsibility of the school or agency to apprise the parents of the proposed action and their rights to due process safeguards. According to P.L. 94-142 Section 615 (C) and (D) the following steps are required:

(C) Written prior notice to the parents or guardian of the child whenever such agency or unit—

(i) proposes to initiate or change, or

(ii) refuses to initiate or change,

the identification, evaluation or educational placement of the child or the provision of a free appropriate public education to the child;

(D) Procedures designed to assure that the notice required by clause (C) fully inform the parents or guardian, in the parents' or guardian's native language, unless it clearly is not feasible to do so, of all procedures available pursuant to this section.

Right to Hearing

Parents and legal custodians must be provided a formal opportunity to present complaints on any matter relating to the identification, evaluation, or educational placement of their child. This process is designed to afford parents, schools, and agencies the opportunity for an objective and structured hearing, the outcome of which will ostensibly lead to the most appropriate educational placement possible for the child. Hearings can be held by the state, intermediate, or local educational agency, depending on the situations and locale.

School districts and agencies must apprise parents of their due process rights under P.L. 94-142. These rights include the following:

- the right to a fair and impartial hearing that is open to the public. This right specifically affords the disputing parties the opportunity for an orderly hearing coordinated by a qualified and objective hearing officer who has neither a professional or personal conflict in the outcome of the hearing. Hearing officers thus cannot be employees of the school or agency involved in the action.

- the right of the parents to have both the child and counsel of their choice present at the hearing. Individuals functioning as counsel can be professionals (e.g., attorney, educator, or psychologist) or another parent or confidant whom the parent or legal custodian considers to be appropriate for representing their interest and those of the child. Both the parents and their counsel are guaranteed access to information and data employed by the school or agency in recommending the disputed action. The parents and their counsel also have authority to present expert witness and testimony (e.g., educational, medical, or psychological) in support of their position and to cross-examine individuals presenting information on behalf of the agency or school. Only evidence that is disclosed at least five days prior to the hearing can be presented.

- the right of the parents to a verbatim recording of the hearing. This record must be made by a mechanical recording device or an official court reporter. Unless the involved parties agree to an extension, the hearing must be held and a final decision rendered by the hearing officer within 45 days after the request for hearing is made. The parents must be provided a copy of the decision report.

• the right of both parents and school districts to appeal the decision of the hearing officer. The first level of appeal is to the state education office. However, further appeals can be made through the traditional court system. Between the time of the request for a due process hearing and extending through the appeal process, or until a satisfactory compromise can be obtained, the child is entitled to remain in the setting he or she was assigned to prior to the recommended action.

It should also be noted that the provisions of due process are not only extended to parents and legal custodians but also to agencies and schools. Thus, a school or agency is entitled to a hearing on its recommendation to initiate or refusal to initiate evaluation or placement procedures.

While due process procedures exist as a necessary and essential safeguard, this option must not serve as a routine mode for arbitrating differences. Individuals having been involved in formal due process hearings are quick to point out that this process rarely leads to mutually satisfying decisions. Accordingly, both educators and parents must develop other means for resolving differences and gaining appropriate services for children. Only after all other options have first been exhausted should due process proceedings be considered.

Whelan (1980) developed a procedural due process checklist for parents, school district personnel, and hearing officers in Kansas. This instrument, as shown in Exhibit 10-1, was specifically designed to ensure that the rights of all parties have been explained and guaranteed.

PLACEMENT IN THE LEAST RESTRICTIVE ENVIRONMENT

According to this provision of P.L. 94-142, handicapped children and youth must be educated to the maximum extent appropriate with nonhandicapped students. Handicapped children and youth can be provided placement outside the regular classroom environment only when the severity or nature of their handicap demands a more restrictive setting. Stephens (1977) referred to this process as the placement of handicapped students in situations "as near normal as their performance and their competencies and creativity of school personnel allow" (p. 146). The National Association for Retarded Citizens (1973) also emphasized this concept, noting that handicapped persons should be aided in obtaining "an existence as close to the normal as possible, making available to them patterns and conditions of everyday life as close to the norms and patterns of society. Specifically it refers to the use of means that are as culturally normative as possible to elicit and maintain behavior that is as culturally normative as possible" (p. 72).

Exhibit 10-1 Procedural Due Process Checklist

Section	Item	Parent		District	
		Yes	No	Yes	No
District Written Prior Notification to Parents of Proposed Special Education Action	1. Proposed action and reasons.				
	2. Parent right to consent to action in writing on forms provided by district.				
	3. Parent right to object to action at a hearing held upon request of parent within 30 days from date on which notification received.				
	4. Parent informed of free or low cost legal or other relevant services available in the area.				
	5. Parent notified in primary language.				
District Written Prior Notification to Parents of Initiation or Change of Special Education Program	1. Description of rights and procedures for due process hearing.				
	2. Opportunity to obtain an independent evaluation of child at district expense unless a hearing on this issue declares district evaluation appropriate.				

3. Right to access school records related to proposed placement.

4. Child remains in present placement until decision following hearing, or until placement accepted by parent and district.

5. Parent has 30 days to request hearing during which period the district will not change child's placement.

Hearing Officer's Responsibilities to Parties Prior to Hearing

1. Verify that parent understands right to:
   a. Independent evaluation.
   b. Access school records related to proposed placement.

2. Verify that parent and district understand rights of parties in due process hearing to:
   a. Have counsel of their choice present and to receive advice of such counsel.
   b. Have parent present at hearing.
   c. Have child and counsel to hear or read full report of testimony from witnesses including those responsible for recommending proposed placement.
   d. Cross-examine witnesses.

Exhibit 10-1 continued

Section	Item	Parent		District	
		Yes	No	Yes	No
Hearing Officer's Responsibilities to Parties Prior to Hearing.	e. Present witnesses in person or testimony by affidavit, including expert medical, psychological, or educational.				
	f. Have child testify in own behalf, and give reasons for or against proposed placement.				
	g. Prohibit evidence or testimony not disclosed to other party at least 5 days prior to hearing.				
	h. Have an orderly hearing.				
	i. Have fair and impartial decision based on evidence.				
	j. Have a record of hearing made.				
	3. Presence of interpreter required.				
	4. Notice of hearing date, time, and place 10 days prior to hearing.				
	5. Obtain from both parties:				
	a. Written summary of evidence each will present at hearing.				
	b. List of persons who represent parties, and/or appear as witnesses at hearing.				

6. Use of subpoenas for attendance of witnesses and/or production of relevant records required.

7. a. Parent/child decision to have child attend/testify at hearing.

   b. Hearing officer finds that child under age of majority may _____ attend all of, _____ be _____ attend parts of, _____ excluded from hearing.

8. Hearing closed/open to public.

9. Prehearing conference held at least 5 days prior to hearing to provide each party with a hearing agenda that includes written summary of evidence, and a list of representatives/witnesses.

Hearing Officer's Responsibilities to Parties Subsequent to Hearing

1. Render a written decision based on evidence and send such decision by restricted mail to both parties not later than 5 days after hearing concluded.

2. The decision, without personally identifiable information, will be sent to the State Advisory Council for Special Education.

3. Arrange for each party to have summary of hearing proceedings, including such materials or statements either party wishes to appear in the record.

Exhibit 10-1 continued

Section	Item	Parent		District	
		Yes	No	Yes	No
Hearing Officer's Responsibilities to Parties Subsequent to Hearing	4. Description of appeal procedures for State Board review which require:				
	a. Filing a written notice of appeal with the State Commissioner of Education not later than 10 days after receipt of hearing officer's decisions.				
	b. The district to submit to the State Board of Education a complete record of hearing and all affidavits, documents, or other evidence produced at the hearing.				

Source: Courtesy of R.J. Whelan, used with permission.

The position of assigning handicapped children to regular classrooms, whenever possible, revolves around two basic arguments. The first is that evidence exists to support the position that the separate special class is a model that has consistently produced less than adequate academic and social results (Dunn, 1968). In spite of the continued popularity of special classes and programs, both professionals and parents appear to be highly aware of the lack of efficacy surrounding this model. The second argument relevant to the desirability of the regular classroom is based on theories of homogeneity and heterogeneity. Brown, Nietupski, and Hamre-Nietupski (1976) have advocated that heterogeneity in classroom populations, whereby children and youth with differences in a number of areas are placed in the position of learning to experience and interact with one another, is highly superior to the establishment of homogeneous groups. These authors emphasized the necessity of such interactions if handicapped individuals are to be expected to function successfully in a heterogeneous community environment later in life. Although parents have not advocated the advantages of regular class placement in such an esoteric manner as these researchers, they have voiced concerns based on many of the same principles and concepts.

While regulations pertaining to the least restrictive environment advocate the use of the regular classroom as the desired arena for instruction, this policy does not apply to children and youth whose needs cannot be met in that setting. The identification of the least restrictive environment, which is reviewed and determined at least annually, must be based on each pupil's ability and performance, as translated through the individualized education program (IEP). Since parents or legal custodians are major participants in this decision, it is apparent that such a disposition cannot be made by school or agency personnel independent of family input.

While the concepts of mainstreaming and the least restrictive environment are different, they are frequently confused, often to the detriment of all concerned. Mainstreaming has, in fact, been the stimulus for a great deal of agitation and, according to Turnbull and Turnbull (1978) has "the potential for encountering the same levels of opposition, misunderstanding and ill will as the requirements for racial desegregation of the schools" (p. 137). Given the controversial nature of mainstreaming and the interpretation of the least restrictive setting, it is imperative that professionals work particularly closely with parents in establishing this component of a pupil's program. Included should be the following (Deno, 1970):

- In determining the least restrictive environment the educator should be reminded that the parent is not an opponent but that a common goal is shared. Pursuant to that end, the allegiance of the educator should be to the child. Thus, the least restrictive environment should be determined by each pupil's needs and the educators and parents' interpretation of those needs rather than by the services that are available in the district.

- As has been suggested previously, parents can be expected to be active participants in the various activities related to gaining an appropriate education for their child only when the proper interpersonal conditions exist. The conferencer must be able to establish conditions of trust and rapport in order for consensus to be reached on significant educational decisions, including the least restrictive environment.

- Educators should not be overly zealous to mainstream pupils in instances in which special classes or settings are producing desirable results. There is evidence to support the argument that many parents view special class placement favorably (McKinnon, 1970). If a more structured setting is an appropriate environment and is supported by the parents, educators should carefully evaluate the advantages of recommending the transfer of a child to a less restrictive setting.

- Even in instances in which full-time regular class placement is inadvisable, educators should promote the advantages of having handicapped children and youth participate with their regular class peers in extracurricular and nonacademic school and community activities. Since many parents are reluctant to give up programs that they have struggled so hard to obtain in order to return their son or daughter to a setting that has been historically unrewarding, attempts should be made to phase exceptional pupils back slowly into more normalized situations. This phasing process can frequently serve to make parents more amenable to other less restrictive environments.

- Educators must be able to offer parents a variety of educational alternatives for their exceptional child. That is, the lesser restrictive alternatives must not exist as either regular or special class placement. Rather, parents and educators must be able to select from a variety of services those that are most appropriate for a given pupil.

INDIVIDUALIZED EDUCATION PROGRAM

Although each of the major components of P.L. 94-142 has received significant attention by parents and educators, the section that has been given the most fanfare has been the requirement that an IEP be developed and monitored for each handicapped child or adolescent. This regulation specifies that each state and local educational agency must provide an IEP for each pupil identified as requiring special education.

The term ''individualized education program'' means a written statement for each handicapped child developed in any meeting by a representative of the local educational agency or an intermediate educational unit who shall be qualified to provide, or supervise the provision of, specially designed instruction to meet the unique needs of handicapped children, the teacher, the parents or guardian of such child, and whenever appropriate, such child, which statement shall include (A) a statement of the present levels of education performance of such child, (B) a statement of annual goals, including short-term instructional objectives, (C) a statement of the specific educational services to be provided to such child, and the extent to which such child will be able to participate in regular educational programs, (D) the projected date for initiation and anticipated duration of such services, and appropriate objective criteria and evaluation procedures and schedules for determining, on at least an annual basis, whether instructional objectives are being achieved. (P.L. 94-142)

Under the requirements of the Education for All Handicapped Children   Act, an IEP for every child or adolescent must be written or revised at the beginning of each school year. Although the IEP format can vary between states, school districts, and agencies, certain basic components, as previously noted, must be included. While the IEP is not intended to be a legally binding contract, whereby districts and agencies are bound to demonstrate that progress specified in the annual goals and objectives has been met, it does serve to solidify the cooperative involvement of parents and educators.

The development of the IEP is so structured that it is functionally impossible to comply with the established protocol and not produce a cooperative document. Thus, the development of an IEP prior to the official IEP conference or by a limited number of personnel constitutes a severe breach of policy. As noted in guidelines to parents in a national publication designed to apprise parents of their rights under P.L. 94-142 (Parents Campaign for Handicapped Children and Youth, Fall 1977), ''If you have reason to think that school people met 'behind the scenes' to agree on the IEP, effectively keeping you out of the act, you have grounds to complain loudly'' (p. 7).

Individuals that should be involved in the IEP conference include a representative of the school or agency providing the services (other than the teacher); the teacher(s) who will actually implement the IEP; the parent(s) or legal custodians; the student, when appropriate; and others, at the discretion of the parents or school. During the development of the initial IEP, the district or agency recommending the program modification should also have available someone who can interpret testing and diagnostic procedures to parents.

Because parents are considered such an integral part of the IEP conference, provisions exist for guaranteeing their participation. Specifically, parents must be provided advance notice of the IEP conference, including the purpose, time, location, and those individuals who will be in attendance. Districts and agencies must also guarantee that these conferences will be held at times and places mutually convenient to the parents and educators. Those individuals coordinating the conference must also ensure that parents will be able to comprehend and have input into the session (e.g., interpreters must be provided for deaf or non-English-speaking parents) or in the event that parents are unable to attend the session, that the school use other methods to allow their participation (e.g., conference telephone calls). Although IEP conferences can be held without parental representation, the district or agency must be able to document that parents were provided an opportunity to participate. This documentation must include accounts and results of telephone calls made or attempted, copies of letters and responses to letters sent, and reports of the results of home and employment visits. While this information is not required for every case in which parents are not involved in an IEP conference, it must be available in situations in which parents claim that they have been excluded from the conference.

Because the concepts, principles, and protocol involved in P.L. 94-142 are both numerous and complex and because school districts often provide parents limited or incomplete information, educators frequently find it necessary to develop alternative procedures for apprising parents of their rights and responsibilities. While published books and periodicals may be able to meet this need, they frequently are threatening to parents and will, at the very least, lack precise information about a specific program, class, or district. As a result, educator-developed parent handbooks may be used more effectively to disseminate the information that parents require. The rights of parents listed in a portion of one such parent handbook, developed by Jody Huxman, a teacher of handicapped children, for use in a rural area of central Kansas, are shown below:

- the right to notice before the agency initiates or changes (or refuses to initiate or change) the identification, evaluation, or placement of your child. Your school must notify you of any change in your child's program.

- the right to have that notice in writing and in your native language or other principle mode of communication, at a level understandable to the general public. You have the right to request any information passed on to you in your native language or the language of the home. If you as a parent are handicapped in some way that reading in the normal fashion is impossible or difficult, you may request any and all information translated into your principal mode of communication. All information should be in terms of what you can understand.

- the right to have the notice describe the proposed action, explain why it is proposed, describe the options considered, and explain why those other options were rejected. Your notice must describe the program selected for your child and why it was considered the best possible choice. All other options must be considered without regard to availability, and an explanation of why each of the other options was rejected.

- the right to be notified of each evaluation procedure, test, record, or report the agency will use as a basis for any proposed action. When the results of tests administered to your child will be used in placing your child will be placed in your child's records, these tests cannot be administered without your permission. However, evaluations written into the IEP can be administered as the teacher sees fit provided you have signed the IEP, unless you wish to make other arrangements.

- the right to have a full and individual evaluation of your child's educational needs.

- the right to have more than one test or procedure used in determining an appropriate educational program for your child. This right and the previous one guarantee you that your child cannot be placed on the basis of one test. You may request a full evaluation given individually (as opposed to a group) to be used as a basis for determining a child's placement.

- the right to have the evaluation performed by a multidisciplinary team. This means that each test given shall be administered by a qualified team member. For example, the psychologist will give intelligence test, speech clinician will give language and speech assessments, etc.

- the right to have your child assessed in all areas related to the suspected disability. For example, if your child has a speech or language problem, you may wish to have your child's hearing evaluated if such an evaluation has not yet been conducted.

- the right to have a re-evaluation on a regularly scheduled basis or more frequently if conditions warrant or if you or your child's teachers request it. Your child will be fully evaluated periodically as he was initially to see if the present placement is still the most appropriate placement for your child.[1]

Even though the efforts involved in scheduling and conducting a functional IEP conference are extensive and time consuming, it should be obvious that such a process carries numerous benefits. In addition, it must be pointed out that complying with minimum federal requirements may do little to ensure parental cooperation. As noted by Meyen (1978), "merely setting up procedures which comply with the law and thus allow for parental participation is not sufficient. Emphasis needs to be placed on establishing relationships which capitalize on parental involvement" (p. 22). While not an easy task, there are several procedures that, when correctly identified and planned for, can serve to allow the educator to include the parents more effectively in the IEP process.

The Need for Trust

Replete in this text has been the message that only under conditions of shared confidence in the integrity and honesty of professionals and parents will the true intent of the IEP conference be realized. Although this position has been advocated by many (Kroth, 1975; Kroth & Simpson, 1977; Rutherford & Edgar, 1979), and thus should be an acknowledged principle, its importance cannot be underestimated. Schools and parents have all too often had an adversarial relationship, making the development of trust less than an easy matter. However, without this basic ingredient even the most precise adherence to mandated requirements will be meaningless.

The staff of a federally supported public school demonstration program for severely emotionally disturbed pupils thought it somewhat peculiar when the mother of an adolescent being considered for placement in the program presented two rather strong demands. The first was that the initial parent-teacher interview, conducted as one component of the evaluation, be held in the home and, second, that a former teacher, residing in a community some distance away, be contacted regarding the subject's past performance. Both requests were honored. After the IEP conference, at which the parent actively participated, the mother revealed that she had been "testing" the staff. She indicated that although she had received a number of promises over the years from school personnel regarding the services to be provided her severely handicapped son, few had been honored. She confided that if the school personnel who contacted her were willing to come to her house and to contact a teacher whom she personally respected "then they probably had the best interests of Calvin in mind." She also reported that this demonstration convinced her that her input into the development of her son's IEP would be considered worthwhile.

The Issue of Administrative and Bureaucratic Restraints

Even though teachers and other educational personnel may understand the components and protocol involved in developing an IEP, the standards adopted by school districts or agencies may be in direct conflict with these standards. District policy statements, albeit unwritten, may specify that only services readily available in the district are to be noted on the IEP, regardless of the needs of pupils. Other policies may require authors of IEPs to word components of the document in such a fashion as to be intentionally nebulous or difficult to interpret. The unfortunate thing about these relatively common practices is that educational personnel are unceremoniously thrust into the awkward position of demonstrating allegiance either to their employer or to the children they serve. Although individuals may argue to the contrary, the adoption of either position, regardless of how cleverly presented, cannot serve to accomplish the goals originally intended.

One director of special education for a large midwestern school district, although knowledgeable of IEP guidelines, required that evaluation criteria for short-term instructional objectives be stated in nonspecific and nonmeasurable terms. For example, goals were frequently stated in terms of "demonstrating indications of improvements" rather than in more empirical and easily evaluated terminology. Although the special services staff did not agree with this approach, they understood that the policy was a nonnegotiable dictate that they were required to follow if they wished to keep their jobs.

The Issue of Language

In order for parents and educators to develop an individualized program for a handicapped pupil, they must share a common language and vocabulary. Frequently, educators become so accustomed to using sophisticated terms and concepts that they assume that other individuals, including parents, share their vocabulary. Parents may be somewhat reluctant to reveal their lack of understanding and, in some instances, may actually employ terms and phrases for which they have little comprehension. It is essential that the importance of a shared language not be underestimated. The selection of appropriate words and phrases, as free from jargon as possible, will ensure that parents will feel more like contributing members of the IEP team.

One mother, when asked about the IEP conference she attended, coolly replied that she learned that "the CEC is aiding the SEA's and LEA's in interpreting the rules and reg's of 94-142 so as to ensure the proper development of IEPs and IIPs for MRs, LDs, EDs and other DDs."

The Problem of Intimidation

Because the development of a pupil's IEP requires wide representation, parents are often in the position of being in a planning conference with up to 15 other individuals, most of whom are professionals. While this wide participation has a number of advantages, it has the obvious disadvantage of intimidating many parents. Since the majority of these parents will have had little or no prior contact with the other IEP participants nor the guidelines of these meetings and may very well be attempting to come to grips with having an exceptional child, it should come as no surprise that a number of parents have reported a great deal of apprehension and discomfort at these sessions. In addition, a number of parents have reported that since they are not professional people they feel somewhat ill equipped to make a realistic contribution. Yet, because parents do represent a significant resource in the IEP conference, they must be made a contributing component of the planning delegation. Even though this is not an easy task to accomplish, there are procedures that can be used to facilitate the process:

- No more participants in the meeting than necessary should be allowed. Although individuals should not be denied admission when their contribution may be of benefit, neither should the composition of the group be obscured by a number of marginally involved persons.

- Nonessential and nonproductive "professionalism" should be removed from the session. In particular, an informal and friendly conference style can most effectively create an atmosphere of warmth for parents.

- Parents should be persuaded to bring a friend or confidant to the conference, particularly someone who is familiar with the IEP process.

- Parents should have at least one professional person with whom they are familiar and to whom they can relate at the conference. It is simply unrealistic to assume that parents can enter into a group of professional strangers, without the benefit of having at least one previously established relationship, and function as a contributing member of an IEP team.

The mother of the recently identified retarded child reported that she felt the same anxiety at entering her son's IEP conference as she does "when I walk into my dentist's office." She reported being particularly overwhelmed at "entering a roomful of strangers who knew more about Arnie than I did." Although she acknowledged that periodically someone would ask for her opinion, she reported that she felt too intimidated to respond "even though later on I wish I had since I knew some things they didn't." This mother later reported that "if I had just known someone at the meeting or if I had someone to go with me I wouldn't have felt so scared."

The Need for Training

In order for parents to be meaningful and legitimate IEP conference participants, they must be provided appropriate training. As was suggested earlier, it is extremely unrealistic to assume that parents of exceptional children can function in a productive manner with professionals to develop an IEP for their child if they lack adequate training and experience. A 1978 study by the National Education Association endorsed the need for this type of systematic training, noting that only with such instruction could parents be expected to fulfill their responsibilities.

Goldstein, Strickland, Turnbull, and Curry (1980) reported that parental participation was limited in their study of parents of mildly handicapped mainstreamed children. These researchers also suggested the need for parental training, noting that "The implications of this study point to the need for systematically training parents to fulfill their roles and responsibilities associated with IEP involvement and for training professionals to involve parents as *full* partners in this significant educational task" (p. 285).

Turnbull and Strickland (1981) identified specific procedures for facilitating the participation of parents in IEP conferences. Included were strategies for involving parents in active decision making, training sessions to prepare parents in fulfilling their roles and responsibilities in the IEP conference, and specific suggestions for facilitating their actual participation during the session.

Again, as has been suggested previously, parents must be given instruction in serving as members of the educational planning team. As noted by McAfee and Vergason (1979) "The issue is not whether parents should be involved, nor the extent of involvement, but rather how the situation can be structured to best utilize parents in efforts to maximize the educational achievement of children" (p. 4). These efforts must include planned and sequenced parental training activities.

CONCLUSION

For decades, parents were required to shoulder the task of raising and educating their handicapped children alone. Presently, however, both parents and professionals are being aided in their common task of providing appropriate services to handicapped children and youth by a series of laws, legislative positions, and court decrees. However, these elements are nothing more than tools and, as such, must be employed to facilitate the development of services and programs for handicapped children and youth. This tooling process, if it is to be successful, cannot be based exclusively on litigation contingencies but rather on a partnership whereby parents and educators plan together for the common good of children. Accordingly, procedures guaranteeing mere minimal legislative compliance will not be sufficient in and of themselves to produce desired results. Without an emphasis on the development of parent-educator relationships, the level and quality of involvement necessary to ensure the educational gains possible for every pupil will not be achieved.

Exercises

1. Prepare a handbook on P.L. 94-142 for parents of the children in your classroom.
2. Prepare a list of procedures that you could use in training parents to serve more effectively as advocates for their children and in becoming more involved participants in IEP conferences.
3. Conduct a simulated due process hearing.
4. Conduct a simulated IEP conference using the role-playing materials provided in Appendix C. Since these simulation scripts are extensions of those presented for previous simulation exercises, you should continue with the same materials (i.e., mentally retarded, physically handicapped, learning disabled, behavior-

ally disordered, or gifted). In conducting this exercise, one individual should assume the part of the parent. Another person, taking the part of the teacher, should structure his or her response around the educator materials. These materials, although in need of refinement, will serve to structure the content of the conference. Although individuals assuming the parent's role have not been provided script materials, they should participate in the conference by reacting to IEP suggestions made by the teacher and through using the simulation materials provided for the initial conference exercise (Appendix A). A third individual should assume the role of evaluator, using the evaluation form provided.

As a part of the session, educators should complete the IEP form that has been provided. Individuals should change roles after completing the exercise.

NOTE

[1]Courtesy of Jody Huxman, used with permission.

REFERENCES

Brown, L., Nietupski, J., & Hamre-Nietupski, S. Criterion of ultimate functioning. In M.A. Thomas (Ed.) *Hey, don't forget about me*. Reston, Va.: Council for Exceptional Children, 1976.

Deno, E. Special education as developmental capital. *Exceptional Children,* 1970, *37,* 229-237.

Dunn, L.M. Special education for the mentally retarded—Is much of it justifiable? *Exceptional Children,* 1968, *35,* 5-21.

Goldstein, S., Strickland, B., Turnbull, A., & Curry, L. An observational analysis of the IEP conference. *Exceptional Children,* 1980, *46*(4), 278-286.

Kroth, R.L. *Communicating with parents of exceptional children*. Denver: Love Publishing, 1975.

Kroth, R.L., & Simpson, R.L. *Parent conferences as a teaching strategy*. Denver: Love Publishing, 1977.

MacMillan, D.L. *Mental retardation in school and society*. Boston: Little, Brown, 1977.

McAfee, J.K., & Vergason, G.A. Parent involvement in the process of special education: Establishing the new partnership. *Focus on Exceptional Children,* 1979, *11*(2), 1-15.

McKinnon, A. Parent and pupil perceptions of special classes for emotionally disturbed children. *Exceptional Children,* 1970, *37,* 302-303.

Meyen, E.L. *Exceptional children and youth*. Denver: Love Publishing, 1978.

National Association for Retarded Citizens. *The right to choose*. Arlington, Tex.: Author, 1973.

National Education Association. *Education for all handicapped children: Consensus, conflict, and challenge*. Washington, D.C. Author, 1978.

Parents Campaign for Handicapped Children and Youth. *Closer Look*. Washington, D.C.: Author, 1977.

Pennsylvania Association for Retarded Children (PARC) v. *Commonwealth of Pennsylvania,* 343 F. Supp. 279 (E.D.Pa., 1972).

Rutherford, R.B., & Edgar, E. *Teachers and parents: A guide to interaction and cooperation*. Boston: Allyn & Bacon, 1979.

Stephens, T.M. Teaching learning and behavioral disordered students in least restrictive environments. *Behavioral Disorders*, 1977, 2(3), 146-151.

Turnbull, A.P., & Strickland, B. Parents and the educational system. In J.L. Paul (Ed.), *Understanding and working with parents of children with special needs*. New York: Holt, Rinehart & Winston, 1981.

Turnbull, H.R., & Turnbull, A. *Free appropriate public education: Law and implementation*. Denver: Love Publishing, 1978.

Wallace, G., & Larsen, S.L. *Educational assessment of learning problems: Testing for teachers*. Boston: Allyn & Bacon, 1978.

Whelan, R.J. Special education procedural due process checklist. Unpublished manuscript, University of Kansas, Lawrence, 1980.

Chapter 11

Progress Report Conferences

Individual parent-educator conferences that focus on students' school progress are among the most common and significant of all parent-professional interactions. These sessions serve to allow for the clarification of information exchanged via less formal means (e.g., notes and grade cards) and to allow for the direct dissemination of information relevant to a pupil's education. In addition, progress report conferences allow for an informal evaluation of individualized education program (IEP) goals and objectives and as a mechanism for maintaining contact between parents and educators.

While there may be disagreement regarding the most appropriate timing for the progress report conference, there is consensus that these sessions should be held on a regular basis. Kelly (1974) suggested that these meetings should at least coincide with report card or grade reporting schedules and that they not be exclusively held at times of crisis. It is also agreed that these conferences should be scheduled to meet the individual needs of parents and pupils. Just as exceptional students are provided individualized schedules that correspond to their unique needs, so must their parents be provided individually scheduled feedback conferences.

Even though the professionals' preparation for and skill in the progress report conference will be significant, it is important to note that the most crucial factor related to a favorable conference outcome will be the success of previous parent-educator contacts (Schulz, 1978). In particular, it is somewhat unrealistic to expect a completely satisfactory progress reporting session if prior positive contacts, including a mutually fulfilling IEP and initial conference, were not provided. In such instances it is highly probable that parents will lack the trust and/or prior information required for effective participation. Consequently, the educator must recognize the cumulative nature of parent-educator interactions and in particular that regardless of the skill of the educator in conducting the conference, success will be dependent on prior positive contact.

DISSEMINATING CHILD PROGRESS INFORMATION

The specific agenda for each progress report conference will be dictated by a variety of factors, including the nature and severity of a pupil's exceptionality and the needs of the parents. However, there are several common areas that should be examined as a part of each session. These areas include a cursory review of factors associated with the diagnosis and intervention procedures employed with each pupil. In addition, academic growth and performance, social/behavioral factors, and educationally related physical variables should be discussed.

Parents should be provided prior written or verbal notice of the nature and purpose of the conference and the areas that will be reviewed. In addition, this prior notice should inform the parents that they will be allowed to discuss any concerns related to their child's program that they may have. Thus, the conferencer should be able to structure the session without communicating to parents that all aspects have been predetermined. Without this direct message parents may either assume that they have no input into the direction of the conference or may attempt to discuss matters that would be more appropriately dealt with in other types of conferences.

Structuring the Conference

Especially with parents who may be relatively unfamiliar with special education and their child's specific educational or treatment program, an overview of the events that led to the pupil's diagnosis and placement in a program and the current status of the program should be provided. While the degree of attention given this phase of the conference will depend largely on the familiarity of individual parents with this information, each conference should include this material. Specifically, this should include a cursory examination of the factors and issues that led to a referral for evaluation. This information on the presenting problems should be followed by a cursory review of diagnostic findings, the pupil's IEP, the educational and intervention program being used, and a summary evaluative statement. The intent of this overview is to provide the parents an overview of the somewhat complicated process that led to the diagnosis and placement of their child and the nature and efficacy of the resulting intervention program. In addition, parents should be provided an opportunity to raise issues or ask questions about any of these factors.

Providing Parents Feedback on Academic Progress

Independent of the presence or type of an exceptionality, parents will be concerned with the academic progress of their child. Hence, even in instances in which a program modification was implemented for other than learning problems, parents will still want information on their child's academic performance. Academic, in this context, refers not only to traditional school-related subjects and skills but also to self-help, prevocational, vocational, and similar areas.

The format for disseminating academic information to parents will be similar to that used in providing a general progress report overview. The exception will of course be that the content will relate specifically to academic and academically related performance. Accordingly, parents should first be provided with a brief review of the academic problems existing prior to the program modification and the diagnostic findings relative to this exceptionality. This process is designed to establish a historical basis for the intervention program and to aid the parents in more adequately understanding the nature of the exceptionality. The extent to which this content area will be discussed will be based on the parents' needs and interest, the characteristics of the academic exceptionality, and the general familiarity of the parents with this information. Consequently, a conferencer may invest relatively little time in discussing this topic with parents whose child has grade-level academic skills or with parents who have had opportunities to discuss the diagnosis and diagnostic implications prior to the conference. Thus, it is essential that the educator be able to gauge the needs of parents in this area accurately, taking care to provide sufficient information to answer their questions and to form a basis for other components of the interpretation process without excessively reviewing materials with which they are familiar.

An aspect of this interpretation and review will be to discuss with parents those tests and procedures that were employed in the diagnostic process. Since these procedures will at least in part consist of formal, standardized tests that will have been administered by other than classroom teachers, the classroom teacher, if he or she is to conduct the interpretation, must be familiar with the measures and the manner in which they were used in the evaluation process.

The ability to review test data and interpret diagnostic findings to parents (especially standardized assessment measure data) will necessitate the conferencer having a thorough knowedge of the instruments being discussed. Since standardized procedures are designed to compare a child's performance with normative data, it is imperative to the accurate interpretation of this data that the professional be thoroughly familiar with the procedures being discussed. This must include a knowledge of the standardization samples regarding the reliability, validity, and adaptability of the procedure for use with exceptional children and youth. Only when the conferencer has this information should an attempt be made to interpret test data to parents. Individuals lacking this background should request assistance from individuals with specific expertise in this area.

Conferencers who may lack formal training in administering and interpretating standardized tests and formal measures should also recognize that informal assessment results, trial teaching findings, and other criterion referenced assessment data will not only be more easily disseminated by teachers but may also be far more meaningful to parents. Above all, the conferencer should remember that the intent of reviewing assessment procedures will be to recapitulate for the parents, in language they can understand, the nature of the problems existing at the time of referral for special service and the nature of the evaluation findings relative to these problems. Wallace and Larsen (1978) noted several advantages to informal procedures, which also serve as strengths during the process of disseminating information to parents. These strengths include the similarity of the assessment items to the skills that are under development in the classroom, the involvement of the classroom teacher in the assessment procedure, the relative ease of administering and interpreting informal techniques, and the wide range of skills that can be evaluated. The reliance on informal measures, including a review of the "Present Levels of Educational Performance" section of the IEP, should also aid the conferencer in minimizing the use of esoteric diagnostic findings and in facilitating the dissemination of functional information. As suggested by Deno (1971), the commitment of the educator "should be to make the assessment as worthwhile as we can in terms of its contribution to improved learning on the part of the child" (p. 3). Certainly this same commitment must also guide the educator in his or her interpretation of assessment information to parents.

After discussing the nature of a child's academic exceptionality with the parents, the conferencer should shift to an analysis of the academic intervention or curriculum modification program and the effect that this system has had on the child. In particular, this process will involve a discussion of the academic remediation model, curriculum, and programming procedures in use and the measured efficacy of these treatments. Although the progress reporting conference is not exclusively designed to serve as an IEP evaluation session, an interpretation of academic progress can be facilitated through following the format established on the IEP. That is, each annual goal should be presented to the parents for review and discussion. Following a discussion of each annual goal should be a statement of the various short-term academic objectives that were developed to accomplish the annual goal and the means for accomplishing each objective. Finally, the conferencer should discuss with the parents the effectiveness with which the curriculum or academic remediation program was able to achieve the desired goals. This model for disseminating information is shown in Figure 11-1.

Again, it is obvious that there are situations in which aspects of academic progress reports may be somewhat independent of a child's IEP; however, for most situations, academic progress can best be disseminated through adherence to the IEP model. This process has the major advantage of making use of an instrument in which it is hoped that parents have had prior input. In addition, this strategy allows for an interpretation of progress made on a previously agreed-upon approach. In particular this can serve as a demonstration that the conferencer is truly following a joint parent-educator plan. While this message is frequently given to parents, the present strategy represents one means for actually demonstrating the authenticity of the message.

Figure 11-1 Model for Disseminating Academic Progress Information to Parents

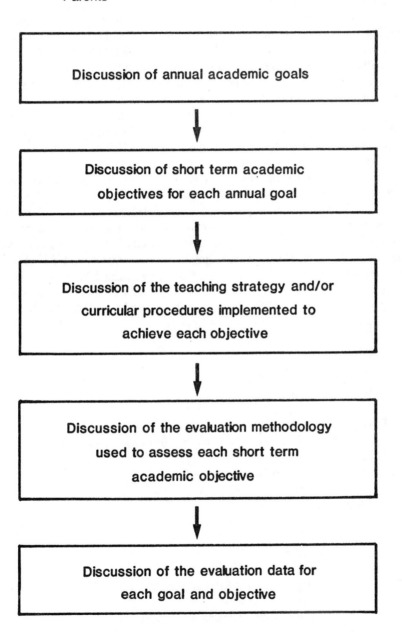

Discussion of annual academic goals

Discussion of short term academic objectives for each annual goal

Discussion of the teaching strategy and/or curricular procedures implemented to achieve each objective

Discussion of the evaluation methodology used to assess each short term academic objective

Discussion of the evaluation data for each goal and objective

Providing Parents Feedback on Social Progress

In addition to requiring information on their child's academic performance, parents are also interested in their child's social functioning. The format for providing this information is similar to that used for disseminating academic progress. That is, the interpretation should involve a discussion of a child's school social history and any particular behavioral or social problems associated with the referral for program modification. This information should be followed by a discussion of the assessment findings relative to these problems, the intervention procedures employed to manage these concerns, and an evaluation of these procedures. Just as with academic functioning, this dissemination process can be facilitated, at least in part, through an interpretation of IEP annual and short-term social goals and objectives.

The conferencer should also be able to comment on social or behavioral problems that have developed since the time of referral or placement. Patterns of conduct disturbance, shyness, immaturity, or social withdrawal, particularly when representative of a marked change in behavior, should be items for discussion. While educators are encouraged to discuss these social patterns with parents when they are first observed rather than to hold them as agenda items for a scheduled progress dissemination conference, they frequently can be dealt with at regularly scheduled progress sessions. Particular social/behavioral patterns that the conferencer will want to be sensitive to include the twenty items listed below:

1. Rejection by peers
2. Shyness
3. Preoccupation
4. Excessive daydreaming
5. Social withdrawal
6. Excessive anxiety
7. Depression
8. Inability or unwillingness to sustain effort and complete tasks
9. Confusion
10. Rigid patterns of behavior
11. Extreme sensitivity
12. Patterns of regression
13. Truant or chronic tardiness
14. Impulsiveness
15. Physical aggression
16. Defiance
17. Responses suggesting that rules and regulations only apply to others
18. Disruptiveness
19. Difficulty in responding to authority figures
20. Hostility

While the above list is in no way complete, it does suggest those general patterns of behavior to which educators should be sensitive and to which appropriate attention should be given in parent-educator conferences. In discussing this information it is important that the educational conferencer not attempt to place the responsibility for a social problem with parents. While it is of course appropriate to apprise parents of the nature of a classroom social behavior and to solicit information on the nature and cause of the problem, it is essential that the conferencer also provide a possible solution or intervention strategy. While it is justifiable for the conferencer to suggest ways in which the parents can be involved in the program, it is grossly inappropriate for a school-based social problem to be identified in the absence of a possible solution or for the conferencer to attempt to make the parents responsible for arriving at a solution to the problem.

It is also important that when social/behavioral excesses, deficits, or other problems are identified in the progress reporting conference that they be presented in a empirical fashion. That is, rather than relating to parents that their child is "defiant," "withdrawn," "hyperactive," or "inattentive," for example, without an adequate explanation of the nature and extent of the problem, a more scientifically based analysis of the situation should be provided. This may take the form of a line or bar graph that illustrates the nature and significance of a particular social behavior or similar procedure. The important element is that the parents be able to understand the nature of the problem and that they be convinced that the professionals have thoroughly analyzed the situation. In addition, the data presented must demonstrate that the child's behavior represents a change and/or that the pattern is outside the classroom norm. This can probably best be achieved by offering a comparison of the child's behavior with that of his peers. Finally, this process can serve as the basis for entering into a discussion of the intervention strategy that has been formulated and later as a means of evaluating the procedure. An example of one situation in which this empirically based interpretation process was employed follows.

A nine-year-old fourth grader was of concern to his teacher because of his erratic completion of assignments. The teacher noted that the child was a disruptive element in the classroom but that he "had good potential." With regard to completing assignments, the teacher was most concerned about his chronic failure to hand in written assignments. In preparation for a progress reporting conference, the teacher began keeping a record of the daily English, spelling, social studies, and writing papers completed and handed in within the appropriate class periods on the given day assigned. The measure did not include homework assignments nor did it impose quality criterion for the material submitted.

The teacher found that the child's mean percent of completing assignments was 31.2 percent, while that of the other class members was 88 percent. The teacher noted, however, that there were differences in his rate of assignment completion as a function of his becoming aware that he was being observed. In particular, his mean rate of performance prior to becoming aware of being observed was 21 percent; this rate increased to 55.6 percent after he determined that his behavior was under scrutiny.

During the regularly scheduled parent-teacher conference this information was shared with the parents, along with a proposed strategy for managing the problem. It was explained to the parents that the child would be exposed to a three-point reinforcement program to increase his number of completed assignments. It was explained that this program would involve (1) social reinforcement immediately following his submission of papers; (2) a self-charting program; and (3) the privilege of being the "teacher's errand boy" on days when at least 90 percent of his assignments were completed. At a follow-up conference, the results of this program, shown in Figure 11-2, were shown to the parents.

Providing Parents Feedback on Physical Progress

Parents of children and youth for whom a physical exceptionality is the basis for a program modification or curriculum adaptation will of course be interested in receiving feedback in this domain. In such cases, a format similar to that employed in the academic and social/behavioral areas should be used. That is, the educational impact of the physical exceptionality and the diagnostic findings relative to the handicap should be discussed with parents. This information should be followed by a discussion of the intervention and curriculum strategies that are being employed to deal with the problem and the efficacy of these strategies. Just as with other progress report components, the parents' interpretation should be based on each child's IEP.

While the majority of exceptional children and youth will be receiving services for other than physical problems, it is nonetheless important for the educational conferencer not to dismiss routinely this category of information as unrelated. Indeed, even in situations in which a child's exceptionality is thought to be a cognitive or social problem, the conferencer should consider the physical domain in preparing for the parent feedback conference. Included should be sensitivity to possible sensory problems. Items from the Keystone-Mast, Inc. Checklist for Visual Difficulties should be considered. Examples of items from this scale are shown below:

Appearance of the Eyes

☐ Eyes crossed—turning in or out at any time
☐ Reddened eyes
☐ Watering eyes
☐ Encrusted eyelids
☐ Frequent tearing

Figure 11-2 Results of Program to Increase the Completion of Written Assignments

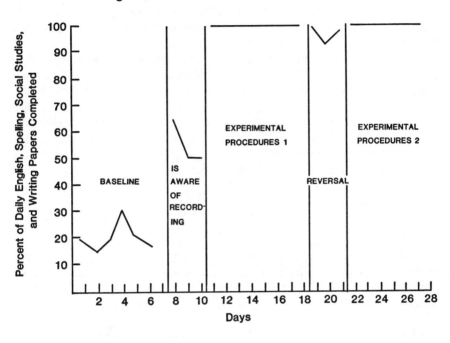

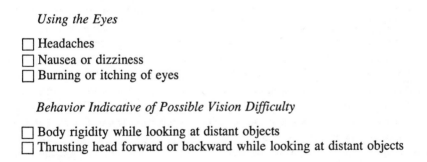

Using the Eyes

☐ Headaches
☐ Nausea or dizziness
☐ Burning or itching of eyes

Behavior Indicative of Possible Vision Difficulty

☐ Body rigidity while looking at distant objects
☐ Thrusting head forward or backward while looking at distant objects

The educator should be equally as sensitive to possible signs of hearing impairment. Signs such as language delay, deviant speech patterns, inattentiveness, erratic school performance, apparent inability to follow oral directions, confusion, and cupping of hands behind ears or favoring one ear in conversations are potentially educationally significant and should be both discussed with the parents and professionally evaluated.

In preparation for the progress dissemination conference, the educator should also be sensitive to other physically related symptoms, signs, and patterns that may require further investigation. For example, indications of substance abuse or dependence, illnesses, frequent school absence or tardiness, signs of extreme fatigue, poor gross and/or fine motor coordination, enuresis, encopresis, and slovenly physical appearance are all potentially significant indicators and thus become necessary items for discussion with parents. While the educator may simply request information from parents regarding these patterns, it is mandatory that the conferencer be ready to suggest a method for acquiring further information regarding the situation or an intervention strategy for dealing with the problem. While ownership of problems (Kroth, 1975) must be clarified, it is nonetheless necessary for professionals to avoid presenting educationally significant problems and concerns without also offering intervention alternatives.

THE PROGRESS REPORT CONFERENCE

In addition to having a set dissemination format for providing parents information, the educational conferencer must have an appropriate style, guidelines, and methods for structuring and transmitting data. These skills should both allow for the effective transmission of information and for the successful disposition of problems and issues that may arise in the course of a session.

Satisfying the Information Needs of Parents Through a Discussion Process

According to Langton and Stout (1954), progress reporting conferences are designed to allow parents and educators an opportunity to discuss a child's school behavior and academic performance. Although these conferences are designed as an opportunity for sharing, the typical progress report conference has been typified by a one-way flow of information (Redl & Wattenberg, 1959). Consequently, the conferencer must be assured that the session represents a discussion process. That is, while some individuals may consider the progress reporting conference to be a one-way communication exchange in which parents are solely the receivers of educational data, the process can only be successful when it involves educators and parents discussing and sharing information, attitudes, concerns, and positions. As noted by Chinn, Winn, and Walters (1978), effective communication requires interaction. Furthermore, they noted that "through a 'two-way' process we are able to learn from one another, share our ideas, provide feedback and enhance the probability that quality communication will take place" (p. 60). It is essential then that the educational conferencer not lose sight of this basic fact and that regardless of time restraint and the amount of information to be dispensed that the educator *discuss* information with parents rather than serving as a lecturer. In particular, this will involve being sensitive to the emotions and feelings of the parents and to the goal of achieving a satisfactory state of understanding. Specifically, this will involve being attentive to questions presented by the parents and to making them a sharer in the progress report rather than exclusively a receiver.

Notifying Parents of the Progress Report Conference

Although it might be logically argued that a professional text should not deal with matters as mundane as getting parents to attend conferences, the fact remains that lack of attendance is a major problem confronting educational conferencers. Since it is obvious that progress conferences cannot proceed without parents being present, educators must identify procedures for securing the presence of parents at these meetings.

First, it must be recognized that parents will be motivated to attend parent-educator conferences only after having been exposed to prior reinforcing experiences with school professionals. Therefore, it is necessary that the conferencer recognize that successfully conducted initial conferences, IEP planning sessions, problem-solving meetings, and other contacts with parents will all serve to promote the attendance and participation of the parents in progress report conferences. As part of American Education Week, the Sandpoint, Idaho, public schools organized a "substitute student day." This involved having parents attend school for one day in place of their sons and daughters. This or similar programs should serve to sensitize parents to their child's educational program and should facilitate the development of rapport upon which attendance and participation in parent-educator conferences is based.

Clements and Simpson (1974) reported that parents were most responsive to handwritten notices of scheduled parent-educator conferences that were sent through the mail. These researchers also noted that parental attendance at conferences was increased when transportation and a baby-sitting service was provided.

Other considerations can also serve to promote the attendance of parents:

- Provide sufficient notice of the scheduled conference for parents to plan accordingly. This may involve announcing the schedule for the progress conference early in the school year and then following up at a later time with a letter regarding the specific schedule for the conference. These announcements should specify the time and place of the meeting, time allotted, topics to be discussed, and specific expectations for the parents. Parents should also have input into scheduling the time of the conference.

- Employ whatever means are necessary to be assured that parents know how to reach the site of the conference. Maps, guides, or well-planned directions should be provided if necessary.

- Identify community resources that can facilitate the participation of parents in conferences. Agencies providing transportation and baby-sitting are particularly important.

- Be willing to conduct the session in the parents' home, if necessary.

Allotting the Correct Amount of Time for the Conference

Ideally, the conferencer should be able to individualize the time requirements of each conference to best meet the needs of parents and pupils. However, administrative personnel frequently schedule progress conferences, including time allotments, for entire buildings or districts. Consequently, the conferencer may not have a major role in determining the amount of time available for the conference. At a minimum, no less than 20 minutes should be available. In addition, it is suggested that a time limit be established for the session. This frequently will serve to keep both parents and professionals "on task." In addition, there is good evidence that setting time limits serves to facilitate growth and reduce irrelevant discussions (Shlien, Mosak & Dreikurs, 1962). Parents should of course be advised that additional time can be provided at a later date if required. In particular, the limited time available for most progress conferences may require that follow-up sessions be scheduled to deal with special problems or other agenda items that the parent or conferencer may wish to discuss.

Preconference Planning

The success of the parent-educator progress report conference will be highly correlated with preconference planning efforts (Barsch, 1969). These planning efforts should involve attention to the following:

- The child's records, including the IEP and previous parent-educator conference notes, should be reviewed carefully.

- An outline of those items to be discussed should be prepared.

- The conferencer should review standardized test data that may need to be reinterpreted to the parents.

- A careful selection of papers and work samples should be made in preparation for the conference. These samples should be representative and illustrative of particular concepts and should be dated and sequentially arranged for comparative purposes.

- Parents should be provided a folder of their child's work to take with them after the conference. This work sample should be representative of their child's performance and consistent with feedback provided by the conferencer. Evaluative comments should be provided on the papers in order to aid parents in understanding the concepts being illustrated.

- The teacher should plan for an acceptable environment for the session. This should include a professional and confidential setting. In addition, the conferencer should make arrangements for adult-size furniture for all participants and pad and pencil for note taking.

- The parents should be prepared to participate in the conference. This important component will be addressed in depth at a later point in this chapter.

- The educator should prepare each child for the conference. This will basically consist of apprising the child of the purpose and nature of the session to be conducted with the parents and the materials to be reviewed. The pupil should be offered an opportunity for input into the agenda. Finally, it is recommended that participation of the pupil in the session be considered. In instances in which such participation is appropriate, the pupil should be provided training (e.g., information, discussion opportunities, and role playing) in participating in the conference.

These preliminary efforts can aid in reducing the anxiety of both the pupil and the parents.

Conducting the Conference

According to a number of practitioners and theorists, the parent-professional relationship is basic to effective communication (Ginott, 1957; Gordon, 1970). Consequently, as an integral component of the conferencing process, the educator must be able to establish and maintain rapport with parents. This relationship can be initiated by means of a warm greeting and a positive lead.

The conferencer should attempt to create as informal an atmosphere as possible. It is important that in addition to communicating aspects of a child's progress to the parents, the conferencer must also listen to parents. As noted previously, providing parents the opportunity of being exposed to a good listener is frequently the most effective relationship builder.

Other preliminary procedures include reviewing the purpose of the conference with parents and clarifying the role of the conferencer or other individuals involved in the session. That is, the sophisticated nature of educational service delivery systems and their related personnel may require some explanation for parents. Thus, for example, it is important for parents to recognize the role of a resource or consulting teacher and the manner in which this individual is a part of the service delivery team and impacts on students and their families. In addition, it is helpful for the conferencer to remind the parents of any time limitations for the session and that agenda items not covered in the time allotted or not related specifically to the progress conference can be dealt with at a later time. Finally, the conferencer, in initiating the meeting, should encourage the parents to participate in the session through asking questions or commenting on the observations of the educator or related matters that the parents have observed.

The conferencer should address areas of growth and progress prior to focusing on problem issues. This strategy should be employed throughout the various stages of the conference. That is, in the overview process and in reviewing the academic, social, and physical areas, the conferencer should address areas of success and growth prior to attending to less positive components. It is also important to realize that for these positive comments to have maximum impact, they must be specific. The conferencer must be able to specifically detail and document the nature of the gains shown by a child for this information to be most meaningful. Typically, this can be accomplished by showing the parents samples of work and curriculum completed by the child. As suggested previously, these materials should be given to parents to take home following the conference.

Following a review of growth components, parents should be apprised of the nature of areas of weakness or areas in which additional improvement is needed. It is suggested that this information, just as with growth feedback, be provided in clear and empirical terms. Especially with regard to social problems the conferencer must be able to explain and document the nature of a problem clearly. Thus, for example, the conferencer should be able to share a graph of the number of times a child is out of his or her seat without permission as opposed to telling parents that their child is "hyperactive" or "noncompliant." In addition, it is mandatory that the educator provide possible solutions to any weaknesses that are identified. That is, rather than only identifying a problem, the conferencer must also provide a possible solution. This process should also include allowing parents an opportunity to discuss the nature of the problem and to offer possible solutions. This will take the form of specifying what the educator intends to do to remediate the problem (e.g., "Jerry will work 20 minutes extra per day with the class aide on his math flash cards") and those things the parents can do, if they so desire, to aid in the solution to the problem (e.g., "I would like to start a note home system that will allow you to praise Sue Ellen daily for good social behavior"). Also to be included should be a time and mechanism for providing parents feedback on the effectiveness of the agreed-upon intervention strategy.

Although the conferencer will want to establish a warm and accepting atmosphere, where parents can feel free in expressing their concerns, it is important that professional ethics and decorum be maintained. In particular, parents should be given an opportunity to share concerns about their child and the individuals who work with their child without creating a forum for criticizing other educators, agencies, or school policy. The conferencer must thus be able to offer the parents an opportunity to be heard on matters related to their child's education without allowing parents an opportunity to gripe and gossip about issues only tantgentially related to the true factors under scrutiny. In instances in which parents focus on complaining about other teachers or educational personnel, it may be necessary to direct the discussion to more appropriate areas. In particular, the conferencer may wish to remind the parent that a limited amount of time is available for discussing their child and that they should attempt to focus on that task. While prompting the parents to attend to the conferencing task may be required in some situations, it is also important to note that parents must be given an opportunity to be heard, even if the subject of their discussion is not specifically related to their child's school progress. Consequently, the conferencer must not be too quick to direct the attention of parents away from a topic they consider worthy of discussion. Only in instances in which this focus dominates the session or when the intensity of the content raises ethical issues should the session be redirected. Given the nature and the frequency of this situation, the conferencer can listen to the concerns of the parents without agreeing, can refer the parent to the individual most able to effect some type of appropriate change (e.g., principal, school board member, hospital superintendent) and can employ subtle redirection techniques, such as reinforcing and attending to content more directly related to the session, as alternatives to direct confrontations regarding the appropriateness of content.

It is also significant for the conferencer to attempt to apply appropriate reinforcement procedures with parents. In particular, the educator should attempt not only to provide parents feedback concerning the progress of a child but also to reinforce parents for their efforts relative to specific gains or successfully implemented procedures. Thus, for example, in instances in which parents have functioned as tutors with their own children, positive feedback should be provided. As suggested by a number of authorities (Fine, 1980), parents have long been criticized by professionals but rarely praised for their positive efforts.

The conference should be concluded with a summary of the discussions that occurred. Included should be a brief review of the high points of the child's progress and a restatement of those activities that will be implemented to deal with identified weaknesses and problems. In particular, this should include an identification of role responsibility for the various programs to be followed, methodology for evaluating success, and the manner and dates for exchanging this information.

Just as the conference was initiated on a positive note, so should it be concluded. In particular, this should involve reinforcing the parents for their participation in the conference, extending an invitation for the parents to contact the conferencer when they experience a problem or require further information (this may, of course, involve scheduling a follow-up conference on the spot to discuss agenda items not covered or items not specifically related to the progress conference), and encouraging the parents to maintain their interest and participating attitude.

After the Conference Has Been Completed

Even though the conclusion of a parent-educator conference will most likely be celebrated through feelings of relief and possibly feelings of optimism and accomplishment, it is important to remember that the responsibilities of the conferencer do not end when the parents leave the session. Rather, the conferencer must attend to the following tasks: record the results of the session; provide feedback to other appropriate school or agency professionals; perform activities agreed upon in the conference and promptly provide feedback to parents regarding the results of these efforts; review the progress report conference with the child; and evaluate the conference.

Record Results

Making an accurate and meaningful record of the progress report conference is a basic professional skill that is integral to not only that particular conference but also future interactions. Since it is not at all unusual for significant and elaborate information to be exchanged and for cooperative intervention programs to be devised in parent-professional conferences, it is essential that information be placed in written form. Included in these written reports should be an integrated summary of discussions that ensued, including academic, emotional/social, and physical information exchanged. The conferencer should take care to present this information in a fashion reflective of the discussions and parent reactions that occurred in the session as opposed to providing only a summary of the child's progress. While the report should contain a summary of progress, it should also capture the interactions that occurred between the parent and professional.

The summary report should also make reference to recommendations that were made and the manner in which these recommendations will be implemented. Included should be items that later will be discussed at the annual IEP review meeting. Finally, the report should include reference to the individual responsible for carrying out each agreed-upon recommendation or activity, follow-up activities, and evaluation procedures.

Conferencers are cautioned to make records of discussions taking place in progress report conferences in as accurate a fashion as possible. Since professionals must be able to validate the accuracy of their reports and inferences, it is essential that extreme care be taken in preparing parent conference reports. As observed by Kroth and Simpson (1977) "some school records may contain potentially libelous material, and not only can parents challenge the accuracy of information contained in their child's record, but they also have legal recourse in situations where the recorded information provides an unsupported or damaging picture of the student" (p. 118). Consequently, it is mandatory that parent conference reports provide clear and functional summary information that is free of damaging data and inferences.

Provide Direct Feedback to Other Professionals

In addition to preparing a written report of the conference, the educator may wish to disseminate information to some individuals directly. This should occur especially in instances in which information may directly result in curriculum, attitude, or procedural modification and when there are questions regarding the degree to which information will be seen if available only in written form.

For example, a junior-high level learning disabilities resource room teacher learned from one of her student's parents during a progress report conference that their son had recently been started on a regimen of antihistamines for hayfever. She had noted that the child had been extremely lethargic and distractible for the past several weeks during the two hours he was in her resource program. Although this teacher was not aware that similar problems were occurring in the child's mainstreamed classes, she made individual visits to his other teachers following the conference to apprise them of his medical condition.

Again, it cannot be stressed enough that even in the best of programs, reports may go unseen by those individuals who most need the information. As a result, highly significant data should be disseminated in a face-to-face manner to ensure that in fact it is shared.

Perform Agreed-Upon Duties

While initial rapport and trust can be established through the use of basic interpersonal skills, ultimate satisfaction and trust in an educator and a program will come only with the performance of agreed-upon tasks and the communication of results to the parents. In the final analysis, delivery on promises will be the ultimate determinant of rapport.

Review the Results of the Conference with the Child

In instances in which a pupil is not a part of his or her own progress report conference, feedback should be provided by the teacher and/or parents. This feedback process should consist of providing the pupil with an overview of the items discussed, with progress results, and with recommendations made. As much as appropriate, the pupil should be exposed to the same format and information as the parents. Pupils should also be provided an opportunity to raise questions, to be made part of any problem-solving efforts, and to have input into the various recommendations. Among the most significant components in this process will be the need to stress to pupils that the purpose of the conference is to alert their parents of their school progress, an effort that will directly be of benefit to them, and that progress report conferences are routinely scheduled for all parents.

Evaluate the Conference

The evaluation of educational efforts is a byword of the decade. School and agency personnel, along with almost every other professional, are required to demonstrate the efficacy of their efforts. While assessment efforts may appear to be a cumbersome burden that requires unnecessarily extensive resources and that is associated with few positive gains, suggestions are that evaluative strategies serve to provide feedback necessary for change. Especially with regard to self-evaluation, the conferencer should be in a position of streamlining any assessment system such that it yields data directly associated with desired goals and objectives. This need for evaluative feedback is further highlighted by noting that personal satisfaction with a conference may not always be indicative of true success. Thus, a teacher who talks incessantly during a conference may conclude that the session, from this teacher's perspective, was a success. However, in spite of this personal feeling of satisfaction, the teacher may have given the parents few opportunities to voice an opinion or offer information and may have actually failed to provide certain basic information. Consequently, the conferencer should, as a regular part of each conference, conduct an evaluation of the session. As noted by Carkhuff and Berenson (1976) "at every point where the helpers intervened in the lives of their helpees, the effects could be 'for better or for worse' " (p. 16).

One suggested procedure for obtaining this feedback is provided in Exhibit 11-1. This instrument can be used as a self-evaluation measure or as a means of allowing one's colleagues (or the parents!) to provide feedback. This procedure can also serve as a preconference checklist for reminding the educator of those specific components that should be addressed.

RESPONDING TO QUESTIONS FROM PARENTS

Parents of exceptional children will have questions regarding their child and the future long after an initial diagnosis has been made and special educational provisions have been provided. Consequently, the conferencer should expect that questions will arise in the course of the progress report conference that may or may not be directly related to the professionals' agenda. While it is, of course, important for the conferencer to keep the discussions related to the task at hand, it is also mandatory that the educator address the issues and questions raised by parents. As a result, the professional must be able to contain the content of the session within certain parameters without being so rigid as to extinguish items not associated with the preconference agenda. Making this discrimination while at the same time providing appropriate feedback to parents, all within a somewhat unrealistic period of time, can in no way be considered an easy task.

Perhaps one of the more important points that the conferencer must be reminded of is that parents may raise a "question" for which they are not seeking a response

Exhibit 11-1 Progress Report Conference Evaluation Procedure

Date: _____

Pupil's Name: _____

Conferencer: _____

Person completing evaluation: _____

		Yes	No	Needs Improvement
I.	Preconference evaluation:			
A.	Was the conferencer familiar with the pupil and family's background and related information, including the IEP?			
B.	Was an agenda developed and followed?			
C.	Was a review of previous test data conducted such that a reinterpretation of results could be conducted if necessary?			
D.	Was a folder of the pupil's representative work prepared for the parents?			
E.	Was an adequate environment prepared for the conferencer?			
F.	Was the pupil prepared for the conference?			
G.	Were the parents prepared to participate in the conference?			
H.	Was sufficient time allotted for the session?			
I.	Were the parents appropriately notified of the conference?			
II.	General conferencing evaluation:			
A.	Were the parents appropriately informed of the purpose of the conference?			

Exhibit 11-1 continued

	Yes	No	Needs Improve- ment
B. Was the session conducted in a systematic and sequential manner?			
C. Was the conferencer able to keep the interview flowing and on course?			
D. Did the conferencer provide the parent with an opportunity to ask questions?			
E. Was the conferencer able to attend to the parent rather than to notes?			
F. Did the conferencer appropriately rephrase when necessary?			
G. Did the conferencer summarize the session?			
III. Evaluation of specific conference content:			
A. Was the conferencer able to provide a general progress report to the parents?			
B. Was the conferencer able to provide an adequate report of academic progress?			
C. Was the conferencer able to interpret previously administered tests/evaluation procedures?			
D. Was the conferencer able to explain the pupil's academic program (remediation strategy) to the parents?			
E. Was the conferencer able to interpret the pupil's success as a function of the academic program (remediation strategy)?			
F. Was the conferencer able to interpret to the parents the future progressions/expectations for the pupil?			

Exhibit 11-1 continued

	Yes	No	Needs Improvement
G. Was the conferencer able to provide an adequate report of social/emotional progress?			
H. Was the conferencer able to provide the parents with a remediation plan if a social/emotional problem was targeted?			
I. Was the conferencer able to provide an adequate report of physical progress?			
J. Was the conferencer able to solicit and respond to questions raised by the parents?			
K. Was the conferencer able to identify information that would later be used to amend the pupil's IEP?			
IV. Additional comments			

but which will provide them an opportunity to redirect the session. Thus, for example, a parent who asks "Why is our child retarded?" may wish to offer his or her own perceptions. On one occasion this very question was raised by a parent. When the conferencer noted that that was a difficult question that had many possibilities, and asked the parent for her perceptions, the mother related that she believed that it was related to her heavy cigarette smoking during pregnancy. She revealed that both her mother-in-law and father-in-law chided her for smoking during her pregnancy with the child and specifically warned her that such behavior could produce mental retardation, poor health, or small stature in children. Although the mother had previously been told that her smoking was not the responsible agent for her son's handicap, and thus did not need another professional to repeat the message, she did feel a strong need to talk about the situation. As revealed in this example, the conferencer must attempt to determine when parents desire information and when they need someone to listen to them. As noted by Benjamin (1969), "Not every question calls for an answer, but every question demands respectful listening and usually a personal reaction on our part" (p. 74).

Frequently conferencers observe that they are asked to respond to "difficult" or "sensitive" questions only after having had several prior meetings with the parents. That is, only after rapport and trust have been satisfactorily established will parents feel sufficiently comfortable in sharing information of this type with the conferencer. Thus, the conferencer should perceive the asking of these difficult questions, many of which have no answers, as a sign of rapport and a request for the professional to listen to the parent.

Attwell and Clabby (1971) identified a list of common questions (with suggested responses) that parents of mentally retarded children are likely to ask. Among those questions most frequently asked are those referring to cause, why the condition affected their child or family, whether or not their other children will have a similar condition, and the impact of the child's condition on their children and family. As noted previously, the situation demands that the professional be sensitive to the nature of the question and whether it is a request for information or an opportunity to talk.

PREPARING PARENTS TO PARTICIPATE IN THE CONFERENCE

With ever-increasing frequency parents are being asked and expected to participate actively and productively with professionals in developing and maintaining appropriate educational services for their children. As a result of the work of parent groups, legislators, and other forces, parents have been awarded the rights and privileges commensurate with a colleague relationship. More than ever before professionals seem to be adopting Hobbs' (1975) position that professionals must learn to be consultants to parents. Some researchers, such as McAfee and Vergason (1979), have focused on more immediate and practical issues. In particular, they suggest that "The issue is not whether parents should be involved, nor the extent of involvement but rather, how the situation can be structured to best utilize parents in efforts to maximize the educational achievement of children" (p. 4). With respect to progress report conference participation, this approach suggests the need to prepare parents to engage in planning and participating in the various activities associated with their child's educational program. This must include information on being a legitimate component of the parent-educator progress report conference. As noted by Simpson and Poplin (1981), "In order for the educational program of a child to be truly a joint effort between home and school, parents must be supplied the knowledge to be effective treatment surrogates and to effect change within given school situations'' (p. 24).

Accordingly, greater emphasis has been placed on making parents more acceptable conference participants. In pursuit of this goal, Turnbull (1978) suggested that educators prepare parents for conferences by equipping them with questions to think about prior to the session. Turnbull included questions about the skills the parents are most interested in the child developing, the strengths and weaknesses of the child, and other related information.

Without doubt, parents can be trained to engage in conference activities that will facilitate their participation. Listed below are suggestions that educators may wish to provide parents to aid them in becoming more functional conference participants.

- Arrange your schedule so that you can arrive on time; if you are not familiar with the school or neighborhood ask for directions or secure a map of the area.

- Arrange for a sitter for your other children. Nothing is more disruptive to a conference than children who distract the educator and parent.

- Determine how much time has been allotted for the session and stay within that time frame. If you are not able to complete your business within that period you can make another appointment.

- Discuss the upcoming conference with your spouse and the child. Ask for input from these individuals, especially if they will not be in attendance. If you feel comfortable with the idea, discuss with the educator the possibility of including your child in the conference. A number of educators recommend including students in their own conferences. This strategy may demonstrate to the pupil that the responsiblity for an education is a personal one. It also eliminates the problems associated with disseminating second-hand information to the pupil.

- Do not gossip about other teachers, students, or families. However, be candid in relating information that may be beneficial to the teacher.

- Review any notes and school documents (including the child's IEP) that you have prior to the conference.

- Bring a written list of questions and items that you want to discuss with the teacher. Do not rely on your memory. Included should be information related to academic, social/emotional, and physical areas. Specific questions, such as "Is he reading at grade level?", "What is his reading level compared with children his age who are in the regular classroom?", "Do you have disciplinary problems with Sue?", "How do you discipline Hector?" can all be useful in eliciting specific feedback.

- Do not come to the conference looking for a fight or an apology from the teacher for the child's school-related problems. Rather arrive at the conference ready to work for the benefit of the child. However, if you feel the professional is in error or does not understand the entire situation, share information that you have. Nonetheless, you should constantly be looking for ways to resolve conflicts and to solve problems associated with your child's educational program.

- Make a list of information you believe should be shared with the child's teacher and other professionals. Included should be particular likes and dislikes and attitudes of the child and specific information that may aid the teacher in better understanding the child's particular situation.

- Take notes during the conference. After the conference attempt to summarize the important points and happenings that took palce.

- Praise the teacher and educational system for things they do well.

- If the conferencer uses a term or concept that you are unfamiliar with, ask for an explanation.

- Accept responsibility for problems that are yours. Likewise, follow through with any plans or activities that you agree to.

- Do not expect the conferencer to solve your personal problems or those of your family. The person conducting the progress report conference will most likely be a teacher. Although educators may be able to make referrals they are not family therapists.

This list is of course far from comprehensive. Messineo and Sleeman (1977), for example, developed a protocol form for aiding parents in gathering information and structuring their participation in conferences. Above all, the educator must be reminded that the maximum growth of a child will be facilitated by parents and educators working together. However, in order for parents to be most productive in conferences they must be provided appropriate training. As suggested by Drucker (1976), parents who are educated in school-related matters will be more satisfied with the system because they will have been involved in the establishment of its design.

CONCLUSION

Progress report conferences remain among the most common of all parent-educator interactions and consequently are among the most significant. These meetings afford the opportunity for parents and teachers to exchange information and thus form a cooperative relationship to be maintained. In addition these meetings provide an opportunity for significant information to be exchanged for the benefit of children and youth. However, in spite of the potential significance of these meetings, it must be remembered that the success of the parent-professional progress report conference will be closely aligned with the establishment of prior rapport and trust and with the training the parents have been provided in participating. As a result, the educator cannot realistically expect the progress report conference to be effective in the absence of prior positive associations. However, when parents and educators who have well-established relationships make use of the progress report conference as one means of sharing information, the results can be highly facilitative of the goals of both parties.

Exercises

1. Conduct a progress report simulation conference using the materials in Appendix D. Descriptions are provided for the cases previously presented for other role-play exercises (i.e., mentally retarded, physically handicapped, gifted, behaviorly disordered, and learning disabled). Consequently, you should use those materials most aligned with your area or those that you have used in previous role-playing exercises.

   In conducting the simulation exercise, one individual should assume the part of the educator. These persons should employ both the materials labeled ''for teachers'' and the IEP that they previously developed for their respective pupil in structuring their responses.

   Although individuals assuming the parent's role have not been provided script materials, they should participate in the conference by reacting to the information provided by the teachers and through reviewing the initial interview simulation materials outlining the parent's role. A third individual should play the role of evaluator, using the attached evaluation form.

   Individuals should change roles after completing the exercise.
2. Conduct a progress report conference with parents. Following the session, ask the parents, a colleague, or both to evaluate your performance using the instrument shown in Figure 11-2. Compare the ratings you gave yourself with those assigned by the others. Based on this feedback, develop a list of procedures that will enable you to function more effectively in your conference.

REFERENCES

Attwell, A.A., & Clabby, D.A. *The retarded child: Answers to questions parents ask.* Los Angeles: Western Psychological Services, 1971.

Barsch, R.L. *The parent-teacher partnership.* Arlington, Va.: Council for Exceptional Children, 1969.

Benjamin, A. *The helping interview*. Boston: Houghton Mifflin, 1969.

Carkhuff, R.R., & Berenson, B.G. *Teaching as treatment: An introduction to counseling and psychotherapy*. Amherst, Mass.: Human Resources Development Press, 1976.

Chinn, P.C., Winn, J., & Walters, R.H. *Two-way talking with parents of special children: A process of positive communication*. St. Louis: Mosby, 1978.

Clements, J.E., & Simpson, R.L. Establishing parental support. *Pointer*, 1974, *19*(1), 70-71.

Deno, E. Some reflections on the use and interpretation of tests for teachers. *Focus on Exceptional Children*, 1971, *2*(8), 1-14.

Drucker, P.F. Managing the educated. In R.A. Sutermeiter (Ed.), *People and Productivity*. New York: McGraw-Hill, 1976.

Fine, M.J. *Handbook on parent education*. New York: Academic Press, 1980.

Ginott, H.G. Parent education groups in a child guidance clinic. *Mental Hygiene*, 1957, *41*, 82-86.

Gordon, T. *Parent effectiveness training*. New York: Wyden, 1970.

Hobbs, N. *Issues in the classification of children*. San Francisco: Jossey-Bass, 1975.

Kelly, E.J. *Parent-teacher interaction: A special educational perspective*. Seattle: Special Child Publications, 1974.

Kroth, R.L. *Communicating with parents of exceptional children*. Denver: Love Publishing, 1975.

Kroth, R.L., & Simpson, R.L. *Parent conferences as a teaching strategy*. Denver: Love Publishing, 1977.

Langton, G., & Stout, I.W. *Parent-teacher interviews*. Englewood Cliffs, N.J.: Prentice-Hall, 1954.

McAfee, J.K., & Vergason, G.A. Parent involvement in the process of special education: Establishing the new partnership. *Focus on Exceptional Children*, 1979, *11*(2), 1-15.

Messineo, L., & Sleeman, P.J. A parents guide to special education. *International Journal of Instructional Media*, 1977, *4*(4), 364-368.

Redl, F., & Wattenberg, W.W. *Mental hygiene in teaching*. New York: Harcourt, Brace & World, 1959.

Schulz, J. The parent-professional conflict. In A.P. Turnbull & H.R. Turnbull (Eds.), *Parents speak out: Views from the other side of the two-way mirror*. Columbus, Ohio: Merrill, 1978.

Shlien, J.M., Mosak, H.H., & Dseikurs, R. Effects of time limits: A comparison of two psychotherapies. *Journal of Counseling Psychology*, 1962, *9*, 31-34.

Simpson, R.L., & Poplin, M.S. Parents as agents of change. *School Psychology Review*, 1981, *10*(1), 15-24.

Turnbull, A.P. Parent-professional interactions. In M. Snell (Ed.), *Systematic instruction of the moderately and severely handicapped*. Columbus, Ohio: Merrill, 1978.

Wallace, G., & Larsen, S.C. *Educational assessment of learning problems: Testing for teaching*. Boston: Allyn & Bacon, 1978.

Chapter 12

Unplanned Conferences

It is becoming increasingly apparent that in order for parent-educator conferences to be successful, educators must be trained and prepared for a variety of encounters and situations (Hobbs, 1975). In particular, conferencers must be:

- aware of the various factors impacting and influencing families of exceptional children

- competent in establishing and maintaining effective relationships with parents

- knowledgeable of basic communication skills

- competent in sharing information with parents

- skillful in apprising parents of legislation relating to the handicapped, including methods for aiding them to serve as advocates for their own children and as more effective consumers of educational services

- effective in training parents to function as change agents within the natural environment

- competent in solving problems and resolving conflicts with parents

- skillful in conducting a variety of group conferences

- adroit in aiding parents and families to more effectively accommodate and integrate their exceptional children into family units.

In addition to acquiring skill and competence in these areas, educators must be prepared to contend and interact with parents at times other than during scheduled sessions. As any public school educator can attest, there are numerous situations in which parents expect to see or talk with their child's teacher or other educational personnel during nonscheduled times and without first having called for an appointment. In fact, since many schools require that teachers be in their classrooms before and after school to talk with parents who want to "drop in," it is likely that many parents rightfully assume that conferences can and should occur at their discretion. In addition, many educators have painfully determined that some parents may wish to discuss their child's progress while waiting in the checkout line of the neighborhood supermarket or over the telephone. Finally, a number of conferencers have discovered that it is during unscheduled meetings that they are most apt to see parents manifest their most intense emotions and sentiments, including anger, sorrow, guilt, and despair. Thus, educators must be equipped with suitable attitudes and skills to deal with parents on these and similar occasions. While unscheduled conferences have received far less attention by researchers and writers than more traditional parent-educator meetings, this should in no way be interpreted as an indication of a lack of importance of these interactions.

DEVELOPING SUITABLE ATTITUDES AND STRATEGIES FOR UNPLANNED CONFERENCES

While educators might understandably prefer scheduled and structured meetings, they must nonetheless acknowledge that at least some of their contacts with parents will be unplanned. Conferencers must not only accept the inevitability of these contacts but also develop appropriate attitudes and strategies for enhancing their success.

Educators must be able to understand themselves and their behavior as related to unscheduled parent meetings. That is, they must be able to assess realistically their beliefs and feelings about parents calling on them unexpectedly, telephoning them at home to talk about their children, and attempting to conduct conferences in noneducational settings. When professionals become cognizant of their own anxieties, fears, and resentments at being unprepared to deal with certain issues, values, and educational philosophies regarding unplanned interactions with parents, they will usually be more adept at dealing with these situations.

Educators must accept all types of parental involvement as a basic component of program success. A premise that is basic to the effective involvement of parents and educators is that parents must be perceived as integral and legitimate components of any educational or treatment program for children and that a variety of options for serving the needs of parents and families must be made available, including unscheduled interaction opportunities. Unless educators are willing to accept this position, little can be anticipated from the implementation of parent programs. Both parents and educators must be able to perceive the other party as having a justifiable role in facilitating a child's growth and development and in being worthy of cooperative involvement for a child's benefit. In particular, both planned and unplanned conferencing opportunities must be made available to parents as a means of facilitating the development of children and the enhancement of parent-professional communication.

Educators must have confidence that planned change can occur with and through parents. Educational conferencers must believe in their capacity to influence the behavior of parents and families in a positive manner as well as in capacity of parents to facilitate the growth and development of their children. Thus, the conferencer must accept the premise that exceptional children and their parents can positively change when exposed to appropriate conditions and contingencies and that educators can engineer and effect such changes. However, in order for parents to effect desired changes they must be provided a variety of interaction and communication opportunities with educational personnel, including both planned and unplanned meetings. The acceptance of parents' ability to change and conferencers' recognition of their own ability to facilitate this change process through both planned and unplanned interactions are basic ingredients of the successful implementation of a number of parent-related programs.

Educators need to be assertive in unplanned conferences. While educators must recognize that some meetings with parents of exceptional children will be unplanned and that these sessions may be both necessary and productive, it must also be recognized that circumstances surrounding these conferences are characterized by variant levels of acceptability. For example, one teacher became concerned because the mother of one of her pupils, who had never attended a planned conference, routinely called her at home after 10:00 P.M. to discuss her child's school progress. That these and similar situations regularly occur can be attested to by anyone who has ever worked in an educational setting. As a result, educators must be able to utilize appropriate assertiveness in structuring unscheduled conferences. While educational conferencers must be tolerant and accepting of unplanned meetings, including an awareness of their potential value, they must also be appropriately expressive relative to the circumstances surrounding these sessions.

Assertiveness, a process associated with the tenets of behavior therapy (Bandura, 1969), can both serve to reduce an educator's vulnerability during unplanned parent meetings and to help direct interactions into more productive areas. That the process can aid conferencers in expressing their rights without infringing on the interests of others (Alberti & Emmons, 1974) and evincing positions in a positive and productive manner makes assertiveness an obviously desirable trait for conferencers to possess. While educators must be appropriately accommodating of parental requests for unplanned meetings, they must also recognize that they need to be able to offer structure and guidance regarding these requests. In particular, educators must know when it is appropriate to say "no"; to be able to express emotions and perceptions truthfully; and to know when to continue, reschedule, and to terminate meetings with parents. Failure to utilize assertiveness in conferencing will facilitate neither the parent-professional relationship nor a child's school progress.

Educators need to provide structure and guidelines for unplanned conferences. Informing parents of guidelines, protocol, and rules of conduct for unscheduled conferences is one essential means of enhancing the productivity of these meetings and of avoiding misunderstandings. While such information may be provided verbally, it should also be disseminated in written form. Some educators verbally provide such ground rules during initial conferences and then as a follow-up provide parents with a written reference (and an additional explanation) at "open house" meetings. The information should include an explanation of when an unscheduled conference is appropriate, the hours available for such meetings, situations that may be inappropriate for a "drop in" session, and conditions and times during which an educator will accept calls from parents at school and at home.

It is essential that administration staff aid in establishing and implementing such guidelines so as to ensure district or school endorsement and some consistency across programs. Finally, information regarding unplanned conferences should be considered for dissemination through other modes, such as meetings of the parent-teacher association, local newspapers, parent-coordinated service organizations, and educational television.

Parents will in all likelihood need information regarding their participation in unscheduled meetings. Therefore, just as parents must be trained to be functional participants in individualized education program conferences and other school-related sessions, so must they be made aware of the variables and procedures associated with unscheduled meetings. Such structure is necessary to make unplanned conferences an appropriate and maximally beneficial form of parent-educator communication.

Educators need to have effective communication skills. As suggested earlier, parents who arrive at unscheduled times for conferences with educational personnel will frequently have a particular concern or need. In conjunction with these absorbing and acute needs will frequently be atypical manifestations of emotion. That is, parents who want to see their child's teacher without the delay of first scheduling an appointment are likely to be concerned about a specific incident at home or school, overwrought with a particular feeling, or in some other way agitated and disquieted. Thus, conferencers can expect to encounter a greater proportion of angry, guilty, and otherwise discomposed parents at unscheduled conferences.

As a result, educators must be prepared to apply appropriate communication skills. While good communication is an integral component of any parent-educator conference, special attention to the characteristics associated with maximizing interactions should be considered at unplanned encounters. In particular, conferencers should strive to attend to parents' messages, both manifest and affective content as well as nonverbal behavior; recognize and value parents' perceptions and concerns (even if the educator does not agree with them), accepting rather than interpreting parental perceptions; and address the conflict directly. Consideration of these and similar communication facilitators may enable conferencers to convert potentially unhealthy situations into joint problem-solving sessions.

Educators need to prepare for unscheduled conferences. While, by their very nature, unplanned meetings between parents and educators exclude comprehensive planning, conferencers can anticipate and prepare for many unscheduled encounters. For instance, educators should consider maintaining well-organized and up-to-date files on each pupil; having lists of names, addresses, and telephone numbers of school and community agencies available for parents; having available written guidelines for parents to use in structuring their child's home-study schedule; and being familiar with the use of conflict resolution strategies. Even though educators may be unfamiliar with the specific types of unplanned meetings they will have with parents, they can anticipate and make general arrangements for most of the types of sessions they will encounter.

SPECIFIC TYPES OF UNPLANNED PARENT-EDUCATOR MEETINGS

Although a variety of unscheduled encounters with parents can be expected, educational conferencers are most apt to contend with a recurring series of meetings: telephone conferences; meetings in noneducational settings; and encounters with angry parents, emotionally overwrought individuals, garrulous parents, parents who are seeking counseling or therapy for their own problems, and parents who insist on observing their child or talking with an educator during class time.

Telephone Conferences

Just as no business person could hope to be successful without making appropriate use of the telephone, neither can educators. This mode of communication affords the professional an easy and personalized means of interacting with parents. Furthermore, it reduces the problems of misinterpretation and message delay so often experienced when notes are sent home. Yet, in spite of the numerous advantages, telephone interactions present a variety of concerns. First, the telephone must always be considered a "less than equal" alternative to face-to-face meetings. Not only do telephone conversations deny the educator full access to an individual's and his or her nonverbal responses and demeanor, it can also limit a conferencer's capacity to provide clear and meaningful feedback. That is, the conferencer will not be able to rely on or produce visual displays, examples of academic work, or other permanent products. Accordingly, telephone interactions are totally dependent on the ability of parents and conferencers to send and receive messages effectively, a capacity that cannot always be depended on (Rabbitt, 1978). The telephone is a particularly weak mode of communication in attempting to resolve conflicts, reach joint solutions to problems, or respond to emotions. While conferencers may be required to respond to the initial needs of parents on the telephone, they are well advised to follow such initial interactions with face-to-face meetings during problematic situations.

Educators would also be well advised to structure their telephone interactions with parents early in a relationship. This structure can be offered at initial conferences or "open house" meetings in the form of suggestions as to when parents should call, matters that are appropriate for telephone communication, and under what conditions parents should telephone educators at home. In a similar manner, conferencers should obtain permission from parents to call them at home or work as well as convenient times for their conversations. The telephone can be a particularly effective tool when used by conferencers to reinforce children and parents, to maintain open lines of communication, and to provide ongoing feedback. In a like manner, parents can facilitate communication with educators by primarily relying on the telephone as an information exchange device. However, correct use of telephones by parents can be anticipated only with appropriate training.

A teacher of adolescent learning disabled pupils provided parents a specific time when they could call her at school to discuss matters of concern. She arranged with the secretary in her school to take messages and to remind parents who called at other times that she would only receive nonemergency telephone calls at specific times (previously negotiated with the parents). This same teacher routinely requested that parents telephone to alert her of changes occurring in their home or with their child's behavior, to clarify notes sent home, or to discuss other matters of their choice.

Meetings in Noneducational Settings

One teacher of learning disabled children confided that she had transferred her church membership to another community so that she would not have to contend with parents of students in her class on Sundays. Other educators have noted that they are apprehensive about meeting their students' parents in public or nonschool settings because of similar experiences. While this represents a chronic and significant issue for professionals, an easy solution can be offered. That is, educators must insist on conducting their conferences only at particular times and places. When approached by parents outside the classroom, the educator must politely, yet assertively, instruct parents about the appropriate manner for setting up a conference. Just as physicians and dentists are reluctant to discuss professional matters with their patients at ball games and restaurants, so must educators be equally resistant.

While some professionals might assume that the protocol associated with this matter is so universally understood that it does not require further attention, it is recommended that parents be informed of educators' perceptions regarding this matter. Only then can the assumption be made that a mutually understood expectation exists.

One special education teacher who was new to a small rural community found that she was constantly being approached by parents wishing to discuss their children in a variety of settings outside of school. As one means of contending with this situation she began carrying cards with her name and school telephone number. When approached by parents hopeful of conducting an on-the-spot conference the teacher would give them a card along with instructions for setting up an appointment. As a part of these instructions she also indicated that without the necessary time or materials she was unable to serve their informational needs adequately.

Meetings with Angry Parents

For many educators there is no situation quite as intimidating as the prospect of an angry parent arriving without prior notice. Yet, as unfortunate as these situations may be, they do occasionally occur. Even good relationships between parents and professionals can be expected occasionally to involve conflict. Hence, even in situations in which conferencers have invested time and effort in establishing prior rapport with parents, conflicts and misunderstandings may develop. Furthermore, the frustrations experienced by parents and families of exceptional children may result in periodic displays of anger toward a child's teacher or other educational personnel independent of these individuals' behaviors. Recognition of these basic factors may enable the conferencer to maintain a suitable frame of reference and a willingness to involve parents in joint problem solving. In fact, the major problem associated with these conflict situations is its potential impact on future relationships. Failure to contend with parental anger effectively can result in reduced cooperation, exacerbated suspicion, and eventual destruction of good communication. On the other hand, conferencers who are able to contend with parental anger effectively and to convert these situations into opportunities for joint problem solving can enhance feelings of trust and the value of parents and educators cooperatively searching for solutions to problems.

It is readily apparent that conferencers' communication skills will determine their success in unplanned meetings with angry parents. In particular, the conferencer must be able to listen to parents accurately and creatively without becoming defensive; recognize and appropriately respond to emotions; maintain a willingness to solve problems rather than to patronize or retaliate against aggressive individuals; communicate to parents that it is acceptable for them to have different values and opinions than educators; maintain an adult-to-adult relationship rather than a superior-subordinate affiliation; and be willing to offer explanations and information without being sanctimonious.

In addition, conferencers may wish to consider the following when interacting with angry parents:

- Allow parents to talk about their concerns without interruption. Rather than attempting to respond as issues are raised, the conferencer should allow parents to exhaust or fully explain their problems.

- Attempt to record the concerns voiced by parents; however, first consideration should be given to maintaining an acceptable listening environment.

- Be aware that some of the issues raised by angry parents may not actually be significant concerns to them. Conferencers must recognize that in their anger parents may comment on items that are obviously not relevant issues, and thus educators must be able to aid angry parents prioritize their concerns.

- Be aware of your own body language and the nonverbal responses of parents during these exchanges. Concentrate on keeping your voice low, relaxing, and avoiding defensive or intimidating gestures.

- Avoid attempts at discounting problems or parents' feelings regarding issues (e.g., "Now let's not overreact," "You couldn't possibly feel that way").

- Avoid arguing with parents.

- Respond to parent feelings without putting them on the defensive (e.g., "You are very angry," "I see a great deal of hostility in you today") and without using clichés (e.g., I feel that you are saying to me . . .").

- Avoid strong emotional reactions and insensitive responses, including sarcasm, disbelief, pain, anger, and disapprobation.

- Request clarification from parents on points you do not understand but avoid constantly interrupting, asking two questions at once, or using leading questions.

- Attempt to keep angry parents on task without eliminating the opportunity for them to voice additional concerns.

- Avoid attempts to engage parents in joint problem solving before they have had an opportunity to express fully their concerns and to vent their anger.

- Be sensitive and sympathetic to parents' problems without assuming responsibility or ownership.

- As much as possible, avoid responding to wrongful and generalized allegations (e.g., "If you were a decent teacher this wouldn't have happened") or threats (e.g., "You can expect to hear from my lawyer," "I plan to call the superintendent of schools").

- When confronted by parents with a confirmed history of being physically abusive toward professionals, ask that a colleague sit in on the session.

- Recognize that most anger is motivation that can be translated into productive problem-solving efforts.

The teacher of a group of intermediate-grade orthopedically handicapped children was surprised one day after school by an irate parent. This individual, whom the teacher had known for several years, accused her and her colleagues of several wrongdoings, including a lack of concern over the well-being and future of their pupils. By simply allowing the parent to talk about her concerns and by not responding defensively, the educator was able to determine that her family had recently been under a severe emotional stress and that this situation had been aggravated by a note sent by the teacher to the parents outlining a new "mainstreaming" and integration program. After the parent had an opportunity to vent her feelings and concerns a discussion of the new program ensued. In addition, the educator was able to suggest several alternatives for alleviating the stress factors in the home.

Meetings with Emotionally Overwrought Parents

As suggested previously, parents and families of exceptional children and youth can be expected to have a number of strong emotional reactions to their childrens' conditions (Roos, 1978). Included may be shock (Ross, 1964), grief (Solnit & Stark, 1961), guilt (Ziskin, 1978), and frustration (Akerley, 1978). Accordingly, educators can anticipate to be required periodically to interact with emotionally upset parents.

While the process of effectively responding to overwrought parents consists of a number of components, the conferencer must keep in mind two basic points. The first relates to the need to confirm and legitimize parents' emotions and to indicate that it is acceptable for parents to have certain feelings. Furthermore, educators must be willing and able to communicate to parents that they are comfortable and capable of aiding them in contending with such feelings. Thus, more than anything else, conferencers must assure parents that their behavior is both acceptable and understandable.

Second, conferencers must recognize that responding to the emotional reactions of parents must take precedence over other agenda items. For example, parents who become emotionally upset in the course of an unscheduled conference ostensibly initiated to deal with other matters should be dealt with as if their emotional response were the single most salient issue rather than a concern that must be eliminated so that attention can be refocused on the initially identified topic. Frequently, when parents arrive at unscheduled times for meetings with educators and subsequently manifest strong emotions, their major concern is associated with their own feelings rather than with the stated issue.

Conferencers are also encouraged to consider the following during interactions with emotionally upset parents:

- Listen to parents; avoid attempts at talking them out of their feelings or aiding them in denying their responses.

- Become aware of your own reactions when confronted with emotionally overwrought parents. Such self-examination will aid educators in becoming aware of their anxieties, including avoidance of eye contact, shifts in body posture, and body movements.

- Recognize that emotionally overwrought parents are in a highly vulnerable position. Therefore, conferencers must be able to verbally support parents (e.g., "It's OK for you to cry"), physically offer assurance (e.g., touch parents, offer tissues), and psychologically communicate a sense of understanding. At all costs, conferencers must avoid being critical (e.g., "Come on, pull yourself together") or intolerant of emotional responses (e.g., "My job as teacher only allows me to talk with you about your daughter's performance in school not that other stuff").

- As much as possible, avoid talking or offering solutions; frequently, the best strategy for dealing with emotionally upset parents is to allow them to talk without interruption.

- Avoid patronizing remarks and clichés when interacting with emotionally upset parents.

- Do not discount or refute the description of feelings or events offered by emotionally upset parents; rather, the emphasis should be on understanding these perceptions.

During one unscheduled conference initiated by a parent ostensibly to discuss her daughter's school progress, it became obvious that the mother's major concern was not her daughter's academic development. This parent had been traumatized by a severe accident that had befallen her daughter and while she had begun to recognize her child's need for special school services, she continued to have a number of strong feelings associated with the accident and its effects. As a result, the educator redirected the focus of the conference toward the mother's feelings and emotional concerns. This session was later followed by a scheduled progress report meeting.

Meetings with Garrulous Parents

Parents who chronically show up for unscheduled conferences without any more serious purpose than an interest in chatting can be very exasperating. While conferencers may hold open portions of each day or week for unplanned meetings, such opportunities must be restricted to discussions of particular and relevant items. When a loquacious parent fails to make appropriate use of this time resource, conferencers must firmly and positively structure the situation. Failure to do so can result in a waste of professional time, interference with parents actually requiring legitimate attention, and a deterioration in parent-educator relationships.

Educators confronted with garrulous parents may wish to consider the following ideas:

- Apprise parents early in the school year that, while unscheduled meetings can be held, these sessions should occur on an aperiodic basis and that they are not designed for casual visitations.

- Confront parents who consistently arrive for unplanned conferences without a purpose or agenda. Such a straightforward strategy is typically much more profitable than devising more circuitous measures for ending or avoiding these meetings.

- Consider setting a time limit for all unplanned conferences. While conferencers must be willing to make adjustments according to the needs of individual parents, this strategy can serve to reduce time spent in nonpertinent areas.

After having tried a number of more subtle approaches, one teacher finally confronted a parent of one of her pupils who routinely showed up in her classroom after school without an appointment. When confronted, the parent explained that she enjoyed seeing the teacher and hearing about her child's progress, albeit in an indirect fashion. After being made aware of her behavior and the restrictions it placed on the teacher and other parents, the mother became more appropriate in her conferencing behavior.

Meetings with Parents Who Are Seeking Counseling for Themselves

Occasionally, conferencers find that parents who frequently call on them to discuss their children are actually seeking counseling for themselves. This may particularly be the case when parents arrive without prior notice and when the focus of each session revolves around the parent and the difficulties experienced by that individual. In such instances, it is extremely important that educators be able to distinguish individuals who simply want to chat from those needing psychological counseling. In situations in which parents require psychological counseling, the conferencer should refer them to other professionals better qualified to serve their needs. Hence, conferencers must be cautious not to dismiss a parent who chronically "drops by" as someone who simply wants to pass the time of day when that individual may indeed be seeking professional services.

While educational conferencers must be cognizant of their role and recognize their professional limitations, they also must be aware of their obligations. That is, educational conferencers must not simply terminate a relationship with a parent because it is determined that that individual is in need of in-depth counseling. Rather, educators must rely on their relationship with a parent along with their clinical skills to reach a point when they can be assured that a parent will not be threatened by a referral to another person or agency and when the recommendation may be rejected. Failure to act in this manner may result in parents both rejecting referrals for counseling and discontinuing relationships with educators that may be needed for their children's continued growth and development.

As a strategy for dealing with a father who was obviously seeking help for himself, an educator initially concentrated on building a trusting relationship. Subsequently, she suggested that this parent consider seeking counseling from an individual associated with the school system who was more adequately trained to provide psychological services to parents. The offer of this suggestion after the relationship had been developed aided the father in giving it serious consideration.

Meetings with Parents During Class Time

Occasionally educators may be confronted by parents who either wish to observe their children without having made prior arrangements or who wish to engage in a teacher conference during class time. Obviously, these situations can be both exasperating for educators and disruptive to pupils.

One of the mechanisms for clarifying procedures for parents wishing to observe their children in class or to meet with educators is to inform them of the protocol surrounding these activities. This information should be provided to parents at the time their children are placed in a program and followed by periodic updates dictated by changes and individual needs. While these guidelines may be provided verbally, they should also be disseminated to parents in written form for later reference.

Frequently, educators may determine that allowing a parent to observe a class without prior arrangements does not constitute a severe problem. However, even in such instances it is suggested that, rather than immediately allowing them to observe, the educator request that they wait in an office area until the teacher or another educator can determine if the parent has a particular concern and what he or she is specifically interested in observing and has a chance to remind the parent of guidelines and rules for classroom observation. Taking the time to attend to these considerations can often convert a potentially distressing situation into a good learning experience for parents. Conversely, in instances in which parents have not made prior arrangements to observe a class and when doing so would not be in the best interests of a program, the educator must courteously, yet firmly, insist that the parent make arrangements to visit on another occasion.

Educators confronted with parents desiring an immediate meeting must be able to determine whether the circumstances warrant an on-the-spot conference. While school psychologists, counselors, and some itinerant and consulting personnel may be able to see parents under these conditions with only minor difficulties, classroom teachers face a much more difficult situation.

One particular policy that can eliminate problems in this area is to require that all visitors to a school or agency check in at the central office. If this policy is followed, classroom teachers will not be required to contend with a parent and a class simultaneously. Rather, an administrator, counselor, or another person can make judgments regarding the needs of a parent and whether or not a teacher's presence is required in a conference. Finally, when warranted, these same individuals can make arrangements for a teacher's class to be covered by another individual or for the meeting to take place during a free period.

After receiving a note from his child's teacher describing a behavior problem, one father of an emotionally disturbed boy arrived at school the following day just as classes were starting with the intent of meeting with his son's teacher. This individual was allowed to confer with the school counselor until the teacher's planning period. At that time, the counselor, parent, and teacher were able to meet regarding the incident. This session led to more adequate evaluation systems and a more regularly scheduled series of conferences.

Undoubtedly, parents who arrive at their child's school during class hours demanding to hold a conference will not be particularly welcome. Nonetheless, educators must not be so rigid and insensitive as to deny parents access to professional services. Rather, efforts should be made to negotiate a time when pertinent parties can be brought together. In addition, when a parent wishes to see an individual who is not available at the moment, arrangements should be made to have the parent meet with someone else. Frequently when the concerns of parents are so pressing that they arrive at a school without prior notice, they must be provided immediate attention. Failure to do so can often lead to unfavorable outcomes.

CONCLUSION

Even though educators may prefer to hold conferences with parents at scheduled times, it must be recognized that unplanned meetings will occur. Consequently, educators can and must be prepared for these encounters if they are to work successfully with parents.

Exercise

Conduct unplanned role-play conferences with another individual. Your sessions should be structured around the following:

- a parent-initiated telephone conference

- attempts by a parent to conduct a conference in a noneducational setting

- a meeting with an angry parent

- a meeting with an emotionally upset parent

- a meeting with a garrulous parent

- a meeting with a parent seeking personal professional help

- a meeting with a parent who insists on observing a child or confering with a teacher during class time.

In conducting the exercise, one individual should assume the part of a parent; another, the part of the educator; and a third, the role of an observer and discussant. Following each session the observer should discuss with the participants those procedures that were employed to deal with the situation and the strategies that might have been more appropriate.

Each group of three should assume each role in the exercise.

REFERENCES

Akerley, M.S. False gods and angry prophets. In A.P. Turnbull & H.R. Turnbull (Eds.), *Parents speak out: Views from the other side of the two-way mirror*. Columbus, Ohio: Merrill, 1978.

Alberti, R.E., & Emmons, M.L. *Your perfect right: A guide to assertive behavior*. San Luis Obispo, Calif.: Impact Publishers, 1974.

Bandura, A. *Principles of behavior modification*. New York: Holt, Rinehart & Winston, 1969.

Hobbs, N. *The futures of children*. San Francisco: Jossey-Bass, 1975.

Rabbitt, J.A. The parent-teacher conference: Trauma or teamwork? *Phi Delta Kappan*, 1978, *52*, 471-472.

Roos, P. Parents of mentally retarded children—misunderstood and mistreated. In A.P. Turnbull & H.R. Turnbull (Eds.), *Parents speak out: Views from the other side of the two-way mirror*. Columbus, Ohio: Merrill, 1978.

Ross, A.O. *The exceptional child in the family.* New York: Grune & Stratton, 1964.

Solnit, A.J., & Stark, M.H. Mourning and the birth of a defective child. *Psychoanalytic Study of the Child*, 1961, *16*, 523-537.

Ziskin, L.Z. The story of Jennie. In A.P. Turnbull & H.R. Turnbull (Eds.), *Parents speak out: Views from the other side of the two-way mirror*. Columbus, Ohio: Merrill, 1978.

Chapter 13

Group Conferences

In spite of indications that it may be highly beneficial to hold individual conferences with every parent (Duncan & Fitzgerald, 1969; Kroth & Simpson, 1977), group sessions are more desirable in certain situations. In particular, group conferences can serve as follow-ups to individual parent-educator meetings and as a means of allowing for dynamic interactions between a number of parents with similar types of children.

One of the most obvious advantages of group conferencing or training is a reduction in time and effort requirements: it is much more efficient to have conferences and train parents in groups than individually (McDowell, 1976; Rose, 1969). Hence, just as public schools are limited in their capacity to provide individual instruction to children, so, too, are many educators restricted in their individual conferencing resources. In addition, there have been some indications that group models offer the most efficacious means of accomplishing certain goals (Kelly, 1974). For instance, by having conferencers transact general business in group settings and disseminate basic information of interest to all parents, they may be able to accrue the necessary time to conduct individual sessions with parents who require more specific or specialized attention. As suggested by Wyckoff (1980), "The time savings noted with the group delivery over the individual delivery has been attributed to the opportunity the grouped parents had to exchange ideas and learn how others solved problems with their own children" (p. 295).

In addition, and perhaps most importantly, group interactions can be both enlightening and stimulating for the participants. In some instances parents may discover that there are other parents with problems similar to their own, or they may gain the confidence necessary to apply new techniques with their children. In still other situations, group sessions may provide parents a forum for discussing their perceptions and feelings about their offspring with a truly empathic group. As observed by Rutherford and Edgar (1979), "group training provides support for parents who feel socially isolated from parents of normal children. In some cases, the friendships formed during these training sessions have been maintained long after the training sessions have terminated'' (p. 161). When provided an opportunity to interact in the right kind of group setting, parents of exceptional children frequently respond by becoming more actively and productively involved with their children and the educators who serve them.

While the structure, characteristics, and goals of each parent group meeting are dictated by the needs and distinctive features of the participants and by the objectives and training of the educator conducting the session, most will focus on one of the following five areas: (1) group information exchange meetings, (2) training sessions to aid parents in their role as educational consumers and child advocates, (3) parent-applied intervention and tutor training programs, (4) group counseling and education programs for parents, and (5) service programs for parents.

GROUP INFORMATION EXCHANGE PROGRAMS

While parents should be provided an opportunity to exchange information with educators on a one-to-one basis when their child first enters a program and thereafter as required, many of their basic information needs can most effectively be satisfied through group meetings. Thus, even though group sessions must not supplant individual conferences, they can be used as a vehicle for disseminating common information, discussing shared issues, and allowing for communication between parents with collective concerns. In particular, sessions focusing on the nature, characteristics, etiology, and prognosis of an exceptionality, a description of the general educational program being utilized, and the manner in which pupils are evaluated are highly compatible with a group format. As suggested by Kelly (1974), "To be successful, the teacher-planner must take care to select a theme which is most relevant to her children's parents. All other aspects of planning revolve around the theme selected" (p. 33).

Information Regarding an Exceptionality

One of the most common needs expressed by parents of exceptional children is for information on the nature, characteristics, etiology, and future implications of their offspring's condition (Chinn, Winn, & Walters, 1978). The search for this kind of information represents both an immediate reaction to an exceptionality as well as an ongoing concern of parents and families. Accordingly, educators should be aware that information relating to an exceptionality is a commonly requested agenda item. In this connection it should be noted that parents may benefit as much (if not more) from being allowed to discuss their own perceptions and to share their own information regarding an exceptionality than from facts disseminated by a professional.

The importance of addressing the characteristics, etiology, and prognosis of an exceptionality cannot be underestimated. First, the complexity of these issues may make their comprehension by parents extremely difficult. Certainly, if indeed professionals have as much difficulty in understanding the various exceptionalities as they appear to, parents can be expected to share the same plight. In addition, even when parents have a cognitive understanding of a condition and its related factors, they can still be expected to demonstrate emotional needs that require attention. Group interactions and the support that can come from parents meeting together can frequently serve to satisfy this need. While group sessions focusing on this type of information must not take the place of individualized and in-depth interpretation, planning, and evaluation conferences, they can serve to clarify and facilitate understanding and acceptance by parents and families.

One teacher of learning disabled children held a parent group session each year on factors associated with her pupils' exceptionality. As a part of her discussion she focused on a definition of learning disabilities (National Advisory Committee on Handicapped Children, 1968), including an interpretation of the various components of this somewhat esoteric and cumbersome definition (e.g., "a disorder in one or more of the basic psychological processes," "minimal brain dysfunction," "developmental aphasia"). Furthermore, she made available a list of common terms associated with "learning disabilities" (e.g., hyperactivity, attention disorders, poor self-concept, dyslexia, vocal encoding) and discussed these items with parents. Finally, she employed her list of terms as a vehicle for stimulating discussions with the participants. This veteran educator revealed that when she gave parents lists of terms she not only was supplying them with a future reference but was also able to generate questions and stimulate lively discussions that might not otherwise have been forthcoming.

Other means of structuring informative group sessions on characteristics and related issues include filmstrips, guest speakers focusing on a particular topic, and handicapped adults commenting on their personal experiences. However, regardless of the format used, time should always be allotted for discussions. As suggested earlier, parental interaction opportunities typically are the most salient part of any group meeting.

Educational Program Description*

Parents of exceptional children can also be expected to be particularly interested in the educational program and procedures designed for their children. When taken up in group sessions, topics on these issues should serve to support (not replace)

*The following two sections are based on the work of Cathryn R. Thomas.

information provided in individual conferences and to provide items for general discussion. Areas of discussion and information exchange will be on topics similar to those pursued during initial parent conferences, including classroom and school schedules, policies, and orientation; academic and social remediation programs; ancillary services and personnel available to students; and parent and family programs. Since parents should have had an opportunity to pursue these matters individually at the time of the initial conference, these group sessions should be designed to reacquaint parents with the original information and any changes that may have taken place and to allow for discussions among the participants.

A number of educators address general information relating to educational programming at annual "open house" meetings. In addition, parents are invited to make individual appointments at a later time to discuss specific matters.

One teacher of learning disabled children provided parents a written description of her educational program at the time she provided a verbal overview. She reported that this strategy both served to provide parents a resource for later referral and to stimulate discussion. The meeting took place in the classroom and was structured to accommodate questions, demonstrations, and comments, all of which aided in facilitating a discussion. A description of the information provided in the group sessions and through the written document is shown below (Thomas, 1974):

Description of daily routine:
Every morning begins with roll. This is also the time when your child brings his daily report back to me. We then have sharing time so that the children can share with the others anything they would like them to know about. From this point the children begin working on their individual work which is charted out for them on their daily program sheet. We also have our individual or group reading sessions at this time, and the children can receive help on work they do not understand. This independent work block lasts until the first recess. After recess the children finish up their work and make corrections on those books which need it. We then do our group work—either in small groups or the class as a whole. Group work includes activities such as handwriting, spelling or language activities. Following these activities the children are given their lunch and noon recess. The afternoon activities are somewhat varied, but still adhere to a basic pattern. Most of the special activities such as art, music, physical education, and library are scheduled during this time. Through teaching units we also get to other areas such as science and history. These activities last until our final recess.

After recess the children are responsible for cleaning and straightening their own desk areas, while I make out their daily reports. I then read aloud to the children until the bus comes.

Attached is a sample of a daily-weekly schedule. Although this is the basic routine it is subject to change on occasion for special events such as field trips, school-sponsored activities (including outside guests), or the yearly holiday parties which the whole school celebrates. However, you shall be informed of these events as they are scheduled.

The classroom schedule (Table 13-1) was also discussed with the parents. During this time the teacher elaborated on (and demonstrated) the various elements involved in the daily routine and gave parents an opportunity to raise questions and discuss items related to this matter.

Table 13-1 Classroom Schedule

	Monday	Tuesday	Wednesday	Thursday	Friday
8:30-9:00	Roll & sharing time	Roll & sharing time	Roll & sharing time	Roll & sharing time	Roll & sharing time
9:00-10:30	Independent work & reading	Independent work & reading	Independent work & reading	Independent work & reading	Independent work & reading
10:30-10:45	Recess	Recess	Recess	Recess	Recess
10:45-11:15	Finish work & make corrections	Finish work & make corrections	Finish work & make corrections	Finish work & make corrections	Finish work & make corrections
11:15-12:00	Group work small or whole class	Group work small or whole class	Group work small or whole class	Group work small or whole class	Group work small or whole class
12:00-1:00	Lunch & recess	Lunch & recess	Lunch & recess	Lunch & recess	Lunch & recess
1:00-1:30	P.E.	Music	P.E.	Music	Special Friday
1:30-2:00	Unit work Activities	Art	Unit work Activities	Art	Privilege
2:00-2:15	Recess	Recess	Recess	Recess	Recess
2:15-2:30	Prepare to go home	Prepare to go home	Prepare to go home	Prepare to go home	Prepare to go home
2:30-2:50	Story session	Story session	Story session	Story session	Story session
2:50	Dismissal	Dismissal	Dismissal	Dismissal	Dismissal

Source: Courtesy of Cathryn R. Thomas.

The teacher also provided a description of the reinforcement system she used in her class. Again, this topic was structured so as to facilitate discussion:

Reinforcement is an integral part of our program. By this I mean, the children receive encouragement for good work and good behavior in both direct and indirect ways. As mentioned before, their work is planned in such a way that success is built in. They begin with work that is very easy for them and are then *gradually* given more difficult work so that they can still achieve well and build up their skills at the same time. And again, the smaller class size allows for more communication with each child and through this social interaction the child begins to feel somewhat important, which in turn, boosts his self-confidence.

Probably equally important to these children is the direct type of reinforcement they receive. Since failure has been an unfortunate part of many children's past school experience, they are often hesitant—or afraid—to try again, lest they should fail. The child is eager to please his parents and teacher and wants to look good in front of his peers, but his lack of motivation to try is understandable. Thus, tangible (material) reinforcement adds an extra "little incentive" to at least try. Or for some children, the reinforcement might be what they need to achieve at their best level, rather than doing just enough to get by.

Reinforcement in our room can take many forms. It might be candy, an extra chance to go to P.E., music, or art, extra recess, free time, listening to records, helping another teacher, playing a quiet game with another child, etc. Again, the child often determines what his reinforcer will be, because what is reinforcing for one child may not be so for another. What the child's reinforcement will be is decided upon by the child and teacher ahead of time. Any of the reinforcers mentioned thus far could easily be used with the classroom at any time the child has earned such a privilege. They are used as "immediate reinforcement."

Another type of reinforcement is also used; this may be termed "long range." This also is a tangible reinforcement, but it is much larger than the immediate reinforcement and usually comes on Friday afternoon. Thus, the children must work all week to earn a Friday privilege. Normally this reinforcer is designed to provide social interaction more than academic skills. It is a chance for the children to enjoy being with others in a "fun-type" situation. Such activities might include an in-class party with a film, bowling, swimming, skating, or a special field trip. The program is set up so that only the children who actually earn the privilege may enjoy it. Arrangements are made so that a child who has not earned his privilege because of poor work or unacceptable behavior may stay with another teacher during this time.

The children can see from day to day how well they are doing. They usually know anyway, but we keep a chart on each child's desk so they can easily remember in case they forget. A "happy face" is awarded each time a child completes his work and each time he has an "excellent" or a "good" day. Whenever the child does not complete his work or has only a "fair" or an "unacceptable" day, a "sad face" is placed in his box for that day. To earn the Friday privilege, the child must have three happy faces in the Good Work row and three in the Good Behavior row. These need not be three days which include BOTH Good Work and Good Behavior—again they're viewed individually. This allows for days when a child may work extremely well in the classroom but may not be able to control his temper on the playground, or the child may be quiet and cooperative all day but doesn't seem to be able to finish his work. We all have our "off" days and children are no different.

Information about a school and the operation of an educational program is of great interest to parents. Furthermore, this topic typically lends itself well to a group discussion and interaction format.

Evaluation Procedures

Group meetings may also serve as an appropriate vehicle for reacquainting and discussing the manner in which a child will be evaluated within a particular program and the mode in which this information will be communicated to parents. In many instances, exceptional children will enter alternative or remedial programs with a long history of school failure, making the topic of evaluation of particular interest to parents. Just as with other topical areas within this domain, information should serve as a follow-up to discussions during individual conferences and in a fashion facilitative of group interaction.

The following is a description of evaluation information provided in written form (Exhibit 13-1) and discussed in a group setting with parents of children assigned to one learning disability classroom (Thomas, 1974).

Evaluation System
Our report system does not include the standard report card used by the school. Since our program is built on the idea of individualization it is difficult to place a grade on the child. The grade would refer to his performance in relation to other children while at this point we are more concerned with the child's growing strengths and abilities within himself. The exception comes when the child has built himself up both academically and socially to the point where he is in a regular classroom

Exhibit 13-1 Evaluation Information Form

Child _____

Date _____

Behavior	*Work*
□ Excellent	□ Totally Complete
□ Good	□ Mostly Complete
□ Fair	□ Incomplete
□ Unacceptable	

Teacher's Signature _____

Parents' Signature _____

Comments:

Source: Courtesy of Cathryn R. Thomas.

---

part of the time. When this occurs, the regular classroom teacher prepares a report card for him on the subjects he has within her class. But until we reach that point, I prefer to use a daily report system and rely heavily on communication between you and me. In fact, I feel this communication is urgent if your child's program is to succeed. First of all, he needs to know that we are working together and supporting each other. His efforts and achievements are more totally appreciated in this way, and he receives a certain amount of security knowing that we will be fair with him. Secondly, it is important that we tell each other anything which may be important to the child and which might otherwise be overlooked. For example, if your family is planning a special trip somewhere, your child will be apt to be a bit more excited than usual. Or even something like a sick pet will undoubtedly upset the child. Likewise, if your child might have a little argument with a friend at school, you should be given a few clues as to what it was about so you can talk more confidently and/or objectively with your child. And finally, we need to be aware of any changes in your child, either positive or negative, so that we can either continue our program or alter it accordingly.

We can talk frequently through phone calls (home or school), school visits any time before or after school, or by our daily report system. Your child will bring a card like this one home to you each night. I ask that you sign it to indicate you have seen it and return it with your child the next day. There is space at the bottom or back for any comments either of us may have.

In addition, there are three scheduled conferences throughout the year—one before the start of school, which enables me to meet both you and your child, and vice-versa, one in November and one in March. The latter two are to discuss your child's progress and any other topic we feel is necessary. But don't ever hesitate to talk with me between times.

To facilitate discussions the conferencer should carefully plan ways of assuring parental participation. Without such prior planning the major benefits of group conferences may go untapped.

GROUP-ORIENTED CONSUMER AND ADVOCACY PARENT TRAINING PROGRAMS

Instruction on procedures for aiding parents to become better consumers of educational services and advocates for their children is particularly well suited for group training. While this training can be provided individually and through printed materials that parents can use independently, optimal training success seems to be associated with group processes. This is particularly true when group sessions allow for discussions along with simulation, role-playing, and modeling opportunities. Specifically, training sessions are needed that familiarize parents with their rights and responsibilities relative to their exceptional child and methods for more effective participation in educational conferences.

The role of parents as chief advocates for their exceptional children requires that they be able to determine whether or not their offspring are receiving appropriate services and that the schools serving their children are in compliance with local, state, and federal guidelines. Without information and training on these topics, parents will probably not be effective representatives for their children. Hence, a primary training activity for educators must be to familiarize parents with the guidelines and procedures associated with P.L. 94-142 and Section 504 of the Rehabilitation Act of 1973.

An example of one unit of a training document used to transmit information about P.L. 94-142 in group conferences is shown below. The training format was structured around a booklet, which parents were allowed to keep. In addition, discussions were planned to ensure that parents were familiar with the various concepts presented. The parents were instructed that according to P.L. 94-142 they had the following rights:

- the right to have your child educated with nonhandicapped children to the maximum extent appropriate. When at all possible, your child has the right to remain in a regular classroom situation to receive his or her education as presented to the rest of the class. However, a regular classroom placement at any time may not be appropriate for the more severely handicapped child. If your child would not benefit from such a placement, as deemed by you with the placement team, then all instruction would take place in a setting designed for your child's needs.

- the right to have your child removed from the regular educational environment only after supplementary aids and services were tried and found unsatisfactory. This means that a full-time placement that would mean complete removal from the child's regular classroom should only be initiated after a part-time placement or other arrangements have been shown not to provide all the needed instruction your child needs.

- the right to have supplementary services such as a resource room or itinerant instruction to make it possible for your child to remain in regular class placement.

- the right to have placement in the school your child would attend if nonhandicapped unless the individual education plan requires some other arrangements. If the school your child would normally attend does not house the appropriate instructional services your child needs, your school district shall provide those services elsewhere (perhaps in another school within the district), and shall also be responsible for your child's transportation between home and his instructional site.

- the right of your child to participate with nonhandicapped children in nonacademic and extracurricular services and activities such as meals, recess, counseling, clubs, athletics, and special groups. Your child has the right to participate in any of the above activities with nonhandicapped children unless such activities are deemed inappropriate jointly by you and the placement team.

In addition, parents must also be given instruction in how to participate in the various types of conferences they will be asked to attend, including initial, interpretation, individualized education program (IEP), and progress report sessions. Without appropriate training, parents cannot be expected to be effective conference participants and to best represent the interests of their child. Again, training in this area can most effectively be provided in group situations, in which discussions, role models, simulation activities, and encouragement can be made an integral part.

Turnbull (1981) suggested that educators provide parents a list of questions they should consider prior to attending a conference. The list included skills parents would like their children to learn, areas of behavior and socialization that they would like to see dealt with at school, parental perceptions of their children, and their attitudes regarding their child interacting with nonexceptional children. Turnbull (1981) noted that with such training parents can be expected to become more productive conference participants.

One group training program designed by a teacher of emotionally disturbed children focused on instructing parents in their role during IEP conferences. Specifically, the training sessions focused on providing parents information regarding their role prior to an IEP conference, during the actual meeting, and after the session. An example of the type of information provided parents is shown below:

- Review all records regarding your child's exceptionality (including school, medical, and social).

- Review and familiarize yourself with the procedures associated with P.L. 94-142, particularly the section on IEPs.

- Hold a family meeting to discuss the goals, procedures, curricula, and other elements that you would like to see incorporated in your child's IEP. Be sure that your child is included in the meeting.

- Discuss with your family the manner in which you will make the suggestions you have identified and which items you consider to be most significant.

- Record all the above information in a form you can easily read so that you can refer to it during the conference.

- Invite a friend or another parent to go with you if you feel uneasy about attending the conference alone.

- Familiarize yourself with the names and positions of the individuals who will be in attendance, the time and date of the meeting, and the location of the school (and room within the building) where the session will be held.

- Develop a positive attitude regarding the outcome of the meeting. Tell yourself that the people involved will each have your child's best interests in mind and that your input is just as significant as that of the professionals who will be in attendance.

The above guidelines were presented to and discussed with groups of up to 10 to 12 parents. After reviewing the various elements within a particular training module (e.g., holding a preconference family meeting), participants were provided a role model by the teacher or other parents who had previously completed the training program. That is, the teacher or several parents would role play a

25

preconference family meeting, for example. After being given an opportunity to react to the demonstration model, participants were encouraged to role play the unit themselves. According to the teacher who conducted the sessions, those parents who regularly attended the training meetings, participated in discussions, and engaged in role-playing exercises were much more confident and productive in their children's IEP conferences.

With proper training, parents of exceptional children can be expected to function with skill and authority as consumers of educational services and advocates for their children. The training associated with developing this proficiency in parents may best be delivered via a group format.

GROUP BEHAVIOR MANAGEMENT AND TUTORIAL TRAINING PROGRAMS

An additional area for which a group format can be highly appropriate is the training of parents to serve as behavioral change agents and tutors for their own children in nonschool settings. As demonstrated by a number of researchers, parents can be trained as both managers of social behavior and academic tutors, thereby extending the service options available to exceptional children beyond the classroom environment (Berkowitz & Graziano, 1972; O'Dell, 1974; Sasso, Hughes, Critchlew, Falcon, & Delquadri, 1980).

An example of an instructional program designed to train groups of parents of exceptional children in the use of behavior management procedures is presented below. This program, designed by Simpson and Combs (1978) to instruct parents of autistic and autistic-like children and youth, is based on a three-part slide/tape presentation (Simpson & Swenson, 1978). Part I provided an overview of behavioral techniques, including procedures for identifying a target behavior. Part II focused on training parents to employ behavioral measurement procedures and Part III dealt with graphing behavioral records and applying intervention techniques. The program was designed to operate for a minimum of four consecutive weeks, with the fourth meeting serving as follow-up.

Listed below are selected sections from the training manual that was written to provide structure to educators and other users of the training model.

Guidelines for Program Use and Selection of Participants

Careful planning has gone into the development of the workshop procedures described in the following sections. The validity of the program will depend on the appropriate implementation of the procedures described in this manual. For that reason, it is mandatory that workshop leaders follow the suggested guidelines.

This training program is designed for use by workshop leaders with professional training and experience in both parent counseling and behavior modification. Specifically, the program is designed for individuals holding at least a master's degree in counseling, child development, special education, psychology, or a related field. In addition, the level of professional expertise of manual users should enable them to screen prospective participants. Specifically, it should be recognized that a group format is not equally appropriate for all parents and that some individuals may be in need of more intensive or individualized intervention. Equally important, it should be remembered that the direct teaching of behavior modification techniques may be inadvisable with some parents. At a minimum, participants in the workshop should be emotionally stable, literate, "normal" or "near normal" intellectually, and be able to speak and understand basic English.

Planning and Organizing the Workshop

The behavior management workshop is not only adaptable to a variety of parents and children, but also to a number of situations. For instance, the series can be used with a group of parents who will continue to meet after completion of the behavior management program, as an initial means of organizing a group, or as a program for parents who will meet only for the management workshop. Regardless of the design, it is imperative that parents participating in the workshop attend all sessions. Equally important, parents and guardians participating in the program must agree to complete all exercises and assignments, including some home-based activities. Since the workshop content is sequentially arranged, parents who do not attend one or more sessions will probably experience a significant amount of difficulty in successfully completing the program and in correctly applying the concepts of behavior modification.

As an aid in securing parental cooperation, it is recommended that participants be notified in advance of the importance of attending all sessions and that they sign an agreement form acknowledging their willingness to complete the program. Use of a contract has been found to be a functional procedure for increasing the probability of attendance, although the parents should be made aware that the contract is legally nonbinding and that they are not required to sign it to take part in the sessions.

An example of a workshop invitation (Exhibit 13-2) and a sample participation contract (Exhibit 13-3) are provided for illustrative purposes. It is suggested that the invitations be sent to the parents through the mail and that the contracts be presented verbally as a means of increasing the probability of success. Basic information about the child must also be elicited in planning the workshop (Exhibit 13-4 and Exhibit 13-5).

Exhibit 13-2 Sample Letter of Invitation

Dear Mr. and Mrs. (Jones):

You are cordially invited to attend a Parent Workshop on behavior management techniques. The workshop will meet on Thursday evenings for four consecutive weeks beginning September 14. The sessions will be coordinated by (Dr. Sally Smith) and will meet in room (31) at (Central Junior High School).

The purpose of the workshop series is to share information about procedures for more effectively allowing parents to manage the behavior of their children. Parents will be encouraged to participate in the program and to apply the techniques with their own children. Since the four-part workshop series is sequentially arranged, it is imperative that parents attend all sessions.

If you would like additional information about the workshop, please call the district administrative offices (849-1403, extension 41). If you do plan to participate, please complete the attached forms [Exhibits 13-4 and 13-5] and return to the district office in the enclosed stamped envelope. This information will be used in applying the workshop principles to your child.

Sincerely,

(Peter Foxx)
(Director of Pupil Services)

Exhibit 13-3 Sample Participation Contract

I wish to participate in the workshop on behavioral management techniques sponsored by the school district. I have been informed of the nature of the workshop series and I understand the importance of attending each of the four sessions. In addition, I agree to participate in all activities related to the workshop.

_____
Parent or Guardian Signature

_____
Date

Exhibit 13-4 Child Information Form

Name of Child:
Name of Person Completing Form:
Relationship to Child:
Date:
  I. List the things which your child does that you like, that other people like, and that he or she does well or relatively well.
   1., Etc.
  II. List the things that your child does too often, too much, or at the wrong times that get him into trouble. List everything you can think of.
   1., Etc.
  III. List the things that your child fails to do, refuses to do, does not do properly, does not do often enough, or does not do as you would like.
   1., Etc.
  IV. Considering the above, list the three things that you consider to be the most important and in need of change or strengthening. List these in order of importance.
   1.
   2.
   3.

Exhibit 13-5 Reinforcement Inventory

Child's Name _____
Name of Person Completing Form _____
Relationship to Child _____
Date _____
Please complete this form according to your knowledge and observation of your child. You may wish to directly ask your child many of these questions since it is important that the answers truly represent the child's likes and dislikes.
  1. What sorts of things does your child like to do?
  2. If given a choice, how does your child spend his (or her) time?
  3. What privileges does your child have?
  4. What does he (or she) frequently ask you for?
  5. If school-aged, what does he (or she) like to do after coming home from school?
  6. What games does your child like to play?

Exhibit 13-5 continued

7. What are your child's favorite things to eat?
8. How does your child spend time on the weekends?
9. Who does your child like to visit? (friends, grandparents, other relatives, other adults)
10. Where does your child like to go? (swimming pool, library, grocery, certain stores, shopping, the park)
11. What are your child's favorite television programs?
12. What are your child's favorite indoor activities?
13. What are your child's favorite outdoor activities?
14. What does your child like most to do with mother?
15. What does your child like to do most with father?
16. What does your child like to do most with brothers and sisters? (list each sibling)
17. List three things your child least likes to do.
18. List three things your child would most like to have.

The Workshop Environment

Experienced counselors and group facilitators generally agree that physical and environmental factors can either augment or detract from the desired goals of a workshop. However, the exact design of the workshop environment is difficult to specify because of resource limitations and individual differences. More importantly, workshops are frequently conducted in situations that allow for only limited environmental manipulation. Nonetheless, it is essential to secure a setting that is characterized by both professionalism and comfort. Professionalism, as shown in the physical environment, implies an atmosphere that is commensurate with the goals of the workshop. Although difficult to precisely specify, the furniture and facilities should be appropriate for a nonsocial meeting among adults and yet be comfortable. Since it is essential that the environment not interfere with the workshop procedures, session coordinators should provide participants with adequate furniture, lighting, and other physical features.

Since the series format calls for both full-group and small-group participation, appropriate space arrangements must be made. These arrangements include a room large enough to accommodate all participants and adequate for an audiovisual presentation and either several small rooms for small group work or one room large enough to allow several small groups to function simultaneously. Finally, workshop leaders should have available audio-visual equipment, an overhead projector, screen, movable chairs, and work tables.

Conducting the Workshop

Although not totally designed for large groups, aspects of the workshop series can be used with as many as 100 persons. Thus, introductory information, audio-visual presentations, and certain other activities can be presented to relatively large groups; however, a large part of the workshop is designed for small groups of 10 to 12 parents. Each group of 10 to 12 parents should have its own leader. These leaders should have the same training and background as previously described for session leaders and should remain with the same participants during the four-session workshop series. It is also recommended that groups be developed to accommodate parents and guardians of children of similar ages. Although parents and guardians may have children with wide age ranges, they will frequently be motivated to apply the techniques with one child in particular. Thus, as much as possible, parents should be grouped according to the age of the child with whom they are most concerned. In addition, especially with regard to exceptional children and adolescents, attempts should be made to homogeneously group parents according to the characteristics of the child or adolescent. Since some parents may find it difficult to participate in the workshop activities if their offspring is significantly different from those described by other participants, prior grouping arrangements should be made.

As a further example of the use of this program, the guidelines associated with the initial components of the four-part series, on developing and maintaining adaptive behavior, are presented. Readers should note that these guidelines are also appropriate for use in other types of parent programs.

Participant Orientation to Workshop

Purpose. To welcome the parents and to describe the objectives for the workshops, the agenda for the evening, and to give information regarding future meeting times.

Materials Needed:

- name tags and pencils,
- participation agreement forms.

Procedure. The participants should be greeted as they arrive for the meeting. Each parent should be asked to find or fill out a name tag. You may also wish to offer coffee or tea as this can contribute to a more genial and informal atmosphere. In addition, if coffee is readily available, interruption of the session for a special break can be avoided.

At the first session, wait about ten minutes after the scheduled starting time to start. This extra time should allow all participants ample time to locate the meeting site. It should be noted that future sessions will start on schedule.

The leader's introduction, which is designed to orient the participants to the workshop and to give essential information, should last no more than five to ten minutes. The introductory comments should include:

- a welcome to participants and reinforcement for their participation

- the general purpose of the workshop

- the date and times of future meetings

- the importance of attendance and participation

- an overview of the workshop series

- an introduction to the agenda for the evening.

An example of the type of introduction appropriate for this orientation session is provided in Exhibit 13-6. It is suggested that this material be used as a guide and not as information to be read to the participants.

Presentation of Information

Purpose. To prepare the parents for the evening's session and to provide instructions and activities to facilitate the establishment of a cognitive framework to enhance learning.

Materials Needed

- pencils

- slides and tape

- slide projector and tape player

- screen

- posttest questionnaire-A

- overview reference sheet

Procedure. Before the slide-tape presentation is shown it may be helpful to give each participant a sheet specifying the name of the workshop and workshop leader(s); a brief statement of the overall purpose of the workshop; topics to be covered in each workshop; meeting dates, times, and places; and relevant telephone numbers. This information should be accompanied by a brief comment on

Exhibit 13-6 Sample Workshop Welcome

Welcome to our workshop on Managing Child Behavior. Each of you is here to learn techniques for managing and working with your children. In addition, each of you here is demonstrating by your presence that you are aware that your child can benefit from parent-school cooperation and that you are a concerned parent or guardian.

This is the first of four workshop sessions designed to help parents of typical and exceptional children. The purpose of the workshop series is to help each of you learn and apply behavior management techniques. The skills can be used to deal with actual problems encountered in raising typical as well as handicapped children, since behavior management techniques have been shown to be effective with both groups of individuals. We will meet here each (Thursday) night from (7:00 P.M.) to (9:30 P.M.). We will be sure to end on time and after tonight, we will also be starting on time. It is crucial that you attend the next two sessions if you hope to develop a behavior management program for your child. The fourth and final session is also important because at that meeting we will attempt to "put together" previously discussed information.

It is necessary that you participate fully in the workshop by completing "homework" assignments and attempting the exercises given during each session. Parents who attend all sessions and complete all assignments have the greatest chance for successful improvement of their child's behavior.

I would like to talk more specifically about the objectives of the workshops and to give you an overview of the next three sessions, as well as a preview of what we will be doing this evening. But, first, I would be interested in any questions or comments any of you may have.

Our goal for this evening's session is to help each of you identify a specific behavior problem that you would like to work on with your child. You have been asked to complete a child information form [Exhibit 13-4] that we will be using in tonight's work.

During our next session, you will be shown how to observe and record systematically the behavior you wish to change. During the third session you will learn how to design a program to produce actual behavioral changes. During the final session, we will meet to discuss your progress and any specific problems or questions that you may have regarding your own child's program and procedures for setting up future programs.

Exhibit 13-6 continued

By the end of this four-part series many of you should be seeing or beginning to see improvement in your child's behavior. Research has shown that a majority of the parents who systematically follow a behavior management approach are eventually successful in changing the behaviors they identify. However, we must emphasize that attending all sessions, participating in practice exercises, and completing homework assignments are crucial to success.

Tonight and during each of the next two sessions you will be shown a slide-tape presentation that is the basis of the information for these workshops. However, before showing the slide and providing you with additional information, let me answer any questions that you might have up to this point.

the nature of the information. Participants should also be provided an opportunity to ask questions or make comments prior to and following the slide-tape presentation.

In order to provide feedback regarding the effectiveness of the slide-tape presentation and to aid in identifying particular problems or misconceptions, a posttest questionnaire is administered to participants following each slide-tape presentation. It is helpful to prepare participants for the questionnaire by explaining that its purpose is to help determine how well the slide-tape presentation was able to convey the information. Participants should be informed that the sheets will be collected but that no one needs to sign the test.

Additional Guidelines for Working with Parents

While the above program example focuses only on the first of four group sessions and is only one of several such available group training alternatives in the behavior management area (Hall, 1976; Wagonseller, Burnett, Salzburg, & Burnett, 1977), it does demonstrate the specificity and structure required for successful use with parents. When such precision is a part of a program the overall effectiveness will in most instances be significantly increased.

The structured training procedures employed with parents to enable them to modify social behavior can also be implemented to augment children's academic programs (Karnes & Lee, 1978). However, to be functional such programs must be based on previously established home-school cooperation. Kelly (1974) observed that "more than any other form of involvement, active parental facilitation of specific subject matter learning must reflect a marked degree of parent-teacher cooperation. Without this type of working relationship, most specific subject matter involvements, from simple parental encouragement to tutoring can never be fully realized'' (p. 120). In addition, these parent-oriented tutorial programs should always be coordinated by a child's teacher and only after parents have been provided sufficient instruction and structure.

Finally, group tutorial training programs for parents should be based on the following guidelines:

- Only parents who are motivated and who appear appropriate to tutor their own children should be involved. This type of training is definitely not for every parent.

- Parents should receive structured training before being allowed to conduct tutoring sessions with their own children. These training programs should make use of lectures, discussions, role model demonstrations, and simulation exercises.

- Parents should constantly be provided new training to match their child's changing needs and skills. Karnes and Zehrbach (1972) suggested that trainers consider using single-topic and small-group training sessions so that parents with the same specific training needs can be dealt with at the same time.

- Carefully monitored evaluation and feedback systems should be incorporated into every program.

- Educators should design their training and feedback systems in such a manner as to provide regular and systematic reinforcement for parents.

Abundant evidence exists to support the contention that many parents can be used as tutors with their own children and that a group training format may be the most efficient and efficacious means of developing tutorial competency (Adamson, 1970; Stokes & Baer, 1978). However, positive results from such programs can be expected only in conjunction with carefully structured and monitored training programs and ongoing evaluation systems.

GROUP COUNSELING AND PARENT EDUCATION PROGRAMS

As suggested previously, educational conferencers must be able to determine when the needs of parents and families are such that traditional counseling and therapy skills are required. Conferencers must be aware of their own strengths and weaknesses and be willing to refer parents and families to mental health personnel as needed.

In part, the process of determining which parents are most appropriate for group educational conferences as opposed to psychotherapy or psychological counseling depends on the distinction made between conferencing, counseling, and psychotherapy. Unfortunately, attempts to make such distinctions have been extremely unprofitable. Perry (1976), for example, observed that attempts at comparing counseling and psychotherapy have been clouded "by an interest either in making one exclusive of the other, or in making the two entirely indistinguishable. Even less biased comparisons have not been illuminating, for they have referred to peripheral matters of institutional settings, function, or training, seldom to process" (p. 5). Nonetheless, there is relatively good agreement that psychotherapists are more inclined to be involved in situations in which intrapsychic and interpsychic conflict are the most salient issues and in which obvious psychopathology exists. Counselors, on the other hand, are more inclined to work with individuals who evidence specific adjustment problems, especially with regard to role or position. For example, adjusting to the role of being the parent of an exceptional child would in many instances fall within a counselor's domain. In instances in which minimal levels of conflict exist and in which significant pathology is absent, an individual will probably be most appropriate for counseling as opposed to psychotherapy.

The task of differentiating conferencing from counseling is also difficult. However, in spite of the confusion and the significant overlap between the two roles, educational conferencers are more inclined to focus on exchanging information with parents and training them to function more productively relative to their child's educational program, while counselors tend to be more involved with family adjustment problems and related conflicts.

With regard to conducting group sessions, educational conferencers must acknowledge that, in most instances, they are not counselors or psychotherapists and that parents requiring such services are most adequately dealt with by other professionals. In such situations the primary role of the educational conferencer should be one of referral agent.

While educators may be restricted in their capacity to conduct group therapy and counseling sessions, they can play a significant role as group facilitators and trainers in parent education programs. In particular, parents can be provided strategies for facilitating communication and reducing conflict in their homes and with their children and families through involvement with educational conferencers. Two such programs for parents that have been successfully disseminated and implemented through group meetings are Gordon's (1970) Parent Effectiveness Training and Dinkmeyer and McKays' (1976) Systematic Training for Effective Parenting.

Parent Effectiveness Training (PET) Program

According to Gordon (1980), the PET was devised as a strategy for facilitating communication and enhancing relationships between parents and their children.

The model was developed as an educational approach best suited for group situations. After completing a training program, educational conferencers are able to instruct parents in the use of the system.

The PET model is designed to instruct parents in the use of interpersonal skills associated with more effective communication. Specifically, Gordon (1980) described his model as being associated with "reciprocal relationships; relationships in which there is social equity; relationships in which there is mutual need satisfaction; collaborative relationships; humanistic relationships; relationships in which there is mutual respect for the rights of each; and therapeutic relationships" (p. 108).

The model (Gordon, 1970) focuses on a variety of interpersonal skills, including active listening, "I messages," problem ownership, and "no lose" methods of conflict resolution. These and related skills are established and enhanced through the use of discussions, role model demonstrations, and role playing. Through the training program, parents are shown the value of listening and expressing their own feelings and of encouraging their children to do likewise.

The PET model has proved to be used effectively by parents to enhance relationships with their children (Gordon, 1978). Furthermore, the model can be disseminated by educational conferencers within a group environment.

Systematic Training for Effective Parenting (STEP)

The STEP program (Dinkmeyer & McKay, 1976) is also an educational model appropriate for dissemination to parents by educational conferencers in group settings. Based on Adlerian concepts (Adler, 1977), the model makes use of a kit containing a leadership manual, group discussion guidelines, cards and questions, and cassette tapes for use by parents in developing and practicing specific communication skills. The program is designed to instruct parents in a theoretical explanation of behavior and procedures for more effectively communicating and influencing the behavior of their children.

During STEP training sessions, attention is focused on descriptive family conflict situations. Parents are encouraged to discuss strategies for handling the various situations based on STEP-related information and discussions.

The training program also makes use of the "parent 'c' group" concept (Dinkmeyer & Carlson, 1973), a procedure designed to aid parents in acquiring information and evaluating their beliefs and attitudes. The strategy was titled "'c'" group because the components include: collaboration, consultation, clarification, confrontation, concern and caring, confidentiality, commitment, and change. According to Dinkmeyer and Dinkmeyer (1976), "The 'c' group goes beyond the study of principles and involves the sharing not only of procedures and ideas but helps members become more aware of how their beliefs, feelings and attitudes affect their relationship with their children" (p. 5).

While the STEP program is a multifaceted approach, it can be implemented by educational conferencers with the necessary training, time, and motivation. The model is particularly appropriate for ongoing parent groups.

In some ways, the role of the educator as a source of group counseling and therapeutic aid is limited. As mentioned previously, educators must be aware of their therapeutic limitations and be willing to refer parents and families with more intensive needs to trained mental health personnel. Yet, when adequately trained the educational conferencer must be considered a valuable source of assistance to parents interested in enhancing their ability to communicate with their children and families.

GROUP PARENT SERVICE PROGRAMS

Some parents of exceptional children and youth will be interested in involvement in community action programs. Particularly suited are individuals who have had their own basic needs satisfied and who are interested in serving a broader range of handicapped individuals. Community action roles include volunteer, advisory board members, and "parent-to-parent" group workers, for example.

While educators must be cognizant of the importance of these activities and the significance of parent-coordinated service ventures, they must also be aware that the primary characteristic of these programs is that they are structured and governed by parents themselves. Hence, the educator must be cautious in assuming a leadership role in this area. Rather, a more appropriate strategy might be to arrange for an initial group session with interested parents for the purpose of presenting information and alternatives regarding parent service programs. At such a session parents should be encouraged to arrange for leadership from among their own ranks and to structure their own activities. While the educator can and must serve as a resource to these groups, the activities themselves should be undertaken by parents.

While educators will be required to implement certain service program suggestions (e.g., train parents wishing to volunteer as aides in a classroom), they must remember that the positive benefits of groups can and will accrue independently of their presence.

CONCLUSION

Even though parents of exceptional children and youth must be afforded opportunities to interact with educational personnel on an individual basis, the value of group interactions cannot be underestimated. Not only can these alternatives save time and energy, but they also allow parents to benefit from each other's experiences and perceptions. When used judiciously, the group conference can be one of the most valuable and effective tools in the conferencer's repertoire.

Exercises

1. Prepare a group conference agenda for exchanging information with parents in your class or program. Compare similarities and differences between your agenda and those of others. In addition, compare differences in your agenda and that which you would use in an individual information exchange session.
2. Develop handbooks on P.L. 94-142 and parent-educator conference participation appropriate for dissemination and discussion at group meetings. Compare your booklets with those of others who may be involved with different ages and types of children.
3. Conduct a tutorial training or behavior management training program for a group of parents in your class or program. Share your experiences and curricula with others who have conducted similar sessions.
4. Observe a Parent Effectiveness Training (PET) or Systematic Training for Effective Parenting (STEP) session. Discuss with the group leader and participants their particular likes and dislikes of the program.

REFERENCES

Adamson, G.A. *Educational modulation center: Final report*. E.S.E.A., P.L. 89-10, Title III, Unified School District 233, Olathe, Kansas, 1970.

Adler, K.A. Philosophical and sociological concepts in Adlerian psychology. *Proceedings of the symposium: The individual psychology of Alfred Adler*. Eugene, Ore.: University of Oregon, 1977.

Berkowitz, B., & Graziano, A. Training parents as behavior therapists: A review. *Behavior Research and Therapy*, 1972, *10*, 297-317.

Chinn, P., Winn, J., & Walters, R. *Two-way talking with parents of special children*. St. Louis: Mosby, 1978.

Dinkmeyer, D., & Carlson, J. (Eds.), *Consulting: Facilitating human potential and change processes*. Columbus, Ohio: Merrill, 1973.

Dinkmeyer, D., & Dinkmeyer, D. Systematic parent education in the schools. *Focus on Guidance*, 1976, *8*(10), 1-12.

Dinkmeyer, D., & McKay, G. *STEP, systematic training in effective parenting*. Circle Pines, Minn.: American Guidance Service, 1976.

Duncan, L.W., & Fitzgerald, P.W. Increasing the parent-child communication through counselor-parent conferences. *Personnel and Guidance Journal*, 1969, *48*, 514-517.

Gordon, T. *Parent effectiveness training*. New York: Wyden, 1970.

Gordon, T. Parent effectiveness training: A presentive program and its effects on families. In M.J. Fine (Ed.), *Handbook on parent education*. New York: Academic Press, 1980.

Gordon, T. *PET in action*. New York: Bantam Books, 1978.

Hall, R.V. *Parent training: A preventive mental health program*. National Institute of Mental Health Grant T31-HH14543, Department of Health, Education and Welfare, 1976.

Karnes, M.B., & Lee, R.C. *Early childhood: What research and experience say to the teacher of exceptional children*. Reston, Va.: Council for Exceptional Children, 1978.

Karnes, M.B., & Zehrbach, R.R. Flexibility in getting parents involved in the school. *Teaching Exceptional Children*, 1972, *5*, 6-9.

Kelly, E.J. *Parent-teacher interaction: A special education perspective*. Seattle: Special Child Publications, 1974.

Kroth, R.L., & Simpson, R.L. *Parent conferences as a teaching strategy*. Denver: Love Publishing, 1977.

McDowell, R.L. Parent counseling: The state of the act. *Journal of Learning Disabilities*, 1976, *9*(10), 6-11.

National advisory committee on handicapped children. *Special education for handicapped children*. Washington, D.C.: Department of Health, Education and Welfare, 1968.

O'Dell, S. Training parents in behavior modification. *Psychological Bulletin*, 1974, *81*, 408-433.

Perry, W.G. On the relation of psychotherapy to counseling. In G.S. Belkin (Ed.), *Counseling: Direction in theory and practice*. Dubuque, Iowa: Kendall-Hunt, 1976.

Rose, S. A behavioral approach to group treatment of parents. *Social Work*, 1969, *14*, 21-29.

Rutherford, R.B., & Edgar, E. *Teachers and parents: A guide to interaction and cooperation*. Boston: Allyn & Bacon, 1979.

Sasso, G., Hughes, V., Critchlew, W., Falcon, M., & Delquadri, J. The effects of home tutoring procedures on the oral reading rates of learning disabled children. Unpublished manuscript, Juniper Gardens Children's Project, University of Kansas, 1980.

Simpson, R.L., & Combs, N.N. *Parenting the exceptional child: A workshop manual*. Developed under federal contract 300-75-0309 with the Bureau of Education for the Handicapped, U.S. Office of Education, Department of Health, Education and Welfare, 1978.

Simpson, R.L., & Swenson, C.R. *Parts I-III: Parenting the exceptional child: Developing and maintaining adaptive behavior*. An audio-visual presentation developed under federal contract 300-75-0309 with the Bureau of Education for the Handicapped, U.S. Office of Education, Department of Health, Education and Welfare, 1978.

Stokes, T., & Baer, D.M. An implicit technology of generalization. *Journal of Applied Behavior Analysis*, 1978, *11*, 590-620.

Thomas, C. Introduction to a learning disability program. Unpublished manuscript, University of Kansas, 1974.

Turnbull, A.P. Parent-professional interactions. In M. Snell (Ed.), *Curriculum for the moderately and severely retarded*. Columbus, Ohio: Merrill, 1981.

Wagonseller, B.R., Burnett, M., Salzburg, B., & Burnett, J. *The art of parenting*. Champaign, Ill.: Research Press, 1977.

Wyckoff, J.L. Parent education programs: Ready, set, go! In M.J. Fine (Ed.), *Handbook on parent education*. New York: Academic Therapy, 1980.

Chapter 14

Resolving Conflicts between Parents and Educators

In many respects the ideal parent-educator relationship is considered to be one that embodies harmony, unity, understanding, and a conciliatory attitude. In the minds of at least some, this relationship should be free from conflict. The basis for this position, albeit inaccurate, is understandable. That is, much attention has been given the need to establish and maintain rapport and trust and to be sensitive to one's own values and the values of those with whom we relate. The resulting concept has been the need to establish and maintain a working relationship that is consistently free from conflict and differences of opinion.

While the need for an acceptable working relationship and atmosphere cannot be denied, it is important that this not be confused with an association in which conflicts are totally absent. Interactions among individuals with different goals, backgrounds, and motivations will periodically involve differences and conflict. Accordingly, it is necessary that this normal and healthy product of human interaction not be perceived incorrectly. To be totally free of conflicts, individuals in a relationship would either need to adopt a strategy of avoiding situations that could potentially breed differences of opinion or fail to recognize their own feelings and needs. In instances in which differences of opinion and conflict are totally absent, so, too, is effective communication. Jourard (1966) believes that, "Interpersonal relationships, besides being a rich source of satisfaction for the participants, also provide a rich source of problems for each participant. The solution of these problems results either in growth of personality toward health or away from health'' (p. 345). While this in no way is supportive of the need or desirability of severe interpersonal conflicts in parent-educator relationships, it does suggest that differences of opinion among adults will periodically arise and can serve as facilitators in the development of new and creative solutions to problems. Thus, normal differences of opinion between parents and professionals should be viewed as indications of open communication, interpersonal maturity, and the basis for meeting the individualized needs of exceptional children and adolescents most effectively. Consistent with this perception, the educator should not actively seek strategies for avoiding healthy conflicts but rather ways for arbitrating differences and selecting mutually satisfying solutions to problems.

FACTORS ASSOCIATED WITH THE DEVELOPMENT OF UNHEALTHY CONFLICT

In the course of developing and implementing educational and training programs for exceptional children and youth, a multitude of decisions will need to be made. Each of these decisions will reflect the values, training, experiences, and goals of the individuals involved in the process and thus each will potentially be the source of differences and conflicts. In situations characterized by free and open communication, the expression of different opinions and the resulting resolutions can enhance the interpersonal relationship between parents and professionals and subsequentially the appropriateness of the services provided children. There are, however, other conditions associated with the development of conflict that are not products of open communication and that are much more difficult to resolve. These situations cannot be considered healthy and do not reflect differences of opinion based on free and open communication. Rather, these conflicts develop as a reaction to situations in which effective avenues of communication are absent. Solutions to these problems are usually not available through the use of standard conflict resolution models but rather are based on the development of acceptable parent-educator relationships and communication strategies. Ways in which unhealthy conflict situations can develop are discussed below.

Conflict, expressed as anger, hostility, or fear may become the sole form of self-expression. The capacity to express differences of opinion and position exists as a necessary and vital means of maintaining an open and effective relationship. Without the opportunity to express differences, parents will be deprived of a primary avenue of appropriate communication. This situation will frequently result in parents employing strong emotion, such as anger or sorrow, in order to gain attention or to release a buildup of minor frustrations that could have been dealt with by way of more effective communication procedures.

There may be insufficient opportunity for parents and professionals to exchange information. In the absence of an adequate information exchange system, both parents and educators are more likely to misunderstand and to accuse the other for the development of problems. When parents are not a part of the decision-making process and when information is not exchanged between parents and professionals, such that the basis for decisions and changes are not clearly understood, conflicts can be anticipated.

Professionals may fail to offer viable models and direction for problem solving and conflict resolution. Although differences of opinion may be a normal by-product of a healthy adult-to-adult relationship, it is necessary that the professional set the tone and provide directions and a model for managing problems and conflict. In particular, the conferencer must be able to clearly communicate that it is appropriate for parents to have opinions that are different from those of the professional and that strategies exist for reconciling differences such that the needs of their child will most effectively be met. This verbal message must also be supported by actual demonstrations of problem-solving and conflict resolution behavior.

Professionals and parents may lack a shared language and knowledge of established protocol. Anger, despair, or withdrawal can be anticipated when parents are exposed to language and procedures that they fail to comprehend. Long (1971) and Dembinski and Mauser (1977) advised that only language appropriate for each parent's social, cultural, and ethnic background should be employed by the conferencer. Turnbull and Strickland (1981) elaborated on the need for parents to be familiar with the procedures utilized in exceptional education programs. These researchers have each recognized the necessity of making parents an active part of the communication process and of the potential for unhealthy interpersonal discord when there is an absence of a common language and shared information.

There may be an absence of trust and acceptance of value differences. The creation of an effective environment in which communication can occur necessitates a basic measure of trust and an acceptance of one's own values and the values of others. Without this basic ingredient of effective communication, parents and professionals will lack the basis for healthy conflict resolution. Wagonseller (1979) observed that "many confrontations between parents and children could be avoided through the use of good communication skills which assist in settling problems before they turn into major wars" (p. 21).

Parents may lack appropriate methods for influencing their child's educational system. In order for parents and professionals to communicate and arbitrate their differences in an effective and functional manner, they must have acceptable modes of influencing their offspring's educational program. Without this option, parents are left with no alternative but to withdraw from interactions with the school, bitterly accept the situation, or create conflicts.

It should be recognized that conflicts resulting from one of these or related deficiencies or policies can be effectively resolved only with a solution to the underlying issues. While crisis intervention and short-term solutions are possible, ultimate and lasting success will be based on the development of mutually satisfying responses to underlying problems.

THE COMMUNICATION PROCESS: AN ANALYSIS

In the final analysis, the capacity to resolve conflicts effectively or to create conditions in which productive conflict resolution strategies can be applied will be a function of the quality of the communication process. The components of this process, according to Barnlund (1973), are the sender, who encodes a message; the message itself; and the receiver, who must correctly decode the message. In order for effective communication to occur, all components must be coordinated and functional.

The encoder (sender) must be able to transmit information in such a fashion that another individual will be motivated to attend and respond. The success of this endeavor, according to Berlo (1960), will be directly related to the sender's communication skills, attitudes, socioeconomic status, and technical knowledge. In addition, the encoder's nonverbal messages will also be a significant part of the communication process. Gestures, posture, facial expression, body language, and voice tone are only a few of the ways in which nonverbal communication occurs. As suggested by Fast (1971), communication is a multifaceted affair and frequently occurs independent of verbal content.

It should also be apparent that the communication process is dependent on the accurate decoding of the sender's messages. This capacity is directly related to the receiver's attitudes, communication skills, background, experiences, and ability to interpret information. In addition, the accurate reception of messages will be related to the receiver's ability to solicit feedback regarding assumptions made and the exactness of information decoded (Rogers, 1951). In particular, this will involve asking for clarification or examples to verify one's understanding of a message. One need only ponder the many nuances of language and the multitude of ways in which the same stimuli can be interpreted to gain an appreciation of the importance of this process.

A related skill is the ability to provide feedback to senders. While it is important to avoid making moral or value judgments, the receiver must be able to provide appropriate feedback. Without this mechanism the sender has no way of determining whether the message has been accurately received. An additional receiver skill needed for effective communication is the ability to obtain additional information. Benjamin (1969) devoted an entire chapter to questioning, noting that "The question is a useful tool when used delicately and sparingly" (p. 86). One particular area of utility is in obtaining additional and clarifying information from senders.

Finally, receivers, especially educators, must be sensitive to emotional and verbal cues. That is, in addition to the manifest content of the senders' message, receivers must also be able to focus and respond to affect. Numerous researchers and practitioners (Hammond, Hepworth, & Smith, 1977; Rogers, 1951) have concluded that the emotional content of a message may be the most salient feature and that the listening and responding process must consider this feature.

COMMUNICATION: THE KEY TO CONFLICT RESOLUTION

While talking and exchanging information are typical, everyday functions, the actual process of communicating with another individual is much less common.

True communication, whether between parents and professionals, friends, or lovers, requires mutual acceptance, attentiveness, trust, and an atmosphere of "good feelings." In these situations the participants assert an interest and understanding of another person and the information this individual is attempting to impart.

Even though this propitious level of communication is ideal, it is also within the bounds of many parent-educator conferences. It is, of course, naive to expect this level of involvement in the absence of prior parental contact or with every parent. However, without at least a basic atmosphere of effective communication, a fruitful interpersonal relationship will be unattainable. Interestingly, both parents and educators have revealed the need and desire to communicate (Dembinski & Mauser, 1977); yet, there remains a high level of dissatisfaction with communication opportunities. Without question, effective resolution of conflicts will be possible only in a suitable interpersonal atmosphere. In addition, such an atmosphere will aid in preventing irreconcilable disunion and conflict between parents and professionals.

VARIABLES ASSOCIATED WITH CONFLICT RESOLUTION

A variety of factors will impact on any interpersonal conflict and the approach selected for resolving the dissonance. Included are the nature of the conflict and its importance to the individuals involved in the discord, the time and resources required to gain resolution, and the willingness of the participants to compromise and allow for concession. These factors will influence not only the conflict resolution strategy that will be chosen but also the potential for resolution. In situations involving various levels of cooperation, conflict resolution is likely; likewise, it is unrealistic to expect that any strategy will be effective when one or both parties are unwilling to make adjustments. This potential for resolution is illustrated in Figure 14-1.

The Nature of the Conflict and Its Perceived Importance

The nature of the conflict and its perceived importance to the parents and professional will be a major variable influencing any reconciliation. A situation perceived as having significant importance will more frequently be associated with a position of obduracy and steadfastness than one considered to have less consequence. When both the parent and educator perceive an issue to be highly significant, the conflict resolution process becomes even more intricate and difficult.

One set of parents, for example, had toiled several years to establish an association for learning disabled children in their community. They considered

Figure 14-1 Potential for Resolution of Conflict

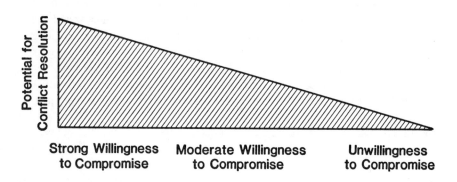

Strong Willingness **to Compromise**	**Moderate Willingness** **to Compromise**	**Unwillingness** **to Compromise**

their efforts directly responsible for the services their 12-year-old learning disabled son was receiving. When the recommendation to mainstream their son was made, the parents openly and firmly resisted, noting that their son had been unsuccessfully "mainstreamed" for several years prior to the development of what they considered to be an appropriate educational program. The child's teacher felt equally strong that the pupil should be mainstreamed, observing that he had made significant progress and was capable of functioning in a regular class setting. The strength with which the parents and teacher assumed their respective positions made the negotiation of a mutually satisfying position much more difficult than if such strong stands had not been taken.

Time and Resources Required for Resolution

While resolution is possible in a majority of conflict situations, the success of the process will be associated with the amount of effort and the number of resources required to reach a solution. Since most educators (particularly classroom teachers) and parents will have time and resource limitations, the resolution of conflicts is possible only when the process is within the means of the participants.

One classroom teacher involved in a conflict with the parents of a moderately retarded adolescent over the youth's curriculum was unable to invest the time necessary to satisfactorily resolve the issue. Although the teacher felt that progress was being made, the amount of time required to work with the parents became inordinate. The teacher ultimately referred the parents to a school psychologist. While not as well versed in knowledge of curriculum as the teacher, the psychologist had more time to spend with the parents in negotiating a resolution.

Willingness of the Participants to "Lose"

Unfortunately the conflict resolution process can sometimes take on an atmosphere in which the involved individuals perceive the inability to gain one's position as a failure. Especially when polarization occurs or when extreme positions are adopted and when strong affect is present, the resolution process, regardless of how strongly based on reason, can take on a "win-lose" flavor. It is mandatory that the conferencer remove this atmosphere if successful conflict resolution is to occur.

APPROACHES TO CONFLICT RESOLUTION

Just as with any problem-solving strategy, there are a variety of ways in which conflicts can be expressed and dissipated. While some are by their very nature more effective and appropriate than others, different situations will create a need for different conflict resolution approaches.

Avoidance

According to Lewin (1935), individuals in conflict situations can either avoid the issues involved, and with it the disunion, or directly deal with them. While avoiding conflicts is an obvious option, it is, by far, the least acceptable. Not only is it difficult to avoid conflicts, but doing so can severely limit the growth potential of any relationship. As suggested by a number of researchers and practitioners (Shafer & Shoben, 1956), open, effective communication occurs only when the participants feel confident in expressing their thoughts and feelings.

Accommodation

While a conciliatory and accommodating attitude is a necessary component of the effective conflict negotiation process, it should be recognized that when accommodation serves as the sole means of resolving issues it is counterproductive. Individuals may avoid conflicts and the placing of stress on relationships simply by always accepting another individual's position. This strategy, however, has at least two major limitations. First, it is virtually impossible to be accommodating in all situations, particularly with individuals who may be quite demanding. Second, this approach will almost always cause frustration and anger, thus serving to strain rather than support a relationship. While an accommodating attitude is a basic requisite for effective conflict resolution it is not an end in itself nor an adequate strategy for resolving conflicts.

Mutual Problem Solving

An alternative to avoidance and accommodation is mutual problem solving. This collaborative strategy has the distinct advantage of providing a means for meeting both the parent and educators' needs while serving the best interests of the child. These circumstances, according to Warschaw (1980), lead to "win-win" situations.

Successful problem solving is dependent on a variety of factors, including an awareness of the needs and emotions of the parent and professional involved in the situation. Above all, it should be recognized that successful problem solving relies on effective communication skills.

As previously noted, a basic feature of effective communication is the use of active listening skills (Rogers, 1961). Active listening involves attention to both the manifest and emotional content of messages. Related to this listening process is the ability to empathically respond. This feedback mechanism is one primary means by which educators can communicate interest and understanding, including an acceptance of parents' feelings. This acceptance will in no way detract from the ability of the conferencer to negotiate; it will, in fact, have the opposite effect. While conferencers may not agree with parents on particular issues, they must be able to understand their position before employing an appropriate conflict resolution strategy. Conferencers who are able to listen effectively provide a supportive environment for parents where they can be heard without fear of blame. This atmosphere increases the parents' feelings of safety and their willingness to engage in problem solving. Without doubt, effective problem solving can occur only when threatening conditions are removed.

The listening and responding process is also designed to provide feedback. This clarification and perception checking mechanism serves to assure the person talking that the message is being accurately received and that the conferencer is truly interested and listening. Listening does not require that the conferencer agree with the position taken by a parent; rather, it simply is a process of communicating interest and understanding. The listener may also find it beneficial to acknowledge particular components of a parent's message. By attending and acknowledging the validity of portions of the parent's position, and looking for areas of mutual agreement, the conferencer is able to maintain an atmosphere conducive to problem solving while establishing a basis for inquiring, questioning, and negotiating on areas of disagreement. Such a procedure is far superior to attempts at arguing with parents independent of this rapport-building mechanism.

Mutual problem solving also requires an atmosphere of constructive openness. While it might be assumed that withholding one's feelings and opinions may reduce the chance of hurting, angering, or alienating parents, it seldom accomplishes that goal. In instances in which the conferencer is not open, the parent is denied access to feedback needed to build and maintain a relationship and to engage in mutual problem solving. Constructive openness, as opposed to undifferentiated candor, is limited to responses that are facilitative of the relationship and problem-solving process. That is, confrontation and openness that are ends in themselves and that do not have the potential to improve the relationship or solve the conflict should be avoided.

Constructive openness does make use of confrontation. While confrontation may generate an image of anxiety and open dissension, and thus be perceived as a detractor to the conflict resolution process, it can be an essential part of the negotiation process. In order to be effective it must, however, be accompanied by other problem-solving tools and communication facilitators. Confrontation is a counterproductive process when employed independently of other basic communication and negotiating procedures. It should also be noted that the intensity of any confrontation be only as strong as the parent-educator relationship. Conferencers would be wise to avoid strong and frequent confrontation in new and weakly formed relationships.

Constructive confrontation allows for the opportunity to authentically identify one's feelings and frustrations. That is, it is one primary avenue for expressing anger, emotion, or concern without producing additional conflict or stress. In particular, "I" messages (e.g., "I am concerned," "I am upset by . . . ") have been identified as being highly useful for this purpose (Gordon, 1970; Hammond, et al., 1977). These responses tend to be safer and more appropriate than "you" statements (e.g., "You are not doing what we agreed on," "You don't seem to be as concerned as you should be").

Constructive confrontation also tends to be most functional when employed in descriptive form. That is, the conferencer should report what is seen (e.g., "I have observed that James has not had his daily report card signed for two weeks"); what is felt (e.g., "I am concerned," "I am uncomfortable"); and what is desired or expected (e.g., "I would like to see us arrive at a mutually agreed-upon plan"). Above all, the confrontation process must focus on the situation or behavior of concern rather than an attack on the parents. Personal attacks simply do not facilitate the goal of improving communication or interpersonal openness.

While constructive confrontation is not an easy tool to use, it is one means of voicing concern while creating an atmosphere of openness and effective communication. It must thus be maintained as one possible strategy in the conferencer's repertoire.

Gordon (1970, 1980) developed a conflict resolution strategy that is based on active listening, "I" messages, bilateral decision making, and active negotiation. In addition, this approach is designed to allow for resolution of conflict without making one individual a "winner" and the other a "loser."

Gordon's model (1970) has six major components, the first of which is the determination of the problem, its owners, and the individuals who are associated with the conflict. Kroth (1975) also noted the importance of determining the owner of a problem, and Fine (1979) noted the need to determine ownership of feelings. Gordon suggests that the individual experiencing discomfort regarding a particular situation is the person with the problem; he further suggests that only those individuals directly involved in a particular problem should participate in its solution.

In this model, the conflict resolution process is initiated by means of an "I" statement. This response consists of a statement of concern about a particular problem or situation to another individual believed to have joint ownership in the issue. Gordon (1970) notes the necessity of addressing specific issues as opposed to dealing in generalities.

This initiating response is followed by active listening whereby the individual commencing the process attempts to understand the other individual's position and perception. This component of the process requires that a relationship appropriate for conflict resolution exists, that the parents be able to engage in rather sophisti-cated verbal interactions, and that sufficient time be allotted for the process. Finally, the process requires that both parties be willing to work toward a solution to the problem. While elementary in nature, these components of the conflict resolution process are among the most significant.

The second phase of the model involves the parents and conferencer generating possible solutions to the identified problem. The process necessitates that both parents and conferencers participate in this process and that each suggestion be given serious consideration.

The third phase involves evaluating the alternative solutions. Again, the process must be structured such that both the parents and conferencer have equal status in evaluating the alternatives.

The fourth and fifth components consist of selecting and implementing the problem-solving strategy appearing to have the most efficacy. As was noted earlier, the success of this component will be dependent on the willingness of the participants to contribute their efforts to the program. This may involve the use of a contract specifying the role to be played by the various participants.

The sixth phase consists of evaluating the solution and the satisfaction of the participants with the selection. In instances in which success or consensus are not available, the conflict resolution process is reinitiated.

While this process requires that the participants have fairly advanced cognitive and verbal skills, it has proved to be a highly effective approach with many parents. For example, a mother and father were notified by their son's former learning disability teacher that the child, who had been mainstreamed for several months, was having "problems" in his regular class setting. This teacher, who was serving as a consultant to teachers of mainstreamed children in the district, requested that a conference be scheduled to discuss the problem. At the confer-ence, attended by the parents, regular class teacher, and special educator, the parents were informed that while their son's academic performance was satisfactory, he had recently developed a number of behavioral excesses. The parents were shown behavioral charts that indicated excessive vocalizations and noncompliance. Both teachers revealed concern over the behavior and suggested that a strategy for managing the problem be selected. While the educators acknowledged that the problem was in their domain, and thus was their responsibility (and that they were willing to take total charge of the problem), they indicated a desire to include the parents in the solution. This approach was in part undertaken because on several occasions in the past the parents had complained that school personnel had not included them in their planning efforts nor kept them informed.

The parents, when informed of the problem, responded that they had not experienced an increase in behavioral problems at home. However, they did accept partial ownership of the problem and voiced a willingness to be involved in the intervention process.

The parents and educators subsequentially discussed alternatives for managing the problem. Options included additional individualized classroom attention, psychotherapy, periodic visitations to the school counselor, medication, various punishment contingencies, and a cooperative home-school communication program. Once presented, the advantages and disadvantages of each option were discussed.

These discussions resulted in the selection of the home-school communication program as the best option. In particular, this program consisted of the teacher issuing ten behavioral evaluations to the child over the course of each day. Each behavioral evaluation, reported as "satisfactory" or "needs improvement," was made on an index card and given to the child immediately after it was made. The child was required to bring home at least seven satisfactory cards per day in order to receive a reward of his choosing. Following the initital conference between the parents and teachers, the program was discussed with the child and subsequentially implemented. The educators and parents remained in close contact throughout the course of the program in order to judge its effectiveness and make necessary adjustments.

ANALYZING YOUR CONFLICT RESOLUTION STYLE

If educators were to analyze their style in interacting and resolving conflicts with parents honestly, they would probably discover that they have some characteristics that are far more facilitative than others. Therefore, it is important that conferencers be aware of how conflicts arise, the ways in which their manner contributes to conflicts, and the options that are available for resolution.

Exhibit 14-1 "Analyzing Your Style," provides one method for examining the manner in which you interact with parents. In completing the form, be honest with yourself. After completing the survey, ask a colleague or parent to rate you.

Exhibit 14-1 Analyzing Your Style

	Always	Frequently	Sometimes	Never
Are you				
1. Able to stay informed about the parents with whom you relate and their family situation				
2. Irritated by parents who offer alternatives for managing the classroom behavior of their children				
3. Willing to let parents tutor their own children at home				
4. Honest with parents				
5. Able to confront parents				
6. Prone to arguments with parents				
7. Aware of how your emotions are communicated through your body language				
8. Willing to "take risks" with parents				
9. Prone to active listening with parents				
10. Annoyed by parents who suggest curriculum ideas				
11. Threatened by parents who initiate a conference				

12. Threatened by parents who request access to school records and data

13. Willing to engage in joint problem solving with parents

14. Uneasy about admitting to parents that you don't have all the answers

15. Threatened by aggressive parents

16. Uncomfortable with parents who display emotional behavior

17. Prone to make assumptions about the parents with whom you interact

18. Creative in problem-solving strategies

19. Reluctant to make changes in the ways you deal with parents

20. Troubled by what you wish you had said but did not say in conferences with parents

Analyze and discuss with others the manner in which your style impacts on your relationships and conflict resolution approaches with parents. Although this survey does not purport to make quantitative comparisons nor to make predictions, it does offer one means of allowing the educational conferencer to examine his or her problem-solving style.

Problem-solving and conflict resolution skills must be a part of each conferencer's repertoire. In addition, it is important that each conferencer recognize that his or her style, personality, attitude, and demeanor will impact on the resolution process. Even more than the conflict resolution model or problem-solving approach that is followed will be the interpersonal characteristics of the individual. Thus, educational conferencers must not only work to develop their listening and other communication skills but must also find ways of becoming aware of their own interpersonal style. Without such a personal awareness, the most salient component of problem solving will remain an enigma.

CONCLUSION

Planning for exceptional children and youth and coordinating the viewpoints and goals of parents with those of professional educators will periodically result in conflicts. While at times these conflicts are formidable to resolve, the process of negotiating mutually satisfying alternatives can be a growth experience for both parents and educators and can lead to creative planning for pupils. When parents and educators are open and willing to engage in problem-solving and conflict-resolution processes, most issues can be satisfactorily dealt with. While conflict and the resolution of conflict may appear to be an area to be avoided, its pervasive and salient nature in the parent-educator relationship mandates that appropriate strategies be developed for its eventual occurrence.

Exercises

1. Complete Exhibit 14-1, "Analyzing Your Style." Discuss characteristics of parents and professionals that can facilitate and detract from a desirable conflict resolution atmosphere.
2. Conduct a conflict resolution simulation conference using the materials in Appendix E. Descriptions are provided for the cases previously presented for other role-play exercises (i.e., mentally retarded, physically handicapped, gifted, behaviorly disordered, and learning disabled). Consequently, you should use those materials most aligned with your area or those that you have used in previous role-playing exercises.

   In conducting the simulation exercise, one individual should assume the part of the parent, using those materials labeled "for parents." Another person, taking the part of the teacher, should structure his or her responses around the teacher materials. A third individual should assume the role of evaluator, using the evaluation form provided.

It should be assumed by the participating parties that the conference is parent initiated, that is, that the parent in the exercise contacted the educator regarding the described issue. Individuals should change roles after completing the exercise.

REFERENCES

Barnlund, D.C. Introduction: Interpersonal communication. In R.W. Pace, B.D. Peterson, & R.R. Radcliff (Eds.), *In communicating interpersonally*. Columbus, Ohio: Merrill, 1973.

Benjamin, A. *The helping interview*. Boston: Houghton Mifflin, 1969.

Berlo, D.K. *The process of communication*. New York: Holt, Rinehart & Winston, 1960.

Dembinski, R.J., & Mauser, A.J. What parents of the learning disabled really want from professionals. *Journal of Learning Disabilities*, 1977, *10*, 578-584.

Fast, J. *Body language*. New York: Pocket Books, 1971.

Fine, M.J. *Parents vs. children: Making the relationship work*. Englewood Cliff, N.J.: Prentice-Hall, 1979.

Gordon, T. *Parent effectiveness training*. New York: Wyden, 1970.

Gordon, T. Parent effectiveness training: A preventive program and its effects on families. In M.J. Fine (Ed.), *Handbook on parent education*. New York: Academic Press, 1980.

Hammond, D.C., Hepworth, D.H., & Smith, V.G. *Improving therapeutic communication*. San Francisco: Jossey-Bass, 1977.

Jourard, S.M. *Personal adjustment*. New York: Macmillan, 1966.

Kroth, R.L. *Communicating with parents of exceptional children*. Denver: Love Publishing, 1975.

Lewin, K. *A dynamic theory of personality*. New York: McGraw-Hill, 1935.

Long, A. Easing the stress of parent-teacher conferences. *Today's Education*, 1976, *64*, 84.

Rogers, C.R. *Client-centered therapy*. Boston: Houghton Mifflin, 1951.

Rogers, C.R. *On becoming a person*. Boston: Houghton Mifflin, 1961.

Shafer, L.F., & Shoben, E.J. *The psychology of adjustment*. Boston: Houghton Mifflin, 1956.

Turnbull, A.P., & Strickland, B. Parents and the educational system. In J.L. Paul (Ed.), *Understanding and working with parents of children with special needs*. New York: Holt, Rinehart & Winston, 1981.

Warschaw, T.A. *Winning by negotiation*. New York: McGraw-Hill, 1980.

Wagonseller, B.R. The parent/professional education relationship. Unpublished manuscript, University of Nevada Las Vegas, 1979.

Initial Interview Role-Playing Materials

BEHAVIORALLY DISORDERED CHILD

Billy
Age: 10

Teacher Role

The ten-year-old boy described below has been placed in your self-contained class for behaviorally disordered children. Since this youngster is new to your program the information you have about him is from the reports of others.

Report of Regular Class Teacher

Billy was referred for placement in special education because of behavior problems in the regular class. His regular class teacher reports that he has a number of behavioral excesses and academic problems. He was described as aggressive; specifically, the teacher noted that he is constantly fighting with other students. Billy was also described by his teacher as socially immature. For example, Billy "tattles" on other children and has consistently attempted to manipulate the teacher. His teacher describes him as a very insecure and frightened boy and also noted that he will work best for a teacher who assures him that he is capable of good work. He was also described as needing a physically, socially, and academically firm teacher. According to the teacher he was in the lowest reading group and generally worked at about one grade level below his peers.

School Psychologist's Report

Individualized intelligence testing results indicated that Billy is functioning at the low average range of intelligence. Previous test results and teacher observations confirmed this intellectual estimate.

Direct classroom observations indicated that Billy attended to task approximately 25 percent less than his peers. In addition, he daydreamed and was out of his seat without permission significantly more than the others in his class.

Standardized academic assessment measures indicated a reading recognition level of 4.0, a reading comprehension level of 2.5, and arithmetic performance of 3.0.

Parent Role

Parents' Perceptions

Billy's parents are most concerned with their son's destructive behavior. They related three incidents in recent weeks when he vandalized neighbors' homes and tortured neighborhood animals. The mother also recalled a recent episode when a baby sitter found Billy trying to shoot his sister with a bow and arrow. Billy told his mother they were "just playing." Recently, a neighbor asked Billy to go home, and he retaliated by throwing a rock through her front window. Billy, according to his parents, picks on his younger sister, especially when angry with other people. His parents report that he does not interact with the neighborhood children and prefers to stay indoors and watch television or go to his room.

Development

The parents report that Billy's early development appeared normal. In particular, his development was similar to the other children in the family. He was completely toilet trained by 3½ years of age and has had no problem with bed wetting. He began talking at 17 months and was talking in short sentences by 2½ years of age.

Family Structure

Billy lives with his natural parents, a 31-year-old laborer father and a 29-year-old unemployed mother. They have been married 13 years. His siblings include a 12-year-old brother and two younger sisters, aged 7 and 8. The maternal grandparents care for Billy and the other children when the parents are gone.

Interaction

According to his mother, Billy disturbs the entire household. She related a story of Billy chasing his youngest sister with a bow and arrow. When he was confronted, he said that he was "just playing." Following the incident he was taken to the family physician who told the parents that he would probably outgrow his problems.

The mother said they bought another television set so Billy could watch his own programs in his room without disturbing other family members.

Billy threatens his mother. He recently fought her when she tried to spank him. The mother, however, is able to manage Billy's behavior physically. The parents feel his problem is one of behavior and not a learning difficulty. They speak of him as a "smart boy" who learns quickly. The mother notes that Billy causes problems between her and her husband. For example, he annoys his mother, increasing his disturbing behavior when the father is due home. The mother, nervous and distraught, nags at him. The father tells her she is yelling too much, and Billy smiles as he hears the parents "bicker." He tells his dad his mother has been mean all day to him. Billy also makes his mother feel guilty for her treatment of him.

Billy has low self-esteem and often makes remarks that no one in the family likes him, that everybody hates him. He has poor relationships with both his siblings and peers. The parents feel he is selfish and rough in play. He was on the soccer team at his last school but was removed owing to inappropriate behavior.

Discipline

The father indicates he is authoritarian with his son although the mother is able to control him. The father whips him and sends him to bed. If the mother threatens to whip Billy, he threatens to tell his dad.

Significant Medical History

Childhood illnesses included both measles and mumps at age 5. He has no known allergies, but according to his mother, he does have "asthmatic fever." This is characterized by difficulty in breathing following running or hard playing and occurs in the spring. Other than the above, Billy is a healthy boy who is rarely ill.

Sleeping Patterns

Billy's mother reports that Billy seems to need little sleep. He constantly gets out of bed at night and "gets into things." He does complain of occasional nightmares. He sleeps in the basement in a room of his own by his own preference. His mother also stated she feels he "lies" about what he does at night when he gets up.

Family Constellation

The 31-year-old father, who completed ten grades, is employed as a laborer. The natural mother is a full-time housewife and mother. She dropped out of school after completing the ninth grade.

GIFTED CHILD

Howard
Age: 8

Teacher Role

The eight-year-old child described below has been placed in your gifted re-source room. You have neither seen the child nor talked to the parents, but since you attended the staffing on the child you have the following information.

Report of Regular Class Teacher

Howard's problems in his regular classroom were identified as:

1. Doesn't turn work in on time
2. Daydreams
3. Becomes involved in something that interests him and then pays little attention to class activities
4. Is a perfectionist
5. Is very verbal and tends to dominate class discussions
6. Reading: Tests indicate he is two grade levels above his peers but he rarely completes his skill sheets on time.
7. Math: Howard has been working on computation skills as required by the district. His work is sloppy and he makes careless errors. His Key Math scores indicate he is two and one-half grade levels ahead of the average second grader. He used to share some new short cuts he had discovered for dividing but hasn't shared them recently. He has not mastered his addition and subtraction facts.
8. Has barely legible handwriting

Howard's interpersonal relationships with his classmates were described as good. At times his classmates seem to be in awe of his responses during discussions. Some students call him "Brain" or "Smartsy." He says he is bored, but there is a lot of work he could be doing but doesn't. Often when he should be doing his skill sheets in reading or math he is engrossed in a library book instead.

School Psychologist's Report

This 8-year-old is currently functioning in the very superior range of mental ability. In spite of this child's level of ability, he evidenced some anxiety during parts of the test. His overall intellectual functioning was in the 99th percentile on the WISC-R. The score on the performance section was three points higher than that of the verbal section, which is not a significant difference. The scaled scores ranged from a high of 19 (block design) to a low of 11 (coding). Most of the scaled scores clustered close to two standard deviations above the mean. Howard was cooperative and friendly. He has excellent verbal expressive skills.

School Social Worker's Report

Howard is the younger of two children; he has an older sister in junior-high school. The parents reported that his developmental milestones were slightly accelerated. He has had a history of ear infections and has a 10 percent hearing loss in both ears when his ears become inflamed. The parents also report that he has mild allergy problems.

The parents report that Howard attended preschool at age three and remained in this program for one year. He has also attended summer programs at private schools since age five. His hobbies include soccer, working riddles, and reading, which he does one hour per day.

Parent Role

Parents' Perceptions

The parents' major concern is Howard's ability to perform academic tasks requested by the classroom teacher. He expresses a feeling of boredom, and his regular teacher has indicated that Howard is not motivated or achieving. The parents feel that this conflict at school has frustrated him. His self-concept and relationship with his peers are now also major concerns for the parents. Howard appears sullen and withdrawn much of the time. He insists that the worksheets in the classroom are "baby" work, and he frequently refuses to do them. He gets interested in a book or game and "forgets" to turn in many of the other required assignments.

Development

Howard's mother's pregnancy was full-term. The delivery was natural without the aid of any medication. Howard walked at 12 months and talked quite well at 18 to 24 months. He was always active and restless. He had few childhood diseases, but because of a hearing loss caused by fluid build-up in the inner ear, he had ear surgery with tubes inserted at age 14 months. He has a slight hearing loss when his ears are infected, but this clears with medication. He has some allergies, but these are not considered severe.

Because the neighborhood, where the family has lived all of Howard's life, has allowed so much social interaction, a preschool was dropped after one year. He attended this program between the ages of three and four. In addition to attending summer programs at private schools since age five, Howard has attended art classes for children conducted at an art gallery. He was also enrolled in a music awareness class. The family has also been involved in many outings, including frequent trips to the library. The mother is a former teacher and seems to enjoy her time with Howard.

Howard read before entering kindergarten, which presented problems for both him and the teacher. At a conference called because of Howard's disruptive behavior in the classroom, the parents asked the teacher if she was aware that Howard was reading. The teacher was not aware, and because the school policy was that kindergarten students could not check out books at the school library, the teacher was helpful in securing books for the classroom, and Howard was allowed to read after his work was finished.

Howard had a satisfying first-grade experience. One of the things his teacher did was set up a contract arrangement for math. She allowed spelling words to be chosen from the dictionary, and she introduced him to books that were more on his reading level. He also learned to enjoy biographies. Finally, the teacher challenged him and allowed him to progress at his own pace.

The second grade has not been a continuation of the success felt in first grade. Howard has received low marks in areas in which he knew success last year.

Howard did begin piano lessons at the beginning of last summer. He has continued these lessons, and the teacher is pleased with his interest and progress. Howard and his father have talked about his joining a baseball team for the coming summer. Howard has expressed an interest, and if the situation is not too competitive, he probably will enroll in the program.

Family Structure

Howard's family includes his father, age 36; mother, age 36; and an older sister in junior high, age 12. The parents have been married 14 years. They feel that they have a good marriage with positive feelings of commitment for each other. Both parents seem intelligent and concerned. Howard's mother is a housewife and is very spontaneous, sensitive, and expressive. Howard's father is an accountant and appears to be somewhat of an introvert, very analytical, and not too expressive.

Howard receives a great deal of attention from his mother. His father's attentiveness toward him seems less. There does appear to be some inconsistency in the way the parents relate to Howard, with the father's responses tending to be very analytical while the mother tends to be more spontaneous and perhaps emotional in her interpersonal actions with her son.

LEARNING DISABLED CHILD

Sally
Age: 9

Teacher Role

The nine-year-old girl described below has been referred for placement in your learning disabilities resource room. You have neither seen the child nor talked to the parents, but since you attended the staffing on the child, you have the following information.

Report of Regular Class Teacher

The regular class teacher identified Sally's major problems as severe academic deficits and "social immaturity." In particular, the third-grade teacher reports that Sally is able to identify most letters of the alphabet. She also is reported to have a four-word sight vocabulary. In the area of mathematics, Sally is able to do simple addition and subtraction if allowed to manipulate objects. She does not seem to understand most basic mathematical concepts.

The teacher is also concerned as to Sally's ability to comprehend. Specifically, she does not know if she is simply not listening or unable to comprehend. Sally is also described as a sensitive student who is aware that she is not making the same rate of progress as the others. She described Sally's interpersonal skills as immature. She is withdrawn, desiring to be by herself much of the time. The other students in the class are accepting of her and attempt to help.

Report of Social Worker's Home Visit

The mother described Sally's problems as directly related to her academic deficits. She and her husband believe that Sally's academic expectations are relatively high and that she becomes frustrated when she is unable to function on the same level as her class peers. The mother noted that her daughter typically manifests her frustration by becoming sullen and withdrawn. According to the mother, this is the same pattern that her husband employs to demonstrate his anger or frustration. She further noted that this pattern is typical of how Sally interacts with her peers.

To a lesser extent the parents are concerned about Sally's lack of self-confidence. They feel, however, that academic success will improve her self-concepts and her peer relationships. The parents reported that their daughter is not a behavior problem.

School Psychologist's Report

According to intellectual measures, Sally is functioning in the average range of mental ability with some indication of bright normal potential. She was motivated to perform and was goal oriented the entire session. As previously reported, Sally did show significant academic deficits. Educational instruments indicate she is functioning on a readiness level. Relative strength was noted in her mathematical abilities and comprehension when material is delivered via the auditory channel. Deficit areas included sight word recognition. No perceptual problems were noted in Sally's performance. It was also noted that Sally tended to be somewhat shy and withdrawn during the testing session.

Parent Role

Parents' Perceptions

The parents' major concern is Sally's poor academic achievement. Specifically, they are concerned over her difficulties in doing her schoolwork, especially learning to read, and the frustration accompanying this failure experience. The parents further stated that because she expects so much from herself, she becomes frustrated when she is unable to do what she sees the other children doing. She feels that it is at these times when other problems, such as social withdrawal and sullen behavior, occur. Sally's mother believes that Sally is very close to her father and relies on him as a role model. She is concerned over Sally's lack of self-confidence and her poor self-image. Finally, the parents are somewhat concerned over her social withdrawal. They believe, however, that this is a result of her academic problems. The parents are in agreement that Sally is not a behavior problem. The mother stated that the discipline they use, restriction of privileges and talking to her, accomplish the desired results.

Sally's Social History

Sally's mother had a full-term pregnancy and normal delivery. The parents reported that Sally's early growth and development were normal, except that she did not talk until 20 months of age. Sally has been relatively healthy and has not had major illnesses or injuries. When she was four, Sally was enrolled at a preschool in their neighborhood. She was withdrawn shortly after beginning, however, because the parents felt that it placed Sally under severe pressure. They were also dissatisfied with the amount of social interaction that occurred among the students. They had hoped to increase the amount of interaction that Sally had with other children; the school, however, allowed for few contacts of this type. Rather, it emphasized academic preparation.

Sally attended kindergarten and first and second grades at a neighborhood public school. She was reported to be a well-behaved and quiet child. She did, however, experience academic problems in each of her early school experiences. These failure experiences have been difficult for both Sally and her parents to accept.

As noted previously, Sally is a shy, withdrawn child. She tends to model her father who is also a shy and retiring individual who avoids social interactions. Both parents describe Sally as having a "keen respect for books and toys she enjoys." They also feel she wants to read very badly and that she is sensitive and very conscious of others' feelings in all areas of interpersonal interaction.

Family Structure

Sally's family includes her father, age 36; mother, age 31; and one younger brother, age 6. Her parents have been married 12 years. They feel they have a good marriage, although there are areas of conflict. In particular, the mother is quite extroverted and active in community activities while the father is introverted and socially retiring. Both individuals take their parenting responsibilities seriously and strive to do what is right for their children.

PHYSICALLY HANDICAPPED CHILD

Eddie
Age: 6

Teacher Role

The six-year-old boy described below has been placed in your resource room for physically impaired children. You have never seen the child nor talked with the parents but you have the following information.

Previous Medical Records

Eddie was born with a meningomyelocele, which was repaired when he was six months of age. He was the product of a full-term pregnancy and uncomplicated delivery. However, he was reported to have tremors and possible seizures during the first weeks of life. This condition, along with the meningomyelocele, resulted in hospitalization for the first four weeks of life.

At one year of age Eddie began having frequent grand mal seizures. These were successfully controlled with antiseizure medication (Dilantin). At present, he has a grand mal seizure about once very five or six months. These seizures are extremely upsetting to both the child and his parents.

School Psychologist's Report

Intellectual assessment procedures indicated Eddie to be functioning in the bright normal range of mental abilities. He did particularly well on tasks requiring a verbal response. The examiner noted, in fact, that Eddie was quite adept at structuring the tasks on the tests administered and at verbally manipulating the situation (e.g., "I bet you can't do that one;" "If I get this one right will you give me some gum?").

Eddie did experience some difficulty with some of the perceptually oriented tasks. However, this was considered to be more a function of his lack of interest and experience with these tasks rather than an indication of brain damage.

The examiner was particularly impressed by this child's verbal skills and his manipulative strategy. Although his verbal prowess was considered to be a strength, the psychologist also noted that his desire to manipulate people could be a problem.

Academic assessment procedures revealed several readiness skills. He was able to follow four-item commands, match shapes, identify colors, identify basic body parts, string beads, and rote count to 50. He demonstrated a significant weakness in fine motor activities, including writing, cutting with scissors, and duplicating geometric shapes with blocks.

Parent Role

Parents' Perceptions

Although the parents know how to respond when Eddie has a seizure, they confess that they are overcome with a combination of guilt, anger, and embarrassment when they occur.

Development

Except for Eddie's physical impairment, the parents described him as normal. They note, for example, that most major developmental milestones were achieved within normal limits. He was talking at 11 months, for example, and has been walking with the aid of crutches since he was three.

The parents report that they tended to shelter their son for the first few years of his life. He was, in particular, expected to do little for himself, with the mother responding to his every need. The parents also resisted placing him in a preschool for handicapped children, preferring, rather, to keep him at home. During these years at home he was rarely taken outside the house. The parents reported that this was because of the problem in transporting him and the anger they felt when "people stared at him."

The parents are quite impressed over their son's verbal aptitude. Although irritated by his manipulative verbal behavior they believe this skill will allow him to live a relatively normal and independent life. Their expectations are relatively high for Eddie; they anticipate he will be able to attend college and pursue a profession. The parents, especially the mother, are extremely resentful of anyone who suggests otherwise.

Family Structure

The 28-year-old parents are happily married. Eddie's father travels in his selling job and is rarely home except on weekends. Eddie's mother, consequently, is the primary parenting figure for her two sons. She is not unhappy with her full-time homemaking job but does hope to pursue a career some day. She is a high school graduate and worked as a secretary until she became pregnant with Eddie. Her other son, Todd, is a "normal" four year old.

MENTALLY RETARDED CHILD

Barbie
Age: 8

Teacher Role

The eight-year-old girl described below has been placed in your self-contained classroom. You have not seen the child, nor have you ever talked to the parents, but you have the following information.

Report of Regular Class Teacher

Barbie has most recently been assigned to a first-grade classroom where she is repeating that grade. She is assigned to the same teacher she had last year. The first-grade school placement was Barbie's initial experience, having been held out of kindergarten because she was "immature."

Barbie was functioning significantly below the academic and social level of her peers. She has few reading readiness skills (unable to identify the letters of the alphabet or identify colors) or math abilities (unable to rote count to five). In addition, she has poor social skills. In particular, she stays by herself and initiates few interactions. The other children in her class are kind to her, although they tend to treat her like a much younger child. Barbie seems to enjoy this treatment.

Finally, Barbie has poor speech articulation. This deficit, combined with her shy demeanor and soft voice, make understanding her difficult. Both the teacher and her peers are becoming more adept at understanding her, however.

While Barbie is not a behavior problem she is extremely active and appears to have difficulty maintaining attention to any task for even a short time. This "hyperactive" pattern has been effectively controlled by verbal cues from the teacher, individual attention, and individualized academic programs. However, the teacher noted that this control was not immediately gained. Rather, Barbie was in the classroom several weeks before responding appropriately to the teacher.

School Psychologist's Report

The single most significant observation made during the testing session was Barbie's noncompliance and hyperactivity. She required constant attention and vacillated between ignoring and manipulating the behavior of the examiner. She was able to follow directions to a minimal degree and was successful on several items whose difficulty is commensurate with her chronological age. Although she could, at times, be implored upon to attend to the task at hand, she was difficult to maintain at any one task for more than a few minutes.

Barbie gives evidence of adequate receptive language, but her expressive skills are far less developed; at least part of this behavior is believed to be a function of her negativism. She does, on occasion, spontaneously employ language, but for the most part her verbalizations consist of repeating what has been said to her and in answering direct examiner questions. She also gave evidence of having a severe articulation problem.

Intellectual instruments were attempted, but this child's lack of cooperation and oppositional behaviors made strict adherence to testing procedures impossible. Specific strengths were noted in her ability to take disjointed elements and unite them into meaningful wholes and in integrating visual-motor responses into productive reactions. Barbie also demonstrated a deficit in perceptual-motor functioning. She was specifically weak at tasks requiring fine muscle coordination and visual-motor integration. However, since her visual-motor skills are consistent with her tested mental age, it is not known if her perceptual-motor difficulties are a reflection of her intellectual functioning or brain damage.

Indicators of socialization skills suggest this child's social maturity to be below her chronological age. Specific deficits appear to be concentrated in the area of communication; this finding correlates with previous observations.

Parent Role

Parents' Perceptions

The parents are most concerned about Barbie's hyperactivity and noncompliant behavior. Her mother and father are also concerned about Barbie's speech problems.

Both the mother and father report that Barbie has been oppositional for as long as they can remember. She has not responded to the various disciplinary techniques that have been used and typically will do what she wants. The parents also noted that she will occasionally do just the opposite of what she is asked to do or will act as if she does not hear commands. When the mother and father attempt to interfere with this behavior she will throw a tantrum.

Development

The mother's pregnancy was significant in that she was extremely ill much of the first trimester. It was also noted by the mother that ''I was so heavy I could hardly walk with her.'' Barbie was a full-term infant who weighed about eight and· one-half pounds at the time of birth. Barbie was discharged with her mother in good health at the age of four days.

The developmental landmarks are obscure due to the mother's poor memory for detail. Allegedly Barbie crawled at 16 months, walked at 19 months, was toilet trained at age 2, and began talking at age 3. This child, according to the mother's report, has only been speaking in sentences for about three years.

At approximately three months of age Barbie had a number of ''seizures,'' which were characterized by ''rolling her eyes, jumping, and getting limber.'' Barbie reportedly has periodic petit mal seizures today.

School History

Barbie is presently repeating the first grade, having skipped kindergarten. The decision to not place Barbie in kindergarten was made by the parents because of their daughter's ''immaturity.''

Barbie is with the same first-grade teacher she had last year. During the first year in this class the parents were told that she was academically and socially unable to function in the first grade. Although she was described as not being a behavior problem, the teacher described Barbie as ''very slow'' and ''probably in need of special education.'' The teacher further revealed to the parents that their daughter did not have a normal relationship with the other children. Rather, the teacher noted that the other kids respond to Barbie like they do their younger sisters.

While the teacher sought to have Barbie evaluated for special education, the parents wanted to see if their daughter could ''mature over the summer and catch up with the other kids.'' Consequently, it was decided that Barbie would repeat the first grade.

Expectations of the Parents

Barbie's parents are frustrated and overwhelmed by their daughter's poor performance in school. They believe that if she is retarded she should be placed in special education. Yet, they are not sure that that is what she needs. In addition, they are perplexed over the differences in Barbie's behavior at home and school. While the classroom teacher reports that Barbie is not a behavior problem, the parents are experiencing a variety of problem behaviors at home.

Exhibit A-1 presents a sample questionnaire to be completed by the parents after the initial conference.

Exhibit A-1 Initial Conference Evaluation

Date _____

Name of Child _____

Name of Person Playing Parent Role _____

Name of Person Playing Conferencer Role _____

Observer(s): _____

I.   General Conferencing Evaluation

A. Ability of conferencer to inform parents of the purpose of the conference.

1	2	3	4	5
Poor	Below Average	Average	Above Average	Excellent

B. Ability of conferencer to conduct the session in a systematic and sequential manner.

1	2	3	4	5
Poor	Below Average	Average	Above Average	Excellent

C. Ability of conferencer to keep the session flowing and on course.

1	2	3	4	5
Poor	Below Average	Average	Above Average	Excellent

D. Ability of conferencer to solicit and respond to parents' questions.

1	2	3	4	5
Poor	Below Average	Average	Above Average	Excellent

Exhibit A-1 continued

E. Ability of conferencer to attend to the parents.

1	2	3	4	5
Poor	Below Average	Average	Above Average	Excellent

F. Ability of conferencer to rephrase questions.

1	2	3	4	5
Poor	Below Average	Average	Above Average	Excellent

G. Ability of conferencer to summarize the conference.

1	2	3	4	5
Poor	Below Average	Average	Above Average	Excellent

II. Evaluation of Information Requested

A. Chief Complaint

1. Ability of conferencer to solicit the parents' perception of the problems.

1	2	3	4	5
Poor	Below Average	Average	Above Average	Excellent

2. Ability of conferencer to resolve discrepancies in the parents' and professionals' perception of the problem.

1	2	3	4	5
Poor	Below Average	Average	Above Average	Excellent

B. Ability of conferencer to secure developmental history information from the parents.

1	2	3	4	5
Poor	Below Average	Average	Above Average	Excellent

C. Ability of conferencer to secure information about the child's likes and dislikes from the parents.

1	2	3	4	5
Poor	Below Average	Average	Above Average	Excellent

D. Ability of conferencer to secure information about the child's school history from the parents.

1	2	3	4	5
Poor	Below Average	Average	Above Average	Excellent

E. Ability of conferencer to secure information about the parents' expectations for their child.

1	2	3	4	5
Poor	Below Average	Average	Above Average	Excellent

F. Ability of conferencer to secure sociological information about the child and family from the parents.

1	2	3	4	5
Poor	Below Average	Average	Above Average	Excellent

III. Evaluation of Information Disseminated

A. Ability of conferencer to disseminate assessment and diagnostic information to the parents.

1	2	3	4	5
Poor	Below Average	Average	Above Average	Excellent

Exhibit A-1 continued

B. Ability of conferencer to disseminate information to parents about the educational program to be used with their child.

1	2	3	4	5
Poor	Below Average	Average	Above Average	Excellent

C. Ability of conferencer to disseminate information to parents on procedures for evaluating the progress of pupils and the manner in which this information will be communicated.

1	2	3	4	5
Poor	Below Average	Average	Above Average	Excellent

D. Ability of conferencer to disseminate information to parents regarding community and school problem-solving alternatives and resources available.

1	2	3	4	5
Poor	Below Average	Average	Above Average	Excellent

IV.   Summary Information

Behavior Management Role-Playing Materials

BEHAVIORALLY DISORDERED CHILD

Billy
Age: 10

Parent Role

Billy has recently been a concern to his parents simply because of his "pouting" behavior. When displeased, Billy will show his displeasure by making facial grimaces, stomping around the house, and sulking. Although he has always had this behavior in his repertoire, he is currently displaying it to an inordinate degree. He has few friends in the neighborhood and, according to the parents, seems to be spending a great deal of his time pouting.

This behavior is quite pervasive and Billy displays it whenever he is at home, regardless of who is there. Since his mother and the siblings are most frequently at home at the same time, they experience it most.

The parents have tried scolding, isolation, ignoring, and reasoning in attempting to deal with the problem but have had little success in decreasing its rate. Billy's brother and sisters make fun of him for his "baby" behavior and his father threatens "to beat hell out of him."

Everyone in the family is upset over the situation and all are looking at the mother to solve the problem. His mother is upset and is considering leaving the family. She has told Billy this in hopes of "straightening him up." The father's attitude is that Billy is seeking punishment when he pouts and the father is not going to disappoint the child by ignoring it.

GIFTED CHILD

Howard
Age: 8

Parent Role

Howard's parents have recently become quite upset over their son's solitary play behavior. Extremely little of his day is spent in any interaction with other kids in the neighborhood. He typically plays alone in a quiet area of the house and interacts only with his parents. The parents are becoming increasingly upset by his isolated play and feel that he should be spending a majority of his leisure time engaging in social behavior.

The parents have begun nagging their son in hopes of persuading him to adopt more socially appropriate play behavior. The mother especially spends a great deal of time and energy after school and on weekends trying to entice him to play with the neighborhood children. She has even threatened to withhold his allowance until he makes some friends and begins to play on a regular basis with the neighborhood children.

Howard's mother and father disagree somewhat in their perceptions of the future. His father feels that Howard will outgrow his isolation and begin making friends. However, he does not feel that he will ever be an extrovert. His mother, on the other hand, has read in several womens' magazines about the problems that can arise if a child is withdrawn and poorly equipped socially. She is frightened that he may later develop a "mental problem." She thinks that perhaps by displaying to him how much his behavior upsets her that the situation will improve.

LEARNING DISABLED CHILD

Sally
Age: 9

Parent Role

Sally's parents are concerned about their daughter's withdrawn behavior. Sally has always been considered to be "socially immature" and "withdrawn." However, this pattern of shyness and seclusiveness has recently become more acute. In addition, several of the family's relatives have told them that shyness in children can lead to severe problems in later life.

Sally's mother has begun prompting Sally to spend more time playing with neighborhood children. When this has not worked she has resorted to punishment (withholding dessert) and nagging and has recently threatened to send Sally to a psychiatrist if she doesn't start spending more time with children her own age. The mother spends a considerable amount of time and effort on weekends and after school trying to get Sally to be more social. Although this is a pervasive behavior, the mother is by far the most concerned.

The parents vary in their overall perception of the problem and its future implications. Sally's father is somewhat concerned; yet he truly believes that Sally is "just shy" and will outgrow her seclusiveness in time. Her mother is not nearly as optimistic. She feels that Sally will develop other more severe emotional problems if she does not develop a more extroverted personality. The mother also believes that by displaying to Sally how much her behavior upsets her that the condition will be improved.

PHYSICALLY HANDICAPPED CHILD

Eddie
Age: 6

Parent Role

Just recently (past few weeks), Eddie has begun to display rather severe tantrum behavior to control the actions of his parents. Since his father is gone during the week, this action is directed at his mother.

Eddie now demands that the mother remain with him during his afternoon nap and after he is put to bed at night. If the mother leaves the bedroom after putting him to bed, he screams and cries until she returns to the room. As a result, the mother has been unable to leave the bedroom until after Eddie goes to sleep. If the mother tries to read while in the bedroom, Eddie will cry until the reading material is put down. The mother feels that Eddie enjoys his control over her and that he fights off going to sleep as long as possible. For the past two weeks, his mother has been spending from one-half to two hours each bedtime just waiting until Eddie goes to sleep.

The mother has received medical assurance that there is no physical reason for the problem. The family physician has indicated that Eddie will probably outgrow the problem.

The mother feels obligated to stay with Eddie when he begins crying in the bedroom. She feels that if he were not handicapped she would probably be able to deal with the situation. However, she feels guilty about punishing the youngster and even more guilty about ignoring him when he is crying. She thus returns to the child's room but states that she is bitter about his obvious manipulation of her. His mother feels somewhat lost without an effective disciplinary method.

Although the mother does not currently know how to handle the behavior, she feels that he will spontaneously overcome the problem with time. Maturity, she feels, will be the answer to this youngster's problem. In addition, she feels that displaying to Eddie how much of an inconvenience he is to the family will instill a feeling of responsibility that will decrease the problem behavior.

MENTALLY RETARDED CHILD

Barbie
Age: 8

Parent Role

The parents have noted that Barbie has always been an immature personality whose primary concern has been to manipulate her environment. For example, Barbie may state that she will not participate in a task, and if implored to participate will attempt to leave the situation physically or to resort to actively negative behavior.

Recently this negativism has become an even more acute problem. Specifically, both parents have experienced marked difficulties in getting Barbie to obey parental requests or commands. Barbie was described as "headstrong" and "set in her ways." Although expressive language is not this child's primary mode of communication, she does use phrases such as "No-No," "I won't," and "I can't" at a high rate of frequency.

Although this behavior has been rather consistent across environments, the parents notice it more at home. In addition, the behavior appears to occur more frequently in the mother's presence. This may be related to the fact that the mother spends a great deal more time with the child than the father.

Neither the mother nor the father know how to deal with the behavior. They suggest that they have "tried everything." They have talked to her, spanked her, taken her dinner away, and put her in her room by herself. Since they have not employed any procedures consistently though, it is difficult to say what works best.

Presently the parents are tremendously upset about what to do. The father has even talked about institutionalization because of his inability to handle the problem. The mother feels inadequate to handle the problem and considers herself a "bad mother." Presently the parents do not know what to do, but they have the attitude that if they try hard enough they can find an answer to the problem. This attitude of perseverance means experimenting with a number of procedures, hoping to stumble across something that will work.

Exhibits B-1 and B-2 display sample questionnaires to be completed by parents involved in behavioral management conferencing.

Exhibit B-1 Behavioral Conference I

Date _____
Name of Child _____
Name of Person Playing Parent Role _____
Name of Person Playing Conferencer Role _____
Observer(s) _____

I.   General Conferencing Evaluation

A. Ability of conferencer to inform parents of the purpose of the conference.

1	2	3	4	5
Poor	Below Average	Average	Above Average	Excellent

B. Ability of conferencer to conduct the session in a systematic sequential manner.

1	2	3	4	5
Poor	Below Average	Average	Above Average	Excellent

C. Ability of conferencer to keep the session flowing and on course.

1	2	3	4	5
Poor	Below Average	Average	Above Average	Excellent

D. Ability of conferencer to solicit and respond to parents' questions.

1	2	3	4	5
Poor	Below Average	Average	Above Average	Excellent

Exhibit B-1 continued

E. Ability of conferencer to attend to the parents.

1	2	3	4	5
Poor	Below Average	Average	Above Average	Excellent

F. Ability of conferencer to rephrase questions.

1	2	3	4	5
Poor	Below Average	Average	Above Average	Excellent

G. Ability of conferencer to summarize the conference.

1	2	3	4	5
Poor	Below Average	Average	Above Average	Excellent

II. First Session Procedural Steps

A. Target Behavior

1. Ability of conferencer to secure an adequate definition of the target behavior.

1	2	3	4	5
Poor	Below Average	Average	Above Average	Excellent

2. Ability of conferencer to explain how the parents were to evaluate (count) the target behavior.

1	2	3	4	5
Poor	Below Average	Average	Above Average	Excellent

B. Evaluation of Stimulus Situations

1. Ability of counselor in obtaining adequate information on where the problem behavior occurred.

1	2	3	4	5
Poor	Below Average	Average	Above Average	Excellent

2. Ability of counselor in obtaining adequate information about whom the child is with when the behavior of concern occurs.

1	2	3	4	5
Poor	Below Average	Average	Above Average	Excellent

C. Evaluation of Contingencies

1. Ability of conferencer in uncovering the major contingencies that might have been perpetuating the problem behavior.

1	2	3	4	5
Poor	Below Average	Average	Above Average	Excellent

III. Additional Comments

Exhibit B-2 Behavioral Conference II

Date _____
Name of Child _____
Name of Person Playing Parent Role _____
Name of Person Playing Conferencer Role _____
Observer(s) _____

I. General Conferencing Evaluation

A. Ability of conferencer to inform parents of the purpose of the conference.

1	2	3	4	5
Poor	Below Average	Average	Above Average	Excellent

B. Ability of conferencer to conduct the session in a systematic sequential manner.

1	2	3	4	5
Poor	Below Average	Average	Above Average	Excellent

C. Ability of conferencer to keep the session flowing and on course.

1	2	3	4	5
Poor	Below Average	Average	Above Average	Excellent

D. Ability of conferencer to solicit and respond to parents' questions.

1	2	3	4	5
Poor	Below Average	Average	Above Average	Excellent

E. Ability of conferencer to attend to the parents.

1	2	3	4	5
Poor	Below Average	Average	Above Average	Excellent

F. Ability of conferencer to rephrase questions.

1	2	3	4	5
Poor	Below Average	Average	Above Average	Excellent

G. Ability of conferencer to summarize the conference.

1	2	3	4	5
Poor	Below Average	Average	Above Average	Excellent

II. Conference Content

A. Charting and Inspecting Target Data

1. Ability of conferencer to train parents to chart baseline data.

1	2	3	4	5
Poor	Below Average	Average	Above Average	Excellent

B. Intervention Procedures

1. Ability of conferencer to devise and present appropriate consequences to modify the target behavior.

1	2	3	4	5
Poor	Below Average	Average	Above Average	Excellent

2. Ability of conferencer to establish desired interim rates for the target behavior.

1	2	3	4	5
Poor	Below Average	Average	Above Average	Excellent

III. Additional Comments

Individualized Education Program Role-Playing Materials

BEHAVIORALLY DISORDERED CHILD

Billy
Age: 10

Summary of Present Levels of Performance

	Strengths	*Weaknesses*
Reading:	Near grade level sight word vocabulary.	Reading comprehension is significantly lower than recognition (2.5 grade).
Math:	Currently working at the third-grade level and is able to do most of the activities.	Extremely low frustration tolerance for new concepts.
Handwriting:	Making more frequent attempts at cursive writing.	Does not know all the letters in the cursive form and is easily frustrated over assignments.
Language:	Ability to express himself is good, and he is very willing to converse with adults.	His greatest degree of trouble is with capitalization, punctuation, and contractions.

Behavioral/ *Social:*	Anxious to please the teacher; works well for a teacher who demands good work.	Difficulty in getting along with peers and frequently threatens them. Some incidents of stealing from other children.

Possible Annual Goals

Reading: Improved reading comprehension.

Math: Improved accuracy on work at grade level; increased frustration tolerance and fewer incidents of going ''blank'' on previously acquired math skills.

Handwriting: Recognition of all letters in cursive form and legible cursive writing.

Language: Correct use of capitalization, punctuation, and contractions.

Behavioral/   Decreased incidence of threatening others, arguing, stealing,
Social: fighting, and manipulative behaviors.

Regularly Planned Activities with Nonhandicapped Children

Billy will participate daily in a half-hour lunch and twice daily in a quarter-hour recess.

Twice weekly Billy will participate in a half-hour music class with nonhandicapped students. In addition, he will also be involved with nonhandicapped students in one hour of art per week.

Recommendations for Specific Special Education Services

Physical education 30 minutes daily.

Monthly parent meetings with the teacher and school psychologist.

Reevaluation by the school psychologist at the end of the academic year.

Other Information

Medical Concerns:

None

Proved Reinforcers:

Verbal praise
Free time
Reading
Token reinforcement systems

Stimulus Control Information:

Billy responds well to a very structured program, which includes scheduling, behavior modification, token reinforcement, and shaping. He works best for a teacher who assures him that he is capable of good work and a teacher who demands good work.

Precautions:

Billy has at times become very aggressive and physically fought with peers. A highly structured program appears to be the best measure for the prevention of such incidents.

GIFTED CHILD

Howard
Age: 8

Summary of Present Levels of Performance

	Strengths	*Weaknesses*
Reading:	Tests indicate he is two grade levels above his peers.	Does not complete skill sheets and is slow to do his assignments.
Math:	Key Math scores indicate that he is 2.5 grade levels ahead of the average second grader. Able to do complex division problems.	Has not mastered his addition and subtraction facts. Is often sloppy and careless.
Handwriting:	Knows all the letters in the cursive form.	Handwriting is barely legible.
Language:	He is very verbal and his ability to express himself is very good.	

Behavioral/ *Social:*	Displays no acting-out behavior.	Howard has recently decreased his amount of contact with other children. He also displays a weakness in motor skills.

Possible Annual Goals

Reading: Improved comprehension of reading materials; increased incidence of completing assignments.

Math: Increased accuracy on work at grade level; decrease in careless and sloppy work.

Handwriting: Legible cursive writing with appropriate spacing between letters and words.

Language: Increase in appropriate use of capitalization and punctuation.

Behavioral/ *Social:* Increased incidence of interactions with peers; completing tasks; and following through on contractual agreements.

Regularly Planned Activities with Nonhandicapped Children

Howard will be in his regular classroom daily. He will attend the gifted resource room no more than 25 percent of each day.

Recommendations for Specific Special Education Services

Physical education 30 minutes daily.

Thirty-minute remedial handwriting program three times weekly.

Reevaluation by the school psychologist at the end of the academic year.

Other Information

Medical Concerns:

A few years ago Howard had a minor hearing loss caused by fluid buildup in the inner ear. He still has a slight hearing loss, especially when the ears become infected. This condition clears with medication. In addition, Howard has some allergies, but these are not considered severe by his doctor. He is not currently receiving any medication.

Proved Reinforcers:

Verbal praise
Free time
Reading
Time out
Token reinforcement systems

Stimulus Control Information:

Howard responds well to a very structured program, which includes scheduling, shaping, and a behavior modification, token reinforcement program. He works best for a teacher who demands good work.

Precautions:

None

LEARNING DISABLED CHILD

Sally
Age: 9

Summary of Present Levels of Performance

	Strengths	*Weaknesses*
Reading:	Prereading skills, such as identification and discrimination of letters, are well established.	Inability to produce sounds corresponding to letters nor to blend sounds. Sight vocabulary is limited.
Math:	She is able to grasp concepts when allowed to manipulate objects when adding or subtracting.	Unable to understand abstract mathematical concept.
Handwriting:	Letter formation is very good.	Difficulties in spacing between letters.
Language:	Adequate expressive language.	Verbal comprehension deficits and her auditory memory is one to two years delayed.

Behavioral/ Social:	Increase in social inter- actions with peers in the classroom.	Even though there has been some improvement, Sally has a very obvious deficit in peer interactions, especially outside the classroom.

Possible Annual Goals

Reading: Established sight word vocabulary of 65 to 75 words; improved accuracy in reproducing individual sounds.

Math: Improved performance on daily mathematics papers—this will include an abstract understanding of addition and subtraction.

Handwriting: Legible reproduction of a printed model with appropriate spac- ing between letters and words.

Language: Increased verbal comprehension and auditory memory skills.

Behavioral/ Social: Increase in peer interactions.

Regularly Planned Activities with Nonhandicapped Children

Sally will be in her regular classroom daily. She will attend the learning disabilities resource room no more than 50 percent of each day.

Recommendations for Specific Special Education Services

One and one-half hours of training weekly by a language therapist to increase verbal comprehension and auditory memory.

Reevaluation by the school psychologist at the end of the academic year.

Other Information

Medical Concerns:

None

Proved Reinforcers:

Token reinforcement system
Free-time activities
Verbal praise
Looking through books
Parent reinforcement programs

Stimulus Control Information:

Sally responds very well to a high degree of structure, which includes a shaping process, scheduling for predictable activities, and a behavior modification employing token reinforcement.

Precautions:

None

PHYSICALLY HANDICAPPED CHILD

Eddie
Age: 6

Summary of Present Levels of Performance

	Strengths	*Weaknesses*
Reading:	Possesses several reading readiness skills, including the ability to match shapes and colors.	Inability to recognize or match letters.
Math:	Ability to rote count to 50.	Lacks one-to-one correspondence skills; inability to do simple addition or subtraction.
Self-help Skills:	Capable of independent self-help skills.	Lacks motivation in carrying out independent self-help skills.
Handwriting:	Improvement in frustration tolerance and attempts at pencil manipulation and writing.	Fine motor skills are poor. He has difficulty with coloring within the boundaries and cutting with scissors.
Language:	Able to relate personal experiences logically and sequentially; follows four-item commands.	His speech is characterized by misarticulation and his auditory discrimination may be slightly delayed.
Behavioral/ Social:	Displays considerable personality strength; he is outgoing and friendly; interacts appropriately with peers.	Frequently displays manipulative behavior and tantrums; constantly demands attention.

Possible Annual Goals

Reading: Acquisition of all reading skills necessary for beginning first-grade reading.

Math: First-grade level accuracy skills; development of simple addition and subtraction skills.

Self-help Skills: Improvement in independent self-help skills without external reinforcement.

Handwriting: Increased incidence of attempts at writing; legible reproduction of all printed letters; decrease in incidence of carelessness.

Language. Improvement in articulation; improvement in auditory discrimination.

Behavioral/ Social: Decreased incidence of manipulative behavior and tantrums; increase in independent work and compliance.

Regularly Planned Activities with Nonhandicapped Children

Eddie will be in his regular first-grade classroom daily. He will attend the special education resource room no more than 50 percent of each day.

Recommendations for Specific Special Education Services

Speech therapy one and one-half hours weekly.

Physical therapy 30 minutes daily.

Reevaluation by the school psychologist at the end of the academic year.

Other Information

Medical Concerns:

Eddie has a seizure disorder that results in grand mal seizures about once every five months. He is presently taking Dilantin, one tablet twice a day.

Proved Reinforcers:

Verbal praise
Free time
Puzzles
Time out

Stimulus Control Information:

Eddie responds best to a teacher who (1) assures him that he is capable of good work, (2) demands good work, and (3) does not respond to his attempts to manipulate.

MENTALLY RETARDED CHILD

Barbie
Age: 8

Summary of Present Levels of Performance

	Strengths	*Weaknesses*
Reading:	On one occasion Barbie was able to recognize her name, and she scored above average on the Word Meaning subtest of the Metropolitan Readiness Test.	On the Metropolitan Readiness Test her performance was in the low normal category (13th percentile) and she has very few reading readiness skills. She also had very low scores on the copying and matching subtests of the Metropolitan.
Math:	Currently able to count to 3.	Aside from counting to 3 Barbie appears to have no mathematical skills.
Perceptual/ Motor:	Barbie is able to hold a primary-size pencil.	Weak at tasks requiring fine muscle coordination and visual-motor integration. She has a very awkward manner of holding her pencil.
Speech/ Language:	Relatively good receptive language skills.	Barbie makes few spontaneous verbalizations. Subtest scores on the Preschool Language Scale ranged from 3½ to 5 years. Articulation problems.

Behavioral/ Social:	Barbie gets along well with her peers and has shown some improvement in adjusting to the class-room situation.	She tends to be a participant rather than an observer; she has on occasion become extremely negative toward the teacher and refused to carry through with structured demands. Barbie is also "hyperactive."

Possible Annual Goals

Reading: Ability to recognize the letters of the alphabet; increased accuracy in reproducing initial sounds; development of basic sight word vocabulary.

Math: Increased accuracy in rote counting to 20 and in counting up to 20 objects; development of basic addition skills.

Handwriting: Improved performance in legibly reproducing printed letters.

Language: Increase in spontaneous verbalizations; development of expressive language skills comparable to a kindergarten to first-grade child.

Behavioral/ Social: Increase in peer interactions; decrease in negativism; decrease in noncompliance; decrease in tantrums.

Regularly Planned Activities with Nonhandicapped Children

Barbie will participate daily in a half-hour lunch and a half-hour recess.

Barbie will participate daily in a half-hour of academic activities in the kindergarten classroom.

Recommendations for Specific Special Education Services

Physical education 30 minutes daily.

Reevaluation by the school psychologist at the end of the academic year.

Monthly parent meetings in behavior management programming for dealing with Barbie's tantrums and related behavior problems.

Other Information

Medical Concerns:

Barbie periodically has petit mal seizures.

Proved Reinforcers:

Puzzles
Praise
Time out
Edibles (i.e., "Honeycomb")

Stimulus Control Information:

Barbie responds well to a highly structured approach as a means of remediating her social and educational difficulties.

Exhibit C-1 presents a sample of an IEP conference evaluation; Exhibit C-2 outlines a sample IEP.

Exhibit C-1 IEP Conference Evaluation

Date _____
Name of Child _____
Name of Person Playing Parent Role _____
Name of Person Playing Conferencer Role _____
Observer(s) _____

I. General Conferencing Evaluation

A. Ability of conferencer to inform parents of the purpose of the conference.

1	2	3	4	5
Poor	Below Average	Average	Above Average	Excellent

B. Ability of conferencer to conduct the session in a systematic and sequential manner.

1	2	3	4	5
Poor	Below Average	Average	Above Average	Excellent

C. Ability of conferencer to keep the session flowing and on course.

1	2	3	4	5
Poor	Below Average	Average	Above Average	Excellent

D. Ability of conferencer to solicit and respond to parents' questions.

1	2	3	4	5
Poor	Below Average	Average	Above Average	Excellent

E. Ability of conferencer to attend to the parents.

1	2	3	4	5
Poor	Below Average	Average	Above Average	Excellent

F. Ability of conferencer to rephrase questions.

1	2	3	4	5
Poor	Below Average	Average	Above Average	Excellent

G. Ability of conferencer to summarize the conference.

1	2	3	4	5
Poor	Below Average	Average	Above Average	Excellent

II. IEP Content

A. Ability of conferencer to review the pupil's level of functioning, including academic, physical, social, prevocational/vocational, emotional, psychomotor, self-help, etc.

1	2	3	4	5
Poor	Below Average	Average	Above Average	Excellent

1. Was legitimate input obtained (or opportunity for input provided) from the parents in this area?

1	2	3	4	5
Poor	Below Average	Average	Above Average	Excellent

B. Ability of conferencer to develop annual goals for the child.

1	2	3	4	5
Poor	Below Average	Average	Above Average	Excellent

Exhibit C-1 continued

1. Was legitimate input obtained (or opportunity for input provided) from the parents in this area?

1	2	3	4	5
Poor	Below Average	Average	Above Average	Excellent

C. Ability of conferencer to develop short-term instructional objectives (steps between present functioning and annual goals) for the child.

1	2	3	4	5
Poor	Below Average	Average	Above Average	Excellent

1. Was legitimate input obtained (or opportunity for input provided) from the parents in this area?

1	2	3	4	5
Poor	Below Average	Average	Above Average	Excellent

D. Ability of conferencer to develop evaluation procedures (criteria for determining whether the objectives are being achieved) for the pupil.

1	2	3	4	5
Poor	Below Average	Average	Above Average	Excellent

1. Was legitimate input obtained (or opportunity for input provided) from parents in this area?

1	2	3	4	5
Poor	Below Average	Average	Above Average	Excellent

E. Ability of conferencer to identify educational services needed (without regard to availability) for the pupil.

1	2	3	4	5
Poor	Below Average	Average	Above Average	Excellent

1. Was legitimate input obtained (or opportunity for input provided) from parents in this area?

1	2	3	4	5
Poor	Below Average	Average	Above Average	Excellent

2. Ability of conferencer to identify special instructional media or materials needed for the pupil.

1	2	3	4	5
Poor	Below Average	Average	Above Average	Excellent

3. Ability of conferencer to specify when services for the pupil will begin and the specific length of time and extent provided.

1	2	3	4	5
Poor	Below Average	Average	Above Average	Excellent

F. Ability of conferencer to describe the extent to which the pupil will participate in regular education programs.

1	2	3	4	5
Poor	Below Average	Average	Above Average	Excellent

1. Was legitimate input obtained (or opportunity for input provided) from parents in this area?

1	2	3	4	5
Poor	Below Average	Average	Above Average	Excellent

Exhibit C-1 continued

G. Ability of conferencer to justify the type of educational placement/program to be provided the pupil.

1	2	3	4	5
Poor	Below Average	Average	Above Average	Excellent

1. Was legitimate input obtained (or opportunity for input provided) from parents in this area?

1	2	3	4	5
Poor	Below Average	Average	Above Average	Excellent

III.   Summary Information

Exhibit C-2 Individualized Education Program

Child's Name: _____   Date: _____

School: _____

SUMMARY OF PRESENT LEVELS OF PERFORMANCE

_____

_____

_____

_____

_____

_____

LONG-TERM GOALS

1.

2.

3.

4.

5.

6.

Exhibit C-2 continued

SHORT-TERM OBJECTIVES	SPECIAL EDUCATION & RELATED SERVICES	PERSON RESPONSIBLE	BEGINNING AND ENDING DATES	REVIEW DATE

REGULARLY PLANNED ACTIVITIES WITH NONHANDICAPPED CHILDREN (%)

COMMITTEE RECOMMENDATIONS FOR SPECIFIC PROCEDURES/STRATEGIES, MATERIALS, INFORMATION ABOUT LEARNING STYLE, ETC.

CRITERIA FOR EVALUATION OF ANNUAL GOALS

COMMITTEE MEMBERS PRESENT

_____

_____ (teacher)

Progress Report Conference Role-Playing Materials

BEHAVIORALLY DISORDERED CHILD

Billy
Age: 10

Teacher Role

In preparation for a progress report conference you have available the records and information listed below.

Background Information and Diagnostic Data

Billy was originally referred for assessment because of both behavioral and academic problems. In particular, his regular class teacher described him as aggressive with other students, manipulative, "socially immature," and functioning academically about one year below his peers.

Individual intelligence testing revealed this child to be functioning at the low average range of abilities. This finding was consistent with previous assessment results. Observations conducted in the regular classroom by a diagnostician revealed that Billy attended to task about 25 percent less than his peers, that he daydreamed, and that he was out of his seat without permission significantly more than the other children. Educational testing revealed a reading recognition level of 3.5, a reading comprehension level of 2.2, and arithmetic performance at a 3.0 grade level.

While his regular class teacher noted that Billy was anxious to please her and responded to a structured routine, she was not pleased with his presence in her class. Candidly she believed he would be better off in "special education."

At Billy's IEP conference the following annual goals were discussed and adopted:*

Reading: Improved performance in reading comprehension.
Math: Improved performance in math; increased frustration tolerance for math problems; fewer incidents of going "blank" on previously acquired math skills.
Handwriting: Recognition of all letters in cursive form and legible cursive writing.
Language: Correct use of capitalization, punctuation, and contractions.
Behavioral/ Decreased incidence of threatening others,
Social: arguing, stealing, fighting, and manipulative behavior.

At the time of the progress report conference, Billy was working at approximately the fourth-grade level. However, his academic level varied considerably, usually in direct relation to his social behavior. Listed below is a summary of his academic levels and skills:

Reading. While Billy's reading comprehension has improved (4.0 grade equivalent level) it continues to be a problem. He becomes easily frustrated when he is asked comprehension questions that require looking back for specific answers through what he has read. Billy has been using a fourth-grade reader and a workbook that requires locating specific answers from the text to answer workbook questions. He has also been using SRA reading lab materials, the *New Practice Reader Book B,* and the *Specific Skills Series Level D* during the past semester.

Spelling. During the period since the last progress report conference with the parents, Billy has completed *My Word Book 3*. He started in *My Word Book 4* but seemed unable to comprehend instructions in that book and also said he could not read the words because they were written in cursive writing. He was switched to *Spelling Our Language Book 3* because it included both printing and cursive writing. This change seemed to aid greatly.

Writing. Billy has had extreme difficulty with cursive writing, and his handwriting is still almost illegible. He has actively resisted attempts at cursive writing and has had tantrums routinely when confronted with this task. However, he is able to recognize all cursive letters.

Phonics. Billy seems able to function relatively well in the book *New Phonics We Use (Book D)*. Although he is somewhat erratic in his ability to function phonetically, he seems to be less resistive to this academic activity than to most others. He is currently working at the early fourth-grade level in this area.

---

*Individuals are encouraged to use the IEP developed in an earlier simulation exercise.

Language Arts. Billy is presently working in *Keys to Good Language, Book 3*. Specific deficit areas include capitalization, punctuation, and contractions, although he has shown significant improvement in this area since the writing of the IEP.

Math. Billy is currently working in *Modern School Mathematics 3*. He seems able to do most of the activities, although on some days his frustration tolerance is so low that he seems to go "blank" on all previous math skills, including simple addition and subtraction, and will have a tantrum when faced with even the simplest math assignment. This has been a chronic problem since the time of the last progress report conference and one that the classroom teacher has not been able to find a key to, even though she has employed a number of different strategies. He is currently showing a 65 percent to 70 percent third-grade accuracy level.

Social Studies. Billy has been working in a book entitled *A Journey to Many Lands* and the accompanying workbook. Just as in other academic areas, he seems able to comprehend the materials but actively resists answering comprehensive questions. This particular academic area has been the source of a number of tantrums.

Emotional Social Behavior

At the time of the progress report conference with the parents, Billy was still emitting a great number of inappropriate behaviors. He was crying and having tantrums almost daily over academic work well within his capabilities. He also regularly stole articles from the classroom and from other classrooms in the building, was chronically belligerent, and threatened other children. Finally, he was involved in a great many verbal arguments with both students and adults. Two recent examples of Billy's emotional social behavior reveal the current situation:

Situation 1. Billy started out the day in a rather poor frame of mind. He was extremely antagonistic toward the other children in the classroom and was called down several times early in the morning for breaking and knocking over the classroom projects of others in the room. He was sent to his seat for engaging in this behavior.

During academic work, Billy was extremely ill tempered and had his hand raised constantly, wanting the teacher to give him answers so that he would not have to actively search for them. With a great deal of "hurdle help," Billy finished his reading assignment, but as soon as he started spelling, he became extremely agitated and upset. He said that he could not understand what was meant by some very simple instructions. He refused to attempt to respond to these questions and claimed that he could not comprehend the directions. He began crying and had to be removed to the time-out room until he could gain control of himself. While in the time-out area, he screamed, kicked, and cried for nearly half an hour. It was the teacher's impression that the crying was extremely bizarre. Specifically, the teacher noted that the crying was more appropriate for a three- or four-year-old than for a ten-year-old. In addition, he cried for "Mama" almost the entire time while in the time-out area.

Situation 2. Billy did fairly well today until about 11:30 A.M. At that time he was doing social studies. The exercise that he was involved with required that he find words in the index of his book and copy the page numbers where the topics could be found. Billy was extremely uncooperative and refused to even listen to the teacher's explanation of how the task should be approached. Instead, he would raise his hand for each word and say that he was unable to find it. When the teacher insisted on aiding Billy rather than finding the answer for him, he began crying, cursing, and kicking. At this time he was required to go to the time-out room to settle down. This strategy appeared to be successful as Billy was able to calm himself down after only a few minutes. However, when he was allowed to come out of the time-out room, he began yelling at a student in the free-time area to give him a toy gun that Billy had been playing with previously but had allowed the boy to play with.

The teacher also found the following data and records regarding one particular social problem that has been experienced:

During one period between the present and the last parent conference, Billy had been fighting on the playground and had become somewhat isolated in the class. No one in the class during that time would have much to do with him and he was constantly sulking. Billy appeared to be bringing most of this behavior about himself. He was constantly enticing the other kids into fights by verbally abusing them and hitting and kicking them when the teacher was not looking. Billy provoked these problems and then innocently stepped back with an appearance of puzzlement when the other youngsters responded.

The teacher took some data on this behavior during one period of time when the problem was of most concern.

Times fighting on the playground:

M — 2
T — 1
W — 0
T — 3
F — 1

Times Billy has provoked a fight in the class:

M — 7 times
T — 14 times
W — 19 times

T — 13 times
F — 12 times

Although the situation has improved, Billy still has problems in this area.

Physical Information

The teacher has noted no physical problems that she feels need to be discussed with the parents. He seems to be in good health and has had no patterns of absence, illness, or tardiness.

Classroom Structure

Billy's classroom teacher has used a highly structured approach to attempt to remediate emotional and educational difficulties. Initially, this consisted of evaluating Billy's patterns of strength and weakness so that an appropriate program could be developed. This enabled the teacher to select suitable curriculum and materials. The highly structured program also accentuated programming Billy for specific academic materials. The programming consisted of a shaping process whereby defined behaviors were sequentially arranged into incremental units. The goal of this programming process was to increase Billy's productive behaviors and to break the repetitious elements of his maladaptive social and academic behaviors. The structure employed by the teacher also emphasized scheduling Billy for specific predictable activities. This was adopted to aid in reducing Billy's uncertainty and to help him predict the consequences of his own behavior and thus to aid in the alleviation of his failure patterns. A final component of the structured strategy was behavior modification. Specifically, positive consequences occurred when Billy's responses approximated what were considered to be appropriate behaviors.

It has been the teacher's impression that since the time that Billy was placed in special education he has had severe problems in the classroom. Although Billy's behavior, academic work, and general emotional state seemed to deteriorate during the first few months he was in the class, he has just recently started to make some progress. The teacher has associated this with a heightened degree of structure and the use of a token reinforcement system. Specifically, he has been reinforced by earning chips for doing each assignment in an appropriate way (i.e., no crying, throwing books, kicking, or tantrums). These tokens are given immediately after each assignment is successfully completed and can be traded for extra activities at specific intervals during the school day. Based on this recent change of behavior, it is the teacher's recommendation that Billy be maintained in her classroom for emotionally disturbed children and that the strategy of increasing the amount of structure that is being administered be further increased.

Other Information

Billy continues to participate daily in a 30-minute lunch and 15-minute twice daily recess program with nonhandicapped children. This program is working well and the staff feels he should maintain this level of contact. Although Billy continues to participate in a 30-minute "regular" music class twice weekly and one hour of "regular" art per week, he is experiencing problems. These are mainly behavior problems similar to those manifested in his special class.

GIFTED CHILD

Howard
Age: 8

Teacher Role

In preparation for a progress report conference you have available the records and information listed below.

Background Information and Diagnostic Data

Howard was originally referred for assessment because his regular class teacher thought he was bored. She routinely observed that he evaded completing daily tasks so that he could pursue a task of his own choosing. In addition, she was concerned about the following: daydreaming in class, perfectionism, verbal domination of peers and class discussions, lack of knowledge of math facts, and poor handwriting.

The regular classroom teacher described Howard's relationship with his classmates as good. However, she observed that his classmates seemed to be in awe of his verbal abilities and analytical mind.

Individual intelligence testing revealed this child to be functioning in the very superior range of abilities and at the 99th percentile. The examiner was particularly impressed by Howard's ability to verbally express himself.

At his IEP conference the following annual goals were discussed and adopted:*

Reading:	Improved performance in reading comprehension and completing reading assignments.
Math:	Improved accuracy and decrease in carelessly completed work.
Handwriting:	Improved cursive writing.
Language:	Improved use of correct capitalization and punctuation.
Behavioral/ Social:	Increased interactions with peers and improved willingness to follow through on contractual agreements.

*Individuals are encouraged to use the IEP developed in an earlier simulation exercise.

At the time of the progress report conference Howard was progressing well in both his regular class and the gifted resource program. He had also recently been administered an additional series of assessment measures. The procedures included the following:

- French Pictorial Test of Intelligence

- Bender Visual-Motor Gestalt Test

- Detroit Tests of Learning Aptitude (selected subtests)

- (Spache) Diagnostic Reading Scales

- Betts Visual Discrimination Test

- Informal Spelling Inventory

These measures yielded the following results:

Howard was found to be functioning in the superior range of general intelligence and fell two full years above expectations in academic performance. On a pictorial test of intelligence, which required a pointing response, he demonstrated relative strength on receptive vocabulary of single words in isolation, on visual form discrimination, on general information, and on an analogies task. He also showed relative prowess for his age on size and number concepts and on a visual memory task.

   A series of visual-perceptual tasks yielded scores well within normal limits. Visual-motor tasks were performed well within normal limits while Howard earned an above-average score on a task requiring him to draw geometric designs from memory.

Four tasks designed to measure auditory attention span and auditory memory revealed that he performed one year above his age-group on memory for single words and two years above his age-group on memory for related syllables and for a sequence of directions requiring gross motor responses. He was able also to score above average on a pencil-and-paper task requiring a series of steps.

Classroom Structure

Howard's classroom teachers have adopted a highly individualized program to meet his educational needs. Initially, this consisted of evaluating his patterns of strength and weakness so that an individualized program could be developed. This enabled the teacher to select, along with Howard, appropriate curricula and materials commensurate with his strengths and weaknesses. The program also accentuated programming him for certain academic materials. The programming consisted of a shaping process whereby defined behaviors were sequentially arranged into incremental units. The goal of this programming process was to increase his handwriting skills and to emphasize completing assigned tasks. The structure employed by the teacher also emphasized scheduling Howard for specific predictable activities. This was adopted to aid in reducing uncertainty for him. A final component of the structure strategy that was being used by the teacher was behavior modification. Specifically, positive consequences occurred when he has stayed on task and completed assigned material.

In addition, the teacher in the gifted program has implemented the following:

- A reading program that takes into account this child's skills in word recognition, comprehension, and intellectual capacity.

- A program whereby Howard is required to complete any task that he begins. Although he should be given curriculum choices, he is not permitted to begin a new project without completing previous assignments. Contracts are used for this purpose.

- Implementation of a remedial handwriting program.

Emotional Social Information

The special class teacher also found the following data and records regarding one particular social problem that was experienced: Howard's teachers have recently been concerned about his lack of contact with other children. The teachers report that this child consistently stands quietly about the playground while the other children run, play games, and climb on the play yard apparatus. Although the teachers have attempted to encourage him through suggestions or invitations to engage in activities with the other children, he consistently declines. The teachers are also concerned over his apparent lack of strength and motor skills. One teacher took some data on the daily time Howard had spent in social interaction with children during a 30-minute morning recess period.

> Day 1 — 2 minutes
> Day 2 — 1 minute
> Day 3 — 4 minutes
> Day 4 — 0 minutes
> Day 5 — 1 minute

The following relates Howard's behavior during a particular recess period. It was raining, so the afternoon recess was spent in the gym. The children had a choice of two activities during this time: (1) jump rope and (2) kick ball. Howard was requested to turn the rope with the teacher while the other children took turns jumping. He was then encouraged to try jumping the rope and he shook his head "no." When the rope was turned, he just stood where he was and did not attempt to jump. He then walked over to the door and quietly watched the children who were playing kick ball. He was encouraged to participate but declined. When the recess was over, he was requested to help carry the rope back to the classroom and he did.

Although the special class teacher has not initiated a program to increase social interactions, she plans to begin a reinforcement program in the near future to modify this behavior.

Physical Information

The teacher has noted no physical problems that she feels need to be discussed with the parents. Howard seems to be in good health and has had no patterns of absence, illness, or tardiness.

Other Information

Howard continues to be involved in the following:

- He continues to be assigned to his regular classroom 75% of each week.
- Twice weekly Howard participates as a tutor in a peer tutoring math program for regular and handicapped students.
- He participates for 30 minutes three times weekly in a remedial handwriting program.

LEARNING DISABLED CHILD

Sally
Age: 9

Teacher Role

In preparation for a progress report conference you have available the records and information listed below.

Background Information and Diagnostic Data

Sally was referred for evaluation by school district diagnostic personnel because of severe academic weaknesses and "social immaturity." Her regular classroom teacher observed that she was particularly deficient in reading and math. She was also concerned about Sally's tendency to withdraw socially and her apparent inability to comprehend verbal directions.

Individual intelligence testing revealed this child to be functioning in the average range of abilities. Testing also indicated that Sally was academically at a readiness level and that she had almost no sight word vocabulary. Further evaluations revealed an absence of perceptual problems.

The regular classroom teacher was frustrated in her attempts to work with Sally and considered her to be desperately in need of "special help."

At her IEP conference the following annual goals were discussed and adopted:*

Reading:	Establishment of basic sight word vocabulary and improved accuracy in reproducing individual sounds.
Math:	Improved performance on daily math assignments and an abstract understanding of addition and subtraction concepts.
Handwriting:	Improved performance in reproducing a printed model, including appropriate spacing between words and letters.
Language:	Improved verbal comprehension and auditory memory skills.
Behavioral/ Social:	Increased interactions with peers.

At the time of the progressive report meeting with her parents, Sally was making progress both in the learning disabilities resource program and in her regular classroom. Sally had been given a series of formal and informal tests to determine her academic progress. Included in the measures given were visual-motor and visual discrimination tests, a general test of intelligence, the *Detroit Test of Learning Aptitude,* a standardized reading survey, and an informal spelling inventory. These procedures yielded the following findings:

Intelligence testing revealed that Sally was functioning in the average range of general intelligence. On a pictorial test of intelligence that required a pointing response, Sally scored above her chronological age on reception vocabulary of single words in isolation, on visual-form discrimination, on general information, and on an analogies task. She scored below average for her age-group on size and number concepts and on a visual-memory task.

A series of visual-perceptual tasks yielded scores well within normal limits, with the exception of visual-sequential memory for letters, which was slightly below the average range.

Visual-motor tasks were performed well within normal limits while Sally earned an above-average score on a task requiring her to draw geometric designs from memory.

Four tasks designed to measure auditory attention span and auditory memory revealed that she performed one year below her age-group on memory for single

---

*Individuals are encouraged to use the IEP developed in an earlier simulation exercise.

words and two years below her age-group on memory for related syllables and for a sequence of directions requiring gross motor responses. However, she was able to score above average on a pencil-and-paper task requiring a series of steps.

Academic assessment revealed Sally to be about two years below grade level. In particular, visual prereading skills, such as identification and discrimination of letters, were established but she could not reliably produce sounds corresponding to the letters, nor could she blend sounds when individual phonemes were provided for her. Her sight vocabulary included 24 preprimer and primer words.

Emotional Social Information

The resource room teacher continues to be concerned about Sally's contact with other children. She reports that Sally isolates herself and rarely initiates contact or participates in games or other activities with her peers. Rather, she tends to stand by herself and watch her classmates. The teacher routinely attempts to encourage and coax Sally to interact with others but with little success. Data taken on the number of minutes Sally engaged in cooperative or parallel play with her peers during a 15-minute morning recess confirmed this observation. These data revealed the following:

Day 1 — 1 minute
Day 2 — 0 minutes
Day 3 — 0 minutes
Day 4 — 2.5 minutes
Day 5 — 0 minutes

Physical Information

Neither the regular class teacher nor the resource room instructor have noted any physical problems that require discussion with Sally's parents. She seems to be in good health and has had no patterns of absence, illness, or tardiness.

Classroom Structure

Sally's resource room teacher has employed a highly structured educational approach. After having thoroughly evaluated her strengths and weaknesses, the teacher selected curriculum and materials that were commensurate with Sally's strengths and weaknesses. The highly structured program also accentuated programming her for specific academic materials. The programming consisted of a shaping process whereby defined behaviors were sequentially arranged into incremental units. The goal of this programming process was to increase Sally's productive behaviors and to break the repetitious elements of her maladaptive social and academic behaviors. The structure employed by the teacher also emphasized scheduling Sally for specific predictable activites. This was adopted to aid in reducing Sally's uncertainty and to aid in the alleviation of her failure patterns. A final component of the structured strategy was behavior modification. Specifically, positive consequences occurred when Sally's responses approximated what were considered to be appropriate behaviors.

Sally's classroom teacher has also used specific programs for dealing with this child's academic problems. Specifically, a reading program with a strong visual emphasis concentrating exclusively on regular sound patterns has been chosen. The series that she is currently working in is a program using visual stimuli and closure activities to teach visual sequencing.

Sally has also been exposed to one-to-one instruction designed to improve her sight word vocabulary. A whole-word method has been chosen for this program. In addition, Sally has only recently been started in a phonics program.

The special education resource room teacher has been pleased with Sally's response to these programs. In particular, she has assessed the following gains:

Reading: A sight word vocabulary of 14 words has been established. In addition, Sally demonstrated 65 percent accuracy in reproducing individual sounds.

Math: A 75 percent correct score on daily mathematics has been achieved. This includes some abstract understanding of addition and subtraction.

Handwriting: Legible reproduction of a printed model with appropriate spacing between letters and words has been achieved.

Language: Expressive language skills have improved to a level comparable with a 2.5 grade norm, along with 69 percent accuracy in gross motor responses to three-step directions.

Behavioral/ Social: There has been a 10 percent increase in peer interactions, although this pattern is variable.

Other Information

It has been the special education teacher's impression that since the time that Sally was placed in her resource room she has made significant progress. The teacher has associated this with a heightened degree of structure and the use of a reinforcement system. Specifically, Sally has been socially reinforced for doing each assignment in an appropriate way. Based on her progress it is the teacher's recommendation that she continue her present programs and percent of time in the learning disabilities resource room.

PHYSICALLY HANDICAPPED CHILD

Eddie
Age: 6

Teacher Role

In preparation for a progress report conference you have available the records and information listed below.

Background Information and Diagnostic Data

Eddie was born with a meningomyelocele, which was repaired when he was six months of age. This birth defect has resulted in an inability to walk without the aid of crutches. Except for occasional grand mal seizures, Eddie has no other apparent physical problems.

As a part of his referral to a resource room for physically impaired children, Eddie was administered a series of psychological and educational tests. These measures indicated that he was functioning intellectually in the bright normal range of abilities, with particular prowess in verbal areas. Academic measures revealed an ability to follow four-item commands, match shapes, identify colors, identify body parts, string beads, and rote count to 50. Weaknesses were identified in a variety of fine motor areas, including writing, cutting with scissors, and duplicating geometric shapes with blocks.

At his IEP conference the following annual goals were discussed and adopted:*

Reading:	Acquisition of beginning first-grade reading skills.
Math:	First-grade level accuracy skills; development of simple addition and subtraction skills.
Self-Help:	Improvement in independent self-help skills.
Handwriting:	Increase in willingness to write, legible reproduction of printed words; decrease in carelessness in handwriting.
Language:	Improvement in articulation and auditory discrimination.
Behavioral/ Social:	Decrease in manipulative behavior and tantrums and an increase in compliance and independent work activities.

At the time of the progress report conference, Eddie was generally working at a readiness to early first-grade level. The following is a summary of his academic levels and skills:

---

*Individuals are encouraged to use the IEP developed in an earlier simulation exercise.

Reading. Eddie recently completed the McGraw-Hill series, *Time for Phonics* *(Book R)*, and has begun work on *Book A*. He has also worked in the *Little Green Story Book* of the Ginn preprimer series. At the beginning of the year, Eddie's frequency of correct responses for matching shapes and colors was approximately 4 per minute. The incorrect responses were 5 per minute. Presently, Eddie's frequency of correct responses has increased to approximately 17 per minute and incorrect responses have been eliminated.

Eddie displays few functional word attack skills in reading, and comprehension questions must be very specific and immediate for him to respond correctly. He is not able to do his reading workbook without a great deal of guidance.

Eddie is involved in a group phonics program using "phonovisual." This program at present is at the level of identifying initial sounds. He is very successful, but little carry-over has been seen as far as attempting to "sound out" words in his reading.

Math. Eddie has been working in the *SRA Greater Cleveland Math Book I*. He is presently working on "plus ones." However, the resource room teacher is not certain that he has grasped this concept because of his erratic performance.

Self-Help. Eddie has shown about a 70 percent incidence of independent self-help skills without the aid of external reinforcement.

Handwriting. Eddie's attempts to write, when given such assignments, have increased to approximately 90 percent, and he is currently able to reproduce letters legibly about 50 percent of the time.

Language. The incidence of correct articulations by Eddie has improved to 65 percent, and he has shown a 25 percent improvement in auditory discrimination.

Emotional Social Behavior

Eddie remains a somewhat manipulative child, particularly with adults. He is also highly prone to be resistive to following teacher directions. However, he is cooperative and plays appropriately with children his own age.

During the period between the present and the past parent conference Eddie has become extremely demanding in the resource classroom. He has been demanding an inordinate amount of attention, and if the teacher is unable to stand next to him, he will not work. In addition to not working he has occasionally initiated tantrum behavior if things do not go his way. When the teacher explains to Eddie that there are other children who need her help he starts crying.

The following data regarding the number of minutes of tantrum behavior as a function of the teacher not standing next to Eddie have been collected:

Day 1 — 3 minutes
Day 2 — 11 minutes

Day 3 —   7 minutes
Day 4 — 27 minutes
Day 5 —   4 minutes
Day 6 — 11 minutes
Day 7 — 14 minutes
Day 8 — 11 minutes
Day 9 — 13 minutes
Day 10 — 16 minutes

Two recent examples of Eddie's emotional social behavior reveal the current situation:

Situation 1. Eddie's assignment was to "read" silently in his *"Little Green Story Book."* Prior to this he was working on a 1:1 basis in his *SRA Greater Cleveland Math Book I* on "plus ones." As the teacher was leaving his work area to attend to another child, Eddie immediately pushed his book off his desk and started into a tantrum routine. Although the tantrum lasted only a few minutes, it was characteristic of situations where 1:1 sessions were terminated and where Eddie was asked to work independently for a short period of time. Subsequently, Eddie acts as if he cannot do the assigned task unless he has the teacher's attention.

Situation 2. The following situation occurs rather frequently when Eddie and the other children in the class are engaged in a free-time activity (usually after lunch). When it is time to put the blocks, trucks, and other toys into the toy box, Eddie becomes very "stubborn" and continues playing. Even when the other children begin putting things into the toy box, Eddie screams and takes them out again and does not let the other children put them away.

Although the teacher has not initiated a program to decrease Eddie's tantrums, she plans to begin a token reinforcement program in the near future to modify this behavior.

Physical Information

Neither the resource or regular class teachers have noted any physical problems, over and above those previously reported, requiring discussion with the parents.

Classroom Structure

As a means of responding to Eddie's needs the resource room teacher has used a highly structured routine. In particular, the teacher has selected curricula and materials that were commensurate with Eddie's strengths and weaknesses. The highly structured program also accentuated programming Eddie for certain academic materials. Initially the programming consisted of a shaping process whereby defined behaviors were sequentially arranged into incremental units. The goal of this programming process was to increase Eddie's productive behaviors and to break the repetitious elements of his maladaptive social and academic behaviors. The structure employed by the teacher also emphasized scheduling him for specific predictable activities. This was adopted to aid in reducing Eddie's uncertainty and to aid in the alleviation of his failure patterns. A final component of the structured strategy was behavior modification. Specifically, positive consequences occurred when Eddie's responses approximated what were considered to be appropriate behaviors.

Other Information

It has been the special education teacher's impression that Eddie has made progress since being placed in her resource room. However, it is her belief that he still has significant problems, particularly in emotional social behaviors and should be maintained in the resource room for at least 50 percent of each day.

MENTALLY RETARDED CHILD

Barbie
Age: 8

Teacher Role

In preparation for a progress report conference you have available the records and information listed below.

Background Information and Diagnostic Data

Barbie was referred for assessment because of both academic and social problems. Her regular first-grade teacher reported that even after repeating the first grade she was still unable to identify the letters of the alphabet, identify colors, or rote count past 3. In addition, her teacher was concerned because Barbie had poor articulation, initiated few contacts with other children, and was "hyperactive."

Psychoeducational testing revealed a child who was noncompliant and hyperactive. Although no specific intelligence test score was obtained, the school psychologist concluded that she was performing at a level associated with mild mental retardation. The examiner also reported that Barbie demonstrated articulation problems, mild perceptual problems, and weaknesses in social maturity.

While the regular classroom teacher said that she enjoyed working with Barbie, she believed this child to be in need of more intensive and specialized attention. In addition, she thought Barbie would be better off if placed with "other special children."

At the IEP conference the following annual goals were discussed and adopted:*

Reading: Ability to identify the letters of the alphabet; increased accuracy in reproducing initial sounds; development of a basic sight word vocabulary.

Math: Improved performance in counting and addition.

Handwriting: Improved performance in legibly reproducing printed letters.

Language: Improved performance in expressive language, including spontaneous verbalizations.

Behavioral/ Social: Increased interaction with peers and decreased incidence of negativism, noncompliance and tantrums.

Since the IEP conference the teacher has acquired additional diagnostic and assessment data. She administered Barbie the *Metropolitan Readiness Test,* the *Peabody Picture Vocabulary Test,* and the *Preschool Language Survey.* These instruments yielded the following results:

On the *Metropolitan Readiness Test,* Barbie's performance was very inconsistent. Many times she would make a written response (marking a picture) before the directions or instructions were given. It was noted that she had a very awkward manner of holding her pencil. Barbie tended to grip her pencil in her fist, close to the eraser. Barbie made no spontaneous verbalizations. However, she would answer questions when they were directed toward her in a firm manner.

On the auditory comprehension portion of the *Preschool Language Survey,* Barbie obtained an age equivalent of 5-1. The verbal ability scale of this instrument yielded an age equivalence of 4-6 years.

The *Peabody Picture Vocabulary Test* yielded an expressive language quotient of 71. However, Barbie was willing to participate in this activity only when provided food reinforcement for each item she attempted to answer.

The *Metropolitan Readiness Test* revealed that Barbie would probably experience great difficulty in succeeding in a regular first-grade classroom. She received particularly low rankings in the areas of copying and matching.

Emotional Social Information

Recently, Barbie has become extremely negative at school. She refuses to carry through with many structured demands made on her and frequently will act as if she does not hear when told by the teacher to do something. Although she has not displayed any violent or acting-out behavior, she is extremely "stubborn."

The teacher has kept a count on the number of times that Barbie has refused to do something (when told to do so by the teacher) during a five-day period.

---

*Individuals are encouraged to use the IEP developed in an earlier simulation exercise.

M — 11 times
T — 17 times
W — 14 times
T — 19 times
F — 26 times

The teacher has previously used a time-out procedure to deal with this problem and plans to reimplement the program soon.

The teacher also recorded the following anecdotal incidents:

Situation 1. Barbie was assigned to work independently in the workbook of the *Little Green Story Book*. She became extremely negative toward the teacher and said she "didn't want to" and closed the book. Her posture became rigid, she avoided eye contact with the teacher, and she remained seated at her desk, refusing to acknowledge the teacher's request to attempt the assignment. She remained in this state during recess time and refused to perform any assignments for the remainder of the day.

Situation 2. Barbie was involved in solitary play in the free-time area. This was her reward for completing an assignment. When the timer went off signaling the end of her free-time activity, Barbie ignored the cue and continued to play with the toys. When the teacher requested that she put the toys away and return to her seat, Barbie acted as though she did not hear. She had to be physically removed from the free-time area.

Physical Information

No physical information, other than that contained in the original records, was felt to be significant by the teacher.

Classroom Structure

A highly structured strategy has been adopted in an effort to serve this child's needs. In particular, the special education teacher has selected curricula and instructional procedures that are commensurate with Barbie's abilities. This strategy has also involved using a shaping process whereby defined behaviors are sequentially arranged into incremental units. The goal of this programming process has been to increase Barbie's productive behaviors and to break the repetitious elements of her maladaptive social and academic behaviors. The structure employed by the teacher has also emphasized scheduling Barbie for specific predictable activities. This was adopted to aid in reducing uncertainty for Barbie and to help her predict the consequences of her own behavior and thus to aid in the alleviation of her failure patterns. A final component of the structured strategy has been behavior modification. Specifically, positive consequences occur when Barbie's responses approximate what are considered to be appropriate behaviors. This program has been largely responsible for the following gains:

Reading:	100 percent accuracy in recognizing the letters of the alphabet; 70 percent accuracy in reproducing initial sounds; and recognition of four Dolch sight words.
Math:	80 percent accuracy in rote counting to 20; 70 percent accuracy in counting up to 20 objects; 58 percent accuracy in work on the kindergarten to first-grade level.
Handwriting:	Legible reproduction of three printed letters.
Language:	Barbie has demonstrated a 20 percent increase in spontaneous verbalizations.

Other Information

It is the teacher's belief that Barbie should continue to participate in a daily 30-minute lunch and 30-minute recess period with nonhandicapped children, in 30-minute daily academic activities in a kindergarten classroom, and in a daily 30-minute physical education program.

It is also the special education teacher's impression that Barbie has made significant progress in special education. She associates this with a heightened degree of structure and the use of a reinforcement system. It is the teacher's recommendation that Barbie be maintained in a self-contained program and that the strategy of increasing the amount of structure be maintained.

Exhibit D-1 presents a sample questionnaire to evaluate the conference progress report.

Exhibit D-1 Progress Report Evaluation

Date _____

Name of Child _____

Name of Person Playing Parent Role _____

Name of Person Playing Conferencer Role _____

Observer(s) _____

I.   General Conferencing Evaluation

A.   Ability of conferencer to inform parents of the purpose of the conference.

1	2	3	4	5
Poor	Below Average	Average	Above Average	Excellent

B.   Ability of conferencer to conduct the session in a systematic and sequential manner.

1	2	3	4	5
Poor	Below Average	Average	Above Average	Excellent

C.   Ability of conferencer to keep the session flowing and on course.

1	2	3	4	5
Poor	Below Average	Average	Above Average	Excellent

D.   Ability of conferencer to solicit and respond to parents' questions.

1	2	3	4	5
Poor	Below Average	Average	Above Average	Excellent

E. Ability of conferencer to attend to parents.

1	2	3	4	5
Poor	Below Average	Average	Above Average	Excellent

F. Ability of conferencer to rephrase questions.

1	2	3	4	5
Poor	Below Average	Average	Above Average	Excellent

G. Ability of conferencer to summarize the conference.

1	2	3	4	5
Poor	Below Average	Average	Above Average	Excellent

II. Progress Report Conference Content

A. Overview Content

1. Ability of conferencer to provide a general overview of the issues associated with the initial referral for evaluation.

1	2	3	4	5
Poor	Below Average	Average	Above Average	Excellent

2. Ability of conferencer to provide a general review of diagnostic procedures used in the evaluation.

1	2	3	4	5
Poor	Below Average	Average	Above Average	Excellent

Exhibit D-1 continued

3. Ability of conferencer to provide a general overview of the educational and intervention program being used, including a brief overview of the IEP.

1	2	3	4	5
Poor	Below Average	Average	Above Average	Excellent

4. Ability of conferencer to provide a general evaluation statement regarding the child's progress in the program.

1	2	3	4	5
Poor	Below Average	Average	Above Average	Excellent

5. Ability of conferencer to respond to parents' questions and to solicit their input within the overview area.

1	2	3	4	5
Poor	Below Average	Average	Above Average	Excellent

B. Academic Content

1. Ability of conferencer to provide an analysis of the academic issues associated with the referral for evaluation.

1	2	3	4	5
Poor	Below Average	Average	Above Average	Excellent

2. Ability of conferencer to provide information associated with the assessment of academic strengths and weaknesses.

1	2	3	4	5
Poor	Below Average	Average	Above Average	Excellent

3. Ability of conferencer to provide a description and analysis of academic intervention programs, including the manner in which each IEP short-term objective is to be realized.

1	2	3	4	5
Poor	Below Average	Average	Above Average	Excellent

4. Ability of conferencer to provide an evaluative statement regarding the child's academic progress, including future expectations for the pupil.

1	2	3	4	5
Poor	Below Average	Average	Above Average	Excellent

5. Ability of conferencer to respond to parents' questions and to solicit their input within the academic area.

1	2	3	4	5
Poor	Below Average	Average	Above Average	Excellent

C. Emotional/Social Content

1. Ability of conferencer to provide an analysis of the emotional/social concerns associated with the initial referral for evaluation.

1	2	3	4	5
Poor	Below Average	Average	Above Average	Excellent

2. Ability of conferencer to provide information associated with the assessment of emotional/social concerns.

1	2	3	4	5
Poor	Below Average	Average	Above Average	Excellent

Exhibit D-1 continued

3. Ability of conferencer to provide a description and analysis of social/emotional intervention programs, including the manner in which each IEP short-term objective is to be realized.

1	2	3	4	5
Poor	Below Average	Average	Above Average	Excellent

4. Ability of conferencer to provide an evaluative statement regarding the child's emotional/social progress, including future expectations for the pupil.

1	2	3	4	5
Poor	Below Average	Average	Above Average	Excellent

5. Ability of conferencer to respond to parents' questions and to solicit their input within the emotional/social area.

1	2	3	4	5
Poor	Below Average	Average	Above Average	Excellent

D. Physical Content

1. Ability of conferencer to provide an analysis of the physical concerns associated with the initial referral for evaluation.

1	2	3	4	5
Poor	Below Average	Average	Above Average	Excellent

2. Ability of conferencer to provide information associated with the assessment of physical concerns.

1	2	3	4	5
Poor	Below Average	Average	Above Average	Excellent

3. Ability of conferencer to provide a description and analysis of physical intervention programs, including the manner in which each IEP short-term objective is to be realized.

1	2	3	4	5
Poor	Below Average	Average	Above Average	Excellent

4. Ability of conferencer to provide an evaluative statement regarding the child's physical progress, including future expectations for the pupil.

1	2	3	4	5
Poor	Below Average	Average	Above Average	Excellent

5. Ability of conferencer to respond to parents' questions and to solicit their input within the physical area.

1	2	3	4	5
Poor	Below Average	Average	Above Average	Excellent

III   Summary Information

Conflict Resolution Conference Role-Playing Materials

BEHAVIORALLY DISORDERED CHILD

Billy
Age: 10

Teacher Role

As a means of motivating Billy to complete his assignments accurately, his teacher has implemented a program whereby he is allowed to go to recess only after having completed a prescribed amount of work. While the program has resulted in some success, it has also created several problems. Specifically, after having been denied recess Billy will sulk, attempt to create disturbances with other students, and swear at the teacher. Nonetheless, the teacher believes the program should be continued because it seems to be aiding Billy to complete his work accurately. Data supportive of the intervention approach are shown below:

	Percent of assignments completed prior to recess	Percent of assignments completed with at least 85 percent accuracy prior to recess
	(prior to program intervention—baseline)	(prior to program intervention—baseline)
Day 1	77%	5%
Day 2	44%	15%
Day 3	61%	0%
Day 4	57%	0%
Day 5	66%	15%

(after program intervention)		(after program intervention)
Day 1	79%	20%
Day 2	77%	26%
Day 3	80%	39%
Day 4	100%	44%
Day 5	78%	21%
Day 6	90%	70%

Parent Role

Approximately three weeks ago, Billy's teacher called to inform the parents that she would be implementing a program requiring that her students accurately complete their assignments before being allowed to go to recess. The teacher indicated that she was hopeful that this program would encourage Billy to be more diligent in completing his assignments.

Shortly after the program was initiated the parents began to notice a significant increase in Billy's pouting and antisocial behavior. When confronted with this behavior, which typically takes the form of making facial grimaces, stomping around the house, and sulking, he reports that he is angry because he was denied recess at school. While Billy's pouting has always been a problem that the family has had to contend with, it has now become a more significant issue than it ever has been in the past.

The parents are also somewhat concerned that denying Billy recess may further exacerbate his problems of interacting with his peers. They have concluded that if he is kept in at recess, he never will learn to play and work with other children.

While the parents are interested in seeing Billy hand in his assignments, they are troubled by the program designed to facilitate this response. They have concluded that this particular intervention strategy should be abandoned.

GIFTED CHILD

Howard
Age: 8

Teacher Role

The special education teacher is pleased with Howard's performance in her gifted resource room. She feels that he has benefited from the experience and that he should be maintained in the program. However, she strongly believes that he should maintain his primary association with the regular classroom and be in a position of having to relate to his regular class peers. She specifically believes that Howard should be in her gifted resource room no more than 25 percent of each week.

Parent Role

While Howard's parents were initially somewhat apprehensive about his placement in a gifted program, they are currently delighted with the results. Not only has he made significant progress in several areas, but he is showing an interest in a variety of topics. They associate this newly found interest with his placement in the gifted program. They are, in fact, so pleased with the gifted program that they would like to see Howard placed there full time or at least 75 percent to 80 percent of each week. They have concluded that if the current program has been successful, increased placement will lead to even greater success. They have also concluded that Howard's problems in relating to his peers are associated with his gifted status. They are beginning to believe that Howard can only relate to children "on his own level."

The parents believe that their son's exceptionality demands appropriate attention. Accordingly, they are willing to "fight" for increased time for Howard in the gifted program.

LEARNING DISABLED CHILD

Sally
Age: 9

Teacher Role

While the resource room teacher has been concerned about Sally's "social immaturity," particularly her tendencies to withdraw from peers, she has aimed most of her efforts at remediating Sally's academic problems. It has been the teacher's philosophy that while Sally has some problems in interacting with other children, her greatest handicap lies in her academic deficits. Consequently, the teacher has firmly adopted the position that, while in her resource room, primary attention will be focused on scheduling Sally for academic remediation programs. In addition, she believes that these remediation programs will be successful only if implemented in an individualized and structured fashion.

Parent Role

Sally's parents had been hopeful that Sally's learning disabilities resource room experience would result in changes in her social responses as well as academic behavior. However, it is their opinion that while some attention is being focused on persuading Sally to interact more with other children, primary attention is being given to academic pursuits. The parents are not opposed to this emphasis, however, they would like to see the adoption of programs whereby social interaction can also occur. In particular, they would like to see Sally and her classmates removed from individual study carrels and placed in a more traditional seating arrangement, exposed to more group instruction and less individual programming, and with a less structured and rigid setting. While the parents are somewhat hesitant to tell their child's teacher how to teach, they are convinced that Sally will develop socially only if given a different type of educational experience. Candidly, they believe that Sally could make the same academic gains that she is making if provided more opportunities for social interactions.

PHYSICALLY HANDICAPPED CHILD

Eddie
Age: 6

Teacher Role

Eddie's resource room teacher has been generally pleased with his progress in her program as reflected in her evaluations. Specifically feedback to his parents has revealed that Eddie has made good gains in academic areas and marginal progress along emotional/social lines. This information was provided to Eddie's parents via weekly notes, telephone conversations, and regularly scheduled conferences. In addition, as per school district regulations the teacher has completed a "special education report card" on Eddie during each 9-week period. She has specifically evaluated Eddie's progress through the use of descriptive statements and ratings rather than traditional grades. The school district allows teachers to evaluate special education students by whatever means they desire, including the use of letter grades; however, Eddie's teacher believes that she can provide a more accurate and fair report card assessment by using descriptive statements.

Parent Role

Eddie's parents are pleased with his placement in a resource room for physically impaired children. They are also happy with his special education teacher and feel that they are able to effectively communicate with her. However, they are dissatisfied with the manner in which the teacher has chosen to evaluate Eddie on his report card. Rather than her descriptive progress-related comments on Eddie's grade report, they would like to see her use a traditional grading system (i.e., A, B, C, D, F). It is their belief that they have ample opportunity of receiving descriptive reports and that their son should be exposed to a more "normal" grading system. They feel that if his regular class teacher can use a traditional evaluation system, so can the resource room teacher.

MENTALLY RETARDED CHILD

Barbie
Age: 8

Teacher Role

In an effort to decrease Barbie's negativism and noncompliance the teacher instituted a time-out procedure. After obtaining administrative and parental permission, she implemented a program whereby Barbie is required to spend two minutes quietly in a small isolated area each time she demonstrates noncompliant or negative behavior. The teacher is pleased with the program and feels it is yielding desirable results. Data supportive of this position are shown below:

Frequency of negativistic and noncompliant behaviors

(prior to program intervention-baseline)

Day 1 — 14
Day 2 — 20
Day 3 — 17
Day 4 — 16
Day 5 — 7
Day 6 — 14
Day 7 — 16

(after program intervention)

Day 1 — 12
Day 2 — 9
Day 3 — 6
Day 4 — 2
Day 5 — 1
Day 6 — 3
Day 7 — 1

Parent Role

Although the parents gave their permission for the teacher to place Barbie in an isolation area at school for two minutes each time she is negative or noncompliant, they are now having second thoughts. They have heard that this procedure, time out, can cause "psychological and mental damage" in children. Because they are concerned that the procedure may be injurious to their daughter's mental health and because they are aware that she has been able to make good progress without the procedure, they are convinced that they must demand that the program be terminated.

Exhibit E-1 presents a sample evaluation of conflict resolution to be completed by parents.

Exhibit E-1 Conflict Resolution Evaluation

Date _____

Name of Child _____

Name of Person Playing Parent Role _____

Name of Person Playing Conferencer Role _____

Observer(s) _____

I.   General Conferencing Evaluation

A. Ability of conferencer to inform or reach consensus with the parents as to the purpose of the conference.

1	2	3	4	5
Poor	Below Average	Average	Above Average	Excellent

B. Ability of conferencer to conduct the session in a systematic and sequential manner.

1	2	3	4	5
Poor	Below Average	Average	Above Average	Excellent

C. Ability of conferencer to keep the session flowing and on course.

1	2	3	4	5
Poor	Below Average	Average	Above Average	Excellent

D. Ability of conferencer to solicit and respond to parents' questions.

1	2	3	4	5
Poor	Below Average	Average	Above Average	Excellent

Exhibit E-1 continued

E. Ability of conferencer to attend to parents.

1	2	3	4	5
Poor	Below Average	Average	Above Average	Excellent

F. Ability of conferencer to rephrase questions and concerns.

1	2	3	4	5
Poor	Below Average	Average	Above Average	Excellent

G. Ability of conferencer to summarize the conference.

1	2	3	4	5
Poor	Below Average	Average	Above Average	Excellent

II. Evaluation of Communication Skills

A. Ability of conferencer to establish rapport.

1	2	3	4	5
Poor	Below Average	Average	Above Average	Excellent

B. Ability of conferencer to engage in active listening.

1	2	3	4	5
Poor	Below Average	Average	Above Average	Excellent

C. Ability of conferencer to respond to manifest content.

1	2	3	4	5
Poor	Below Average	Average	Above Average	Excellent

D. Ability of conferencer to respond to affect (emotion).

1	2	3	4	5
Poor	Below Average	Average	Above Average	Excellent

E. Ability of conferencer to display empathy.

1	2	3	4	5
Poor	Below Average	Average	Above Average	Excellent

F. Ability of conferencer to provide feedback (i.e., make appropriate use of clarification and perception checking).

1	2	3	4	5
Poor	Below Average	Average	Above Average	Excellent

G. Ability of conferencer to identify areas of mutual agreement.

1	2	3	4	5
Poor	Below Average	Average	Above Average	Excellent

H. Ability of conferencer to be constructively open.

1	2	3	4	5
Poor	Below Average	Average	Above Average	Excellent

I. Ability of conferencer to use "I messages."

1	2	3	4	5
Poor	Below Average	Average	Above Average	Excellent

Exhibit E-1 continued

III.   Application of Conflict Resolution Model

A.   Ability of conferencer to determine the problem, its owners, and the individuals associated with the conflict.

1	2	3	4	5
Poor	Below Average	Average	Above Average	Excellent

B.   Ability of conferencer to generate and aid the parents in identifying possible solutions to the identified problem.

1	2	3	4	5
Poor	Below Average	Average	Above Average	Excellent

C.   Ability of conferencer to evaluate and aid the parents in evaluating the various solutions.

1	2	3	4	5
Poor	Below Average	Average	Above Average	Excellent

D.   Ability of conferencer to select and implement and, in turn, aid the parents in selecting and implementing an appropriate problem-solving strategy.

1	2	3	4	5
Poor	Below Average	Average	Above Average	Excellent

E.   Ability of conferencer to evaluate the solution and to aid the parents in evaluating the solution to the problem.

1	2	3	4	5
Poor	Below Average	Average	Above Average	Excellent

IV.   Summary Information

Index

P

Parent-applied behavior modification program, training, procedures, 152-170
See also Parent training, agents of change
Parent conferencer, educator as, 13-16
Parent effectiveness training, 266-267
Parent/family programs, 135-136, 248
Parent groups, 10, 21, 30, 31, 268
Parent organizations. *See* Parent groups
Parent service programs, 268
See also Parent groups
Parent support group. *See* Parental interaction
Parent-teacher conference
group, 235-268
initial, 120-144
progress report, 205-229
unplanned, 231-243
Parent training
agents of change, 20-21, 30, 64-65, 67-68, 71, 148-170, 200-201, 217, 226-228, 234, 254-265
educational consumers, 20, 30, 52, 67, 68, 71, 253-256
history of, 145-147
importance of, 145-146, 148-149, 159
motivation for, 150, 154, 157, 265, 274
suitability for, 141-144, 257
Parental and family needs, 12-13, 25-37
exercises in meeting, 37, 72
parents of elementary-aged children, 65-68
parents of preschoolers, 61-65
parents of youth and young adults, 68-72
Parental interaction, 245, 246-247, 248, 253, 257
See also Parent groups
Parental involvement in educational

programs, 9-10, 11, 16, 20, 25-27, 30, 31, 59-72, 118, 145, 178, 211, 214-215, 218, 226-228, 232-233, 273
See also Parent training; Parent groups
Parents Campaign for Handicapped Children and Youth, 195
Parsons, J.E., 82
Past school performance, history of, 127
Pennsylvania Association for Retarded Children v. *Commonwealth of Pennsylvania*, 10, 184
Pepper, F., 50
Perry, W.G., 266
Perske, R., 28
PET. *See* Parent effectiveness training
Peterson, R.F., 164
Piers, M., 44, 45
PL 89-10. *See* Elementary and Secondary Education Act of 1965
PL 94-142. *See* Education for All Handicapped Children Act of 1975
PL 93-380. *See* Education of the Handicapped Amendments of 1974
Plato, 117
Pope, B., 110
Poplin, M.S., 226
Poppelreiter, T., 71
Preliminary conference. *See* Initial parent-teacher conference
Problem ownership, 150, 152, 154, 267, 279-280, 281
See also Conflict resolution
Progress evaluation, dissemination of results, 136
letter and notes, 141
report cards, 139-140
telephone contacts, 136, 139
Progress report, 205-214
academic progress, 206-209
physical progress, 212-214
purpose of, 205
social progress, 210-212
Progress report conference, 214-229
evaluation procedure, 223-225

exercises in, 229
planning for, 216-217
postconference activities, 220-222
student participation, 217
See also Progress report
Provence, S.A., 45
Public schools, changing role of, 8-9
Publilius Syrus, 93
Purky, W.W., 106

R

Rapport
importance of, 18, 95, 110, 111,
118-119, 152, 170, 184, 194, 217,
221, 226, 229, 271, 278
See also Trust
Reactions to exceptional child. *See*
Exceptional child
See also Family unit, accommodation
of exceptional child
Regular-class placement, advantages
of, 193
Rehabilitation Act of 1973, Section
504, 52, 59, 177, 253
Reinforcement
conferencer, 110, 112
parents, 110, 112, 170, 215, 219, 265
techniques, 164-165, 250
Reinterpretation, test data, 130,
132-133
Reiss, I.L., 27
Related services. *See* Ancillary services
Remediation strategies. *See* Educational
program
Rights of the handicapped. *See*
Education for All Handicapped
Children Act of 1975; Rehabilitation
Act of 1973, Section 504
Rights, parental, 9-11, 179, 183-187,
196-197, 226, 253-256
See also Due process; Parent
involvement in educational
programs
Risk taking, parental and professional.

See Trust
Risk taking, questionnaire for
professionals, 108-109
Risley, T.R., 164
Rogers, C.R., 17, 94, 106, 113
Role playing activities, 144, 171, 201,
229, 284
Roos, P., 14, 15, 30
Ross, A.O., 149
Ruble, D.N., 82
Rudov, M.H., 45
Rutherford, R.B., 12, 18, 105, 139, 245

S

Santangelo, N., 45
Sasso, G.M., 171
Sawrey, J.M., 29
Scheduling, parent conferences, 7, 86,
97, 196, 205, 215-216, 231-232
Schweid, E., 164
Scott, I.W., 93
Self-acceptance, 107, 110, 112
Siegel, E., 68
Siegman, A.W., 110
Siladi, M.S., 64
Simmons-Martin, A., 34
Simon, S.B., 115
Simpson, R.L., 11, 17, 68, 71, 96, 106,
115, 171, 215, 220, 226, 256
Simulation. *See* Role playing activities
Single-parent or reconstituted families,
exercises in serving, 89
Sleeman, P.J., 228
Sociological information, 128
Solnit, A.J., 45
Special-class placement, 193, 194
Stables, J.M., 164
STEP. *See* Systematic training for
effective parenting
Stephens, T.M., 187
Stout, I., 113, 214
Strickland, B., 68, 200, 201, 273
Sudia, C.E., 79, 81
Sullivan, R., 62

About the Author

RICHARD L. SIMPSON is an Associate Professor of Special Education and School Psychology at the University of Kansas and University of Kansas Medical Center. He has also been a teacher of emotionally disturbed children, school psychologist, clinical psychologist, and director of a program for autistic children.